Marriage License Affidavits

1861–1921

Sonoma County, California

Volume IV
Index to Bride's Surname

Sonoma County Genealogical Society

HERITAGE BOOKS
2011

HERITAGE BOOKS
AN IMPRINT OF HERITAGE BOOKS, INC.

Books, CDs, and more—Worldwide

For our listing of thousands of titles see our website
at
www.HeritageBooks.com

Published 2011 by
HERITAGE BOOKS, INC.
Publishing Division
100 Railroad Ave. #104
Westminster, Maryland 21157

Copyright © 2011 Sonoma County Genealogical Society

All rights reserved. No part of this book may be reproduced or transmitted in any form or by any means, electronic or mechanical, including photocopying, recording or by any information storage and retrieval system without written permission from the author, except for the inclusion of brief quotations in a review.

International Standard Book Numbers
Paperbound: 978-0-7884-5360-1
Clothbound: 978-0-7884-8904-4

Marriage License Affidavits, 1861 to 1921
Sonoma County, California

Introduction

The information contained in this four volume series is taken from Marriage License Affidavits currently housed at the Sonoma County History and Genealogy Library in Santa Rosa, California. These data originated in the office of the Sonoma County Clerk. The information is contained on eight reels of microfilm and contains approximately 14,000 records.

The volumes consist of:

Volume	Data Alphabetized by Groom's Surname
I	A - F
II	G - M
III	N - Z
IV	Index to Bride's Surname

In 1990, the Sonoma County Genealogical Society published *Sonoma County Marriages, 1847 - 1902*, which was an index to marriage records housed at the office of the Sonoma County Recorder. This current publication, unlike the index, in most cases contains the age, residence, and birth place of both the bride and groom. In addition, the consent of a parent or guardian is noted for brides under the age of 18 and grooms under the age of 21. In a few cases, birth dates or other pertinent information is given.

Affidavits are the application for a marriage license and may well include persons who were never actually married. The date may or may not coincide with the actual marriage date of those who did, in fact, get married.

Condition of the Microfilm

In many cases, the condition of the microfilm is exceedingly poor, and the handwritten entries vary from readable to totally unreadable. Forms often varied from year to year, and in some cases, a handwritten note from the parent(s), guardian(s), or a notary was substituted for the form generally in use during that time period. Many of the parental consent forms were handwritten notes and were not always adjacent to the marriage affidavits to which they belonged. Some notes partially obscure the information written on the affidavits.

A clerk apparently filled in the form in most cases, which was then usually signed by the groom, sometimes by both the bride and the groom, occasionally only by the bride, or occasionally by another person. Not infrequently, the spelling of the name made by the clerk did not agree with the spelling of the person who signed the affidavit. In such cases we used the spelling of the person(s) who signed if it was legible. All affidavits were read by at least two persons, and, in some cases, by three persons to try to resolve the correct spelling. If the issue could not be resolved, a question mark (?) appears beside the name, or other information provided.

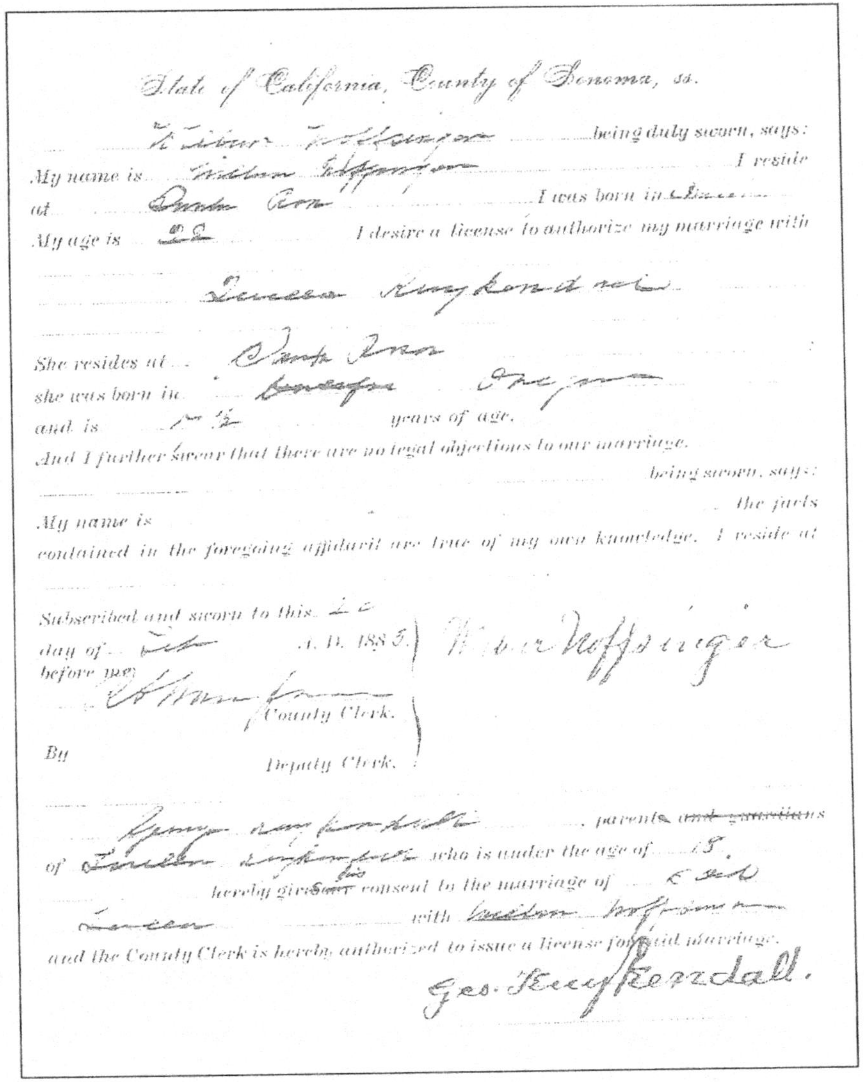
State of California, County of Sonoma, ss.
being duly sworn, says:
My name is … I reside at … I was born in … My age is 22 I desire a license to authorize my marriage with
She resides at …
she was born in …
and is … years of age.
And I further swear that there are no legal objections to our marriage.
being sworn, says:
My name is … the facts contained in the foregoing affidavit are true of my own knowledge. I reside at
Subscribed and sworn to this … day of … A. D. 1883, before me
County Clerk.
By … Deputy Clerk.
parents and guardians of … who is under the age of 18, hereby give consent to the marriage of … with … and the County Clerk is hereby authorized to issue a license for said marriage.

Figure 1: Example of an 1883 marriage affidavit

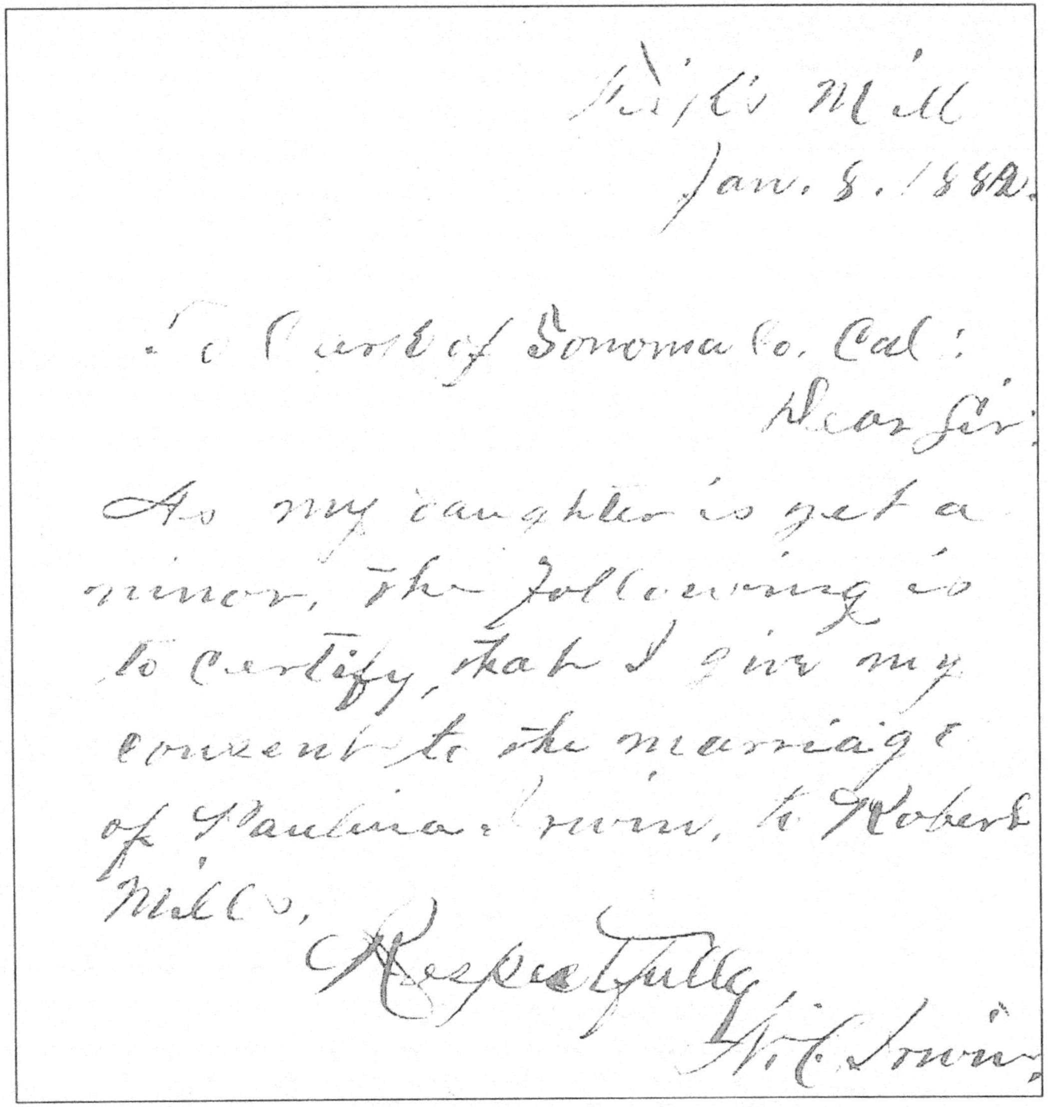

> Skill's Mill
> Jan. 8. 1882.
>
> To Clerk of Sonoma Co. Cal:
>
> Dear Sir:
>
> As my daughter is yet a minor, the following is to certify, that I give my consent to the marriage of Paulina Irwin, to Robert Mill.
>
> Respectfully
> W.C. Irwin

Figure 2: Example of one of the "better" notes of permission

Description of Data Layout

The data are presented alphabetically by groom's surname in three volumes, each volume having two parts. A fourth volume is an index to the bride's surname.

Part	Data Included
I	Name of groom, bride, date of application, comments (includes name of parent or guardian for males under 21 and brides under 18), and occasionally other notes
II	Detailed information on groom and bride: age, residence, place of birth

Example of Use

If you know the name of the groom, locate the appropriate volume, begin with part I, then go to part II for additional information about both parties. If you know only the name of the bride, go to volume IV and locate the bride's name to find the name of the groom. Then located the groom in parts I and II to find additional detailed information.

For place of residence, the town was most frequently given. The state can be assumed to be California unless otherwise noted (using standard postal codes). State codes may be designated for smaller/lesser known towns in California and other states. State codes are not used for well-known cities (Chicago, New York City, New Orleans, etc.).

Place of birth is most often given as state or country; standard postal codes are used for the USA, as shown in Table 3. A three-character code is used for other nations, as shown in Figure 4. However, some birth places may be given as a city or town, township, county, or region in the USA or in another nation. Those cities or other locations that are most frequently used are also coded to conserve space and are shown in Figure 5.

Acknowledgments

Project Director
Carmen Finley

Data Entry
Maggi Andrews
Kerri Bailey
Kay Clegg
Phyllis Kuehn
Joe Panaro
Helen Strickley

Proofreaders
Anna Conley
Doris Dickenson
Carmen Finley
Lois Nimmo

Editor
Doris Dickenson

Camera Ready Copy
Carmen Finley

Special acknowledgment goes to Anthony Hoskins, head of the History and Genealogy Library in Sonoma County and Sonoma County Archivist who made the microfilm available for abstraction. Also, thanks to Mairi Barsky, Branch Manager of the Guerneville Regional Library for the use of their library facilities.

Bride		Groom	
Surname	Given Name	Surname	Given Name
Abario	Rose S.	Marshall	A. F.
Abbinante	Lena	Tiozzo	Asgostino
Abbott	Mabel Louise	Tarleton	Frank William
Abdou	Mabel	Weyl	Frank
Abeel	Lola Elizabeth	Carrington	Bartine
Abraham	Dorthey E.	Finley	Allan W.
Abraham	Mary	Pinschaer	Simon
Abraio	Clara J.	Rezendes	Antone G.
Abraio	Marie K.	Kelton	Clarence F.
Abrams	Nettie L.	Lytte	George W.
Abramsky	Katie	Meyers	Henry
Abshire	Alice	Bunch	John B.
Abshire	Callie A.	Parrott	J. W.
Abshire	Laura P.	Turner	Wm. A.
Abshire	Laura P.	Bean	Eben D.
Aced	Pilar S.	Bowman	James C.
Acker	Eolim (?)	Blundell	Vance D.
Ackerley	Sarah Anna	Willis	Francis M.
Ackerman	Harriet B.	Keig	William C.
Ackerman	Jennie	Patterson	Samuel Charles
Ackley	Ida May	Sellers	James D.
Acquistapace	Amelia	Frati	Abramo
Acquistapace	Elena	Pedroncelli	Frank
Adam	Catherine M.	Chisholm	Donald
Adams	Abbie Mary	Lincoln	Ulysses G.
Adams	Alice P.	Corville	Richard
Adams	Allie	Campbell	Geo. S.
Adams	Amanda E.	Taylor	Isaiah
Adams	Anna M.	Haynie	Wm. M.
Adams	Annie Mary	Hansen	John G. E.
Adams	Carrie	Stewart	Daniel R.
Adams	Clara Violet	Chahon	Gustave Cecil
Adams	Delcina, Mrs.	Hudson	W. T.
Adams	Ellen	Lemay	Josiah
Adams	Emma	Lehn	Charles
Adams	Emma D.	Beagle	William H.
Adams	Ethel	Russell	Preston
Adams	Georgietta	Peterson	Andrew
Adams	Gladys Eleanor	Bovett	George Harold
Adams	Ida H.	Willey	John J.
Adams	Iva May	Jones	Edward Robert
Adams	Jennie	Haehl	Edward Oliver
Adams	Jennie Aileen	Weber	Carl
Adams	Jennie M.	LeFebvre	Eugene O.
Adams	LaVerne I.	Kennedy	Charles E.
Adams	Lillie D.	Bell	Walter C.
Adams	Lora Z.	King	William
Adams	Lucy K.	Chaffee	E. S.
Adams	Lulu May	Rhodes	Arthur
Adams	Margaret, Mrs.	Love	Wm.
Adams	Martha	Adamson	John Martin
Adams	Maruella (?) J.	Trosper	Francis D.
Adams	Mary Etta	Hopper	William Thomas
Adams	Mary L.	Lawson	Grover E.
Adams	Mattie I.	Warboys	John L.
Adams	Minnie, Mrs.	Nixon	William R.
Adams	Nellie May	Baum	John Wesley
Adams	Nina	Petit	Louis W.
Adams	Rena M.	White	Hale B.
Adams	Rose A.	Jurd	Andrew J.
Adams	Sadie	Doda	Victor
Adams	Sarah M., Mrs.	Bradford	George W.
Adams	Viola, Mrs.	Hunt	Byrd A.
Adams	Pearl	Casassa	Louis

Adamson	Mary	Cornell	Reynolds T.
Adamson	Rena	Tornblinson	John
Adcock	Dora	Gresham	Joseph Francis
Adcock	Icapena	Rector	John L.
Adcock	Lois J.	Hobbs	Charles C.
Addisen	Eliza J.	Foster	William E.
Addison	Eliza J.	Foster	William E.
Adel	Annetta	Echelmeier	Fred
Adell	Violet Emily	Van Gordon	Jasper Gerome
Adgate	Nannie	Bigelow	Frank L.
Adney	Laura Lucile	Snyder	D. E.
Agnew	Ella V.	Cooper	Charles Alexander
Agnew	Ida A.	Dunbar	John J.
Agnew	Lizzie	Champlin	Charles V.
Agostini	Sofia	Tonella	Camillo
Aguiar	Maria S.	De Rosa	Roque P.
Aguillon	Gabrielle F.	Heggie	Norman J.
Aguirre	Marguerite P.	Whybark	Ralph
Ahern	Bella	Green	Louis H.
Ahl	Ruby Ada	Ball	Raymond Oliver
Aiken	Florence	Banks	Louis Albert
Aiken	Inez Mabel	Hartin	Richard
Aiken	Mary Edith	Laird	Thomas F.
Aikin	Hattie	Rathcke	Fred C.
Aitken	Elenor M.	Maggart	Edward F.
Akers	Blanche Louisa	Lawson	Jesse Herbert
Akers	Malinda C.	Armstrong	Frederic W.
Akers	Willie	Cook	Archibald
Akmann	Lillian G.	Hourtani (?)	Alphonse J. P.
Aladalo	Sadie M.	Hinshaw	Clyde C.
Albee	May Edith	Ludwig	Peter H.
Alberigi	Amelia	Cuicci	Filippo
Alberigi	Ancilla	Lencioni	Henry
Alberigi	Annie	Simi	Louis F.
Alberigi	Mary	Pedrini	Angelo
Albers	Emma	Keller	Peter
Albert	Pearl Ione	Felis	Fred R., Jr.
Albertson	Amy Frances	Wagers	Derral Deronda
Albertson	Ella	Holloway	James Henry
Albini	Angela	Mazzucchi	Martino
Albini	Elvira	Albini	John
Albini	Emelia	Girolo	Gabriele
Albini	Ersilia	LaFranchi	Robert
Albini	Maria	Mafia	Antoni
Albini	Mary	Pozzi	James
Albini	Mary	Fomasi	Peter
Albini	Mary	Mache	John A.
Albini	Mary	Benelli	Harry
Albini	Rosie	Barlieri	Italo
Albini	Victoria, Mrs.	Asti	Erminio
Albrecht	Hulda	Hedel	Henry
Albreigi	Madelina	Francesconi	Federico
Albright	Leone Thelma	Smith	Thomas Edgar
Alcott	Myrtle I.	Travis	Anly M.
Alden	Priscilla B.	McCarter	William Ernest
Alderson	Sue E.	Whelan	Lawrence J.
Aldridge	Crystal G.	Bray	Frank Jerome
Aldridge	Lulu G.	Kidd	William H.
Aldridge	Myrtie May	Nowell	John Warren
Alessandri	Dina	Bonini	Olivero
Alexander	Alice Maria	Crawford	Andrew Kerr
Alexander	Carrie	Striening	M. J.
Alexander	Hannah	Henshaw	Iram
Alexander	Idelia M.	Van Auken	Henry J.
Alexander	Lillie	Walk	Edward G.
Alexander	Lily M.	Keechler	Bloss F.
Alexander	Lucille B.	Engelhardt	Richard R.
Alexander	Mary Ida	Stearns	Ernest
Alexander	Pearl L. G.	Hollingsworth	Harry M.
Alexander	Selma	Harris	Claude

Alexson	Gabrella	Owen	Fred Milton	Allen	S. A.	Wooldridg	M. D.
Algeo	Wanda	Zanolini	Fredrick Alfred	Allen	Sarah	Silva	F. M.
Alkire	Florilla Florence	Parker	Henry	Allen	Lizzie M.	Hendrick	James M.
Allan	Lucille Dorothy	Vicars	Gilbert Howell	Allen	Rebecca H.	Knott	Warren T.
Allaway	Sarah E. (?)	Carr	T. M.	Allenbury	Evelyn	Hall	Walter R.
Alleman	Jessie, Mrs.	Schmacher	Jacob	Allesandri	Elisa	Bianchini	Mariano
Allen	Alice Elizabeth	Dorsett	Fred Edward	Alley	Nina B.	Price	William
Allen	Alta W.	Wheeler	George W.	Allison	Elizabeth	Draper	John
Allen	Annie	Gossage	Chas. S.	Alloway	Mary	Baldwin	C. A.
Allen	Annie K.	Mesa	Joseph	Alonso	Ruth C.	LeFever	Eugene
Allen	Belle	McPherson	Walter	Alten	Anna E.	Allen	George O.
Allen	Catherine	Mather	William	Alten	Elizabeth	Collins	George W.
Allen	Cleora	Whitehouse	John V.	Altman	Emma	Culler	Albert Roy
Allen	Cornelia	Martz	Samuel Anderson	Alton	Mary Agnes	McConnell	William S.
Allen	Eloise	Riddell	Foster J.	Alves	Amelia	Jason	Frank
Allen	Ethel Lillian	Hoadley	Mervyn J.	Alves	Gladys Clark	Jelbert	Richard H.
Allen	Ethel Mae	Garner	Walter A.	Alves	Mary C.	Bettencourt	John M.
Allen	Grace G.	Walker	E. J.	Amavisca	Matilda	Martino	Giovanni
Allen	Hattie L.	Corcoran	William D.	Ambrogio	Annie E.	Quilici	Henry
Allen	Hattie W.	Marble	Edward R.	Ambrose	Marguerite Gertrude	Stoddard	Albert Lauren
Allen	Huldah	McKillap	Dugald				
Allen	Ione May	Fry	Albert S.	Ambrose	Mary	Fernandez	Clemente
Allen	Juanita	Griffith	Clyde E.	Amci (?)	Harriett Dorothy	Pond	Samuel F.
Allen	Kate L.	Woodward	Gemane P.	Amer	Alice G.	Rodgers	B. F.
Allen	Luella Rebecca	Muller	Daniel L.	Ameral	May E.	Wilcox	Almond L.
Allen	Lydia Jane	Dorsett	William A.	American	Martha Jane	Simpson	Charles Rouelle
Allen	Maggie E.	Miller	Elmer F.	Ames	Annie L.	Marshall	William
Allen	Mary C.	Harmon	Robert A.	Ames	Arvilla	Saxe	Edward Arthur
Allen	Mattie M.	Jones	Homer A.	Ames	Clementine	Anderson	Thomas W.
Allen	Molly	Hixson	John	Ames	Gertrude Francis	Ruggles	Jesse Robert
Allen	Nattie J.	Palmer	J. Irving	Ames	Gladys H.	Swart	Luther W.
Allen	Nellie Angeline	Abbey	William Newton	Ames	Phebe E.	Hubbell	O. B.
Allen	Nellie May	Hoss	Frank Blair	Amons	Susannah	Clark	Alfred Churchill
Allen	Nina	Barnhart	Frank McGowan	Amos	Villa	Graham	James W.
Allen	Rosie J.	Turner	J. H.	Amstael	Gina Matildos	Carpenter	Charles Thomas

Ananos	Joaquina	Catarina	Antonio	Anderson	Mary E.	Cox	E. Morris
Anderegg	Annie	Segessenmann	Christian	Anderson	May Etta	Hunger	Elmer G.
Andersen	Anna Margaret	Crocker	Earl F.	Anderson	Meta Catherine	Haag	Michael Peter
Andersen	Annie	Hansen	Walter	Anderson	Myrtle	Camerlo	James A.
Andersen	Caroline Amalie	Henningsen	Knudt Theodor	Anderson	Nellie	Rivers	Frank
Andersen	Henrieta	Paviso	Louis	Anderson	Nellie V.	Leephart	James H.
Andersen	Hilda Helena	Pellascio	Miglio John	Anderson	O. E.	Praetzel	A. H.
Andersen	Josie E.	Corstensen	Henry M.	Anderson	Rosalie N.	O'Connell	Elmer C.
Andersen	Julia Jane	Finke	Joseph H.	Anderson	Ruth	Phillips	John P.
Andersen	Theresa M.	Mathiessen	Henry A.	Anderson	Ruth M.	Gaston	George R.
Anderson	Alice H.	Geary	Michael	Anderson	Theresa	Pomi	Henry
Anderson	Alice Missouri	Smith	Harlon Pearl	Anderton	Gertrude A.	Larsen	Albert O.
Anderson	Amanda A.	Vandor	Paul J.	Anderton	Mabel	Riewerts	C. W.
Anderson	Anna	Voris	Phillip	Andrews	Alice M.	O'Leary	Franklin T.
Anderson	Anna C.	Schneider	Samuel	Andrews	Alice May	Clark	Charles Raymond
Anderson	Anna C.	Vallier	Henry S.	Andrews	Bernice V.	Baker	Albert Marion
Anderson	Anna M.	Broyles	Fred H.	Andrews	Carrie E.	Josselyn	Joel S.
Anderson	Botella	Carrico	Charles E.	Andrews	Kathryn	Tovani	Ernest L.
Anderson	Byrtee	Singletary	William S.	Andrews	Lilian Grayce	Lippold	Alfred E.
Anderson	Catherine Mildred	Gregory	Canfield Burrell	Andrews	Lucile M.	Johnson	Milton H.
Anderson	Clara J.	Wooten	Thomas M.	Andrews	Mary E.	Eakle	George H.
Anderson	Dorothy M.	Wolf	Sidney J.	Andrews	Nettie B., Mrs.	Peterson	Frank B.
Anderson	Elizabeth M.	Pfoff	Frank T.	Andrews	S. Libbie	Stullen (?) Hutten	C. E.
Anderson	Ella Marguerite	Webb	James Paul				
Anderson	Florence	Foutch	Thomas G.	Andrieni	Maria	Sanguinetti	August J.
Anderson	Frieda Cecelia	Branigan	Charles Floyd	Angeli	Madalain	Bebagliati	Eugene
Anderson	Gussie	Harman	William A.	Anglade	Ida	Delbary	Marcel
Anderson	Hanna	Roden	John	Anglade	Katy	Galard	Nicholas
Anderson	Helen Marie	Peoples	Stuart Zeno	Anholm	Marie B.	Cutts	Lloyd C.
Anderson	Johanna L.	Gabrielson	Carl O.	Annike (?)	Minnie	Kietsinger	George W.
Anderson	Josephine	Presswood	Jesse	Annis	Nettie	Wilson	John T.
Anderson	Lila V.	Standley	Lester R.	Ansbro	Sabrina	Keenan	George
Anderson	Lillian Hannah	Whittington	Richard Lee	Ansell	Fannie V.	Turner	W. Arther
Anderson	Lizzie	Robertson	Lawrence W.	Anselmi	Martini	Baccala	Antonio
Anderson	Mabel J.	Hoosier	Charles Rasmond	Anthony	Anna E.	Rhymes	Ernest R.

Anthony	Anna M.	McCraken	Alexander	Ariasi	Rose	Mora	Laurence
Anthony	Mary E.	Reed	John J.	Arkland	Mabel E.	Knight	Bert P.
Anthony	Ruby Alma	Wheeler	Rollo Abbey	Arland	Lela D.	Ayers	George W.
Antognini	Gabriella	Antognini	Alfred	Armbruster	Carrie	Sammy	Richard
Antonietta	Manne	Acquistapace	Pietro	Armbruster	Louise M.	Rasmussen	Arthur L.
Antonietti	Angelina	Lorenzi	Luigi	Armbruster	Marie W.	Burtner	Jesse H.
Apodaca	Fermina Saturnina	Aguirre	Amadeo	Armeau	Elisabeth Anne	Bryant	George E.
Appiarius	Victoria B.	Batsakis	Nicholas	Armstrong	Alice	Delehanty	James E.
Appleton	Carrie S.	Burlingame	Claude	Armstrong	Bessie	Cassidy	Albert H.
Appleton	Eliza G.	Gottenberg	Hartley W.	Armstrong	Elizabeth	Jones	William L.
Aquisttapace	Domenica	Aquisttapace	Giovanni	Armstrong	Ella L.	Cockrill	Travis Lee
Aragona	Lena	Viarengo	Joe	Armstrong	Fannie	Kleiser	James H.
Arata	Angela	Mazza	John	Armstrong	Fannie	Dunton	Oscar
Arata	Rose	Crandall	Edward	Armstrong	Flora A.	Cochrane	Marcus Edward
Arbuckle	Violet C.	Smeeton	Walter S.	Armstrong	Florence	Lowry	Herbert L.
Archabal	Julia	Aguirre	Martin	Armstrong	Florence	Todd	Samuel Cavin
Archambeau	Agnes M.	Smith	George A.	Armstrong	Frederica	Rohrer	Karl George
Archambeau	Mary O.	Davidson	Allen	Armstrong	Hazel D.	Pollock	Lester A.
Archambeau	Minerva Belle	Stewart	George F.	Armstrong	Irene Esther	Wright	Arthur G.
Archamlean	Ilene M.	Vaughan	Benjamin W.	Armstrong	Lizzie O.	Pryal	James A.
Archer	Berdena E.	Isaacs	Ernest A.	Armstrong	Lucy	Barnes	P. D.
Archer	Grace Dorothy	Laughlin	Perry Raymond	Armstrong	Lusettie	Hansen	Carl Emil
Archer	Ida M.	Roberts	Charles E.	Armstrong	Mabel F.	Bucknell	Roy
Archer	Laura	Murray	Paul	Armstrong	Margaret V.	Weber	John H., Jr.
Archer	Nellie	Lukeer	Charles R.	Armstrong	Mary Ann	Truitt	Elliott Andrew
Archer	Nellie R.	McCracken	William J.	Armstrong	Ruby Ann	Fuller	Frank Leslie
Archer	Rubie Isalene	Morris	John Reuben	Armsworthy	Olive E.	Vanhutton	Karl Hermann
Archer	Ruth E.	Andrews	Walter J.	Arnett	Alice May	Sheldon	Lute A.
Arfsten	Dora Lizzie	Estes	George Henry	Arnold	Alberta L.	Agnew	James F.
Arfsten	Emma D.	Baum	Thomas J.	Arnold	E. Mina	Peterson	John L.
Arfsten	Engeline	Nichelsen	Ocke	Arnold	Emma	Hill	William C.
Arfsten	Eva M.	Brower	Walter J.	Arnold	Florence L.	Weir	J. G.
Arfsten	Giene	Boien	P.	Arnold	Josephine L.	Dyer	Roy C.
Arfsten	Katie	Timon	Cornelius	Arnold	Katie A.	Hendley	Chas. Bacon
Ariasi	Margaret	De Martini	John	Arnold	Lucile Frances	Mobley	William H.

Arnold	Margaret Elizabeth	Lander	Eugene	Atchinson	Lella	Cooper	Sash D.
Arnold	Nellie M.	Goodman	James W.	Athey	Edith V.	Young	Edgar C.
Arnold	Philippina	Cirimele	Angelo	Athey	Olive M.	Close	Frank D.
Arnold	Rose L.	Armstrong	Oatie M.	Atkins	Maggie, Mrs.	Ward	George B.
Arnold	Ruby Pearl	Voss	James Claus	Atkins	Rosa J.	O'Neill	Alfred H.
Arnold	Mary	Wilhoit	Henry	Atkins	Venia	Owen	C. W.
Arrasati	Catalini	Ruiz	Felipe	Atkinson	Elizabeth	Orth	Walter
Arrighi	Ernestina	Ghiselli	Anacleto	Atkinson	Frances M.	Voorheis	Edward C.
Arrigoni	Kate	Pasero	Paul	Atkinson	Irene	Gow	George Buchanan
Arrigoni	Rosa	Steffe	Joseph	Atkinson	Laura M.	Gregg	Edward E.
Arsnip	Sarah	Isola	Alphonso	Atkinson	Laura M.	Benton	Henry Benjamin
Arthur	Louise Elizabeth	Weldt	Joseph Ambrose	Atkinson	Mary M.	Jones	Nathan H.
Arvilla	Florence, Mrs.	Crockett	Edmund Bowden	Atkinson	Maud Eleanor	Scrutton	Hugh Campbell
Ashcraft	Edith	Kelly	Henry Clay	Aubaille	Victoria	Vruwink	Garrett
Ashcraft	Rebekah, Mrs.	Beckner	W. S.	Augeir	Adelia Anna	Boardman	Edward Madison
Ashe	Pearl Lucille	Rhodes	Harry E.	Auger	Annie Irene	Duryea	Stanton Bun
Ashley	Louisa R.	Buck	Charles	Augsperger	Rosa J.	Struve	C. William
Ashley	Mary A.	Moore	Gideon J.	August	Malvina	Pippert	Peter
Ashley	Sarah F.	Steele	Julius A.	Augusta	Clara	Continho	Joseph
Ashmore	Emily F.	Blythe	Frank	Augusto	Mary	Azevedo	Tony Thomas
Askam	Lillian	Blake	Frank T.	Ausehmi	Gulia	Ricci	Luigi
Askins	Lucretia J.	Potter	A. B.	Ausseresses	Marie Louisa	Goobi	Julius
Asmann	Mabel I.	Sassemath	Julius J.	Austin	Agnes	White	Thomas
Asnip	Ellen	Massimo	George	Austin	Alice E.	Gill	Charles W.
Aspenwall	Georgiana F.	Hanna	Daniel N.	Austin	Essie Mae	Vanghan	Marvin S.
Aspesi	Giuseppina	Rinaldo	Tomazini	Austin	Eva M.	Simmons	Mardis C.
Assenti	Lillian F.	Boudin	Lucien Victor	Austin	Gula B.	Mills	Ernest M.
Assenti	Maybelle	Rossi	Victor T.	Austin	Harriet L.	Spridgen	W. T.
Astengo	Maria	Saitone	Antonio	Austin	Hattie H.	Holmes	Marvin P.
Asti	Edith	Sprague	Homer	Austin	Ida M.	O'Connor	James
Asti	Ersiglia	Barbieri	Peter	Austin	Jessie M.	Archer	John W.
Asti	Josephine Lucy	Cayla	Raymond Marcellin	Austin	Lulu	Nowlin	George
				Austin	Rose, Mrs.	Cowen	Joseph A.
Asti	Lizzie	Babbini	Alvise	Autonovich	Marguerite L.	Stone	Byron Franklin, Jr.
Asti	Mary J.	Newman	Frank T., Jr.	Aveil	Maria	Bettencourt	Manuel

Averill	Margaret	Ramsey	Charles	Bach	Adeline W.	May	Henry C.
Avila	Mary Ruth	Louvis	Steven	Bachman	Sophia	Minaglia	John
Avilla	Mary	Arfsten	Adolph	Bacigalupi	Irene May	Pedersen	Jay Fred
Axford	Alice May	Smith	William F.	Bacigalupi	Lena	Canobbio	Serafino
Ayer	Gladys E.	Ross	Fred L.	Bacigalupi	Maria	Bacigalupi	Giovanni B.
Ayer	Lizzie	Miller	Daniel Erskin	Bacigalupi	Sophie	Williams	Robert Edward
Ayers	Alice	Bee	Milliard F.	Bacigalupi	Virginia Angelina	Schwab	Frances Eugene
Ayers	Alice May	Oeltjen	William Fred	Bacigalupi	Josephine	De Matei	Louis Paul
Ayers	Anna	Ross	Frank	Backer	Elizabeth	Lutgens	Henry Chas.
Ayers	Edith	Chapman	H. E.	Bacon	Adrienne	Torliatt	Peter
Ayers	Elise May	Armstrong	James C.	Bacon	Iona A.	Cook	F. R.
Ayers	Elsie	Ray	Frederick	Bacon	Lillie T.	Derrick	Geo. W.
Ayers	Hattie M.	Wood	Frank W.	Bacon	Mildred E.	Hawkins	Christian H.
Ayers	Martha J.	Campbell	Wm.	Bade	Augusta	Heitter	Henry
Ayers	Rosalie	Blakely	T. M.	Badell	Ellen M.	Bradford	Branch Johnson
Ayers	Veryl D.	Lauritzen	Lewis	Badger	Basha	Cook	Isaac N.
Azari	Cicira	Triaca	Francisco	Badger	Blanche	Burt	Roy J.
Azevedo	Mae M.	Silva	Manuel J.	Badger	Blanche H.	Martz	Roy
Azevedo	Mary Cecilia	Fitzgerald	James R.	Badger	Grace P.	Strong	Samuel H.
Baago	Lola M., Mrs.	Parsons	Charles E.	Badger	Kathryne C.	Gosney	Charles J.
Baagoe	Andre	Nielson	Niels Peter	Badger	M. E.	Patocchi	Charles
Baagoe	Carrie	Kruse	Charles G.	Badger	Vernon	Thorp	James
Babbini	Katherine G.	Babbini	Arthur	Baettge	Sophia	Manuel	H. S.
Babbino	Angeline F.	Vest	James B.	Bagan	Emma M., Mrs.	Dillon	James E.
Babbino	Carlotta	Francard	Ernest	Baggs	Violet Mary	Shelly	Charles Henry
Babcock	Edith M.	Beal	S. Pryor	Bagley	Amy L.	Hatch	Frank R.
Babcock	Sylvania E.	Lugo	John A.	Bagley	Mary L.	Colwell	Abner M.
Babcook	Edith C.	Pepin	George E.	Bahr	Bertha	King	John
Baber	Nellie G.	Sanger	John F.	Bahr	Elsie	Beck	Christian Hansen
Baboe	Annie Laureta	Perry	Arthur Raymond	Bahr	Sophie	Bundesen	Martin
Baccala	Carrie	Magetti	Robert	Bailer	Honora E., Mrs.	Hicks	John H.
Baccala	Louise Marie	Ramos	Manuel	Bailey	Annie	Bennett	W. J.
Bacci	Beppa	Franchi	Nildo	Bailey	Bania (?) Mary	Chapman	Rockwell Jerome
Bacci	Gussie E.	Venturacci	Edward	Bailey	Clara V.	McComb	Barron N.
Bacci	Louisa	Papera	Lorenzo	Bailey	Elizabeth	Cooper	Thomas J.

Bailey	Elma G.	Allen	James T.
Bailey	Emily E.	Burdick	Fred E.
Bailey	Ethyl A.	Brown	H. H.
Bailey	Hester Drew	Lane	Ernest
Bailey	Ima Mae	Woods	Paul C.
Bailey	Margaret	Patteson	Charles H.
Bailey	Nellie C.	Griffin	John M.
Bailey	Nina E.	Jacobs	James B.
Bailey	Olive L.	Taylor	Ethan A.
Bailey	Rose E.	Stone	John T.
Bailhache	Juanita	Waldrop	Oda
Bailhache	Ruth	Abbey	Alfred
Bailiff	Geraine M.	Dillon	Charles
Baine	Dora	Howard	Harry
Baine	Emma	Green	Raymond L.
Baine	Lola	Cox	Homer M.
Baines	Irene	Block	George Henry
Baiocchi	Marianna	Puccinelli	Giuseppe
Baiocchi	Marie	Pigoni	Paolo
Bair (?)	Elizabeth	Williamson	Howard A.
Baird	Leona Lovel	Campbell	Ira Samuel
Baird	Luretta	Tyler	Frank
Baird	Mary	Jeans	Newton
Baitey	Minnie Elvie	Fitsimmons	Miron Ray
Baker	Alma E.	McKibbin	Edward L.
Baker	Amy T.	Blank	John
Baker	Annie Elizabeth	Ireland	James David
Baker	Annie Laura	Perry	Charles Oscar
Baker	Atlanta	McPherson	Ernest I.
Baker	Bertha H.	Chambers	E. W.
Baker	Crystabel K.	Foster	Charles L.
Baker	Ethel F.	Johnson	Harrick T.
Baker	Eva M.	Blank	Louis
Baker	Georgia M.	Steinbeck	Eugene H.
Baker	Grace A.	Stanley	Allan J.

Baker	Harriet F.	Bradford	Elbert
Baker	Hazel Magnes	Pierce	Edgar Bellisle
Baker	Jane Frances	Reilly	Henry Anthony
Baker	Jennie Cecelia	Bennetts	Herbert Franklin
Baker	Julia	Darby	Martin Ernest
Baker	Julia J.	Button	Ray E.
Baker	Lillian Emma	Maringo	Steven
Baker	Matilda	Canfield	Albert
Baker	Maude	Nicklos	Chris
Baker	Mildred	Naylor	Orlando
Baker	Nyza N.	Scott	Ira Lee
Baker	Roxie Dell	Knight	Francis Marion
Baker	Sarah M., Mrs.	Rodgers	William D.
Baker	Susie R., Mrs.	McDonough	Michael
Baldi	Amelia	Monotti	Eugene
Baldocchi	Julia C.	Castiglio	Louis
Baldocchi	Lizzie Mary	Giovannoni	Adolph Joseph
Baldridge	Louise Cathr.	Smith	Sydney F.
Baldrusch	Katie	Beyer	Edward
Balducci	Rosa	Granucci	Angelo
Baldwin	Cora B.	Loukes	Harris Fisk
Baldwin	Joan	O'Donnell	John
Baldwin	Kittie	Read	John M.
Baldwin	Mollie Dell	Mason	George B.
Bale	Caroline	Murchie	William T.
Bale	Francisco Josephine	Patterson	Lester
Bale	Loletta	Leard	Charles M.
Balemi	Giacomina	Cavagna	Emile
Bales	Della Morton	Fawver	James Clark
Bales	Minnie Estella	Scott	Thomas
Balestracci	Adele	Andreini	Silvio
Ball	Addie L.	Bradlee	Adelbert S.
Ball	Agnes	Congleton	Geo. W.
Ball	Mary M.	Butt	George A.

Ball	Sue	Baker	Joel F.	Baraldi	Leontina	Matazzoni	Guiseppe
Ballard	Beryl C.	Stahlman	Fred E.	Barba	Joaquinna	Mattos	Joseph
Ballard	Effie E., Mrs.	Johnston	Richard I.	Barbarin	Augustine	Cantoni	Romeo
Ballard	Mae B.	Dana	Alfred H.	Barber	Flora G.	Fletcher	Wm. F.
Ballati	Ursula	Mastai	Battista	Barber	Josephine	Agnew	Hugh C.
Ballenger	Laura C.	Stanley	James M.	Barber	Marjorie V.	Pedersen	Arthur A.
Balletti	Emilia	Quartaroli	Leonido	Barber	Mary	Robbins	Lander
Ballik	Anna	Young	Virgil A.	Barberie	Rose Lee	Fanucchi	Angelo
Ballou	Althea L.	Leggett	A. E.	Barboni	Celestina	Levens	Harry Stocking
Ballou	Margaret J.	Johnson	David Q.	Barboni	Mae	Martinoni	A. H.
Balozs	Rose M.	Binggeli	George	Barbour	Clementine	Farley	William T.
Balser	Mabel Almira	Worth	Edmund Lionel	Barella	Amellia	Albini	John
Balsley	Edith Evalyn	Condeff	Harry P.	Barella	Elena	Maffei	Gaetano
Bamber	Elsie	Bell	Noah	Barella	Emilia	Albini	Peter
Banducci	Clara	Rosaia	Felix	Barella	Madelena	Poncia	Guiseppe
Bane	Eleanor, Mrs.	Bledsoe	John H.	Barff	Mary Eleanor	Hoffman	John Walter
Baney	Elsie R.	Fouts	Clyde E.	Bargagliotti	Louisa	Forgett	Isadore
Banfield	Ida F.	Call	George B.	Bargaglotti	Della	Baley	Joshua
Banfield	Mary Jane	Whitney	E. D.	Barger	Viola	Smith	Morris W.
Banks	A. Varde	Akers	Edward W.	Barham	Hattie L.	Mason	Fred B.
Banks	Bertha	Bisordi	Angelo	Barham	Lena May	Thompson	Edward Allen
Banks	Caroline M.	True	Thomas J.	Barham	Lucy	McCulloch	James Henry
Banks	Emma A.	Johnson	D. W.	Barham	Luda V.	Coffee	S. R.
Banks	Esther E.	Davis	Charles Louis	Barilani	Maria	Pedroncelli	Giuseppe
Banks	Helen Grace	Johns	Harvey Raymond	Barker	Beatrice Miriam	Swift	Robert
Banks	Lenora	Hansten	Herman	Barker	Bertha B.	Bathurst	Roland L.
Banks	Louise Manilla	Tibbetts	Joseph Kimball	Barker	Ruth	Meyer	Walter
Banks	Maud Eveline	Kee	James Hamilton	Barker	Sophie	Dodge	A. C.
Banks	Susan R.	McKenzie	James	Barlow	Anna Maude	Newman	Rea C.
Bannister	Libbie E.	Wilson	Albion P.	Barlow	Elizabeth L.	McNeil	Wilbur J.
Banta	Evalyn F.	Baker	Fred Lester	Barlow	Ethel Maud	Twichell	Fred S.
Banta	Mary Alice	Craig	George Washington	Barlow	Mary Elizabeth	Hallberg	Oscar A.
				Barman	Clara B.	Coyne	Lawrence J.
Banty	Clara B.	Coffey	Charles	Barnard	Panchita C.	Brunings	John H., Jr.
Baptiste	Lena Mary	Paula	John L.	Barndt	Ruby Belle	Northrop	Percy L. E.

Barneburg	Alice Maude	Wells	Marvin
Barnell	Barbara	Barrie	Nelson T.
Barnes	Alethea M.	Rowland	Thomas E.
Barnes	Alice M.	Colburn	Leroy H.
Barnes	Anna M.	Andersen	Paul
Barnes	Annie	King	David
Barnes	Annie	Deeds	William W.
Barnes	Cora E.	Rayner	William
Barnes	Daisy	Owens	George S.
Barnes	Dora Harlan	Duggan	Edward Bernard
Barnes	Edna Gay	McNeil	Justin Louis
Barnes	Eliza Lownes	Larsen	Julius Anton
Barnes	Emily L.	Greer	Earl C.
Barnes	Ethel E.	Thompson	Joseph G.
Barnes	Etta	Christensen	Clarence
Barnes	Eva E.	Urton	William
Barnes	Florence Madeline	Schieffer	Robert Arthur
Barnes	Frances Gordon	Quinn	Edward
Barnes	Harriet Florence	Chenoweth	Hardin Talman
Barnes	Henrietta A.	Decoe	T. C.
Barnes	Ida F.	Earll	F. A.
Barnes	Jennie Grace	Thompson	Jean Ed.
Barnes	Lottie H.	Rayner	James S.
Barnes	Lyda Ann	Thorne	Jno. H.
Barnes	Lydia	Russell	William A.
Barnes	Marien E.	Barkway	Wm M.
Barnes	Mary E.	Freeman	Albert J.
Barnes	Mary Susannah	Beattie	John
Barnes	Mattie Veale	Wilkinson	Thomas
Barnes	May E.	Knight	George W.
Barnes	Mildred	McDermott	William, Jr.
Barnes	Myrtle Blanche	McNulty	Charles Augustus
Barnes	Nettie A.	Chisholm	William C.
Barnes	Ruby Rhomance	Gein	August Carl
Barnes	Sarah Baronetta	Jones	Josiah
Barnes	Sarah C.	Walford	Fredrick
Barnes	Cora	Landis	Arthur L.
Barnes	Ida M.	Miller	James R.
Barnes	Zella	Chandler	Joseph
Barnett	Emma B.	Gale	James A.
Barnett	Fannie A.	Nisson	Theodore M.
Barnett	Lillian May	Beebe	John Franklin
Barnett	Loretta B.	DeBolt	Ralph A.
Barnett	Lottie	Smith	Perry, Commodore
Barnett	Mary	Peterson	Peter A.
Barnett	Mary Amelia	Cox	Alvin Joseph
Barnett	Minnie Della	Matthews	Alvin Wesley
Barnett	Nettie J.	Johnson	Martin
Barney	Ophelia	Lindsey	Calvin
Barnhardt	Minnie	Cameron	Fred J.
Barnum	Evaline	Fouts	Edwin Lee
Barnum	Francis A.	Ward	Walter A.
Barnum	Inez Mildred	Alderson	Earl Ray
Barnwell	Gail	Munk	William N.
Baron	Julia Adeline	Kirby	Charles F., Jr.
Baron	Sarah	Peterson	Anton
Baroni	Isabel	Ramatici	Romeo
Barr	Maysel	Morgan	John Albert
Barr	Myrtle	Beckman	Albert
Barrass	Mayme Lowery	Anderson	Albert Gustav
Barrett	Kittie C.	Smith	Owen
Barrett	Linnie Mary	Freitas (?)	Frederick Augustius
Barrett	Luella B.	McCombs	John F., Jr.
Barrett	Mary	Hefferman	William H.
Barringer	Matilda	Kellogg	Edward L.
Barrows	Leah Louise	Hoyt	Franklin Lowe
Barrows	Mary J.	Heid	Conrad G.
Barrows	Olive M.	Fuchs	Ewald A.
Barrows	Edith Ainslie	Dietz	Henry Werner

Barry	Agnes Claire	Nieman	James E.	Baruch	Anita	Cottle	Edmund J.
Barry	Alice E.	Johnson	Ober J.	Barz	Louise	Suesman	Richard
Barry	Honora	Graban	John	Barzi	Angelina	Masini	Sante
Barry	Julia M.	Sweeney	John J.	Basaglia	Amelia E.	Banchiero	Antone T.
Barry	Margaret M.	Bill	Frank B.	Basaglia	Angeline	Gori	Michael
Barsi	Abbina	Cassine	Frank	Basford	Ida Ellen	Bertron	Albert
Barsi	Della	Maffini	Ernest	Bassett	Alice	Seybold	Arthur P. C.
Barsi	Rosina	Wagner	Frank H.	Bassett	Lillian E.	Matthews	James L.
Barsi	Silvia	Fanucchi	Angelo	Bassetti	Amelia	Mossi	Achille
Barsuglia	Josie	Diceare (?)	Salvatore	Bassetti	Claudina C.	Pesenti	Tido
Barth	Mae	Morgan	Carey	Bassi	Julia	Laveroni	Dave
Barth	Mary E.	Matthews	Charles W.	Basso	Leveria T.	Smith	James Monroe
Barth	Susie A.	Campbell	Walter G.	Bastoni (?)	Mary R.	Simi	William Anthony
Barthold	Edna V.	Simpson	Arthur C.	Bata	Grace	Heyneman	David H.
Bartholdy	Elsie	Volonte	Arthur P.	Batchelder	Ona R.	Wiig	George H.
Bartholdy	Ottilie	Cristofani	Louis	Bateman	Harriett N.	Duerner	William, Jr.
Bartholomew	Yula D.	Harrison	Francis Richard	Bates	Charlotte	Herbert	William
Bartle	Fannie Myrtle	Beeson	Charles Wesley	Bates	Laura E.	Crigler	Albert P.
Bartlett	Clara	Brown	William	Bates	Lottie	Cotter	William
Bartlett	Delia	Ross	George Breabner	Bates	Marion	Grant	Frederick T.
Bartlett	Ella Lillian	Brown	Frank J.	Bates	Nancy C.	Olin	Silas W.
Bartlett	Frances Gertrude	Lewis	J. Hall	Bates	Pauline C.	McMullin	Joseph E.
Bartlett	Sibyl	Bendorf	Derby	Bates	Sarah E.	Potter	Stephen D.
Bartlett	Ella M.	Moody	Harry E.	Bathaglia	Lena	Bonfigli	Alvise
Bartlow	Edith Mable	Cussins	William Edison	Batt	Alice E.	Whalen	William E.
Bartlow	Mary Elizabeth	Jinks	William Woods	Batt	Alice May	Evans	Merle Lester
Bartoli	Edith	Camotta	Laurence	Batt	Faith Ray	McLennan	James
Bartoli	Palmira	Zanetta	Giovanni	Batt	Lillian	Stibi	John
Bartolomei	Amelia	Gionnoni	Eugene	Batta	Katie	Figone	August
Bartolomei	Sabina	Galli	Verginio	Battaglia	Luisa	Bindi	Acille
Barton	Adda Ella	Washington	C. A.	Battaglia	Mary, Mrs.	Rose	Frank Steven
Barton	Annie A.	Taggard	Fred A.	Battaglia	Polissene	Giannecchini	Aladino
Barton	Nellie	Melton	William	Battaglia	Valeria	Pelletti	Aristo
Bartow	Gladys	Taxon	J. L.	Batten	Mattie H.	Fairchild	Fred F.
Bartow	Helen	Gwin	Andrew J.	Batten	Sarah, Mrs.	Lockard	Joseph H.

Batterfield (?)	Ida	Paparo (?)	Bartisti	Beard	Gertrude V.	Copsey	Lumin
Batti	Regina	Pagani	John	Beard	Jennie	Browning	Edmond
Batto	Louise R.	Groskoff	Albert, Jr.	Beardin	Mary E., Mrs.	Laughlin	Joseph P.
Baudendistel	Annie	Winter	Bernhardt	Beardon	Martha E.	Blakley	Thos. S.
Bauder	May	Cole	Nathaniel J.	Beardsley	Ada	Patrick	Corydon A.
Bauer	Caroline	Eferly	John	Beasley	Bessie C.	Corrick	William B.
Bauer	Jennie	Cantor	Nathan	Beattie	Alice M.	Bassett	Henry W.
Bauer	Valesea C.	Kane	Thomas	Beattie	Edith I.	Miller	Raymond F.
Baum	Arvilley K.	Heffelfinger	William	Beattie	Friedia	Garofalo	Bert
Baum	Pearl J.	Cuicello	Frank Louis	Beatty	Bessie Helen	Roland	Eugene W.
Bauman	Emma Christina	Shaffer	Ruben Hilman	Beatty	Maggie	Clawson	Cyrus R.
Bauman	Clara E.	Seymour	William R.	Beatty	May V.	Gammill	Charles F.
Baumann	Ida	Hopcroft	Charles	Beauchamp	Lellah Myrtle	Rego	Dan James
Baumberger	Alice B.	Zehnder	Rudolph A.	Beauchamp	Ruth	Shriver	Realford
Bavricklow	Emma Alice	Carah	J. H.	Beaufils	Marie C.	Turk	J. A.
Baxman	Alice	Caughey	Chester	Beaulieu	Marie H.	Harwood	John F.
Baxman	Hattie Laurietta	Dicke	George	Beaver	Clara B.	Simmons	Thos. S.
Baxter	Delia D.	Westrup	Alexander	Beaver	Mary Alice	Rommel	George Bernhard
Bazzano	Edith	Venturino	John	Beaver	Rosa E.	Cox	William M.
Beach	Agnes	Newburgh	A. S.	Beaver	Susannah	Ross	William T.
Beach	Bertha	Ferguson	Edward	Beaver	Sylvia	Beaver	W. J.
Beach	Clara M.	Fogarty	James V.	Beccaria	Maddelina	Parravicini	Antonio
Beach	Della E.	Mayes	Ernest E.	Bech (?)	Elisabeth	Koebeli	Rudolph
Beach	Helen G.	Cox	William Toliver	Beck	Belle	Gibson	G. W.
Beach	Jeannette	Lacque	Clarence Andrew	Beck	Estena M.	Wipner	Antone H.
Beagley	Emma Violet	Zimmerman	Albert C.	Beck	Maryanne	Waldow	William F.
Beal	Bessie M.	Snyder	Herbert B.	Beck	Maven	Nielsen	Hans Thomsen Beck
Beall	Mattie A.	Varney	Oscar R.				
Beam	Alice May	Craig	Francis A.	Beck	Metta	Peters	Henry
Beaman	Nellie E.	Rollins	Martin	Becker	Alice M.	Bogusch	Herbert W.
Bean	Harriet Newell	Lawrence	Frank	Becklund	Olge	Hemmarberg	Edward
Bean	Helen A.	Guptill	Roscoe Volney	Beckman	Emma Lena	Makee	George William
Bean	Jessie May	Hessel	Andrew Conrad	Beckmann	Lillie	O'Brien	John W. F.
Bean	Luvica	Painter	James	Beckner	Carrie O.	Mussleman	Jesse A.
Bean	Zella	Melton	Thomas	Beckner	Lillian E.	Callahan	Walter H.

Beckner	Lulu	Rennison	Arthur W.	Beitels	Jewel	Andersen	Cyril Harry
Beckwith	Catherine E.	Strickland	Oliver P.	Bel	Ida May	Biddings	Henry A.
Bedford	Elise	Lentz	Walter Edward	Belcher	Gertrude	Windt	Henry C.
Bedwell	Annie Alberta	Mann	Frank B.	Belcher	Ruth A.	Dalton	Edwin P.
Bedwell	Belva	Drake	Jacob Hopper	Belden	Grace A.	Kragel	Adam H.
Bedwell	Jane	Niles	Annias	Belding	Jessica	Brodie	Louis F.
Bee	Maud M.	Sicotte	Frederick	Belgum	Marie	Jennings	C. S.
Bee	Myrtle May	West	Wilbur P.	Belin	Agnes	Carlson	Gust
Beebe	Christina M.	Heyward	Jesse	Bell	Alice	Young	Robert
Beebe	Frances J.	Davis	B. F.	Bell	Alice Ruth	Hewlett	Louis Clifton
Beebe	Grace E.	Sutherland	James T.	Bell	Amanda Lydia, Mrs.	Maltman	Francis D.
Beebe	Maggie	Mumay	William				
Beebe	Olive D.	Heckley	Thomas B.	Bell	Carrie V.	Callen	S. H.
Beebe	Stella S.	Gisel	Herman	Bell	Geneva	McCutchen	James B.
Beedle	Addie	Alfiere	Joseph	Bell	Hazel C.	Streeter	Alvin D.
Beedle	Bella	Jones	Noah	Bell	Lilly Amelia	Turton	Luther Mark
Beedle	Georgie F.	Todd	Marion E.	Bell	Lucinda	Adamson	Isaac Newton
Beedle	Josephine	Kingwell	B.	Bell	Maggie E.	Kelly	William S.
Beedle	Lena E.	Decvursoy (?)	John	Bell	Mary E.	McBride	Murrie J.
Beeson	Anna	Bowbeer	C. W.	Bell	Mary E.	Wilson	Charles
Beeson	Ella Frances	McPherson	Harry Moore	Bell	Myrtle M.	Ross	William H.
Beeson	Elva Marie	Grant	Ralph Delano	Bell	Sarah Emma	Cox	Thomas W.
Beeson	Eunice Naomi	Ferguson	John N.	Bell	Vivian Phillis	Hennisch	Albert G.
Beeson	Ida	Romine (?)	Thomas	Bellah	Eldora May	Wilson	Clifford John
Beeson	Kate	Miller	David	Bellah	Viola N.	Kelly	Mark P.
Beffa	Lillie	DeRosa	Manuel	Bellah	Mildred M.	Martin	Ira P.
Begbie	Jeanne	Halliday	William J.	Bellesi	Domenica	Bellesi	Achelli
Beguhl	Emma	Bell	Holly E.	Belli	Faustina	Pieroni	Enrico
Behler	Helena	Gorman	James B.	Belli	Flora	Cottini	Erico
Behrens	Gertrude Louise	Tomlinson	Walter Leland	Belli	Marguerite	Masconi	Pasquale
Behrens	Henrietta	Asher	Sidney	Bellingham	Maggie	Middagh	William A.
Behrens	Irene	Stack	James J.	Bello	Mary	Rogers	Frank P.
Behrens	Tillie	Hermann	Albert	Bellotti	Mary	Mazzucchi	Adorno
Behrs	Minnie	Steinweg	Ernest	Bellotti	Minnie	Bassignani	Cesare
Beier	Mette M.	Degn	Jorgen Andersen	Belsardi	Mary Ida	Pellascio	William Oliver

Beltrametti	Teodolinda	Alessi	Ignazio	Benton	Beulah	Smith	Henry Claude
Benatti	Italia	Borelli	Matteo	Bentsen	Carola	Matson	Hjalmar
Bender	Anna	Ramos	Frank	Bentz	Eda M.	Smith	Albert K.
Bender	Madeleine L.	Ambler	J. Raymond	Bentzan	Amelia	Scott	Niels C.
Benedetti	Agnes	Caseri	Arthur	Benvenuti	Lena	Pera	Giuseppi
Benedetti	Amalia Rosa	Burmester	Charles F. D.	Beretta	Olivia	Ghisletta	Antonio
Benedetti	Charlotte M.	Maggiora	Costantino Delbi (?)	Beretta	Theresa D.	O'Connell	John M.
				Berger	Anna E.	Daw	J. M.
Benedetti	Clarinda	Bogale	John	Berger	Clara Lee	Larimer	Robert E.
Benedetti	Edith M. (Tela)	Belluomini	Palmiro	Berger	Ermma Amalia	Witherell	Alonzo D.
Benedetti	Marriana	Peri	Zelindo	Berger	Flora	Posh	Edward Nanthiel
Benelli	Carmelinda	Vannucci	Angelo	Berger	Flora Helen	Martin	Robert Edward
Benelli	Madalena	Vannucci	Luigi	Berger	Hattie E.	Jarvis	L. B.
Benelli	Rosa	Mastrado	Angelo	Berger	Mollie	Poznansky	Solomon
Benjamin	Penelope F.	Hammell	Fred R.	Berger	Ruth E.	Jarvis	Eugene L.
Benner	Etta M.	McKeand	William J.	Bergersen	Magdalena	Ivarson	A. G.
Bennett	Alice H.	Dei	Henry	Bergmann	Mary R.	Jenkins	Gilbert C.
Bennett	Clara L.	Thompson	Arthur E.	Bergmann	Minna	Oster	Henry
Bennett	Ethel A.	Houghton	Wm. H.	Beria	Ernesta	Saraiba	Marcelino
Bennett	Eunice	Wilson	W. F.	Berka	Regina	Beukers	Peter Gerard
Bennett	Freda, Mrs.	Manning	Lincoln	Berkman	Eva Josephine	Parkhouse	Mark Cowell
Bennett	Mary	Roberts	Charles	Berling	Elsie M.	Rathke	Adolph W.
Bennett	Mary A.	Banta	John H.	Bernardi	Inez M.	Mundell	Oliver A.
Bennett	Susie Edna	Douglass	Stephen Chester	Bernasconi	Della	Chicca	Americo
Benninghoven	Emma	Gilder	Alfred	Bernauer	Frieda	Egenhoff	Julius A.
Benoit	Dixie	Payne	Charles A.	Berndt	Gladys	Miller	Raymond J.
Benson	Bertha J.	Turner	Oscar Clinton	Bernetti	Lizza	Bertoli	Paulo
Benson	Laura E.	Ward	Thomas B.	Bernier	Frances Ellen, Mrs.	Crawford	Jesse Blacker
Benson	Mabel E.	Brunings	John H.				
Benson	Marcia E.	Foster	Charles Simpson	Bernstein	Sophie	Wiener	Louis
Benson	Martha E.	Miller	Chas. S.	Berry	Anna Belle	Mays	John Burton
Benson	Rowena	Downing	Arthur B.	Berry	Carrie Ella	Barnes	Thomas Sturgis
Benson	Velma Lee	Brunk	Hugh Dennis	Berry	Ethel	Combs	George
Bentley	Jessie Lerona	Surryhne	John Calvin	Berry	Gertrude	Linebaugh	Robert
Benton	Alice	Hughes	Judd	Berry	Gladys G.	Wright	Winfield R.

Berry	Ina	Odell	George P.	Bettencourt	Mae Erneline	Petersen	Walter Chester
Berry	Isabelle Lavonia	Staley	Clarence Carl	Bettiga	Anna	Cerutti	Paul
Berry	Lelia	Harris	Bert A.	Bever	Cleo Maud	Kistner	Lester Alfred
Berry	Lovonia J.	Ward	John E.	Bew	Jennie	Prindle	Henry
Berry	Mary E.	Schneider	August T.	Beynon	Evelyn F.	Strasser	Edward D.
Berry	N. L.	Young	C. M.	Biaggi	Marta	Vitali	John
Berryessa	Rose D.	Swetters	Joe F.	Biagi	Lottie	Ambrose	Frank
Bert	Mary	Underwood	G. C.	Bianchi	Eugenia	Geremia	Massente
Berta	Anna	Gilardi	Joe P.	Bianchini	Dora	Puffer	Bruce
Berta	Emma Mengere	Birkle	Nickolas	Bianchini	Giulia	Guffanti	Emilio
Bertini	Cattina	Rosselli	Mario	Bianchini	Sarah	Rawson	Ralph J.
Bertino	Rose N.	Bianchini	Giovanni W.	Bianchini	Sarah, Mrs.	Bianchini	Mario
Bertod	Angiolina, Mrs.	Violetti	Giuseppe	Bice	M. E.	Bell	Geo. K.
Bertolani	Mary C.	Schmidt	Henry W.	Bice	N. E.	Sargent	Henry
Bertoli	Assunta	Pelletti	Louis	Bice	Sarah	Kelly	Thomas Lamb
Bertoli	Carmella	Lombardi	Guiseppe	Bickers	Mary	Turner	W. H.
Bertoli	Erminia	Alessandrini	Charles	Biddings	Hazel	Skelton	John W.
Bertoli	Maria	Gozzarino	John	Biddings	Ida M., Mrs.	Stone	T. B.
Bertoli	Stella M.	Motroni	Herbert J.	Biddle	Edna	Stone	Mark V.
Bertolucci	Liduina	Bandiera	Emil	Biddle	Ruth M.	Hilder	Henry D.
Bertolucci	Lieta	Micheli	Giovani	Bidetti	Frances Nora	Ward	Francis Moore
Bertoni	Amelia	Furia	Quinto	Bidwell	Antonia P.	Brooks	Henry W.
Bertoni	Maria	Porta	Fred	Bidwell	Eva	Siemer	Diedrich, Jr.
Bertoni	Maria	Colombani	Primo	Bidwell	Frances E.	St. Clair	Frank C.
Bertoni	Natalina	Frati	Giuseppe	Bidwell	Freda M.	Caldwell	J. G.
Bertoni	Rose I.	Carniglia	Charles A.	Bidwell	Lennie G.	Cunmmings	Charles E.
Bertossi	Josie	Buzzi	Joseph L.	Bidwell	M. Callie	Johnson	Andrew E.
Bertossi	Liberata	Ariasi	Peter	Bidwell	Nancy Jane	Anderson	James H.
Bertossi	Teresa	Marcucci	Faustino	Bidwell	Rena	Pugett	Henry J.
Bertozzi	Pascuina	Cecchi	Pietro	Bidwell	Sarah J.	Gober	B. F.
Bertres	Marie, Mrs.	Lestingue	Jean	Biedermann	Marie B.	Trowbridge	N. S.
Beteneur	Marianna Teadora	de Silva	Manuel R.	Bierkle	Emma Christine	Belvail	John H.
Bethel	Dora	Head	Albert P.	Bigham	Lula Jane	Coburn	William
Bettencourt	Belmera	Avilla (?)	A. I.	Biglin	Rosa	Pedigo	Grayson E.
Bettencourt	Elvira S.	Kreidler	Carl W.	Bigllow	Mary E.	Scott	Charles

Biglon	Maggie	Ronsheimer	Peter H.	Bisordi	Emilia	Bourbeau	Joseph
Bigsby	Macueleta	Abbey	Alfred B.	Bisordi	Emma M.	Del Bianco	Attilio
Bigsby (?)	Bell	Beaver	J. S.	Bisordi	Lizzie	Ponti	Baltromeo Carlo
Bihli	Eliza	Brittisigi (?)	Leo	Bispo	Mary E.	Davila	Antonio S.
Bill	Estelle L.	Chambers	William D.	Bither	Nellie E.	Smith	John K.
Bill	Lucy A.	Alexander	John	Bither	Susie	Nordyke	Wm.
Billing	Edith C.	Goodman	Daniel O.	Bitter	Annie M.	Nichols	William A.
Billings	Nellie I.	Corrillo	Leo Arthur	Bittner	Ella Emile	Huph	Henry Philip
Billman	Susie A.	Haley	Charles F.	Bittner	Martha	Glynn	Burr Augustus
Bimmerle	Emma	Gercich	Fred	Bittner	Mary H.	Genazzi	Charles E.
Bin	Lena	Marin	George	Bittner	Nellie	Redmond	Patrick J.
Bin	Theresa	Tonelli	Agostino	Bizzini	Bessie	Rock	Peter
Binggeli	Rosa	Mini	Olindo	Bjornskob	Nicolina Christina	Cartwright	Aubrey Badger
Bingham	Agnes H.	Pattini	Ernest	Black	Ada	Hirschman	J. C.
Bingham	Margaret	Cruz	Joe	Black	Alice	Beggs	W. H.
Bingham	Olga R.	Brand	Fenton M.	Black	Annabelle	Ornbaun	Breck
Binner (?)	Elizabeth	Deaueare (?)	John	Black	Ellen C.	Shelford	Levi L.
Binton	Luc?? M.	Woodward	Orrin T.	Black	Elsie M.	Williams	Walter W.
Bioletti	Beatrice	Spaulding	Thomas W.	Black	Harriet Isabel	Clark	A. N.
Bird	Emma L.	McKee	Harry B.	Black	Jessie F.	Lowrey	George W.
Bird	Grace L.	Plum	James M.	Black	Mabel C.	Putman	John Wesley
Birkenstock	Eleen	Glinden	Harry	Black	Marie	McCready	Thomas
Birks	Elizabeth Richmond	McFadden	Joseph	Black	Mary J.	Shelford	Erastus M.
				Black	Mary M.	Kidd	David W.
Biscarro	Nettie S.	Slover	James E.	Black	Myrtle E.	Forbes	Alfred L.
Bischoff	Albertine Louise	Junge	Walter Frederick	Black	Villa	Cook	Frank A.
Bischoff	Louise	Schilling	Louis	Blackall	Bertha	Seymour	Louis C.
Bish	Maria Ann	Wells	Pleasant	Blackmon (?)	Emily A.	Elgin	Ira P.
Bishop	Ada R.	Owen	Llewelyn	Blaha	Catherine	Korbel	Frank
Bishop	Bessie M.	Reid	David P.	Blain	Audrey Jane	Madison	James
Bishop	Delia	Robinson	John W.	Blain	Mary E.	Wright	Paul Jones
Bishop	Effie	McFeely	John	Blaine	Lillian M.	Fischer	William R.
Bishop	Florence	West	Frank	Blair	Huldah	Moore	Fred T.
Bishop	May M.	Cannon	R. D.	Blair	Josephine	Bignell	James
Bishop	Nellie M.	Bones	Benjamin Marcus	Blair	Julia	Ormsby	Charles W.

Blair	Mary	Huderson	Robert G.	Bloch	Rose	Otley	Fred, Jr.
Blair	Nellie M.	Orr	Roy R.	Block	Clara M.	Rossi	Albert
Blair	Gertie	Beach	Gordon S.	Block	Lora	Kloustermeyer	Wm. J.
Blake	Ada	Pierce	Eugene I.	Block	Mamie M.	Coutts	Maxwell C.
Blake	Effie M.	Kirkland	David J.	Blockinton	Cora A.	York	August A.
Blake	Ella	Hansen	Orin F.	Blodget	Anna	Horak	Ferdinand
Blake	Lulu E.	Horton	Arthur	Blodgett	Bessie May	Williams	Benjamin Clay
Blake	Maggie M.	Gwin	Andrew Jones	Blonquist	Amanda	Miller	Francis W.
Blake	Minerva	Burling	William B.	Bloom	Anna M.	Linser	Frederick W.
Blake	Minnie	Quant	William E.	Bloom	Beniamina	Traversi	Joseph
Blake	Minnie A.	Richardson	Charles H.	Bloom	Celia Virginia	Filippini	John Ernest
Blake	Ruth W.	Morrow	Harrison E.	Blosser	May Pearl	Saunders	Eugene Walter
Blake	Wilmot	Shultz	Theodore F.	Blum	Theresa	Herbst	John Frank
Blakesley	Delina May	Tyrrell	Harry	Blumenthal	Valerie	Blumenthal	Albert M.
Blakesley	Lillie Maud	Meranda	Howard E.	Blunden	Grace Lancefield	Slye	Franklin Albert
Blakley	Annie	Fisher	David	Blunden	Violet	Hall	Albert Leroy
Blakley	Mary E.	King	William	Board	Neva J.	Watson	Benjamin Franklin
Blakley	Oliva M.	Walton	Jay A.	Bocca	Clementina	Maccagno	Joseph
Blanchard	Lizzie Eveline	Lane	Louis M., Jr.	Bocca	Mary	Toronto	Joseph
Blanck	Annie	Hillman	Theodore	Bock	Kate	Magoon	Wm. H.
Blanck	Katherine M.	Johns	Frederick	Bodwell	Charlotte Elizabeth	Morgan	Ross
Blandini	Armenia	Boida	G.				
Blandini	Ermini, Mrs.	Reed	Peter	Boechen	Anna	Golsch	Henry
Blank	Grace, Mrs.	Holst	Joseph A.	Boehm	Annie	Miller	Garnet W.
Blank	Ismpie (?)	Johnson	Dudley H.	Boehm	Ella L.	Chambers	Benjamin H.
Blankstein	Belle	Moose	Edward Henry	Boehrner	Annie E.	Gemmer (?)	John C.
Blattenberger	Zoe N.	Aaronson	Phillip V.	Boettcher	Oreon E.	Weber	Hermann
Blazer	Ethel Rae	Enzenauer	Joe	Boettcher	Pollie A.	Berka	F.
Blazer	Lena A.	Benepe	W. Weimer	Bogart	Julia R.	Short	Orville B.
Blazer	Lois	Sanborn	Ralph C.	Boghkert	Augsta	Pitt	J. W.
Blazer	Mabel Edna	Dutra	John E.	Bohen	Josie	Breen	John M.
Bledsoe	Sarah Amanda	Sprague	James Henry	Bohn	Edna M.	Anderson	Albert V.
Blessing	Josephine	Carman	Harry Vanoy	Bohn	Ida E.	Arfsten	Conrad H.
Blindhein (?)	Alma	Lee	Edward P.	Bohn	Jennie	Dibble	Leroy Earl
Bloch	Rosa	Austin	Chas.	Bohn	Leona G.	Williams	Clayton S.

Bohn	Mary Lena	Estes	John	Bone	Maud, Mrs.	Hutchison	Lawrence
Boicelli	Rachele	Passalacqua	Francisco	Bone (?)	Ellen	Harding	William A.
Boido	Francissa	Stradella	Louis (Luigi)	Bonee	Nancy	Vasser	Nicholas
Bojorques	Elizabeth L.	Evans	Charles E.	Bones	Alice	Garcia	Chick
Bojorques	Mary A.	Farley	George F.	Bones	Electa Z.	McCord	Robert B. M.
Bolden	Nettie C.	Hindson	Francis	Bones	Elizabeth A.	Lovell	David J.
Bolla	Domenica	Bizzini	Joseph	Bones	Ella Bessie	Lunger	Elmer S.
Bolla	Eda	Quanchi	Gilio	Bones	Elsie D.	Lapham	William C.
Bollard	Marguerite M.	Heintz	John H.	Bones	Hattie	Brians	Benjamin
Bolle	Sopha M.	Mulhall	Thomas J.	Bones	Hazel Celia	Ahern	George F.
Bollinger	Catherine	Manch	Gottfried	Bones	Hila	Hatler	Joseph E.
Bollinger	Dora Francis	Gebharth	Christian	Bones	Lida M.	Dillon	John H.
Bollinger	Maggie	Hargens	Charles	Bones	Lillie	Means	Thomas Jefferson
Bologna	Lina	Forno	Alasandro	Bonetti	Claudina	Tamba	Vittoria
Bologne	Lizzie	Babbini	Paul	Bonfigli	Nazarena	Langero	Giovani
Bolton	Emma M.	Millee	C. T.	Bonham	Alma Ruth	Williams	Roy Henry
Bolton	Sallie, Mrs.	Hicks	Moses C.	Bonham	Lucia M.	Peterson	Carl Herbert
Boman	Hilda	Rasmussen	Peter	Bonham	Mattie	Mitchell	John H.
Boman	Marian Beatrice	Acorne	Melville G.	Bonham	Mattie Olive	Smithers	George Edward
Bommer	Ella	Nitchman	Jno. A.	Bonham	Murrel Agatha	Story	Alonzo Louis
Bona	Annie E.	Johnson	George C.	Bonham	Rena Lucile	Allen	James Rodney
Bonaccorsi	Mary	Lombardi	Peter	Bonhan	Rose M.	Snyder	Charles M.
Bonacina	Emily	Sbarboro	Augustus John	Boning	Marie H.	Hansen	Albert
Bond	Bertha Elizabeth	Juler	George Albert	Bonini (?)	Felicita	Graglia	John
Bond	Calra F.	Rasmussen	James W.	Bonkofsky	Willamena	Henry	Charles P.
Bond	Carrie M.	Winterberg	Dan	Bonnardel	Benaite, Mrs.	Wallace	Boladen L.
Bond	Frances G.	McGlauflin	Hallam C.	Bonneau	Laura N.	Augustus	Martin
Bond	Jessie Mae	Johnson	John Berger	Bonnel	Edith, Mrs.	Gill	George Willard
Bond	Julia	Turner	James E.	Bonnemason	Louise M.	Bonnecaze	Joseph
Bond	Lizella Edith	Hollingshead	Edward	Bonnemazon	Catherine	Labat	Jean
Bond	Lola Ethel	Hibbard	Charles Elbert	Bonner	Grace I.	Granice	Harry H.
Bond	May Emily	Harkness	Raymond L.	Bonner	Jean C.	Weeks	Frank P.
Bond	Rosie May	Pomeroy	George W.	Bonner	Lavinia	Wooden	John
Bondi	Claudina	Bellazzini	Senio	Bonner	Mary D. Irwin	Weeks	Parker H.
Bondi	Mary	Ciavarelli	Nello	Bonnula	Inez M.	Norton	James C.

Bonsell	Ada	Herald	E. H.	Bosqui	Emma	Simmons	Joseph C. A.
Bonter	Lillian J.	Pippin	John H.	Boss	Ada May	Peters	William Charles
Booher	Mary Luemma	Allen	Thomas Edgar	Boss	Laura	Stark	Geo.
Booker	Caroline	Harwell	George O.	Bossen	Sophia	Dodge	Milton
Boone	Renette Emogene	Hughes	Henry F.	Bostick	Mary	Myers	D. P
Booth	Eugenie M.	Hooper	Thomas R.	Bostick	Louise M.	Hunt	Elmer H.
Booth	Jennie L.	Renner	Jacob F.	Boston	Ethel	Steen	William H.
Booth	Nettie L.	Taylor	John W.	Bostrom	Anna C.	Hansen	Antone M.
Boothby	C. M., Mrs.	Hatton	J. E.	Boswell	Clara J.	Jennison	Alfred M.
Boradori	Nettie	Antognini	Carlo	Boswell	Cora L.	Dale	J. W.
Borba	Margaret Genevieve	Anderson	Mose A.	Boswell	Daisy	Winkler	Arthur S.
				Bosworth	Cora May	Hanlon	Newton B.
Borba	Maria	Oswill	Charles E.	Bosworth	Fannie L.	Cramer	John F.
Borboni	Laudivini	Patterson	James H.	Bosworth	Georgie	Rose	H. W.
Borchers	Clara	Gruenhager	Henry	Bosworth	Mary Etta	Hale	John F.
Borchert	Iva A.	Williams	Wm. J., Jr.	Bosworth	Viola	Wyckoff	Amos
Bord	Dixie O.	Casey	Thurman G.	Bottorff	Mary	Whitehom	George
Borden	Frances Lynes	Smith	Clarence Cushing	Botts	Ethel	Howard	Frederick W.
Bordessa	Juiliana	Bordessa	Antonio	Boud	Effie	Michael	David Benj.
Bordocchi	Carlotha	Simoni	Geremia	Bour	Emma	Schwan	Fred
Borer	Florence A.	Herbert	Victor	Bourdens	Emilie	Sioli	Victor E.
Borges	Mae Clara	Souza	Bartholomew C.	Bourgon	Amelia	Halvarsen	Herbert T.
Borges	Mary	King	Joseph G.	Bourke	Mary E.	Conway	Edward P.
Borgess	Mary Amelia	Zappa	Alfredo A.	Bourne	Anna L., Mrs.	Reale	Antonio L.
Borghi	Rosalia Grace	Poncia	Jerome	Bourras	Catherine	Ash	Frank E.
Borgo	Stella	Wilson	John	Bouse	Urith	Cooper	James M.
Borgonovo	Erminia	Sala	James	Bovee	Helen, Mrs.	Wahrman	Leopold H.
Borhinger	Margaret, Mrs.	Beatty	James H.	Bow	May	Rosasco	George
Bork	Lizzie Sophia	Zimmerman	Frederick John	Bowe	Josephine	Jackson	Arthur V.
Boronda	Jennie	Smith	Earle	Bowen	Elenore C.	Metzger	George V.
Borotra	Grace, Mrs.	Ungewitter	John Franklin	Bowen	La Verne	Leclileiter	Joaeph A.
Borreo	Thelma M.	Spencer	Robert M.	Bower	Emma Katherine	Hayt	William A.
Borsen	Ella M.	Peoples	Curtis V.	Bower	Grace Lillian	Cox	Stacy Verne
Bosch	Katherine	Levey	Morris	Bower	Margaret Belle	Salisbury	Ralph Francis
Bosch	May B.	Rochat	Fuller A.	Bower	Marguerite Evelyn	Schneider	Joseph Charles

Bower	Mary L.	Scheidecker	Albert F.
Bower (?)	Sarah	Patchett	Benjamin E.
Bowers	Bertha Blanche	Lambert	Lewis A.
Bowers	Eliza M.	Hicks	George M.
Bowers	Elizabeth A.	Huntley	Albert
Bowers	Elizabeth Clara	Floyd	Fred
Bowers	Ilene	Webber	L. Ross
Bowersmith	Lottie V.	Day	Carl F.
Bowie	Mae Josephine	Duttweiler	Frederick
Bowie	Vera	Francis	William A.
Bowles	Veda A.	Hart	Leo Blair
Bowman	Bertha May	Mount	John Clayton
Bowman	Estella May	Matthews	Frederic Hamilton
Bowman	Gertrude	Pitts	Charles
Bowman	Hazel E.	Schlinkmann	Frederick W.
Bowman	Jessie Z.	Black	Charles M.
Bowman	Lela E.	Smith	Walter R.
Bowman	Mamie Francis	Clinesmith	Fred
Bowman	Minnie	Tryon	A. E.
Bowman	Rebecca	Shader	G. C.
Bowmer	Abbie W.	Cozzins	Davenport
Bowse	Nellie F.	McKee	Samuel
Boxall	Katie	Tyler	Geo. H. W.
Boxold	Margaret E.	Ireland	Claude C.
Boyce	Lillian A.	O'Brien	Edward W.
Boyce	Ruth Alice	Tilden	William Richard
Boyd	Belle	Shaw	Daniel Berkeley
Boyd	Dorothy Juanita	Butler	Vernon Miller
Boyd	Elizabeth L.	McCown	George M.
Boyd	Ella Vinora	McMillen	James William
Boyd	Emma	Simpson	A. W.
Boyd	Lodeemah	Ross	George
Boyd	Lottie Moore	Pannell	Alfred Thomas
Boyd	Viola	Brittian	George McAlpine
Boydston	Grace Eloise	Smith	Lester Merritt
Boyer	Gertrude Emily	Hicks	Walter Eugene
Boyer	Mabel C.	Albright	Frederick W. H.
Boyer	Margerette A.	Endicott	Perry A.
Boyes	Emma California	Wise	Charles Henry
Boyes	Lola M.	Boysen	Clarence Constant
Boyes	Polly H.	Hill	James M.
Boyle	Catherine J.	Duncan	James A.
Boyle	Mary	Wegener	Julius
Boyle	Sara Hilarita	Morgan	Patrick H.
Boynton	Eunice A., Mrs.	Taubert	Charles Theodore
Boyse	Varena	Williams	Joseph McKeney
Boysen	Helena	Stahl	Jacob F.
Boysen	Sophie Catherine	Wade	Frederick
Boysen	Flora Ellen	Wilsey	Hayes Centennial
Boyson	Gertrude E.	Flohr	Marcus
Bozza	Phyllis Leigh	Lane	Howard A.
Brachman	Maud	South	James
Brackett	Fannie E.	Jewell	Jesse I.
Bradbury	Eva	McCormick	Charles E.
Bradford	Emma A.	Wannop	Chrisopher T.
Bradley	Lydia F.	Bradley	A. F.
Bradley	Margaret	McGrath	Patrick J.
Bradley	Mary Ellen	Curtis	Robert Ross
Bradley	Sallie Ann	Peabody	Henry Adams
Bradshaw	Isabelle	Stevens	Charles O.
Bradshaw	Meita	McGuire	Bert
Bradsley	Delia	Pallo	Willie
Brady	Anna, Mrs.	Mortimer	John K.
Brady	Annie S.	Patocchi	Eugene G.
Brady	Bertha B.	Turner	Frank
Brady	Delia	Brockman	Joseph
Brady	Julia May	Mills	Allen Davis
Bragg	Lulu	Nystrom	Clarence
Braime	Martha	Winkler	Clayton
Brain	Alice P.	Carr	Charles F.

Brainerd	Maud Shafter	Strobridge	Tullius Albert	Brazil	Nellie	Azevedo	Joseph A.
Brake	A. Edith	Benns	Clarence F.	Brazil	Rose Helen	Affonso	Joseph T.
Braman	Mary	Benson	Henry	Brazil	Vetra A.	Morais	John P.
Branaum	May, Mrs.	Hough	Martin	Breakes	Katie A.	Moses	Isaac Newton
Brand	Julia	Wagner	Edward	Breakey	Mary Annie	Sample	Simon Neil
Brand	Katie	Austin	Mervyn Maison	Breaks	Blanche Edna	Hill	Robert Elmer
Brand	Marie Ellezene	Philpott	Bert Roy	Breaks	Florence F.	Foster	Edwin J.
Brand	Stella L.	Singmaster	Henry L. H.	Brechwoldt	Mabel Josephine	Wilder	William Ernest
Brandlein	Alma Theresa	Comstock	Horace William	Breckwoldt	Agnes C.	Tuttle	Joseph W.
Branick	Mary P.	Clement	Walter L.	Breckwoldt	Alma Lillian	Hickey	William Joseph
Brannan	Ida	Peterson	Peter H.	Bree	Eva	Biaggi	John Robert
Brannum	Felitha F.	Snelson	Benj. Frank	Breheny	Katie E.	Curtin	Daniel J.
Brannum	Lutitia	Pickrell	Reuben A.	Breitenbach	Emma Anita	Leiser	George
Brannum	Myrtle E.	Meyer	Fritz	Breitenbach	Gertrude I.	Grokopf	Frank D.
Branscomb	Sarah L.	Meeks	Robert G.	Breitenbach	Mathilde	Ward	Charles H.
Branson	Minnie	Coke	Joseph Homer	Breitling	Matilda	Horn	Frank Charley
Branstetter	Daisy Dean	Harris	Jesse Winfred	Breitling	Matilda	Gober	Charley Van Buren
Branstetter	F. Marie	Tenter	Herman A.	Bremer	Elmira G.	Leveroni	Victor L.
Branstetter	Sylvia S.	Mendenhall	Roy D.	Bremner	Luella May	Sohler	Frank Ernest
Braren	Edna M.	Sims	Fred C.	Brennan	Catherine	Wallis	Albert E.
Braren	Inge M.	Rorden	George	Brennan	Florence M.	Jennings	John
Brasher	Irene I.	Dwyer	James J. B.	Brennan	Hetty	Morton	John J.
Braughler	Florence I.	Cowan	William F.	Bressman	Genevieve	Jacobson	Roy
Braun	Anna J.	Vogel	Ernest Richard	Brewer	Bertha	Huffman	Eddie
Braunton	Blanche	Edwards	Arthur S.	Brewer	Fannie	Rector	W. H.
Brava	Edith	Kuhi	Henry	Brewer	Kate	Green	John
Bravo	Meri	BalVelde	Antonio	Brewitt	Augusta T.	Rickard	John
Brawley	Evaline May	Sowers	William R.	Brewitt	Lucille Elviara	Graham	James Hunter
Bray	Jessie M.	Newcomb	Walter I.	Brians	Nellie Isabelle	Holman	Edward Kingwell
Bray	Louisa J.	Mitchell	F. M.	Brians	Olive May	Chick	D. A.
Bray	Mae	Cassin	Richard J.	Brians	Ruth E.	Banks	Lester D.
Bray	Sarah Jane	Gott	William	Brick	Bettie M.	Ronsheimer	Tony A.
Brayton	Ester Ruth	Endicott	Charles L.	Brickley	Hattie	Crull	Frank M.
Brazil	Marie	Siqueira	Manuel	Brider	Erminie	Toon	Charles Tod
Brazil	Mary	Perry	Napoleon	Bridges	Katie L.	Daniels	Claude William

Bridges	Minnie	Freck	Louis P.	Brogan	Frances Catherine	Donohoe	Patrick
Bridges	Pearl May	Cliff	Ernest Henry	Brokins	Sarah Jane	Hansen	Christian C.
Bridgford	Edna A.	Starkweather	Beverly Randolph	Bronsert	Anita M.	Formway	Utah S.
Brien	Laura	Bucher	Conrad	Brooke	Annie A.	Petray	Henry C.
Briggs	Alice	Paul	Frank	Brookfield	Marie R.	Curtis	Jos. S.
Briggs	Amanda	Rose	J. E. B.	Brooks	Edith Nellie	Lane	Carlton A.
Briggs	Belle	Hanks	William W.	Brooks	Emma	Bigham	M.
Briggs	Birdie	Elphick	Henry, Jr.	Brooks	Leslie E. M.	Hunter	Eugene W.
Briggs	Elsie L.	Rowe	Frank T.	Brooks	Levinia Elizabeth	Solomon	Louis
Briggs	Grace I.	Worster	William D.	Brooks	Lucy	Hanks	Geo Lewis
Briggs	Leorah Belle	Workover	Stephen Edward	Brooks	Lucy A.	Stine	Arthur C.
Briggs	Lizzie	Harmon	Owen	Brooks	Mamie Louise	Taylor	Austin Edward
Briggs	Ruth	Schram	Leland W.	Brooks	Marjorie M.	Parks	Thomas I.
Brigham	Bertha A.	Sargent	Ulysses G.	Brooks	Mary	Chitwood	John F.
Brigham	Mamie L.	Foreman	Lorin	Brooks	Mattie	Bedwell	S. J.
Brighouse	Henrietta C.	Heald	William Thomas	Brooks	Ora F.	Von Krusze	Harold E.
Brightenstein	Maggie	Dunlap	J. L.	Brooks	Pauline	Cook	Walter D. B.
Brightenstine	Nettie E.	Ciancio	Charles	Brooks	Viola Marie	Fiege	Carl William
Bringham	Arvilla May	Jackson	Clarence S.	Brower	Lillie Bell	Scott	Albert Charles
Brining	Margaret M.	Hagler	John M.	Brower	Mary Elmira	Went	Jack Thomas
Brink	Ella Helena	Rogers	Ethan L.	Brown	A. D., Mrs.	Schnelle	Chas. Feo.
Brink	Evaline	Vanderkuy	Henry	Brown	Abbie E.	Howe	Chas. W.
Brisino	Mabel	Keller	Charley C.	Brown	Ada E.	Waite	Lester Edwin
Brittain	Grace C.	Fournier	Arthur, Dr.	Brown	Adelaide M.	Adams	Wallace A.
Brittain	Jennie M.	Tomlinson	Isaac J.	Brown	Alta Maud	Zilhart	Charles F.
Brittain	Ora C.	McDonald	Thomas J.	Brown	Amelia	Wilson	David Alex.
Broback	Naomi	Bennett	Ralph	Brown	Ann, Mrs.	Wylie	Edwin R.
Brochier (?)	Eulalie	Dusserre	Vincent	Brown	Anna W.	Shain	Elijah A.
Brockmann	Agnes M.	McCulley	T. A.	Brown	Annie I.	Douglass	Geo. V.
Brockmann	Wilhelmina Marie	Sayers	William Albert	Brown	Bernice Luretta	Fobes	Charles Fitch
Brockmon	Elizabeth J.	Anderson	Mathew	Brown	Bertha E.	Hesse	Walter E.
Brodbeck	Elizabeth	Baldocchi	Lawrence	Brown	Birdie Estella Neva	Miller	James Pierce
Broderson	Anna P.	McFarlane	James D.				
Brodie	Annie, Mrs.	Markham	Henry C.	Brown	Caroline M. N.	Von Frank	Vasil E.
Brodie	Mabel Gray	Carter	C. Gilbert	Brown	Carrie	Clark	Benjamin Henderson

Brown	Carrie	Fitch	Charley	Brown	Leatha M.	Jones	James L.
Brown	Carrie C.	Williams	Charles J.	Brown	Leila Emma	Libby	George W.
Brown	Cassie	Weyl	James	Brown	Lena May	Brown	Robert Curtis
Brown	Catherine	Grant	Ben E.	Brown	Leona	Hughes	Michael J.
Brown	Catherine A., Mrs.	Harris	John W.	Brown	Lida E.	McDonald	James P.
Brown	Cecilia Frances	Keating	William Joseph	Brown	Lillian Nathalie	O'Connor	John James
Brown	Della Louise	Morton	Charles	Brown	Lillie	Janssen	George
Brown	Edith M.	Trumbull	Robert H.	Brown	Lillie	Vogel	Charles A.
Brown	Edna Catherine	MacGowan	Henry	Brown	Lilyan F.	Smith	John Hall
Brown	Edna L.	Wesner	Fred E.	Brown	Lizzie R.	Espey	George E.
Brown	Edna L.	Fallon	John Franklin	Brown	Mabel E.	Stewart	Sidney Joseph
Brown	Elizabeth	Nail	James	Brown	Maggie	Ayers	William M.
Brown	Ella F.	Dornbach	Fred	Brown	Mamie	Wendt	Fred Berthald
Brown	Elsie I.	Batt	Elmer M.	Brown	Marguerite	Rogers	Willis
Brown	Elyda, Mrs.	Bertsch	Frank	Brown	Marguerite J.	Garrison	Charles H.
Brown	Emma	Hand	Wm. E.	Brown	Marian	Martin	Lewis
Brown	Emma G.	Fites	Charles E.	Brown	Martha E.	McFall	Frank
Brown	Erma B.	Matheson	Charles J.	Brown	Martha J.	Hays	James W.
Brown	Esther E.	Crispin	Charles A.	Brown	Mary	Price	Clyde C.
Brown	Eva R.	Peterson	James B.	Brown	Mary	Kennedy	William H.
Brown	Fannie	Moore	Charles	Brown	Mary A.	Stone	Edwin Newell
Brown	Florence	Dunlap	Robert E.	Brown	Mary E., Mrs.	Knapp	Marion O.
Brown	Francis E.	Brown	John	Brown	Mary J., Mrs.	Hansen	Edward
Brown	Georgia A.	Clark	Frank A.	Brown	Mary, Mrs.	Hutchins	Horatio
Brown	Gertrude E.	Barry	John J.	Brown	Mildred	Farnham	Leroy T.
Brown	Gladys B.	Harder	Oscar C.	Brown	Minnie	Benjamin	Frank E.
Brown	Hallie B.	Martin	Eugene E.	Brown	Minnie Wilhelmine	White	Joseph Willie
Brown	Hattie	Shinn	George Edgar				
Brown	Hazel Violia	Millerick	William Dennis	Brown	Myrtle Ellen	Nesbitt	Joseph A.
Brown	Helen Margaret	Perry	Manuel William	Brown	Myrtle M.	Choquette	Stephen A.
Brown	Hester	Ream	Elmer A.	Brown	Nina B.	Phillips	Walter L.
Brown	Josephine M.	Winkler	Ollie W.	Brown	Sallie Marie	Turner	John
Brown	Katie Maybell	Crist	Wm. H.	Brown	Sarah	Ward	George Franklin
Brown	L. Fern	Ruebenack	A. O.	Brown	Utilla	Hitchcock	John
Brown	Laura	Bennett	Grant	Brown	Virginia K.	Wightman	George E.

Brown	Malinda	Hammon	William Henry	Brush	Annie	Wilson	Thomas
Brown	Mary, Mrs.	Nixon/Hixon	Alexander	Brush	Dorothy Alice	Reams	Mannie Ellsworth
Brown (?)	Nellie	Martin	John S., Jr.	Brush	Jennie M.	Clasby	Michael M.
Browne	Ida Lee	Dukes	Elmer Frank	Brush	Lucetta Adeline	Tomasini	Walter Ernest
Browne	Minnie	Fellers	Lorenzo	Brush	Lucie	Schmid	John
Browning	Ada, Mrs.	Sebring	Wm. P.	Brush	Mame E.	Merritt	Edson C.
Browning	Catherine L.	King	Charles W.	Bryan	Angie	Chase	Frank J.
Brownlee	Ida Mabel	Myers	Frank H.	Bryan	Iva May	Breaks	Gent D.
Brownlee	Linnie	Walsh	Joseph F.	Bryan	Jessie E.	Gregg	Walter T.
Bruce	May Lena	Head	Clarence Elmore	Bryan	Marie E.	Hardin	James Taylor
Bruce	Ruth Helen	Marshall	Charles Wilson	Bryan	Maud R.	Lundholm	Charles E.
Brucher	Hazel G.	Hansen	Chris P. F.	Bryan	Susan	Barnhill	A. F.
Brucker	Isabella	Holcomb	William	Bryant	Bertha	Heaton	Charles C.
Brucker	Jeane J.	Wharton	Archie	Bryant	Caroline Augusta	Hopkins	Oliver Clay
Brugge	Loretta R.	Davidson	John	Bryant	Della D.	Garlow	J. A.
Bruhn	Mary	Bruhn	Andrew Peter	Bryant	Effie Lyle	Lovejoy	George P.
Bruhn	Nandina Rosina	Mastrup	Christian Theodore	Bryant	Ida E.	Childers	J. S.
Brumfield	Margaret Jenette	McPherson	Perry Lewis	Bryant	Lucy May	Wisecarver	Emory Lloyd
Brumfield	Priscilla	Hudson	William H.	Bryant	Lulu	Parkerson	John Carter Herbert
Brundige	Angie Fay	Walker	Benjamin F.	Bryant	Margaret J.	Chaffee	Joseph E.
Brundige	Bessie M.	Gilmore	Carl F.	Bryant	Margery	Evans	Robert H.
Brune	Anna	Breeding	Charles	Bryant	Mary	Muller	John
Bruner	Ada B.	Laymance	Henry J.	Bryant	Mary E.	Benton	C. C.
Bruner	Amanda	Esmond	Frank L.	Bryant	Ruth	Hall	Isaac K.
Bruner	Belle	Veirs	Ernst	Bryant	Susan F.	Martin	James C.
Bruner	Edith M.	McFarling	Clarence H.	Bryn	Carrie	Marshall	Thomas
Bruner	Olive L.	Doelling	Harry J. W.	Buchan	Marjorie L.	Fisk	Arthur M.
Bruner	Wilma	Wahrman	Edward H.	Buchanan	Anna	Bernnan	Patrick
Bruning	Natalie Lucile	Buger	Henry Antes	Buchanan	Effie	Martin	James Delea
Brunutti	Lucy	Sciaroni	Peter	Buchanan	Eleanor M.	Sears	Edward Ewing
Bruphacher	Elisabeth	Bernhard	Rudolph H.	Buchanan	Hilah Norine	Wallace	William
Brusa	Julia	Asti	Joseph	Buchignani	Fannie	Meschi	Ostiglio
Brusa	Mary	Pieroni	John	Buckbee	Violia	Chaffie	Weaver S.
Brusa	Rosie	Tollini	Ambrogio	Buckland	Jeff	Gorman	Syrem
Brusco	Emily J.	Pedrozzini	Clay A.	Buckle	Elsie G.	Flechner	Lloyd L.

Buckley	Margaret J.	Chace	Ernest B.	Bunn	Mable Mary	Parent	Arthur William
Buckley	Viola I.	Cooper	Lawrence H.	Buns (?)	Josephine F.	Speers	Cyrus C.
Buckman	Kathleen W.	Gibson	Floyd E.	Buonaccorsi	Penelope	Giorgi	Nicola
Buckman	Mary Jane	Harrod	W. W.	Bur	Louise M.	Stephens	Ernest J.
Bucknell	Hazel	Gowan	Francis W.	Burbank	Edna H.	Hayes	Stanley W.
Buckner	Arcadia	Richardson	Lewis	Burbank	Emma L.	Beeson	William I.
Buckner	Mary C.	Richardson	Lewis	Burch	Celesta Jane	Curtner	Alan E., Jr.
Budworth	Hester Lorene	Robinson	Harold Carleton	Burckhalter	Agnes	Adair	C. H.
Buell	Ida M.	Ely	Albert W.	Burdick	Claudia E.	Roberts	Ernest G.
Bueno	Maria	Kinney	John H.	Burger	Alta	Johnson	A. R.
Buffi	Gina	Micheletti	Stefano	Burger	Florence	Thompson	Eugene M.
Buffi	Rosaria	Micheli	Eisani	Burger	Jessie	McCarty	Eugene G.
Bugbee	Evalyn	Dirvin	Peter	Burger	Katie L.	Ross	Marvin J.
Bugby	Della M.	Terry	T. F.	Burger	Pearl J.	Mobley	John Elmer
Bugghard	Minnie	McDonald	Glen	Burgess	Beatrice	Garland	Harry
Bughani	Dahlia	Puccioni	Angelo	Burgess	Ella	Burbank	David B.
Buhl	Dorothy Inez	Lock	Ernest Lawrence	Burgess	Ethna Mae	Hamilton	Durley LeRoy
Buhl	Josie Mabel	Formschlag	August Elias	Burgess	Jennie	Brain	William H.
Buletti	Delfine C.	Todd	William Raymond	Burgess	Mary Alice	Jones	Richard
Buletti	Elvezia	Corfir	Carlo	Burgess	Mary Ann	Lang	August B.
Bull	Emma	Thurston	C. A.	Burgess	Sarah Ethel	Halleran	Joseph Francies
Bullard	Iva Irene	McEntire	Ernest J.	Burgess (?)	Maud Stella	James	Orie (?) Edward
Bullen	Clara J.	Kruse	Herbert M.	Burgett	Laura	Keller	John
Buller (?)	A.	Miner	E. E.	Burgstrom	Alice B.	Taylor	Simpson P.
Bullis/Butler (?)	Mabel Ella	Brown	John McA.	Burgstrom	Maud	Smith	Fred F.
				Burk	Jessie	Barnes	Aaron
Bulotti	Gina	Bulotti	Lee	Burk	Mrs.	Driscol	John
Bulotti	Lillian S.	Goeffert	Edward Raymond	Burke	Anna Matilda	Lopez	Charles Paul
Bulotti	Mary	Bulotti	Alexio	Burke	Annie (?)	Pickrell	Charles
Bumford (?)	Mary I.	Lehman	George	Burke	Evelyn Lucille	George	William Edgar
Bundesen	Alma Catherine	Sornsen	Fred William	Burke	Ida	Palmer	Eugene F.
Bundesen	Catherine Magdalene	Olsen	Hans Ejnar	Burke	Lillian M.	Burke	Walter A.
				Burke	Mabel P.	Jones	John P.
Bundesen	Josie Magdalene	Peters	John H.	Burke	Margaret May	Garguilo	Fred
Bundesen	Marie	Hasper	Henry	Burke	Minnie	Norrbom	Fred
Bundy	Edith	Fisk	W. C.				

Burkett	Helen M.	Girder	Clyde H.	Burroughs	Edith A.	Bury	John F.
Burkhardt	Evelyn	Hackmann	William	Burroughs	Ivy F.	Wugan	Louis G.
Burlando	Amelia	Leonardi	Joseph	Burrows	Catherine Mabel	Williams	Frank Joseph
Burman	Ellen	Pickle	Thomas Frederick	Burrus	Lizzie	Yerger	Theodore
Burnardi	Magareta	Morniga	Lugi	Burrus	Mary C.	Bousse (?)	Daniel
Burne	Mary A.	Burke	Walter A.	Burston	Francis E.	Abraham	Louis F.
Burnett	Leonora	Cardoza	John H.	Burt	Blanche A.	Bell	Walter C.
Burnham	Emily L.	Jacob	Thomas	Burtenshaw	Elizabeth	Spotswood	Joseph W.
Burnham	Isabel W.	Sylvester	James W.	Burton	Marie	Streiff	Harry
Burnham	Phebe	Enzenauer	Louis	Buschini	Maria	Malfante	Victor
Burns	Anna J.	Howell	Thomas Wm.	Bush	Ella M.	Brainard	W. H.
Burns	Bernice	Price	Malcolm E.	Bush	Lesa	Dioke	Joseph
Burns	Carrie Mable	Lawler	John Gardner	Bush	Lillian P.	Murphy	William G.
Burns	Carrie Virginia	Maxwell	John R.	Bush	Lotta	Wilhite	Lawrence R.
Burns	Elsie Viola	Boivin	Emile Peter	Bush	Margaret, Mrs.	Nelson	Leonard
Burns	Ethel G.	Hall	Eugene F.	Busher	Marion Gladys	Loney	David M.
Burns	Jennie T.	Eldridge	Joseph B.	Bushnell	Linda F.	Templeman	Robert
Burns	Jessie E.	Blakeley	Leslie A.	Bushnell	Sarah N.	Pitken	D. W.
Burns	Mae	Murray	Charles L.	Bussard	Ruth E.	Swerger	Frederick A.
Burns	Margaret	Butler	Edward H.	Bussman	Annie	Cline	Joseph V.
Burns	Mary E.	Ward	Charles A.	Bussman	Harriett I.	Hemenover	Dudley A.
Burns	Nellie T.	Laux	John Frances	Butcher	Florence E.	Rine	George W.
Burns	Rose A.	Beggs	Thomas G.	Butcher	Grace Inez	Tibbetts	John P.
Burns	Sadie R.	Thomas	William	Butin	Elsie Lee	DeLaney	Everett M.
Burns	Sarah, Mrs.	Bennett	James	Butler	Annie S.	Hassett	William Henry
Burnside	Mary D.	Taber	Elmer E.	Butler	Bessie	Dibble	William I.
Burr	Eva E.	Young	Wm. M.	Butler	Bettie	Moore	James E.
Burr	Flora I.	Bishop	E. L.	Butler	Clara	Jarred	George Carl
Burright	Retta	Berryhill	Joseph F.	Butler	Grace V.	Coolidge	Homer H.
Burris	Eudora	Glaisty	Skelton D.	Butler	Harriette M.	Early	J. Frank
Burris	Mary F.	Hopper	Henry	Butler	Ina Belle	Sharp	William Thomas
Burris	Nellie, Mrs.	Beffa	Caesar F.	Butler	Julia Emma	Spencer	Robert A.
Burrison	Alice	Hawkins	W. H.	Butler	Leonora	Wilson	Charles H.
Burriss	Ruby M.	Smith	Guy H.	Butler	Lillian R.	Locke	Albert
Burrough	Carrie Frances	Severen	Charles L.	Butler	Rosa B.	Riddle	Ulysses G.

Butler	Rosa E.	Kiester	Charles C.	Cabaup	Marie G.	Bonnard	Constant
Butler	Sarah A.	Gibson	Henry	Cabelleira	Lucia	Steven	Jose
Butler	Clara L.	Brown	M. V.	Cabral	Emilia	Andre	Anton
Butner	Cora	Walgren	John	Cadd	Alice G., Mrs.	Wheaton	John T.
Butteer	Henriette	McNeil	John	Cadd	Ethel Mae	Gibson	Henry Frank
Butterfield	Carrie	Green	Henry H.	Cadd	Frieda E.	Zanzi	Mario G.
Button	Eva A.	Gregson	Paul V.	Cadd	Lillian Rebecca	Martin	Frank F.
Button	Flossie	Bobst	George M.	Cadd	Mary I.	Goddard	Elmer F.
Button	Jennie	Dow	Geo. W.	Cademarton	Elvera Rose	Torliatt	Charles Lewis
Button	Jessie R.	Colburn	Frank N.	Cadenazzi	Rosa	Pinelli	Agostino
Button	Ruby Irene	Patteson	Harry Leroy	Cadoza	Francis	Silva	Manuel
Button	Theodosia C.	Murphy	Frank J.	Cadwell	Josephine M.	Towne	Walter
Butts	Marietta	Patton	Sylvester	Caetoft	Eunice	Nielsen	Niels
Butts	Mary E.	Fairman (?)	William J.	Cain	Hazel R.	O'Neill	William T.
Butts	May L.	Spencer	Oscar J.	Caito (?)	Belle	Harris	George F.
Butts	Nellie	McDonald	Casey	Cake	Mary Emma	Howard	David Jackson
Buzza	Jennie	Sims	Clemuel F.	Calbreath	Maggie A.	Kirkpatrick	Josiah M.
Buzzell	Lucinda	Williams	J. B. P.	Calcote	Eva Ethel	Mosely	Gus
Buzzi	Carrie	Cassini	Charley	Calder	Mary Jane	Adams	William
Buzzi	Mary	Bianconi	Mansueto	Calderwood	Elizabeth	Wright	Frederick L.
Buzzi	Nora	Filippelli	John	Caldweil	Sarah O.	Chapman	Lawrence L.
Buzzi	Rosie Nonie	Poncetta	Rocco	Caldwell	Alice Grace	Roberts	Albert Edward
Buzzini	Kate	Moni	Frank	Caldwell	Ethel Frost	Yorki	Frank Arthur
Buzzini	Teresa	Grossi	Domengo	Caldwell	Georgia	Maurer	Ed
Bwinham	Alice Ada	Upp	Arthur Frank	Caldwell	Jane	Dickson	J. C.
Byce	Eveline	Laufenburg	George	Caldwell	Lissie S.	Gugg	Roy I.
Byce	Hazel Irene	Guthrie	Vernon Hamilton	Caldwell	Martha H.	Morton	Martin Tuller
Byers	Ruth E.	Smith	Chester A.	Caldwell	Ora Helena	Lampson	Everett D.
Byington	Josephine S.	Jacks	Lorenzo D.	Calestini	Freida E.	Bush	Joe
Byler	Lucie May	Taylor	Alfred De Frees	Calhoun	Margaret M.	Wright	William A.
Byrne	Agnes	Crimmings	Ernest Fulton	Calhoun	Marguerite A.	Singmaster	Owen S.
Byrne	Lena C.	Hall	Charles S.	Caligari	Celestina	Foucrault	Edward Chas.
Byrne	Lizzie A.	Gribbin	Thomas H.	Calley	Mildred Madeline	Hodgson	Ralston Winton
Byrne	Mary Agnes	Hatton	William Henry	Callison	Leona E.	Disney	John H.
Cabaup	Maria	Albera	Michele	Calpen	Telitha	Nunn	Joseph G.

Caltoft	Mary	Lausten	Louis Mitchell
Cambra	Jimella	Cook	William E., Jr.
Cambra	Mae A.	Burrier	Edgar V.
Cambra	Mary Roseline	Brooks	Reginald Charles
Cameron	Ama Lulu	Staehlo	Frederick J.
Cameron	Florence E.	Rubottom	Herbert W.
Cameron	Hazel	Fraser	Dan W.
Cameron	Lottie	Lawry	William
Cameron	Maggie	Clark	Joseph B.
Cameron	Martha M., Mrs.	Lowrey	Robert L.
Cames	Justine	Clasquin	Emil
Camesi	Diva	Grandy	Henry
Camfield	Addie	Hoberg	James A.
Camiglia	Marssimiglia	Barsotti	Antonio
Camm	Charlotte Shepard	McNally	Thomas Charles
Camozzi	Esther E.	Wigaard	Theodore A.
Camozzi	Virginia	Pozzi	John
Camp	Eva D.	Bussman	Peter William
Campbell	Alice	Campbell	George
Campbell	Anna May	Roderick	Lawrence David
Campbell	Annie	Snider	George
Campbell	Emma L.	Snow	Harry A.
Campbell	Emma May	Stevens	James Edward
Campbell	Ethel S.	Potter	Charles R.
Campbell	Etta Edith	Enzenauer	Ed.
Campbell	Etta M.	Desin	John N.
Campbell	Florence E.	Ogg	William G.
Campbell	Grace Evelyn	Bolser	Chester Arthur
Campbell	Ida Cynthia	Moore	George Henry
Campbell	Janett	Thompson	Frank William
Campbell	Jennie L.	Bruce	Charles L.
Campbell	Leonore Francorce (?)	Christy	Henry Alfred
Campbell	Lizzie	Painter	Clarence H.
Campbell	Maggie J.	Roemer	Ernest E.
Campbell	Minnie Lucile	Ballagh	Ehrnest Ellsworth
Campbell	Mollie	Ford	William A.
Campbell	Myra I.	Shideler	Quincy N.
Campbell	Ora May	Riddle	David M.
Campbell	Phoebe L.	Gibbens	John W.
Campbell	Theresa J.	Pool	Harry E.
Campfield	Rose E.	Reynolds	Frank
Campigli	Effie	Fredericks	Adolph N.
Campini	Carolina	Modini	D.
Campion	Jessie May	Wooden	Walter Raymond
Campion	Kate	King	Charles W.
Campion	Margaret M.	Barnes	Henry L.
Campion	Margarette Ann	Runyon	Oliver Perry
Campion	May	Crist	Walter K.
Campion	Nellie	Cochran	Horace
Campomenosi	Victoria, Mrs.	Guisti	Paulo
Canale	Elvira S.	Hondaa	Emile J. B.
Canaveri	Louise	Morelli	Orlando
Canell	Nellie Floy	Howard	John W.
Canepa	Clementina	Maxzenti	Amanezio
Canepa	Mabel	Hanold (?)	Nathaniel Gould
Canevari	Clara	Baldocchi	Henry
Canevascini	Bena	Hill	William
Canevascini	Ella	Durando	Felice
Canevascini	Irene	Cavalli	Antone
Canfield	Gertrude	Dixon	William Gordon
Cannon	Julia V.	Brown	E. W.
Cantel	Eugenie	Towne	Lester B.
Cantel	Josephine L.	Schmidt	Auguste
Cantel	Rosette M.	Porter	Frederick C.
Cantell	Henriette D.	Waycott	William B.
Cantrell	Matilda A.	Robison	John S.
Canvascini	Inez	Sdrualeg	Louis
Canway	Mary E.	Miller	George
Capell	Elsie Aline	McPherson	Leon

Capell	Ethel Pauline	Ledford	John Irvin	Carlile	Lulu H.	Soules	Charles E.
Capell	Lula Romona	Murray	Cleve	Carlin	Madeleine E.	Wood	Edward C.
Capell	Margaret E.	McCracken	Geo. F.	Carlson	Esther C.	Vallier	Edwin A.
Capell	Minnie O.	Brumfield	Chas. A.	Carlson	Hilda M.	Hart	John E.
Capell	Ruby I.	Murray	Thos. B.	Carlson	Lillian Emma	Kerrick	Walter Armstead
Capella	Corinne M.	Kivi	Newton M.	Carlton	Ada B.	McMinn	Joseph
Capello	Delila	Corda	Joseph	Carlton	May M.	Stump	Lurnun (?) W.
Capezzoli	Catherine	Rossi	Rocco	Carlton	Rachel E.	Vanlaningham	John
Capitane	Angelina	Signorelli	Frank	Carlyon	Elizabeh	Ballou	Arthur M.
Capri	Maria	Belli	Sante	Carmady	Maggie	LaGrant	Lucon
Capucetti	Rose	Havard	Laurence S. H.	Carmer	Alma Bell	Cooper	John R.
Carassa	Nicoletta	Simi	Giuseppe	Carmichael	Belle	Freeman	Carlos J.
Carberry	Josephine M.	Kretzmer	William J.	Carmichael	Eliza	Wisecarver	I. (?) R.
Cardellini	Maria	Andreini	Pietro	Carmichael	Nannie	Hagler	John
Cardinet	Elva	Harlan	William Christian	Carney	Helen Maude	Reeves	Walter I.
Cardoza	Alice J.	Misner	Horace W.	Carothers	Maggie I.	Stitt	William W.
Cardoza	Josephine M.	Ilg	Fred G.	Carothers	Fannie	Norris	Cecil
Cardoza	Mae	Quigley	Arthur L.	Carotta	Catherina	Bassi	Abramo
Cardoza	Mary	Gonsalves	Manuel	Carotto	Maria	Neros	Frank
Cardoza	Mary Ann	Francisco	Anton	Carpenter	Adelia E.	McNabb	James Henry
Cardoza	Virginia	Cardoza	Thomas	Carpenter	Florence	Weyl	Albert
Carey	Adeline Helen	Goodwin	George M.	Carpenter	Jennie	Savage	E. R.
Carey	Hettie E.	Hart	John T.	Carpenter	Leah	Harris	William E.
Carey	Isabel	Dutra	Manuel F.	Carpenter	Mamie Ellen	Holloway	Calvin Walter
Carey	Joe Mabel	Ryan	Clarence A.	Carpenter	Sallie P.	Hayward	Harry M.
Cargile	Lucina	McClool	Thomas A.	Carr	Daisy Ethel	Hamson	Chris
Cargile	Lucy J.	Phillips	Warren H.	Carr	Mabel Estella	Todd	Carlton Edward
Cargile	Mary E.	Whitaker	Walter L.	Carr	Maggie	Clisbee	Albert
Cariaga	Refuge	Fairclo	Charles	Carr	Margaret	Quinn	Robert
Carithers	Gladys Ellen	Garrett	Vernon George	Carr	Marion Genevieve	Wilson	Andrew C.
Carithers	Mary E.	Carithers	David N.	Carr	Mary A.	Baldwin	D. A.
Carle (?)	Catherine R.	Johnson	William B.	Carr	Mary T.	Moore	Clement J. B.
Carli	Giudita	Barbreri	Agostino	Carr	Ursula A.	McLean	Hector
Carlile	Anna	Reese	Thomas Bert	Carrie	Anna B.	Mays	Larkin B.
Carlile	Etta	Adams	Frank	Carrigan	Agnes	Malone	Joseph

Carriger	Emma	Carriger	I. C.	Carter	Ellen	Donnelly	Thomas F.
Carriger	Margaret F.	Gilbert	William J.	Carter	Flora, Mrs.	Hunt	George M.
Carrillo	Amelia	Barnes	Henry L.	Carter	Laura H.	Ward	Erastus C.
Carrillo	Anita H.	Walden	Frank J.	Carter	Lois York	Smith	Arthur Melvin
Carrillo	Frances Benicia	Welty	John	Carter	Margaret L.	Roberts	Henry J.
Carrillo	Isabel (?).	Grissin (?)	W. H.	Carter	Mary	Murphy	Dennis
Carrillo	Jennie Rose	Carrillo	Paul Abraham	Carter	Mary A.	Price	Joseph A.
Carrillo	Lulu	McCord	Charles	Carter	Mary E.	Green	William A.
Carrillo	Mary Agnes	Moore	Saml. C.	Carter	Pearl L.	Wilson	William M.
Carrillo	Rafelia	Cook	William M.	Carter	Sarah E.	Hutchison	Earnest E.
Carrillo	Ramona	Jackson	George Samuel	Cartmel	Alice S.	Hutchinson	Oliver A.
Carroll	Agnes J.	Guldager	L. C.	Cartwright	Leta May	Adams	Clement Scott
Carroll	Eleanor I.	Smith	Marcel M.	Cartwright	Mary M.	Check	Elliott E.
Carroll	Gertrude	Swanson	Andrew	Carubbi	Graziosa	Pracchia	Emilio
Carroll	Helen E.	Thomasson	Ambrose	Carvell	Lucia E. E.	Delevan	Frederick S.
Carroll	Virginia E.	Becker	Myron B.	Carvelle	Elizabeth	Roberts	James L.
Carroll	Williette	Sydenstucker	Charles S.	Carvey	Mary	Carroll	James P.
Carroz	Mary	Beffa	James	Carvey	Mattie A.	Paschich	John
Carsen	Nancy	McCaughey	James	Casarotti	Mary O.	Bloom	Valenti J.
Carsin	Julia L.	Whitlatch	Frank	Casasnovas	Sara	Garcia	Benigno
Carsin	Margaret L.	Jenson	Albert L.	Case	Ellen M.	Easterbrook	Thomas
Carson	Jennie B.	Wright	Lathrop B.	Case	Leolia Lailia	Philbrick	Samuel Edwin
Carson	Katherine F.	Gleason	David P.	Case	Martha J.	Brown	Chester B.
Carson	Mary	Fleming	William	Case	Mary E.	Brown	George W.
Carson	Mary	Fleming	William	Case	Mollie	Winants	Newell
Carssin	Rosa	Sanchez	Tony	Case	Susie	Davis	Manra (?) J.
Carstensen	Hilaria Christiane	Springer	Frank	Case	Susie A.	Bowers	George
Cartensen	Katy	Samuelson	Norman	Caselli	Angie A.	Bandieu	Alibrando
Carter	Alice Blanche	Freeman	Charles Henry	Caselli	Beatrice	Fortunati	Alfredo
Carter	Alice M.	McClendon	William J.	Caselli	Venerina	Pellegrini	J.
Carter	Alphy Etta	Nielsen	Daniel J.	Casey	Anna J.	Hunter	John J.
Carter	Amy F.	Ross	Chas. H.	Casey	Bridget	Cresante	Sepe
Carter	Annie Elizabeth	Hughett	Ernest Adolph	Casey	Catharine	John	Gregory
Carter	Carrie	Thompson	Walter	Casey	Katherine	Bennett	John C.
Carter	Eirmah E.	Schlotterback	Peter L.	Casey	Mary Ellen	Sheehy	Charles J.

Cashdollar	Algie B.	Logan	Howard	Cattron	Alice	Wright	Herbert
Casini	Emma	Martinelli	Ulesse	Cauckwell	Addie J.	Sullivan	Charles C.
Casini	Ermida	Ragghianti	Angelo	Cauckwell	Minnie Bell	Farley	Thomas Bachariah
Casky	Alta M.	Auten	George M.	Cauckwell	Nancy M.	Kyle	John G.
Casmore	Adella L.	Ames	Irvin E.	Cauckwell	Sarah F.	Norris	Samuel
Cassani	Antonietta	Vitali	John	Cauckwell (?)	Mary E. C.	Lock	Charles
Cassani	Carolina	Vitali	Richard	Caue	Margaret	Plasket	Peter
Cassani	Carrie	Pagani	Giuseppe	Caufield	Marguerite R.	Soberanes	Edward T.
Cassani	Margaret	Rovai	Joseph H.	Caughey	Agnes	Folk	James
Cassani	Nora	Bertossi	Louis	Caughey	Alice	Eagle	Bert
Cassani	Rica	Bartolomei	Salvatore	Caughey	Corinne Alice	Colen	Lewis H.
Cassani	Ricca	Maroni	Louis	Caughey	Elizabeth Annie	Bishop	William Raymond
Cassares	Maria T.	Whittaker	John R.	Caughey	May	Ledford	George Lee
Cassidy	Nellie L.	Webster	Calvin B.	Caughey	Myrtle	Vassar	Cleve
Cassin	Ada I.	Tucker	Ira W.	Caulfield	Catherine F.	Bacigalupi	Louis
Cassina	Margaret	Biocca	Louis	Cauyers (?)	Lucy Ellen	Paschal	Willie Frank
Cassini	Carrie	Lagomarsino	George J.	Cavagna	Cecelia	Sardelli	Anton
Cassini	Giuseppina	Bertulucci	Lorenzo	Cavallo	Catherina	Del Piano	Giovanni
Casson	Dixie L.	Powell	Charles Clifford	Cavanagh	May Alice	Fuson	Amandus U.
Cassoni	Josephine B.	Brichetto	Edmund J.	Cavanough	Nettie A.	Johnson	Robert N.
Castagnasso	Annie	Clerici	August	Cavauagh	Laura A.	Whitney	Wm. B.
Castellino	Maria	Dormetta	Georgie	Cave	Freda Marie	Montgomery	Robert B.
Castello	Frances T.	Tietjen	Henry M.	Cavers	Margaret I.	Meek	Thomas Barney
Casto	Mamie	Lee	W. H.	Cawley	Maria	Moore	John
Castro	Della	Taggart	John F. J.	Cawsey	Clara E.	Viera	Joseph
Castro	Rafael	Williams	Eugene C.	Cayla	Odette	Suez	William Joseph
Catelani	Conchetta	Mangiantini	Narciso	Cazerous	Laura	Heryford	Bennett, Jr.
Catendo	Bertha	Woosbury	Robert Leland	Celeri	Elizabetto	Ginsti	Angelo
Cathcart	Mary	Carter	Oliver C.	Cella	Beatrice	Corts	Frank James
Catlin	Beatrice Lenore	McDonald	Frank Andrew	Cenini	Ersilia	Ferrori	Enrico
Catlin	Delia Reseller	Dow	A. J.	Ceraille	Jennie	Alberigi	Americo
Catlin	Elfie	Ridenhaur	William R.	Cereda	Mary Dorothy	Vogel	Frank Louis
Catlin	Kate	Beckwith	Nelson M.	Cereghino	Mary	Pezzolo	John
Caton	Louisa	Ramos	John	Cereghino	Mary	Hannan	Daniel
Catron	Nellie	Britton	Norris	Cereghino	Nellie D.	Burns	James F.

Cerini	Dell	Focha	Joseph
Cerini	Florence M.	Creely	James H.
Cerini	Nora A.	Cardoza	Joseph S.
Cerini	Olga	Cerini	Henry
Cerini	Evelyn Cecilia	Smalley	David Dunlap
Cerri	Juliet V.	Santarini (?)	Raphael D.
Cerruti	Dominica	Luchetti	Giovani
Cerruti	Rosi	Luchetti	Agostino
Cervinki	Katie	Honsa	Joseph
Cesena	Estelle V.	Peard	John O.
Cesena	Marie Violet	Robertson	Oliver G.
Chadd	Lelia C.	Strait	Louis F.
Chadwick	Belle	Collier	S. F.
Chaffee	Carrie	Bills	Lemuel James
Chaffee	Lenna	Commers	Robert
Chaffee	Mary S.	Henderson	Harry H.
Chaffee	Maud E.	Burdette	Charles O.
Chaffee	Nellie	Chamberlain	William H.
Chaix	Rose	Renfro	John F.
Chalfant	Mattie F.	Porterfield	William H.
Chambaud	Sadie	McCann	Thomas F.
Chamberlain	Georgie	de Neuf	Emil A.
Chamberlin	Carrie	Chandler	Ernest R.
Chamberlin	Charlotte E.	Purvine	Arthur B.
Chambers	Alta	Weaver	Frank
Chambers	California	Boice	John Dudley
Chambers	Elizabeth, Mrs.	Coulter	Charles
Chamler	Fannie Belle	Gauldin	Joseph E.
Chamley	Charlotte E.	Burch	George M.
Champlain	Sarah D.	Hall	Martin V.
Chance	Alice E.	Norrborn	Henry James
Chance	Mary E.	Gaige	Walter Louis
Chandler	Ethel	Joseph	Joe William
Chanmet	Felectie	Dumas	Alphonse
Chanteloup	Marie	Rogues	Alphonse

Chapin	Ethel	Herron	Joseph H.
Chapman	Carmen	Schwartz	Abraham G.
Chapman	Catherine	Blomquist	John
Chapman	Gertrude E.	Plummer	John P.
Chapman	Helen Edith	Anderson	Arthur
Chapman	Ivy R.	Smith	James A.
Chapman	Maria E.	Shine	John
Chapman	Martha	Kellner	Harold C.
Charles	Clara L.	Spooner	Horace D.
Charles	Mabel, Mrs.	Osmon	William G.
Charles	Minnie	Osborne	William H.
Charlton	Ellen T.	Neely	John
Charmley	Gertrude Geneive	Wells	Elbert Edward
Charmley	Helen Tilston	Gregg	Pleasant Wesley
Charnock	Amy	Mack	Charles Westly
Charnock	Annie	Sanders	Charles Fenas (?)
Chase	Dorothy Maud	Von Hacht	William H.
Chase	Lois A.	Pritchett	Orlean A.
Chase	Maggie, E.	Williamson	Hiram L.
Chauvet	Adele M.	Doyle	Charles M.
Chauvet	Henrietta M.	Meller	Reginald D.
Cheda	Amelia	Pedrotti	Martin
Cheeks	Lena A.	Brush	Fred W.
Cheesborough	Mable Teresa	Miller	Addison Charles
Cheetham	Ethel L.	Ring	William B.
Chelini	Adela	Toso	Angelo
Chelini	Anita Mary	Castagnasso	Enrico A.
Chelini	Annie	Sorini	Joseph
Chelini	Josephine	Gainer	Roland L.
Chelini	Julia D.	Repetto	Mario Angelo
Cheney	Clara	Johnson	Claude E.
Cheney	Elsie	Thomas	John E.
Cheney	Irene Margaret	Craig	Robert John
Cheney	Louisa C.	Phinney	Martin E.
Cheney	Sarah E.	Banfield	John T.

Cheney	Susan	Revie	John	Christensen	Karen O. M.	Iverson	Louis
Chenoweth	Josie E.	Stouder	Calvin F.	Christensen	Magdalene C.	Tutt	Philip A.
Chenoweth	Viola T.	McChristian	Wm. E.	Christenson	Cora M.	Severin	Eugene T.
Cheny (?)	Mary	White	Harrison W.	Christian	Mary A.	Hutchinson	F. A.
Cherne	Mollie F.	Frey	Howard L.	Christianson	Minnie	Barham	Abwey
Chester	Mary M.	Ramey	Willard L.	Christie	Evalena Alberta	Shelly	William Newton
Chevalier	Marguerite	Johnson	Williard H.	Christie	Gertrude May	Stedman	Robert Miner
Chevallier	Marie	Moret	Elie H.	Christie	Isabella J.	Morgan	Thomas P.
Chiantelli	Pauline	Pera	Luigi	Christie	Josie Mary	Sailor	Charles William
Chiaroni	Edith Marie	Pelletti	Louis	Christie	Lizzie, Mrs.	Cook	Ernest Ward
Chiesa	Francis	Villata	Romaro	Christie	Mabel F.	Burke	Sylvester
Childers	Emma	Duncan	Geo. B.	Christinsen	Martha B.	Banfield	Frederic H.
Childers	Gussie	Wilson	W. C.	Christoferson	Dina Marie	Michaelson	Otto Emil
Childers	Josephine	Wilson	M. D.	Christoffersen	Ruth M.	Regas	Sam J.
Childers	Sealy	Wilson	Frank Edward	Christophersen	Josephine	Jensen	Christ.
Chinden (?)	Mollie	Skillman	A.	Christy	Myrtle May	Irvin	John H.
Chinn	Mary Ellen	Thrum	James W.	Church	Alice C.	McCauley	Thomas P.
Chinnock	Jessie May	Moffett	L. L.	Church	Bertha L.	Winn	Robert Lee
Chinnock	Mary A.	Thorp	Zachariah	Church	Clara Rosa	Ash	Leroy
Chintelli	Jennie	Martinelli	Fortunato	Church	Deets	Currie	Robert Alvin
Chio	Emma	Cole	Walter Vernon	Church	Juanita Sybil	Behrns	Carl Nisson
Chio	Mary	Thomas	Willard E.	Church	Julia E.	Obermuller	John H.
Chism	Martha	Gaither	William	Church	Linnie	Mack	William, Jr.
Chittenden	Cornelia F.	Frehe	Alfred Louis	Church	Mary E.	Thompson	Robert A.
Chittenden	Katherine	Zimmerman	Caspar	Church	May Adeline	James	Burnie Edgar
Chitwood	Anna Eliza	Chitwood	Joseph Andrew	Church	Myrtle E.	Cox	Willard S.
Chitwood	Mary B.	Hill	Samuel R.	Church	Rena	Weyler	William J.
Chitwood	Sarah M.	Nance	William H.	Churchill	Clara	Tapscott	Robert M.
Chiver (?)	Lena A.	Hocker	Will O.	Churchman	Edith	Davis	H. Ruliff
Chouquette	Ella	Thompson	William	Churchman	Hattie L.	Bower	George A.
Chow	Ah	Wing	Tong	Churchman	Maggie A.	Damon	Myron H.
Chrisman	Lucile E.	Rossen	Robert Pierce	Churchman	Mary	Wahl	C.
Christensen	Anna	Rasmussen	Nes	Churchman	Nello May	Skaggs	William Warham
Christensen	Anna Birgitte	Olson	Minnick	Churchman	Ruth E.	Phair	Carter N.
Christensen	Elizabeth F.	Greninger	George Frederick	Cia	Antoinetta	Magri	Guiseppe

Ciabbatini	Serafina	Checchi	Luigi	Clark	Eva R.	Jorgensen	Julius
Ciancao	Mary	Gonsalves	Frank S.	Clark	Fannie E.	Gilbert	Thos. A.
Ciapusci	Lizzie	Ratto	Charles	Clark	Frances H.	Moore	Francis M., Jr.
Cinnamond	Isabell	Paetzold	Arthur	Clark	Gladys A.	Alves	Frank S.
Cinquini	Isma T.	Poli	Giovanni I.	Clark	Grace Pitkin	Mitchell	Ralph Brown
Cinquini	Clara	Pieroni	Silvio	Clark	Hattie	Murray	John
Cissell	Mary Annis	Godman	Charles Edwin	Clark	Hazel Frances	Hicks	Archibald Lynn
Ciucci	Amelia J.	Walton	John R.	Clark	Hilda Vinden	Wipner	Arthur H.
Claassen	May	Lauritzen	Jesse C.	Clark	Jennie	Conisto	Achille
Cladden	Mary Ella	Cameron	John Willard	Clark	Jennie Alice	Spencer	Henry Jost
Clair	Stella Louise	Compton	John Andrew	Clark	Jennie B.	Clark	Stephen D.
Clairy (?)	Anna	Burns	Eugene	Clark	Katie May	Porter	James Ross
Clancy	Anna Estelle	Haupt	Frank L.	Clark	Lennie	McIntosh	D.
Clanton	Rebecca, Mrs.	McGrath	Peter J.	Clark	Leona	Laymance	Francis M.
Clanton	Victoria Alice	Keller	John Claus	Clark	Lettie A.	Fraser	John N.
Clark	Ada	Alley	Leonard Samuel	Clark	Lillian L.	Vail	Albert H.
Clark	Addie Louise	Bailhache	Frederick	Clark	Linnie P.	Childers	Arnold, Jr.
Clark	Agnes Emma	Evans	Tipton Edward	Clark	Lizzie	Collins	Charles F.
Clark	Alice C.	Walker	Joseph E.	Clark	Lottie J. M.	Gibson	Clyde C.
Clark	Alice F.	Harbine	James L.	Clark	Mary E.	McCloud	Louis Clifford
Clark	Alice L.	Fairbanks	William B.	Clark	Mary Elizabeth	Shepherd	William Phares
Clark	Allice S.	Curries	Wm. H.	Clark	Mary I.	Farquar	Calvin S.
Clark	Annie	Miller	Frank B.	Clark	May Edith	Hill	William James
Clark	Annie J., Mrs.	Yeager	Hyle E.	Clark	Melinda Letticia	Richey	Isaac Calvin
Clark	Annie M.	Olmsted	Lewis C.	Clark	Mollie	Davis	Gilman Bush
Clark	Clara Belle	Dennis	William Whan	Clark	Nancy C.	Forsyth	John Hamilton
Clark	Edith Jerome	Nolan	Walter C.	Clark	Nettie	Cannon	L. L.
Clark	Ella	Gamble	Charles	Clark	Retina (?) J.	Windsor	Wm. Russell
Clark	Ella	McNally	Oscar	Clark	Ruth M.	Fairchild	Olif G.
Clark	Emma E.	Grove	George W.	Clark	Selina C., Mrs.	Matthews	Charles H.
Clark	Emma Nettie	Hussy (?)	Eugene	Clark	Susie	Blow	James
Clark	Ethel Julia	Toucrault	William Patrick	Clark	Tillie	Fisk	Geo. S.
Clark	Ethel M.	Packwood	Laurel E.	Clark	Virginia	Rayner	Moses
Clark	Ethel Mary	Giorgi	Alfred	Clark	Wilma S.	Arnett	Floyd F.
Clark	Eva M.	Russell	James F.	Clark	Zoe Ruah	Bates	Henry Frederick

Clark (?)	Halloween	Popp	Fred W.	Clement	Maggie	Tibbits	Charles A.
Clarke	Agnes T.	Levansaler	Russell J.	Clement	Minnie E.	Rowland	Edwin S.
Clarke	Delia	Bateson	Claude William	Clements	Katherine	Bayol	Frank P.
Clarke	Mary Eleanor	Webley	Frederick D., M. D.	Clements	Lena A.	Groskofs	Joseph F.
Clarke	Maybelle	Maddux	Harry W.	Clements	Maude H.	Miller	D. P.
Clarke	Sibyl G.	Kimble	Thomas H.	Clerici	Angela	Rossi	Charles
Clarkson	Artmchia (?)	White	Robert L.	Clerve	Helen A.	Holt	William T.
Clary	Emma	Allen	George P.	Clery	Mary E.	O'Brien	Joseph P.
Clasby	Catherina	Orr	W. J. T	Cleveland	Flora	Rowland	William B.
Clausen	Anna D.	Momsen	Charles F.	Cleveland	Nellie M.	Poe	Otto
Clausen	Dorothy Helen	Badenhop	John Henry	Clifford	Blanch H.	Goddard	Wellman
Clausen	Magdalena	Jessen	Julius Theodore	Clifton	Ollie E.	Clifton	Thomas K.
Clausen	Minnie	Dalessi	Walter	Cline	Ada	Palmer	Frederick E.
Clauton (?)	Amanda J.	Overton	James M.	Cline	Anna Maria	Gray	Alva C.
Clavey	Dorothy Louise	Larson	Rudolph Otto	Cline	Jennie	Lloyd	Hubert T.
Clavo	Nellie	Stoker	Otto	Cline	Jessie	Hart	Frank
Clawsen	Cynthia A.	Knutsen	Iver	Cline	Mary A.	Fredericks	Martin
Clawsen	Minnie Josine	Jessen	Frank Edward	Cline	Nellie, Mrs.	Treat	C. H.
Clawson	Lucy E.	Derrick	George L.	Cloer (?)	Vada	McMillan	Harmon D.
Clay	Effie E.	Crane	Charles B.	Clos	Rose L.	Jones	Oscar R.
Clayborne	Florence E.	Alten	John H.	Clough	Julia M.	Clare	George A.
Clayman	Margaret McI.	Burnham	Leslie J.	Clover	Leonora	Barnes	Millard L.
Claypool	S. Ella	Welden	D. Ralph	Clover	Martha J.	Keaton	Wheeler M.
Clayton	Alice	Lawrence	James W.	Clover	Minnie C.	Johnson	Archibald M.
Clayton	Edna L.	Rosengarn	Walter J.	Clow	Crystal M.	Berry	John E.
Clayton	Erma	Walton	Jim Hortenstein	Clunan	Esther	Mendelson	Isador
Clayton	Opal E.	Peck	Leo W.	Cluver	Anna C.	Whitmore	John H.
Cleary	Mary Ellen	Pratt	Frank C.	Cnopius	Antoniette Maria	Lauteren	Ferdinand
Clegg	Alice	McReynolds	Melvin J.	Cnopius	Gertrude M.	Much	Herbert N.
Clegg	Grace	McReynolds	Arthur	Cnopius	Gertrude M.	Hamilton	James W.
Clegg	Mary M., Mrs.	Silva	John Pedro	Cnopius	Maria E.	Smissart (?)	Jacob H.
Cleland	Mary Martha	Eaglin	Elmer Harrison	Coary	Gusta	Decker	John T.
Clemens	Maggie	Tibbits	Charles A.	Coates	Levina	Unwiller	Wm.
Clemensen	Freda M.	Wilson	Charles H.	Coats	Emma L.	Trubody	Charles M.
Clement	Loma (?)	Keenan	Walter H.	Cobb	Emma, Mrs.	Solomon	Charles

Cobb	Frances	Freshour	John L.	Colassor	Albertinn	Haberhouer	Karl
Cober	Jane	Ferguson	Newton J.	Colburn	Edna A.	Williams	Frank J.
Coburn	Nettie	Pippin	John	Colburn	Lulu I.	Cockrill	William A.
Cochran	Mattie J.	Morin	Frank L.	Colburn	Mabel	Springer	Earl Leroy
Cochran	S.	Moses	Meyer	Colby	F. A.	Hinshaw	B. B.
Cochrane	Agnes M.	Praetzel	Gustav C.	Colby	Mae L.	Cunninghame	Reuben H.
Cochrane	Alice Myrtle	Perry	George Harvey	Colby	Minnie A.	Codding	George C.
Cochrane	Clare A.	Holles	Clayton W.	Cole	Amy	Sullivan	Jabez B.
Cochrane	Evelyn E.	Barbier	Harry A.	Cole	Annie	Heffron	George
Cocknill (?)	Ida J.	Cannon	James P.	Cole	Arcadia F.	McGrew	Francis H.
Cockrill	Fidella	Cook	Edward	Cole	Beatrice	Carr	William
Cockrill	Ida May	Dressler	J. F.	Cole	Celia A.	Fisher	Francis
Cockrill	Lora T.	McCready	Thomas C.	Cole	Charlotte Sarah	Willey	John
Cockrill	Margaret Allen	Simonet	Albert	Cole	Chrissie V.	Barsot	Robert Eugene
Coco	Ugolina	Battero	Vittorio E.	Cole	Eda F.	Nay	Frank G.
Coddington	G. W., Mrs.	Hamlin	Harry	Cole	Edna C.	Bagley	Herbert L.
Coe	Emma	Stare	Joseph C.	Cole	Elsie Rachel	Johnson	Adolph
Coe	Nannie T.	Lusk	William	Cole	Josie E.	Varner	Thad A.
Cofer	Lottie Edith	Howard	Raymond L.	Cole	Margaret	Proschold	Carlton G.
Cofer	Lydia May	Bumbaugh	Erle Leroy	Cole	Mary E.	Forneris	Albert
Cofer	Mary	Mason	Chas. O.	Cole	Mary Violet	Christenson	James Rasmussen
Coffer	Addie	Hesseltine	Benjamin L.	Cole	May	Behrens	Albert Percy
Coffer	Lillian	Wardell	William Henry	Cole	Nettie I.	Snook	Edward B.
Coffer	Lucy A.	Johnson	Charles L.	Cole	Rosa E.	Turner	James T.
Coffer	Maggie	Duncan	Samuel	Cole	Sylvia G.	Hamilton	Gilbert S.
Coffey	Edith E.	Peterson	Chauncey W.	Coleman	Amanda	Epperly	Hiram
Coffey	Eva	Peterson	Harry	Coleman	Jennie	Davis	Charles E.
Coffey	Mary A.	Schlueter	Rudolph H.	Coli	Eletta	Particelli	Giulio
Coffey	Mary E.	Crowley	Timothy J.	Coll	Edna G.	McFadden	George Reuben
Coffman	Mary Gertrude	Cochran	Arthur Payne	Collier	Louisa Jane	Harris	Richard Alexander
Coggeshall	Catherine	Byce	Malcolm Lyman	Collier	Miriam De Ford	Shipley	Maynard
Cohen	Hannah	Wilson	William	Colling	Elaine Elizabeth	Walker	Douglas
Cohenous	Jennie F.	Dobyne	William H.	Collins	Clara E.	Kingwell	William I.
Cohl	Rose	Robinson	Harold E.	Collins	Ella C.	Hendrix	G. L.
Cohn	Anna	Johansan	Axel A.	Collins	Katherine B.	O'Keefe	John J.

Collins	Loretta M.	Hill	Arthur C.	Condy	Mae E.	McCraney	Harrie E.
Collins	Marie	McCray	William Lloyd	Cone	Kathryn A.	Gentis	Camille
Collins	Mary A.	Meacham	Charles S.	Conecl (?)	Eva	Gale	Leander
Collins	Maud	McKee	William A.	Conelly	May	Mack	Richard
Collins	May Caroline	Morgan	John Franklin	Confette	Eufemia	Lafranchi	John
Collins	Maye	Rutherford	Asa John	Conger	Antoinette Isabel	Loiser (?)	Gustave A.
Collins	Minnie P.	Welch	Harry J.	Conger	Cornelia Constance	Bledsoe	John Henry
Collister	Vivienne E.	Johns	Watson L.				
Colombani	Rosina	Palmieri	Paulo	Congleton	Agnes	Wilson	Albert A.
Colton	Minnie	Rope	Morris	Congleton	Augusta	Brown	Thos.
Colton (?)	Amelia A.	Russell	William J.	Congleton	May	Taeuffer	John N.
Columbo	Catherine Elsie	Sweet	Bryan Abel	Congrave	Mae L.	Wells	James E.
Colvin	Mae E.	Vandre	Lewis W.	Conkel	Addie	Snider	John D.
Comaich	Louise	Johnson	Walter J.	Conklin	E. C.	Lane	J.
Comber	Nora	Collins	James Michael	Conklin	Minnie	Colville	Thomas P.
Combs	Addie	Rayner	Harry	Conley	Clara B.	Heseker	Fred W.
Combs	Amnada M. F.	McCoy	Hugh	Conley	Daisy	Hocking	William Benn
Combs	Clara Edna	Lattin	Perry Raymond	Conley	Marion B.	Goodhart	Lewis E.
Combs	Frances	Kraemer	Herman	Conlin	Nellie A.	Faithful	H. R.
Combs	Genevieve	Krough	Martin L.	Conne	Annie, Mrs.	McNeal	William E.
Combs	Helen E.	Smith	Robert E.	Conne	Isabel D.	Smith	Charles Medred
Combs	Kittie L.	Bidwell	Charles E.	Conne	Josephine M.	Hildebrand	Calvin G.
Combs	Leonore	McCord	David C.	Conne	Margaret	Gage	George S.
Combs	Lizzie	Pritchett	Zeb. E.	Connell	Lizzie	Millerick	John
Comer	Louisa H.	Wambold	David M.	Connell	Mary	Connell	John
Cominos	Johanna	Ives	William S.	Connelly	Mary K.	Munday	Thomas O.
Compagnoni	Teresa	Trabucchi	Luzi	Conner	Jeannette Muriel	Howe	Willard Earl
Compton	Edna Tersa	Shepard	Roy Roderic	Conner	Millie	Stuckey	Harry F.
Comstock	Catherine	Seideneck	George Joseph	Conners	Nama V.	Jackson	Carlisle P.
Comstock	Cornelia	Matthews	Winfield Scott, Jr.	Conniff	Mary Ellen	Bryan	Thomas Welsh
Comstock	Eleanor W.	Miller	Harold K.	Conniff	Annie L.	Conway	Thomas James
Comstock	Lois Mae	Richardson	Fontaine H.	Conniffe	Delia Teresa	Healey	Thomas Matthew
Comte	Blanche	Feliz	Gumisindo, Jr.	Connihan	Julia V.	Coffey	Maurice J.
Condon	Ruth	Booth	John	Connlley	Margaret A.	Swift	Martin I.
Condraz (?)	Nancy Jane	Stark	I. (?) T.	Connolly	Katherine Rose	Dolcini	Arnold Tully

Connolly	Louise Bernidette	Hussey	Edward Otis	Cook	Louise	Sharkey	John
Connolly	Mary V.	Felldin	John Joseph	Cook	Lydia M.	Carrillo	Abraham
Connon	Mildred E.	Crooks	Asa S.	Cook	Mary	Barham	J. A.
Connor	Jennie	Fowler	J. H.	Cook	Mary E.	Hedrick	David M.
Connors	Rose L.	Timmerman (?)	Matthew M.	Cook	Maude Irene	Walz	Louis Oscar
Conran	Margaret H.	Doyle	Peter J.	Cook	May Adeline	McFarling	John Stanley
Consiglieri	Celestine	Paulucci	Vincent	Cook	May M.	French	William
Consiglieri	Josephine	Giambruno	Alberto	Cook	Minnie E.	Ronsheimer	H. L.
Constayscia	Rosa P.	Rose	Joseph	Cook	Nancy Jane, Mrs.	Worden	William D.
Conway	Ida G.	Silvershield	Henry	Cook	Neva	Kelly	C. E.
Conyers	Iva	McNair	Elmer A.	Cook	Salome	Morris	Alfred
Coogan	Carrie M.	Tibbitts	Francis A.	Cook	Susan	Millington	Ira
Cook	Alice Emme (?)	Kunde	Kurt G.	Cooke	Grace E.	Sample	Samuel R.
Cook	Anna	Tarzyn	Joseph	Cooke	L. Constance	Wisecarver	Robert P.
Cook	Anna M.	Whalin	William E.	Cooke	Viola M.	Priest	George L.
Cook	Beatrice Bidwell	Martin	Frederick	Cookson	Ruby E.	Smith	A. G.
Cook	Bella	Swenson	Carl L.	Cookson	Ruth A.	Herman	Franklin A.
Cook	Carrie Belle	Smith	Charles Frederick	Cooley	Katherine	Imrie	George Nicoll
Cook	Cassie	Krueger	Oscar Feasco	Coombs	Lulu M.	Anderson	William I.
Cook	Daisy	Selby	Ellbert	Coon	Josephine	Guerne	Alfred Lucian
Cook	Daisy D.	Hood	Benjamin H.	Coon	Laura	Brown	George G.
Cook	Daisy M.	Jones	Lewis E.	Coon	Sophronia, Mrs.	Ross	James L.
Cook	Della T.	Flaherty	Albert W.	Coon	Stella L.	Johns	Frank M.
Cook	Elsie M.	Gully	Frank J.	Cooney	Mary Eleanor	Ligore	David Claude
Cook	Emily	Hastings	Fletcher D.	Cooney	Stacy L.	Gray	Frank S.
Cook	Emma	Slocum	Drayton Preslin	Cooper	Alice L.	Field	John K.
Cook	Estella M.	Davis	Claude H.	Cooper	Charlotte	Cornalson	Peter
Cook	Evelyn	Glaizer	Walter Oscar	Cooper	Chrilla J., Mrs.	Newton	William
Cook	Fidella	Guisler	Edward T.	Cooper	Clara B.	Alexanderson	Philip E.
Cook	Florence B.	Talbot	Stanwood E.	Cooper	Edith M.	Stidger	Oliver P.
Cook	Gertrude	Keppel	Fred E.	Cooper	Ella J.	Knox	Josiah N.
Cook	Hattie	Edrington	James B.	Cooper	Elsie M.	Norris	Percy E.
Cook	Illiene	Cannon	Earl	Cooper	Emma	Sterling	James
Cook	Jennie	Burnett	Thomas B.	Cooper	Emma J.	McDonald	J. R.
Cook	Katie (?)	Corbaley	Frank R.	Cooper	Eva U.	Emerson	Harry E.

Cooper	Hattie, Mrs.	Shelling	Alexander	Corbin	Ida	Gross	Eugene A.
Cooper	Hazel Grace	Jewett	Joseph Carl	Corda	Catherine	Nichelini	Anton B.
Cooper	Hazel Marguerite	Black	William Earl	Cordano	Rose	Flippi	Toney
Cooper	Ida May	Daley	George	Cordes	Ethel Lucy	King	Albert Roy
Cooper	J??etta Viola	Richardson	Lewis E.	Cordes	Gertrude B.	Stevens	Frank Miles
Cooper	Lillie May	Lund	August	Cordes	Wanda H.	Lascuola	Frank P.
Cooper	Lula May	Fisk	Frank F.	Cordevant	Lilly	Leininger	Daniel W.
Cooper	M. L.	Douglass	W. A.	Cordingly	Lila H.	Cleaveland	H. J.
Cooper	Margaret E.	Luebberke	Benjamin H.	Cordova	Rosie	Marks (?)	Julian
Cooper	Mary L.	Hall	James Otto	Cordoza	Carrie C.	Perry	Joseph L.
Cooper	May E.	Hiatt	T. L.	Coregliano	Domencia	Marinoni	Gaetano
Cooper	May N.	Coltrin	Hugh C.	Corel	Jane	Howard	Horace A.
Cooper	Minnie	Stansbury	W. M.	Corey	Augusta	Hull	Wm. D.
Cooper	Minnie L.	Canevara	Don A.	Corey	Mary	Frazer	Joe E.
Cooper	Rachael	Barker	Henry	Corey	Nora E.	Tanner	James C.
Cooper	Sadie A.	Harvey	Lowell N.	Cork	Mary Elizabeth	Pellascio	William O.
Cooper	Tina	Pierson	Edward E.	Cormer	Nannie M., Mrs.	Stoner	Corvin
Cooper	Willie Margaret	Smith	Joseph E.	Corneilson	Francis	Rose	Adelbert M.
Cooper	Zella R.	Kellogg	Harold G.	Cornelius	Elizabeth L.	Burlingam	Raleigh W.
Cooper	Catherine	Hammond	Frank	Cornelius	Ella M.	Cornelius	George
Cooper	Elanor A.	McGregor	Franklin D.	Cornelius	Matilda J.	Anderson	Charles F.
Cooper	Sarah Alice	Briggs	William H.	Cornett	Edith Luella	Gardner	Robert Elmer
Coover	Anita B.	Held	H. R.	Cornevali	Sarah	Sorini	Attilio
Cope	Hattie May	Tonini	Bernard Ernest	Cornish	Shirley F.	Knight	Russell H.
Copeland	H. Edith	Brown	Earl D.	Cornwell	Bessie Agnes	Kreitler	John H.
Copeland	Josephine	Hembree	Albert Lafayette	Corrall	Caroline	Hastings	A. R.
Copland	Mary J.	Walker	James	Corrick	Lizzie	Potterton	Eugene A.
Coppedge	Nellie B.	Righetti	Henry W.	Corrick	Lucela Catherine	Fay	Wilbert Lee
Copperelmann	Laura	McNeil	John	Corrigan	Bridget M.	Gorman	Timothy J. O.
Copple	Annie	Clark	James H. H.	Corry	Marie	Corry	Julio
Copple	Mary	Long	John Suoddy (?) Beach	Corsi	Angelina M.	Rossi	Enrico D.
				Cortezo	Delores (?)	Stra	Dominick
Corbelli	Argia	Narducci	Louis	Corvi	Antonieta	Zappa	Martino
Corbett	Hazel M.	Brooks	Joseph F.	Cory	Isabelle L.	Amaral	Anthony
Corbett	Julia B.	Peoples	Joseph S.	Costa	Bella	Freitas	Tony

Costa	Lizzie	Meineri	Guy
Costa	Maria L.	Carvalho	J. P.
Costigan	Mary Louise	Koenig	Charles
Cotrell	Minnie E.	Burke	Benjamin L.
Cotta	Delia	Gemetti	Battista
Cottle	Anna W.	Richardson	William G.
Cottle	Ella	Leroux	Arthur
Coul	Annie Laura	McDonald	William Vincent
Coul (?)	Annie	Chisholm	William
Coulter	Martha	Torrance	Samuel
Coulter	Mary G.	Severson	George
Counihan	Mary G.	Smith	Richard J.
Couper	Jennie	Fortier	William
Court	Caroline	Clark	Doane
Court	Ida Belle	Martin	Andrew William
Courtz	Mary E.	Durr	Otto R.
Coutts	Mabel	Havens	Charles I., Jr.
Coventry	Adelle	Deily	James B.
Coventry (?)	Mary A.	Coul	Peter
Covert	Dora L.	Wren	Grant H.
Covert	Gladys	Kellogg	Grant L.
Covert	Emma H.	Morris	James
Covey	Amanda E.	Ross	Alfred
Covey	Cashia Mary	McMichael	John William
Covey	Elizabeth	Barnum	Samuel
Covey	Ella Z.	Ward	Edward L.
Covey	Frances	Badgley	Sherman
Covey	Mary M.	Green	Lewis Ralston
Covey	Pearl Caroline	Scott	William F.
Cowan	Permilla I.	Cook	Delbert R.
Cowles	Eva M.	King	Joseph B.
Cowles	Mollie	Smith	Poten Fillmore
Cox	Alice Almira	Johnson	Cornelius M.
Cox	Anna	Butler	A. M.
Cox	Della V.	Nelson	Samuel S.

Cox	Emma Elizabeth	Cook	John S.
Cox	Evalyn Augusta	Graham	William Emerson
Cox	Florence M.	Murphy	Albert E.
Cox	Irene	Huneke	Robert Carlisle
Cox	Lulu H.	Holtz	James H.
Cox	Mary Catherine, Mrs.	Lovell	John
Cox	Mattie A.	Eastlick	A. D.
Cox	May M.	Brown	W. M.
Cox	Ruby Marie	Fitzgerald	Halcie
Cox (?)	Phebe	Totton	Thomas
Coy	Ethel A.	Luce	Hughbert S.
Coy	Josie, Mrs.	Stone	Robert
Coyn	Anna E.	Cromwell	J. G.
Cozad	Bertha M.	Leneve	Edward
Cozad	Cora O.	Wilson	Cassius C.
Cozad	Dora E.	Cheney	John L.
Cozad	Lulu E.	Walker	William C.
Cozine	Charlotte M.	Jones	Thomas A.
Cozini	Lottie May	Agnew	Newton W.
Cozzens	Pearl Adele	Fallmer	Charles Frederick
Crabbe	M. Florence	Turner	Everett J.
Crabtree	Ella	Harbin	Thomas B.
Crafoot	Annie	Crowley	John
Craig	Belle	Stumpf	William A.
Craig	Bessie	McDowell	William A.
Craig	Cora Allida	Engle	Lewis Joseph
Craig	Ethel	McDowell	Frank
Craig	Henrietta	Brians	John F.
Craig	Ina Margaret	Barnes	Ellis James
Craig	Mary Jane	Sayre	George A.
Crain	Hazel M.	Chaney	Vernon E.
Cramer	Gladys	Anderson	A. F.
Cramer	Hattie M.	Severance	Charles W.
Cramer	Katherina	Pieperling	Joseph

Cramer	Katie	Pickrell	Joseph W.	Crickett	Lizzie	Campbell	William A.
Cramer	Loomda (?)	Wright	Isaac	Crighton	Margaret H.	Prescott	Warren A.
Cramer	Nettie Louisa	McDaniel	Albert Edwin	Crigler	Lottie	Dixon	John T.
Crandal	Annie, Mrs.	Derrick	C. A.	Crigler	Lucy	Hendley	Harry L.
Crandall	Edna	Forsyth	W. B.	Crigler	Sally E.	Murray	Thomas Elmer
Crandle	Jessie	Whitney	Henry Grant	Crilly	Anna Francis	Johnson	John
Crandle	Mary C. G.	Patten	Richard Redmond	Crilly	Mary A.	Woodson	Warren G.
Crane	Catherine H.	Ballard	Robert L.	Crimmins	Agnes Marie	Frasier	Frank B.
Crane	Ella A.	Irving	Joseph O.	Crisp	Sarah J.	McMinn	J. A.
Crane	Eva Grace	Ford	George T.	Crispin	Hazel M.	Batt	Leo F.
Crane	Grace L.	Brayton	William H.	Crispin	Alice	Wann	Emerson R.
Crane	Mattie K.	Ward	Thomas B.	Crist	Cornelia	Peterson	John G.
Cranson	Birdie A.	Showalter	Fred V.	Crist	M. Jennie	Fandre	Crockett
Craumer	Ethel	Schaefer	August	Crist	Wilma L.	McCaslin	Reo W.
Craven	Eva A., Mrs.	Smith	Ernest W.	Cristfani	Maria	Pocai	Libro (?)
Crawford	Alice F.	Peatross	John H.	Cristofani	Teresa	Papera	Battista
Crawford	Alice M.	Weeks	Curtis M.	Critchfield	Lulu	McPeak	Jefferson P.
Crawford	Annie	Freeman	David	Critchfield	Lulu B.	Mann	Robert J.
Crawford	Fay	Pleasants	Samuel A.	Critchlow	Fannie Mirth	Snook	Marcus William
Crawford	Ginerva E.	Patterson	Wm.	Critchlow	Levina Martha	Parks	Harry Bernard
Crawford	Harriet Anna	Adams	Joseph	Critchton	Jessica Isabel	Stumbaugh	Gail Knowles
Crawford	Mary Anderson	Lumsden	Alexander Henry, Jr.	Crites	Nan	Hemple	George
				Criteser	Ella	Moranda	Silva
Crawford	Mary, Mrs.	Coe	Geo. W.	Crivelli	Mary	Storenetta	Charley
Crawford	Nadine E.	Harris	Ralph W.	Crivelli	Lizzie	Chanin	Peter
Crawford	Sarah J.	Johnson	Thomas J.	Crockard	Anna	Thiele	Herman W.
Crayne	Mamie L.	Witham	Walter F.	Crocker	Alice Elizabeth	Sichel	Michael
Creamer	Gertrude Mary	Presley	Hugh Allen	Crocker	Eliza	Baxman	Fred
Creba	Jennie K.	Potts	Jack S.	Crocker	Mary	Winrott	Rufus
Creighton	Elizabeth M.	Levy	Harold Walter	Crogan	Elizabeth	Ketelsen	Ocke
Crepin	Louise Cecelia	Freeborn	Francis Maurice	Crohare	Rose	Dufranc	Isidore
Cretser	Blossom	Stevenson	Joseph L.	Crommett	Sarah A.	Harris	Ephraim D.
Crevison	Cary	Richardson	Samuel N.	Cromwell	Edith M., Mrs.	Deal	John L.
Crew	Minnie M.	Black	George H.	Cromwell	Florence	Mentz	Jack F.
Crewdson	Dobey	Michael	George W.	Cromwell	Pearl Gertrude	Ayers	George Lemuel

Cronin	Catherine E.	Horan	Charles	Cullum	Carrie B.	Ulrich	Charles
Cropley	Adella C.	Manning	James C.	Culu (?)	Ollie	Gray (?)	Luster D.
Crosby	Estella	Prindle	Fred A.	Culver	Katherine	King	George
Crosby	Mary	Chattman	Beverly B.	Cumming	Jean	Wentworth	George H.
Crose	Nellie	Harris	Paul C.	Cummings	A. G.	Gutheil	C. R.
Cross	Emma	Nash	Charles	Cummings	Hattie E.	Martin	Charles J.
Crossfield	Evangelene May	Small	Louis Norman	Cummings	Kate	Medeira	William
Crossfield	Ruth	Ogburn	F. R.	Cummings	Lewella	Smith	L. S.
Crosta	Anna	Barella	Fred	Cummings	Lizzie	Goodrich	Edwin C.
Croste	Madalina	Gobbi	Joseph	Cummings	Lizzie M.	Waterman	Geo.
Crotts	Emily K.	Gardner	Vanness	Cummings	Mary	Doyle	Frank A.
Crow	Charlie Eveline	Branstetter	Charles H.	Cummings	Mary J.	Valchester	Ronald P.
Crow	Lucy A.	Congrove	Jonathan	Cummings	Olive	Clark	Richard L.
Crow	Luella Rains	Livingston	William Jesse	Cummins	Ethel	Strickland	Rollie
Crow	Susie E.	Abshire	Farley A.	Cummins	Loretta Ellen	Godman	Robert Edward
Crowder	Erma May	McCombs	Joseph Franklin	Cummins	Metta H.	Austin	Ashton E.
Crowell	Elizabeth	Armstrong	Walter Ernest	Cuneo	Amelia	Cuneo	G.
Crowell	Evelyn	Walker	Henry L., Jr.	Cuneo	Palma	Fitzgerald	John A.
Crowley	Ceclia Catherine	Coakley	Daniel John	Cunha	Anna	Avilla	Manuel
Crumrine	Stella I.	Norris	Herbert G.	Cunmings	Isabel (?)	Seward	Wm. V.
Crusher (?)	Eliza	Baxman	Fred	Cunningham	Alice M.	Lane	Lonnie
Cruson	Minnie	Caulfield	Daniel Philip	Cunningham	Jennie	Katterfield	Julius Charles Peter
Crutchen	Virginia	Choney	Lawrence	Cunningham	Jennie M.	Terschuren	G. F.
Crutson	Angeline	Hutton	George W.	Cunningham	Lillian N.	Linebaugh	Charles A.
Crystal	Etta	Somes	Albert	Cunningham	Lillie A., Mrs.	Campion	James
Cuadro	Mary	Martin	Manuel	Cunningham	Loura E.	Hogg	Robert O.
Cuadro	Veronica	Park	James Hall	Cunningham	Lucy	Tilli	Carlo
Cuda	Rose E.	Akers	Austin G.	Cunningham	Mattie	Delahunty	Bernard
Cullahan	May A.	McNamara	Thomas	Cunningham	May	Bennett	Charley
Cullen	Frances	Towne	Frank	Cunningham	Minnie	Duncan	C. A.
Cullen	Mary	Marsh	Arthur	Cunningham	Pearl Gertrude	Barham	Byrd
Cullen	Mary Alice	Bennett	Gilbert Louis	Cunningham	Viola W.	Rich	Elliott Pennington
Culligan	Petronilla	Childers	George T.	Cunninghame	Jennie	Parmeter	John C.
Cullum	Alice M.	Bush	Eli F.	Cupp	Olga L.	Cooke	Reuben
Cullum	Annie	Wolcott	Guy W.	Curran	Mary L.	Nelson	Charles W.

Curran	Ruby	Spellman	John	Daffort	Marie	Brundige	A. L.
Curren	Annie	Hurlbert	Fred Yale	Daggett	Jennie N.	Howe	Asa A.
Currier	Kate, Mrs.	Harlan	Joel M.	Daggett	Tirzah May	Spence	Charles
Curry	Bell	Williams	James M., Jr.	Dagnall	Margaret	Page	Ernest Hearne
Curry	Charlotte C.	Dunagan	Alva J.	Dahl	Mole Hansen	Albertson	Iver Magnus
Curry	Elzada M.	Wells	Roy B.	Dahlman	Mary	Perry	John
Curry	Lillian M.	Elkins	John C.	Dahlmann	Alba Flora	Knowlton	Cyrus Dexter
Curry	Lizzie	Maddux	Joe Ferreira	Dahlmann	Augusta	King	James
Curter (?)	Mary J.	Millett	William H.	Dahlmann	Clara	Lauritzen	Christian
Curtis	Hattie	Sharp	Nathan	Dahlmann	Eunice F.	Clemo	William H.
Curtis	Katie L. D.	Drake	George	Dahlmann	Georgia Wilma	Jameson	Arthur Roy
Curtis	Mabel H.	Gellerman	Louis W.	Dahlmann	Gladys Marie	Milner	Joseph B.
Curtis	Mary Ellen	Rich	Henry J.	Dahlmann	Martha	Schumacher	Peter J.
Curtis	Mary J.	Chandler	W. R.	Dahse	Johanna Dorothy	Moss	Lemuel A.
Curtiss	Bessie E.	Smith	George E.	Dakin	Daisy D.	Philpott	Jefferson F.
Curtman	Emily	Kent	Wm. C.	Dakin	Eunice I.	Linn	Allen McLeod
Cusick	Helen Winifred	Matthews	Hiram Walker	Dal Poggetto	Elena	Lattanzi	Emil C.
Cuspin	Peolyn	Williams	John Ralph	Dale	Clara E.	Longley	John A.
Cutter	Mabel Viola	Hagemann	Gustav Henry	Dalessi	Sophie May	Grove	Bert B.
Cutts	Olive	Hansen	Louis	Dalmaso	Olinpia	Dalbalcon	Louis
Cuyler	Anna H.	Luman	William E.	Dalton	Edna M.	Brown	Arthur
Czarro	Margaret L.	Schrader	Henry W. R.	Dalton	Eva C.	Luff	Caleb B.
D' Noximento	Maria	Azevedo	Manuel Jacinto	Daly	Maria	Lancaster	William
Da Shiell	Annie	Davis	Charles M.	Dambrogia	Mary	Braga	John
da Silva	Maria Joze	de Betencur	Joao	Dameron (?)	L. E.	Hall	James
Dabel	Ida	Brown	Robert	Damon	Eliza A.	Hodge	Alexander L.
Dabner	Mary Josephine	Guedet	Joseph Henry	Damon	Florence May	Nelson	William
Dabney	Lida E.	McGrew	James Gale	Damon	Maggie A.	Hollingsworth	Greene
Dabney	Melissa M.	Jones	William H.	Damozonio	Rose Marie	Roche	George H.
Dabney	Rose Zelma	Jobe	Thomas Frederick	Dana	Charlotte	Vassar	Jacob R.
Dabuer	Rosa Emilia	Frates	Manuel Suza	Dana	Emma	Gater	Frank I.
Dado	Evelina E.	Gambonini	Silvio G.	Dana	May L.	Ellingen	Casper W.
Dado	Guilietta C.	Mossi	Emilio	Dandridge	Lucy	Williams	John
Dado	Irene E.	Bloom	Plauso G.	Danehy	Mae C.	Young	Ray L.
Dado	Valeria R.	Silacci	Quinto V.	Danhansen	Louise	McCann	William Charles A.

Dani	Julia	Newsome	George M.	Daveiro	Josephine A.	Silva	John C.
Daniels	Edith	Snow	Clarence E.	Daveiro	Mary C.	Gonsalves	Joe P.
Daniels	Edith Edna	Darling	Floyd Willis	Davello	Mary J.	Thomas	Manuel L.
Daniels	Ethel I.	Houser	Basil L.	Davidson	Adele E.	Hunt	Oscar L.
Daniels	Frances A.	Stuart	Charles D.	Davidson	Alexandra	Woutila	Otto
Daniels	Iola B.	Pine	Andrew N.	Davidson	Alice L.	Meyers	Herman C.
Daniels	Jessie Marian	Conner	Charles W. G.	Davidson	Elizabeth S.	Sullivan	George E.
Daniels	Lilly M.	Dewey	Dean	Davidson	Emma A.	West	John C.
Daniels	Lorena F.	Martin	Christian J.	Davidson	Fannie S.	Cooper	J. A.
Daniels	Lula M.	Johnson	Elmo A.	Davidson	Mable Ann	DeGregorio	Peter Martin
Daniels	Mabel	Price	John H.	Davidson	Maggie A.	Snyder	John H.
Daniels	Minnie M.	Harris	George W.	Davidson	Martha	Davidson	John
Daniels	Myrtle A.	Johnson	Omar H.	Davidson	Mary Jane	Crowford	Thomas
Daniels	Nellie Estella	Lewis	Albert Ray	Davidson	Sarah E.	Ahern	James B.
Daniels	Zella	King	Horace Constable	Davidson	Wilma	McNab	Gavin
Dannhausen	Alvine	Grassman	Otto	Davidson	Zidana	McCord	Smith
Dannhausen	Anna	Thompson	Bert M.	Davies	Florence C.	Clanton	Samuel B.
Dannhausen	Kate	Dukes	Arthur H.	Davies	Harriett C.	Haskell	Greenlief A.
Dannhausen	Meta, Mrs.	Dannhausen	William	Davies	Rose E.	Madden	William
Dant	Jeannette M.	Schneider	Herman	Davini	Antonietta	Martini	Adolfo
Danterman	Priscilla	Holding	George	Davini	Bruna N.	Massoni	William J.
Danules (?)	Alice	Bennett	Warner	Davini	Concetta	Guidi	Angelo
Danz	Rosa	Dont	John G.	Davis	Ada	Dauer	Charles R.
Darden	Jennie	Skaggs	W. W.	Davis	Alice	Carr	George David
Darden	Rosa Belle	Jones	Edward T.	Davis	Amanda	Fouts	Alvin Roy
Darling	Nora M., Mrs.	Bennesen	Peter L.	Davis	Anna E.	Chance	Glenn I.
Darr	Lena	Ledger	Guy Wallace	Davis	Anna E.	Aiton	Wensley T.
Darrow	Lucretia A.	Orth	John A.	Davis	Bessie Smith	Hulbert	Ansel C.
Darwin	Georgia E.	Wills	Thomas C.	Davis	Carrie E.	Humbert	George H.
Das Nevis	Francisco Carloto	Rose	Joseph	Davis	Dara A.	Denison	Joseph N.
Daschwander	Francisca	Langensand	Melchior	Davis	Delecia S.	Nystrom	Milton
Daugherty	Maria Theresa	Belvail	John H.	Davis	Dora J.	Bacon	George Dudley
Davall	Augusta	Unger	Lawrence E.	Davis	Edell	Brattain	Arthur Lane
Davaz	Agnes	Jossler	Chris	Davis	Edith M.	Davis	Charles E.
Davaz	Rose	Daniels	Leroy E.	Davis	Edna Angie	Hanshop	Guy Edwin

Davis	Eliza S.	Frame	R. A.	Davison	Bertha Olive	Jones	George Richard
Davis	Elma Olive	Irwin	Robert	Dawkins	Lillian E.	Logan	Roy Sylvester
Davis	Elmira	Grove	David	Dawson	Annie L.	Taggart	Wilmer W.
Davis	Emmie M.	Robinson	John H.	Dawson	Florence M.	Oryuski	Ralph J.
Davis	Eva F.	Stoll	Leland C.	Dawson	Maude E.	Happersburger	Frank, Jr.
Davis	Fanny	Nippert (?)	August	Day	Agnes Nettie	Gleason	Guy Strahom
Davis	Georgia M.	Kirwan	Louis J.	Day	Alice Eliza	Wagers	Albert C.
Davis	Gertrude L.	Kruse	H. A.	Day	Alice M.	Nalley	George A.
Davis	Hattie L.	Cooper	C. J.	Day	Katie A.	Pack	Barnett W.
Davis	Helen, Mrs.	Le Baron	Harrison M.	Day	Katie K.	Russ	William H.
Davis	Henrietta L.	Roberts	Edwin A.	Day	Laura	Jones	Cethil
Davis	Ida B.	Frey	Frank J.	Day	Lizzie	McCallum	Alphonso
Davis	Ida M.	Roche	Thomas A.	Day	Lyda Edith	Hart	Harold D.
Davis	Ina A.	Cochran	Arthur F.	Day	Mary Alice	White	John Charles
Davis	Jesssina Cline	Smith	Fred	Day	Rose	Wickbaum	Emil
Davis	Kessie Rebecca	Phinney	George Henry	Dayton	Hazel W.	Rego	Frank T., Jr.
Davis	Lena	Foote	W. D.	Dayton	Pearl	Kettendorff	Otto J.
Davis	Lydia A.	Linton	T. S.	Daywalt	Elizabeth	Mather	William Henry
Davis	M., Mrs.	Coleman	George E.	De Bella	Della	Tonelli	Salvatore
Davis	Margaret L.	Butterworth	Thomas C.	De Bolt	Kate	Butler	Willie
Davis	Margaret W.	Ward	David N.	de Cungi	Lina	Borserini	Zeno
Davis	Marion	Bufton	Harvey M.	de Freitas	Isabelle	Gomes	Antonio Jos.
Davis	Mary	Dahlmann	Otto Hugo	De Gassick	Aylene Stewart	Barr	Elmere Roy
Davis	Mary	Redenbaugh	Joseph Isaac	De La Monte	Ollie	Yancey	Oliver H,
Davis	Mary E.	Long	Geo. W.	de Martini	Millie	Diehl	Henry N.
Davis	Mary J.	Derrick	Jesse W.	De Matos	Maria	De Souza	Manuel T.
Davis	Mary L., Mrs.	Davis	Erastus L.	de Shiell	Virginia	Cook	William H.
Davis	Mary Warren	Morrison	Burk Guy	De Silva	Mary	Silva	Domingo Prater
Davis	Medna	Drever	Andrew M.	de Veuve	Anna M.	Finch	Fred F.
Davis	Olga C.	Norton	Samuel R.	Deaborn	Edith Alice	Seaton	Roland M.
Davis	Ona M.	McChesney	Robert S.	Deacon	Martha	Martin	Walter
Davis	Pearl	Marshall	Cleveland H.	Deal	Dorothy May	Camozzi	Walter C.
Davis	Pearl May	Nelson	James B.	Deal	Mary Catherine	Davis	John Elmer
Davis	Rebecca Dorothy	Baxman	Ernest B.	Deal	Minnie Etta	Deal	Oliver Morton
Davis	Sarah J.	Pieratt	John M.	Dean	Eva May	Smyth	Hugh Moore

Dean	Flora Hilton	Goodwin	Henry B.	Del Fava	Gina	Lucchesi	Enrico
Dean	Jeannie	Butts	Thomas J.	Delahanty	May Frances	Brand	Philip Edward
Dean	Maybell	Hosmer	Stanley	Delamater	Mary E.	Bates	George H.
Dean	Sylvia G.	Mitchell	Floyd H.	Delaney	Alice N.	Sherman	Clancy J.
Deane	Norah	Watters	Henry	Delaney	Blanche M.	Beardin	Hubert W.
Dearborn	Ethel	Meeker	Godfrey Hinkley	Delaney	Elizabeth A.	Bowden	Isaac
Dearborn	Mollie Theresa	Claypool	Jerry W.	Delaney	Marguerite M.	Sullivan	John Allen
Dearborn	Nellie	Woodward	John Grant	Delany	Sarelda M.	Covell	R. William
Deardorff	Anna M.	Bailey	Jessie William	DelCarlo	Emma	Barindelli	Charles
Dearing	Alice M.	Phelps	David C.	Delehanty	Josephine	Peacemaker	George W.
Dearing	Josie	Lyttaker	Will	DeLew	Lena	Rand	Walter Stoops
Debats	Marie	Quadrio	John	Delfino	Ethel Victorine	Code	Reginald F.
DeBoet	Alice M.	Wilson	Jesse W.	Dellavedora	Maria	Dagi	Augostino
DeBolt	Lucy H.	Ketterlin	Auguste D.	Dellenbaugh	Madge	Langsdorf	Charles
DeBorba	Mary L.	Lemos	John B.	Dellenbaugh	Viola May	Owens	William
DeBord	Nevada	Bugbee	Troby E.	Delloca	Hazel S.	Presley	Harry C.
DeBow	Sallie	Atwood	Joseph C.	Dellosso	Ida	Tonelli (?)	Vittorio E.
Decanini	Amanda	Minelli	Cesare	Delmue	Mary J.	Marall	Henry R.
DeCarly	Annie	McLaren	Henry Havelock	DeLong	A. Gertrude	Walce	John J.
Dechenne	Rosa	Kinne	Albert B.	DeLong	Harriet S.	(name missing)	
Decker	Emma J.	Jensen	Victor	DeLong	Maud	Wilson	Roy C.
Decker	Josie C.	Hearsey	Mason E.	DeLong	Nellie Alice	Bowers	Oliver Clyde
DeCosta	Annie	Belfils	Ernest	DelSarto	Rosie	Pellegrini	Paul
Deeds	Louisa C.	Fowler	Alfred	DeLude	Martine O.	Hart	Charles E.
Deeds	Millie E., Mrs.	Pfister	John E.	Delzell	Maggie	Bartlett	Alexander
Deering	Martha J.	Hatler	John P.	Delzell	Margaret A., Mrs	Simpson	C. C.
Dees	Berdena	Wilber	Alonzo	DeMartini	Cecilia T.	Hazlett	Emmett M.
DeFries	Gertrude M.	Pedigo	Olney G.	DeMartini	Irene, Mrs.	DeMartini	Benigno
Degardin	Clara	Howard	Phillip	DeMartini	Laura M.	Summ	William H.
Deghi	Prima	Bettiga	Vincenzo	DeMeo	Angelina	Colabella	Carlo
DeGiorgi	Giuseppina	Lodovico	Morgantine	Demeo	Annie	Vossos	Andrew
DeGiorgi	Ottavia	Pomi	James	Demetz	Anna	Geiger	Fred
DeGroot	Flora	Mong	George William	Demol	Claire	Herbst	John H.
Dehay	Louise A.	Forsyth	Jess Thomas	Dempsey	Catherine F.	Fitzpatrick	James H.
Dei	Aneta	Gilliam	George D.	Dempsey	Emogene E.	Hovey	Arthur La Verne

Dibble	Jennie	Meredith	Laurence Milton
Dick	Agnes E.	Street	Thos. B.
Dick	Mayme S.	Birmingham	Winfred W.
Dicke	Lizzie	Day	George Frank
Dickey	Bessie	Luce	Elmer E.
Dickey	Parmelia	McCune	William M.
Dickson	Adela	Mitchell	Robert A.
Dickson	Lizzie B.	Dickson	William M.
Dickson	Mary L.	Hotle	William Marley
Dickson	Rena M.	Hiatt	Ray Isaac
Dickson	Ruth E.	Tuttle	Ovid S.
Dicus	Georgia	Stump	Lewis
Dies	Emma J.	Raymond	Henry J.
Dietz	Gladys N.	McGeein (?)	Roland J.
DiGrazia	Elvira T.	Ponzo	Phil J.
Dill	Catherine Hester	Voluntine	Edwin Earle
Dill	Matilda S.	McCoy	David A.
Dill	Nettie	Betts	Ross Everett
Dillian	Lillian Pearl	Brain	Herbert Roy
Dillingham	Susan M.	Smith	Robert A.
Dillon	Fanny C.	Reed	Charles C.
Dillon	Margaret G.	Dillon	Melville C.
Dillon	Sarah M.	Lyttaker	E. V.
Dimick	Viola	Fulkerson	Bruce C.
Dimmick	Lillian M.	Fearn	John R.
Dinelli	Nonziatina	Luchesi	Angelo
Dinnucci	Giula	Giacomelli	Etalo
Dinnucci	Mary	Coli	Lorenzo
Dinucci	Clara	Barsi	Nicholas
Dinucci	Eleanor	Gonella	Ray N.
Dinucci	Emma	Pieri	Vincenzo
Dinucci	Filomina	Dinucci	Antonio
Dinucci	Katherine	Bacci	Vincent
Dinucci	Mary	Dal Pino	Guiseppe
Dinucci	Julia Katherine	Galgani	Vincenzo
Dishong	Lucinda L.	Doir	Edgar
Ditto	Elizabeth A.	Smith	Merle C.
Dix	Annie M.	DeWitt	Henry C.
Dixon	Helen Louise	Herrick	Albert B., Jr.
Dixon	Jessie	Fowler	Scott D.
Dixon	Lillie May	Roth	George
Doan	Elizabeth	Pohley	Henry
Doane	Lulu M.	Davis	George B.
Dobbel	Dorothy Catherine	Van Coops	Harold
Dobbins	Luella F.	Roberts	Levi G.
Doda	Rosie	Pedroia	Victor
Dodd	Delfina	Garzoli	Alfonso
Dodenhoff	Ceres Wanda	Fenton	Claude Merton
Dodenhoff	Edythe W.	Lockwood	Frank B.
Dodge	A. C., Mrs.	Mills	John
Dodge	Alice Mae	Kee	George Hamilton
Dodge	Florence H.	Meeker	Alexander H.
Dodge	Hattie Azuba	Williams	Willie
Dodson	Mary	Hall	Thos. R.
Dodson	Mary Jane	Adcock	Joseph C.
Dodson	Mary R.	Frazier	Elisha H.
Dodson	Minnie M.	Lewis	Calvin Mc M.
Dodson	Rosa	Adcock	George
Doelling	Eliza	Mehl	Carl Frederick
Doerges	Louise	Hockney	Byron S.
Doggett	Averil Alison	Hadrich	C. F. Hugo, Jr.
Doggutt	Georgie W.	James	Henry W.
Dogia	Anociata	Belli	Albert Joseph
Doherty	Gertrude H.	Gilder	Alfred
Doherty	Sadie M.	McFadden	William H.
Dohl (?)	Effa B.	Allen	Chesley M.
Dohn	Ella	Anderson	Herbert A.
Dohn	Ida G.	Nielsen	Carl H.
Dolan	Anna	Ambler	John
Dolan	Maria	Kent	William Charles

Dempsey	Katherine C.	Healey	William E.	Derrick	Lucy Clawson	Wright	John
Dempsey	Maggie M.	Borland	Lee	Derrick	Lulu Maude	Buxton	Ernest Edward
Dempsey	Mary E.	Hurley	Thomas F.	Derrick	Lydia	Jones	Henry
Denehy	Helen	Buechler	Lewis	Derrick	Maggie Ellen	Proctor	James Monroe
Denham	Ada B.	Campbell	J. Otto	Derrick	Nellie Annie	Eddinger	Charles Winfield
Denham	Bertha	Tenter	Carl W.	Derrick	Sadie Ray	Proctor	Royal Tyler
Denham	Lena Ethel	Barnes	William Julius	Derrick	Sarah	Yancy	Oliver H.
Denis	Linnie C.	Soules	Charles F.	Derrickson	Hila	Bones	Lester
Denise	Vivian	Vellutini	George G.	Dervin	Eliza	Melton	Newton
Denman	Ida Belle	McNear	George Plummer	DeSart	Florence J.	Brubeck	L. S.
Denman	Nellie A.	Lupton	Earl L.	Deskin	Geneva O.	Tipton	Willis O.
Denmark	Kittie M.	Raber	John French	Deskin	Sadie I.	Renwick	Donald P.
Denner	Bessie K. (?)	Clark	James E.	Desmue	Ida	Blomme	John
Denner	Emily Rose	Briggs	Stiles Harlan	DeSoto	Dorthey Christa	Chaix	Emile Adrien
Denner	Fulvia M.	Mossler	Frederick A.	DeSouza	Katie	Azveado	John
Denney	Emma C.	Hunter	Grover C.	DeSouza	Mamie	Ventura	Joel S.
Denning	California	Briggs	William Edward	Deuman	Carrie Elizabeth	Allen	James Edgar
Dennis	Nellie	Armstrong	Charles Newton	Devello	Frances Julia	Colburn	Lester F.
Dennis	Rosa	Ray	Robert M.	Devoto	Carrie R.	Phillips	George C.
Dennis	Sarah E.	Lowrey	Leroy	Devoto	Elsie Clara	Pedersen	Joseph Obert
Dennison	Lucy E.	Gourley	John A.	Dewey	Beatrix C.	Bird	Charles A.
Dennison	Maude Pearl	Hoff	Herman James	Dewey	Beryl Marie	Woodhams	Roy Charles, Dr.
Denny	Sadie Mae	McDermott	Charles Henry	Dewey	Ruby	Feckenscher	Edward R.
Densmore	Christine M.	Williams	Wm.	Dewick	Letitia B.	Norris	B. T., Jr.
Denton	Carrie M.	MacNevin	Wm. V.	DeWiederhold	Amelia	Ross	William G.
Denton	Itasca Mae	Cornwell	Jesse Roberts	DeWitt	Flora E.	O'Connor	Howard V.
DeNye (?)	Freda	Grubb	Merle M.	DeWitt	Mary Lauvira (?)	Malm	Arthur Marian
Deputy	Isabelle	Lerouge	Stephen A.	DeWitt	Ruby Ruth	Laughlin	Lester
Derby	Cora	Benson	L. E.	Dexter	Alice B.	Bryant	John Kenneth
Derby	Linda Burr	Gutermute	Henry Shauer	Dexter	Ella B.	Hannah	Percy J.
Derick	Lena M.	Codd	David E.	Dey	Ella Bell	Anthony	Edward Augustus
Dering	Josephine M.	Simmendinger	Grover C.	DeYoung	Minnie	Gentry	Samuel
DeRose	Lenora	Lewis	Harry D.	Diaz	Isabelle E.	Lawrence	William H.
Derrick	Cassie	Tyler	Arthur E.	Dibble	Avonia	Given	Andrews Logan
Derrick	E. J., Mrs.	Rouse	N. S.	Dibble	Helen	Watson	Valentine

Dolan	Mary	Clements	T. H.	Donati	Mary	Scollari	Eugenio
Dolcibella	Margherita	Rovetta	Lamberto	Donati	Romilda	Albini	Paul
Dolcini	Irene D.	Barboni	Joseph H.	Donati	Romilda	Pontaletta (?)	Andrea
Dolcini	Lydia C.	Respini	Robert M.	Donati	Sophie	Pellascio	John D.
Dolcini	Zelma D.	Lafranchi	Fred L.	Donati	Teresa	Gonnella	John
Dolet	Helen A.	Mann	T. W.	Dondero	Katie	Benedetti	John
Dollar	Alice	Beebe	Elbert E.	Donegan	Marion A.	Warde	John P.
Dollar	Daisy B.	Bigham	Ray E.	Donelin	Eva Marie	Rapp	John
Dollar	Elsie Elma	Mathisen	Jesse	Donnelly	Amelia A.	Faulkner	M. H.
Dollar	Grace E.	Barron	Harold	Donnelly	Elizabeth F.	Hussa	Walter H.
Dollar	Mary E.	Burns	Robert A.	Donnelly	Kate	McGee	Thomas J.
Domenica	Martinovia (?)	Poncia	Peter	Donner	Bettie L.	Coburn	James A.
Domenici	Louisa Agnes	Silva	John J.	Donner	Cora	Wilson	John J.
Domeniconi	Matilde	Mari	Ernesto	Donner	Mary E.	Ungewitter	William P.
Domeniconi	Rachel	Fumasoli	Giacomo	Donohoe	Annie	Orsi	Pete
Domenighini	Lettie	Bruhn	Nickels	Donovan	Annie Elizabeth	Thompson	John Alexander
Domenighini	Maria	Belli	Luigi	Donovan	Mary F.	Parker	Fred E.
Domenipelli	Erminia	Pastori	Constanti	Donovan	Nadine G.	Bachrach	Arthur E.
Dominechelli	Luigina	Berizzi	John	Donovan	Thelma E.	Slusser	Eugene
Domitille	Carlotina	Davini	Joe	Donoven	Mally (?)	Marcell	N. E.
Don't	Mary	Wernecke	William A.	Dooley	Anna	Young	Dolph Henry
Donahoo	Ilma	Kunzler	Ora Archibald	Dooley	Maggie	Ryan	James W.
Donahue	Georgia	Burns	John T.	Dooley	Maude	Rains	Bud
Donahue	Gertrude	Seibert	Leo Anthony	Doran	Josephine E.	Lavin	Joseph E.
Donahue	Margaret	Love	Francis	Doran	Mamie J.	Brendel	Fred W.
Donahue	Margaret V.	Spence	Harold R.	Doremus	Florence M.	Lower	John
Donahue	May	Burns	E. F.	Dorff	Olga L.	Walker	Carol
Donahue	Minnie C.	Clinch	Henry W. R.	Dorman	Ida J.	Otley	Fred
Donahue	Rena	Gallagher	James	Dorman	Marjorie W.	Graves	Joseph L.
Donahue	Violet P.	Elliott	James J.	Dorman	Sarah Ada	Jones	Charles
Donair	Helen E.	McGillwray	William	Dormann	Tillie	Stademann	Herman F.
Donaldson	Ann, Mrs.	Scott	J. Thompson	Dormeau	Albertine	Martin	Louis
Donati	Annie	Camotta	Joe	Dornell	Maria B.	Stevens	Herbert S.
Donati	Dosola	Mazzotti	Ralph	Dornin	Alice	Bryant	Hubert
Donati	Mary	Codiga	Antonio	Dornin	Julia	Eldridge	George G.

Dorward	Anna G.	Giorno	Victor E.
Doss	Bell	Hammell	Charles E.
Doss	Belle	Turner	John H.
Doss	Emma A.	Hunt	William Irvin
Doss	Ida May	Wallace	Henry D.
Doss	Iva	Dillman	Charles
Doss	Laura	Middagh	Samuel
Doss	Pearl Elizabeth	Baugh	Douglas Guy
Doss	S. N.	Gibbs	F. H.
Doss	Wilma Eloise	Murphy	Frank Edward
Doty	Ethel A.	Nichols	Manunde
Doty	Ida H.	Garrison	Elmer B.
Dougherty	Grace	Peck	Stanley S.
Dougherty	Lillian E., Mrs.	Livingston	Charles
Doughty	Lula Amelia	Clark	Charles Raymond
Doughty	Margaret Elizabeth	McHale	William Anthony
Douglas	Edith R.	Douglas	David J.
Douglas	Emma	Shuster	George W.
Douglass	Clara	Stanford	Jerome B.
Douglass	Flora B.	Richards	J. Goldwin
Douglass	Ila T.	Grube	Axcel E.
Douglass	Julia	Hunt	Warren E.
Douglass	Mary E.	Peterson	Mark R.
Dour	Annie E.	Surryhne	Charles E.
Dovey	Eva	Fellows	Fred C.
Dovey	Margaret	Fletcher	William R.
Dovey	Minnie Henrietta	Murphy	Osbort Louis
Dovin	Elizabeth	McCulloch	Irvin Scott
Dowd	Marie G. V.	Roache	Valton G.
Dowdall	Genevieve	Myron	William
Dowdall	Katie	Murray	William
Dowdall	Mary E.	Gale	Archie R.
Dower	Vivienne M.	Wherry	Rixey B.
Dowling	Anna Katherine	Marx	Bert Franklin

Down	Edith	Gabrielsen	William J. A.
Downer	Mae	Cereghino	Nathaniel
Downey	Gertrude Francis	Sahlstrom	Harry A.
Downey	Katie	Woods	Thos. Stanley
Downham	Alma N.	Aanensen	Peider
Downie	Catherine Lilias	Eastman	Tarleton
Downing	Annette Robie	Brown	Edwin Francis
Downing	Annie M.	Brush	Charlie W.
Downs	Annie	Lennard	Edward
Downs	Carrie I.	Saxton	Fred L.
Downs	Catherine H.	Flohr	Frank G.
Dows (?)	Alice M.	Randall	James S.
Doyle	Allien Evelyn	Coldwell	Edrie Sayor
Doyle	Anna	Ames	Raymond J.
Doyle	Louise	Hornberger	Charles
Doyle	Mary Ellen	Morrison	Guy Bryan
Doyle	Mary K.	Askins	Samuel M.
Doyle	Nellie J.	Hood	Frank B.
Doyle	Ruth	Dent	Elmer S.
Drake	Ada Verlina	Murray	Byrd B.
Drake	Clarica	Lawrason	Dinnie Fred
Drake	Dora Luella	Dasquith	Sidney W. G.
Drake	Edith Martha	Burke	Edmund J.
Drake	Ella	Haverlo	Jesse
Drake	Helen N.	Wasson	Louis L.
Drake	Mary Emily	Brown	Alenzo Theodore
Drake	Maud	Davis	John
Drake	Maude A.	Murray	Perry L.
Drake	Pearl A.	Mathis	Ephraim R.
Drees	Johanna E.	Nauert	Henry
Drees	Mary	Holm	Jacob F.
Drennan	Hazel Estelle	Brown	Leo Allyn
Drescher	Lena	Hogeboom	Robert Percy
Dresner	Fannie	Silver	Max
Drever	Harriet	Devow	George

Drew	Annie E.	Traner	Harold W.	Dugan	Edith	Bayes	Lou
Drew	Hester	Bailey	Wilson Roy	Dugan	Linda	Luna	Frank
Dreyer	Helena E.	Denner	Russell L. A.	Dugdell	Martha L.	Woods	Alexander B.
Drickhammer	Meta	Dittmann	Henry	Duher	Catherine	Fallon	Martin
Driscoll	Rinetta	Cullen	William Edward	Duhig	Sarah E.	Whitty	James
Driver	Edith Katherine	Linebaugh	Francis Elmer	Duhring	Agnes J.	Ryland	Cains Tacibus
Driver	Emma Sarah	May	Ernest Clarke	Duke	Ada	Smith	Edson L.
Druck	Elizabeth M.	Fowler	Dewey	Duke	Ethel E.	Bones	R. W.
Druckhammer	Minna	Geils	George F.	Dukes	Eva Della	Young	Clarence Henry
Drummond	Bridgie	Sullivan	Michael	Dunbar	M. A.	Mitchell	L. W.
Dryden	Clara	Richardson	Kinnie Z.	Dunbar	Carrie B.	Jenkins	Arthur G.
Dryden	M. I.	Ridenhour	L. E.	Duncan	Ada M.	Duncan	Richard
Dryden	Olive V.	Ramsey	H. T.	Duncan	Bessie	Hutchins	Jasper Lawrence
Dryer	Bessie L.	Lowe	Herbert E.	Duncan	Estelle	Kettlewell	Richard S.
Du Commun	Lucille	Mack	William E.	Duncan	Gertrude	Ronsheimer	Howard
Du Commun	Marcelle M.	Bailey	Percy D.	Duncan	Helen	Mell	A. William
du Temple	Madeleine	Graham	Patrick	Duncan	Mattie McDonald	Duncan	George Benjamin
Du Vander	Rebecca L.	Elsbree	Charles Dyer	Duncan	May Agnes	Hulbert	Harry E.
DuBois	Hazel M.	Kock	George A.	Duncan	Navarro	Robertson	Harrison
DuBois	Jessie Leta	Thompson	Will Arthur	Duncan	Nellie	Snow	Myol M.
Ducker	Lottie Alice	Lumsden	Charles William	Duncan	Susan A.	Burton	Oliver F.
Ducker	Mary	Cannon	Louis	Duncan	Vella I.	Mell	John W.
Ducker	Minnie May	Cook	Andrew Joseph	Duncan	Vella Irene	Moore	Ray
Ducker	Sarah A.	Ducharm	George	Duncan	Verda	Selvage	James
Ducker	Ella Mae	Lacque	Edward F.	Duncan	Gemma E.	Clark	Winfred P.
DuCommun	Lillian E.	Kerner	Henry R.	Dunckley	Lucy E.	White	James S.
Dudley	Daphne A.	McVay	Clarence L.	Dunham	Addie Bell	Pittman	Charles C.
Dudley	Nellie	Warren	Charles	Dunham	Alta Faye	Alley	Omery Elmo
Duenwald	Ethyl E.	Brown	Arthur	Dunham	Essie	Boyd	Hugh Coleman
Duer	Charlotte	Winkler	Ernest	Dunker	Hattie A.	Hall	Frank J.
Duerson	Elizabeth C.	Elphick	Thomas R.	Dunkley	Mattie J.	Adams	John Henry
Duerson	Mary E.	Stocking	George	Dunlap	Melinda	Foutch	Albert P.
Duffey	Cassandra	Kozminsky	Nicholas	Dunn	Anna M.	MacQuiddy	Oscar Lee
Duffey	Mabel G.	Galindo	Ruperto	Dunn	Daisy B.	Linebaugh	Robert F.
Duffy	Susie	Fitzgerald	Thomas	Dunn	Fannie J.	Cooper	Thomas S.

Dunn	Lillie Caroline	Munfrey	William Osmund
Dunn	Maggie Irene	Hoyle	George Wilson
Dunning	Melissa M.	Schlake	Christian F.
Dunning	Minnie M.	Neasham	Ira A.
Dunton	Audella	Smith	James W.
Dunwoody	Florence E.	Stubbs	Robert H.
Dunwoody	Lizzie	McReynolds	R. E. L.
Dupe	Fannie, Mrs.	Vinclet	Edmund Joseph
Duprey	Elsie Constance	Price	William Lee
Durant	Ella	Cheney	Charles
Durbin	Susie Loraine	Hart	Ellis O.
Durham	Elizabeth	Butler	John Samuel
Duriee	Mima B.	Williams	Ernest V.
Durkee	Caroline A.	Mothersole	Thomas H.
Durling	Flora	Osborn	E. W.
Dutcher	Pearl	Holst	William
Dutcher	Stella V.	Hepworth	Albert
Dutil	Jeanne Harriette	Lalanne	Laurence Marius
Dutra	Margarida P.	Braga	Joe F.
Dutre	Alice E.	Winfrey	Larry Arlington
Dutro	Josephine	Bordges	Joseph S.
Dutro	Josephine M.	Mathias	Antoni B.
Dutton	Ada W.	Carleton	Calvin W.
Dutton	Emma J.	Denicke	H.
Dutton	Ida	Stoffal	Philip
Dutton	Loraine K.	Davis	Barton J.
Duval	Laura M.	Hammond	Grant
Dwane	Agnes	Murray	William
Dwyer	Nellie A.	Gender	Edward F.
Dye	Violet E.	Scott	Charles
Dyozenz (?)	Maria	Marties	Joseph F.
Eades	Nellie	Kuhule	Perry
Eager	Loretta	Frank	James
Eagle	Geneva	Fredson	Chris A.
Eagle	Millie May	Price	Arnold David
Eagleson	Anna May	Lottman	W. B.
Eakin	Mary E.	Campbell	William A.
Ealderton	Mildred	Wright	George M.
Eardley	Eliza Fitchford	Hardin	Andrew Evan
Eardley	Gladys	Klemgard	James G.
Earl	Deta	Boswell	William L.
Earle	Grace L.	Cooper	Peter G.
Earley	Olive J.	Ayers	Robert Charles
Early	Cleora A.	Hall	Louis Williard
Early	Mary L.	Murphy	J. R.
Earnest	Helen Pearl	Heryford	Roy
Earps	Christine, Mrs.	Spear	John B.
Easlie	Nora Emma	Black	Wm. H.
Easter	Lucy J. (?)	Morris	Walter C.
Eastlick	Gussie A.	Patterson	Donald C.
Eastlick	Mabel	Smith	Voyle S.
Eastlick	Dora Belle	Nichols	Walter James
Eaton	Bettie, Mrs.	Prows	Sylvester W.
Eaton	Lillian	Winter	William
Eaton	Nettie, Mrs.	Gould	Frank H.
Eavons	Lydia	Shepperd	M. F.
Eberstein	Ethel	Oakley	Edward B.
Eberts	Berwin E.	Barber	Walter P.
Ebling	Frances, Mrs.	Trautner	Max
Eby	Ida J.	Horton	Samuel
Eby	Jessie Leone	Forgett	Joseph Nelson
Eby	Lucretia	Bane	David A.
Eccles	Grace S.	Davison	George W.
Eckard	Alice Minnie	Stone	Charles Edgar
Eckard	Elsa	Stone	Albert R.
Eckert	Signatoria Oxana (?)	Park	George Edward H.
Eckly	Elmira	Pitt	John W.
Eckman	Clara Lee	Quigley	George Calvin
Eckman	Emma May	Miller	William

Eckman	Minnie	Holaday	Elon R.	Ehrlich	Amelia	Vance	Wm. K.
Eddelbuttel	Henrietta W. M.	Drury	Eugene Vernon	Ehrlich	Miriam D.	Dunn	James
Eddy	Zulpha L.	Eathorne	Alexander	Eichler	Ella, Mrs.	James	John P.
Edgar	Mary Estelle	Wescott	Benjamin Harrison	Einfeldt	Mary Ellen, Mrs.	Bobkiewicz	Louis
Edgewood	Margaret	Bussman	Frank	Einhorn	Clara Webber	Stearns	William Gordon
Edgeworth	Lillian R.	Tremblay	Fred P.	Ekman	Sigrid	Moltzen	Axel
Edgeworth	Rose E.	Newman	John W.	Elburn (?)	Laura	Deter	John
Edington	Eliza Francis	Eakle	Henry P.	Elden	Helena	Lindsey	William A.
Edleman	Anna Marie	Schmid	Gottlieb	Elden	Susie E.	Van Zandt	James Hoyle
Edmester	Grace Amelia	Williams	Wallace W.	Elder	Emma	Morris	Roy
Edmiston	Annie	Mize	Thompson	Elder	Lelia May	Siegle	Arthur Leslie
Edmunds	Ivah Beyrl	Wentz	Coleman Clayton	Elderkin	Edna M.	Hullen	Peter H.
Edringlow	Carrie B.	Bass	Seymour S.	Eldred	Beatrice M.	Purvine	Charles H.
Edrington	Rhea R.	Hannon	Joseph F.	Eldridge	Mary	Smith	James L.
Edwards	Charlotte T.	Denman	Frank H.	Elias	Margaret Josephine	Lowry	Patrick Joseph
Edwards	Evelyn Maud	Blast	Leo A.	Eliasen	Johanne	Iverson	George
Edwards	Helen R.	Blanchard	D. N.	Eliason	Agnes	Grant	Henry M.
Edwards	Jennie	Graham	Arthur W.	Eliot	Florence	Pratt	Oliver W. H.
Edwards	Josephine Letitia	Hannah	David Albert	Elkerton	Ida May	Chaney	William Levi
Edwards	Laura V.	Overton	John P.	Elkins	S?eyphene E.	Smith	George F.
Edwards	Lizzie	Kennedy	Elbert L.	Ellings	Annie	Simoens	Julius
Edwards	Sadie E.	Wyatt	Charles E.	Ellingwood	Bertha May	Miller	Robert Lee
Eefers	Gretchen Anna	Rothenberger	Louis	Elliot	Rachael, Mrs.	Heald	J. G.
Egan	Lena K.	Haub	Theodore G.	Elliott	Alma R.	Struckman	Fred C.
Egan	Nellie V.	McNear	John A., Jr.	Elliott	Amy G.	Griggs	Alvin S.
Eggers	Hermine	Heintz	August Henry	Elliott	Marion G.	Mitchell	Claude D.
Egler	Anna Reynella	Hughes	John Franklin	Elliott	Mary A.	Falanery	Charles A.
Egli	Emma	Clegg	Frances L.	Elliott	Ora	Rosenthal	Louis
Egloff	May L.	Weybe	Charles A.	Ellis	Carrie E.	Childs	George B.
Egner	Martha	Denham	Drury	Ellis	Ethel M.	Spittler	Dudley M.
Egola	Giuseppena	Romeri	Pietro	Ellis	Eva M.	Broaddus	Andrew S.
Ehlers	Margaretta	Butenop	Wilhelm	Ellis	Laura C.	Harlan	Carolus
Ehly	Lucile E.	McCabe	Arthur D.	Ellis	Leona G.	Fay	John F.
Ehmer (?)	Julia	Hickey	John	Ellis	Mary Jane	Maker	Archie
Ehrhardt	Elvesta I.	Jamieson	John A.				

Ellis	Mary Josephine	Robertson	James R.
Ellis	Olive I.	Harlan	James W.
Ellis	Treasure Sterling	McClymonds	Vance
Ellison	Anna	Nicholson	Alfred
Ellison	Bess Evelyn	Sinclair	Alfred Leslie
Ellison	Edith	Icanberry	John M.
Ellison	Grace E.	Herman	Christopher M.
Ells	Inice R.	Lovejoy	Robert T.
Ellsworth	Elsie J.	Sheehy	Edward P.
Ellsworth	Hazel	Sigrist	Jules A.
Elmore	Lois Merrill	Lawrence	George Edwin
Elmore	Ruth Eunice	Reynolds	Harold Vernon
Elphick	Annie M.	Morse	James Grant
Elphick	Blanche	Brown	Chesney E.
Elphick	Clytie	Beffa	James, Jr.
Elphick	Emma M.	Schlener	Albert C.
Elphick	Mattie E.	Hudson	George R.
Elsdon	Winifred J.	Foster	Aubrey M.
Elton	Gratia	George	Joseph M.
Elwell	Myra A.	Setchell	William T.
Ely	Cedora Dell	Peters	Albert Paul
Ely	Sarah E.	Bradley	Henry L.
Emel	Anna, Mrs.	Thormann	John H. C.
Emeldi	Theodora Marie	Garcia	Firmin
Emelio	Caroline	Thomas	Jose
Emeral	Mary	King	E. Manuel
Emerson	Lodia M.	Wheeler	Philip J.
Emerson	Mildred	Treanor	Peter J.
Emerson	Natalie S.	Passalacqua	Louis L.
Emerson	Nellie	Connor	J.
Emerson	S. R.	Henry	J. R.
Emerson (?)	Bessie	Paxton	Blitz W.
Emery	Eva J.	French	Charles F.
Emmerson	Delia M.	Kennedy	C. A.
Emmick	Minnie	McConochie	Thomas S.
Emperan	Anita Vallejo	Thomson	Allen Milo
Endicott	Bertha G.	Rowland	Willis B.
Endicott	Edythe E.	Hulbert	Marion O.
Endicott	Juanita M.	Thompson	Frank
Endicott	Margaret A.	Ornbaun	Herbert N.
Endicott	Margaret R.	Southard	Daniel W.
Enevold	Maria	Hansen	P. B.
Engdol	Mabel E.	Muller	George A.
Engelund	Marie C.	Brown	Henry B.
England	Angeline, Mrs.	Bates	Philip
England	Basha C.	Thompson	C. H.
England	Carrie	Gale	D. R.
England	Cora May	Godman	George G.
England	Elma L.	McKillop	William D.
England	Maron Love	Wood	Merabeau (?) Dallas
England	Martha Isabel	Berry	George Herod
England	Mary	Ledford	Clayton A.
England	Susan A.	Berry	George H.
England	Susan J. (?)	Warner	Alexander L.
Englander	Minnie Diana	Cassab	Elias Kalile
Englebright	Eva	Cartwright	Frank
Englehart	Eliza Ellen	Winder	Joseph
Engler	Annie Marie	Drake	Lennard Arthur
English	Dora	Chambers	King
English	Frankie M.	Warren	Edward D.
English	Margaret M.	Gorman	James
English	Norma Beulah	Lovell	Kenneth Henry
English	Sadie, Mrs.	Miller	James Jesse
Englund	Etta	Cornelius	Emil
Enlow	Ada	Cameron	Charles Edwin
Enlow	Alta E.	Stetson	Bernard L.
Eno	Fannie Vashti	Nickerson	Albert Franklin
Enos	Elsie	Renner	Frederick
Enos	Getrude C.	Willis	William

Enright	Margaret	Carrillo	Albert Frank	Espey	Jessie L.	Miller	Thomas B.
Enslow	Emma A.	Hotz	Gustave H.	Espy	Belle	Poole	James R.
Enslow	Orpha Ann	Stevenson	Robert	Esquien	Marie Rose	Thomas	Ollie Oscar
Entzminger	Elizabeth S.	Oehlman	Otto A.	Esquieu	Louise	Goard	W. F.
Entzminger	Emma	Oehlman	Byron A.	Essner	Joan D.	Edwards	Thomas M.
Enyisch	Martha	Holtchauer	Louis	Esterling	Margaret K.	Warnecke	Carl I.
Enzenauer	Annie	Cadd	Thomas	Esterman	Elsa	Martin	William S.
Enzenauer	Dollie	Reiners	John A.	Estes	Fannie C.	Warren	J. C.
Enzenauer	Ethel R.	Flournoy	Alexander H.	Estes	Fannie E.	Matthews	Fred R.
Eperson	Fannie	Messner	Jacob F.	Estes	Mary C. E.	Smith	W. H. F.
Eproson	Addie	Boyer	Sidney Roswell	Estinghausen	Clara I.	Watson	W. A.
Eproson	Jane	Nossett	Israel	Estinghausen	Phileta J.	Organ	Thomas F.
Equi	Lucy Victoria	Reilly	Thomas Bernard	Eten	Ella Agnes	Farrer	Ernest Eugene
Equi	Marie	Bernard	John Leo	Eten	Olive A.	Dutro	James M.
Equi	Teresa	Mitchell	John	Evans	Alma M.	Cluver	Harold H.
Eraldi	Albina	Quartaroli	Harry R.	Evans	Annie B., Mrs.	Erskine	Alvin Chester
Eraldi	Emma	Garzoli	Joshua	Evans	Catherine J.	Clark	Geo. C.
Erezuma	Tomasa	Scott	Edward F.	Evans	Edith	Crozier	Alfred B.
Ericksen	Dagmar	Andersen	Henry	Evans	Edna G.	Wolfe	L. B.
Ericksen	May	Hurley	Joseph	Evans	Eva L.	Beardsley	J. A.
Erlebach	Mae Asenath	Norrbom	Peter Albert	Evans	Grace M.	Wann	J. T.
Erlish	Wilhel Mina	Siegel	Valentino	Evans	Helen M.	Ross	Ellis E.
Erno	Winifred	Brusco	Henry D.	Evans	Lydia L.	Meulenbrock	Leonard
Erringer	Hattie	Russell	C. W.	Evans	Marie H.	Hobson	Frank S.
Ervin	Katie	Howell	Joseph L.	Evans	May Louise	Winter	John Edward
Erwin	Mary L.	Roux	A. F.	Evans	Rose	Church	John L.
Erwin	May	Fairbanks	Percy M.	Evans	Ruby F.	McGowen	A. L.
Esaia	Julia	Maschetti	Ben	Evans	Vera U.	Strickland	Fred E.
Esaia	Natalina	Damaino	Mike	Evans	Virginia Isabelle	Peoples	Andrew Spencer
Esaia (?)	Jennie	Lazzaroni	Peter	Evans	Vivian Maud	Tolburg	Fred J.
Esler	Della	Lichau	Edward P.	Evanson	Josie	Hultgreen	Gustaf Olof
Eslick	Daisy Belle	Moody	Logan	Everhart	Effie	Dallas	John P.
Eslick	Ida B.	Jenkins	Edgar W.	Everly	Julia N., Mrs.	Hopper	Thomas
Esmond	Fannie L.	Phillips	J. W.	Ewald	Frances	Muther	Frank, Jr.
Espey	Evelyn Blanche	Burris	Shirley David	Ewing	Gertrude	Ingram	Charles W.

Ewing	Grace	Vining	Corney
Ewing	Ida B.	Carithers	William R.
Ewing	Sadie, Mrs.	Crystal	Melvin
Eyton	Lilia A. C.	Hunt	Edward Rowland
Fagan	Cora A.	Morrow	Wilford E.
Fagie	Emma	Huntley	George W.
Fagon	Margaret	Batten	Albert
Fair	Helen	Latell	Harry
Fairbairn	Martha, Mrs.	Gerald	James T.
Fairbanks	Clara I.	Estinghausen	William
Fairbanks	Dacia Dean	Rich	Edwin W.
Fairbanks	Hattie L.	Hill	Alexander B.
Fairbanks	J. Nettie	Highbee	H. B.
Fairbanks	Loretta Louise	Jensen	Hans P.
Fairbanks	Zoe	Bell	Wellie Samuel
Fairchild	Gipsy	Foreman	C.
Fairchild	Lee	Atwood	George C.
Fairclo	Carrie Martha	Luth	Frederick Henry
Fairclo	Hattie	Whitcomb	Dan
Fairclo	Serena	Duncan	Charles W.
Fairman	Ethel Florence	Cochran	Albert Francis
Faith	Mary	Rodd	Samuel
Falena	Salamina, Mrs.	Stefani	Peter
Falkner	Amelia, Mrs.	Lawrence	Henry E.
Fallon	Edna Brown	Day	Charles Eugene
Fallon	Ruth	Christian	Herman B.
Falting	Ella	Zimmerman	William F.
Fambrini	Assuntina	Stefani	Paul
Fan	Lenora	Irwin	Nathaniel
Fan (?)	Harriet F.	Rader	Daniel
Fancher	Gladyst Maud	Mangin	Eugene Louis
Fankhausen	Clara	Baldizzone	Charles Louis
Fanning	Lizzie	Smith	Geo. W.
Fannon	Frances	Walker	Edward D.
Farbstein	Anna	Brown	William Carl

Farish	May P., Mrs.	Edmunds	George R.
Fariss	Bessie	Piver	Albert
Farley	Henrietta	Pettis	Ira N.
Farley	Mamie E.	Nunn	John
Farley	Maud	Sinclair	Samuel
Farley	Ruby	Baker	Theodore
Farmer	Agnes	Meador	Bert L.
Farmer	Carrie J.	Bering	Edward A.
Farmer	Elsie	Standifird	Thomas
Farmer	Frances M.	Griffith	Archer C.
Farmer	Hazel	Still	Samuel S.
Farmer	Lillia Belle	Webb	Edward O., Jr.
Farmer	Margart, Mrs.	Hyatt	John B.
Farmer	Marie G.	Brooke	Robert
Farmer	Olive A.	Von Emmel	Frederick H.
Farmer	Rebecca W.	Lowry	J. W.
Farmer	Sarah Angeline	Fox	Chas. W.
Farnocchia	Mary	Rossier	William
Farnsworth	Clara	Ayers	Andrew M.
Farnsworth	Hazel M.	Grenache	Harry L.
Farnsworth	May	Railsback	F. A.
Farquar	Mary I.	Channel	L. M.
Farrar	Theo	McCarthy	Will
Farrell	Angela Helen	Fevrier	George Taylor
Farrell	Carmeleta U.	Ballard	Augustus Seaton
Farrell	Genevieve M.	Bent	Edwin M.
Farrell	Gertrude M.	Fevrier	Harold C.
Farrell	Maggie	Slattery	Wm. H.
Farrell	Marjorie J.	Goss	William H., Jr.
Farrell	Mary Gertrude	Shott	William Alphnsus
Farrer	Etta Rebecca	Colburn	Orrin E.
Farrer	Jessie Catherine	Lichau	Charles Fabian
Farthing	Delia Marion	Swesey	Weitzel
Farthing	Irma George	Smeltzer	William George
Fassoth	Courdadena	Kinley	Fielden

Faudre	Lusettie	Armstrong	Benjamin	Fees	Nora M.	Storz	Carl F.
Faudre	Francis	Ward	John	Fehrensen	Susie Elizabeth	Bussman	Frederick
Faught	Ella	Rich	William B.	Fehrmann	Matilda	Sherrer	Jacob S.
Faught	Ethel A.	Fowler	William C.	Feige	Julia O.	Richter	Max
Faught	Hazel S.	Ernst	August M.	Feige	Mabel A.	Barbier	Howard E. W.
Faught	Nannie J.	Petray	R. A.	Feinberg	Lillie	Glaser	Abe
Faught	Ruth	Hixson	William H.	Felciano	Mary C.	Moniz	Joseph S., Jr.
Faulconer	Jennie M.	Crane	George S.	Feldner	Nadine	Ross	John W.
Faulkender	Millie M.	Faulkender	Everett F.	Feliz	Cassie	Armstrong	Frank L.
Faulkner	Emma M.	Sprague	John E.	Feliz	Maria Antonia	Winkler	Walter
Fava	Delima C.	Papera	Victor	Feliz	Pauline	Williams	Mark H.
Fava	Rosie M.	Shaw	Charles P.	Felmira	Gacoji	Stephani	Vincenzo
Favilla	Rosa	Paulucci	Alex	Felt	Ella E.	Smith	Charlie A.
Fawcett	Margaret	McElheny	Roy	Felt	Freda Elizabeth	Donlin	Frank L.
Fawcett	Ruth N.	Ramsey	Oliver H.	Feltes	May Caroline	Mulligan	George Julian
Fawcett	Sarah Dorthey	Young	Herbert Edward	Felton	Dollie	Schaefer	John
Fay	Anna	Baines	Latin L.	Felton	Nellie	Hopper	Wesley L.
Fay	Annie	Noble	Frank C.	Feltz	Amelia	Frank	Frederick
Fay	Cora	Dana	George Sherman	Feltz	Elsie	Miller	Jacob B.
Fay	Edith	Dittemon	Loven J.	Feltz	Frieda L.	Flockhart	Robert E.
Fay	Elsie S.	Tallman	Leland O.	Feltz	Mary S.	Blair	William E.
Fay	Laura, Mrs.	Day	Denny	Fennacy	Jeanne A.	Nicholls	William C.
Fay	Lulu A.	Winder	Joseph Q.	Fennell	Mary J.	Bernard	Gerardus
Faylor	Florence M.	Gustafson	Howard Paul	Fenner	Sarah C.	Loomis	Denton W.
Fazzi	Eliza	Simi	Casimero	Fenno	Minnie	Madeira	George D.
Fearnes	Elizabeth M.	Taylor	Leroy A.	Fenwick	Juanita	Bethune	John
Featherly	Fannie	Litton	Bearse A.	Ferguerson	Sarah Jane	Rose	John Henry
Fechter	Esther Ella	Hull	Irving Melvin	Ferguson	Addie M.	Shrivers	James B.
Feddersen	Annie	Ferenbach	Charles	Ferguson	Florence A.	Thornton	Joseph E.
Feddersen	Inka	Hansen	Andrew	Ferguson	Jemima S.	Stratton	Schuyler
Feehan	Gladys Lorene	Hall	Harley A.	Ferguson	Laura Virginia	Chase	Gay Henry
Feehan	Lizzie	Locke	J. B.	Ferguson	Lena B.	Robbins	Bert E.
Feeley	Helen, Mrs.	Haering (?)	Fred	Ferguson	May	McPherson	Early
Fees	D. Gertrude	Thompson	Walter	Ferguson	Minnie Irene	Williams	John Wesley
Fees	Mattie Grace	Moranda	Charles S.	Ferguson	Nettie Lucinda	Rouse	Alvin Emory

Ferguson	Nora	Miller	Fred H.	Field	Rucilla R.	Flack	John
Ferguson	Velma Crawford	Barnes	Ben H.	Fieldler	Mary D.	Baker	Cicero H.
Ferrari	Angelica	Morelli	Lee G.	Fields	Lucinda	Davis	William Henry
Ferrari	Edith Margaret	Bianchi	Antonio	Fields	Maggie	Smith	Frank K.
Ferrari	Elva	Defanti	Albert Alphonse	Fields	Margaret	Londen	Melville Charles
Ferrari	Nettie, Mrs.	Whiting	Frederick A.	Fields	Theresa	Flaherty	Philip Hyde
Ferraris	Annetta	Mazzeri	Enrico	Fienili	Rosa	Lotti	A.
Ferrasci	Theresa L.	DeRoco	Leo U.	Figini	Margherita	Locatelli	Antonio
Ferreira	Mary F.	Silva	Manuel F.	Filebot (?)	Maria C.	Fitch	Joseph
Ferrero	Maria	Audero	Giovanni	Filion	Mary	Klaus	Charlie
Ferrin	Cornelia L., Mrs.	Norris	Joseph J.	Filippi	Adella	Pieroni	Angelo
Ferris	Helen M.	Cepernich	Maxin J.	Filippini	Aurelia	Respini	Giocondo
Ferroni	Marie	Rosasco	Charley C.	Filippini	Clorinda	Traversi	Riziero
Ferry	Maggie E.	Dowdall	Edward J.	Filippini	Elmira Mary	DeCarli	Victor
Ferry	Sarah, Mrs.	Schonbacher	Vincent	Filippini	Elvira Leretta	Mazza	Joseph H.
Fetts	Florence	Taylor	John H.	Filippini	Louise Elvezia	Calanchini	Emil Phillip
Fewel	Addie J.	McCarthy	Eugene G.	Filippini	Nellie Dolphina	Pometta	Silvio Louis
Fewel	Millie C.	Gott	William J.	Filippini	Rose A.	Magona	Peter F.
Fewell	Kate Florence	Harmon	Oliver Lewis	Filippini	Vivian Mabel	Bloom	Americo James
Fick	Annie S.	Breitenbach	Louis	Fillippini	Silvia O.	Martinelli	Ulysses J.
Fick	Emma M.	Kopf	Carl L.	Filloon	Harriet J.	Potter	Harold R.
Fick	Hernine D.	Bayer	Herman Henry	Filosi	Lucia	Foresti	Giuseppe
Fickas	Norrie Elizabeth	Fick	John Frederick	Finale	Josephine	Morris	Rudolph A.
Ficker (?)	May	Maynard	Harry H.	Findlay	Katherine Mary	Kenna	Richard
Fickes	Daisy M.	Whittier	Frederick A.	Findlay	R. Christina	Musgrave	Albert
Fiefer	Della E.	Mason	Troy F.	Findley	C. J., Mrs.	Barnes	Thomas P.
Field	Amanda	Smith	Henry Lee	Findley	Ruby F.	Borello	Pietro J.
Field	Edna	Dasso	Dante A.	Fine	Caroline, Mrs.	McCory	Gene L.
Field	Ella	Shaw	Reed	Fine	Mary E.	Herman	Fred A.
Field	Emma	Robertson	Wm. D.	Fine	Mary M.	Davis	Charles Alva
Field	Emma H.	Hodghead	William Horace	Finerty	Katherine L.	Murphy	Lewis T.
Field	Florence	Stephens	Alexander H.	Fingahl	Nellie	Adolphson	Gustav
Field	Kate	Mason	Ernest	Finley	Abbie J.	Laughlin	Grant A.
Field	Mary	Ford	David	Finley	Anna A., Mrs.	Taynton	Charles F.
Field	Olive B.	Chambers	Edward C.	Finley	Annette	Dei	John W.

Finley	Bessie	Garloff	Walter W.		Fisher	Etta E.	Lowery	Robert D.
Finley	Carrie Ann	McKinstry	George D.		Fisher	Fannie	Middling	Casper
Finley	Elvira Victoria	Richardson	Charles Frederick		Fisher	Florence M.	Lewis	John F.
Finley	Emma	Van Auken	Henry James		Fisher	Harriet J.	Williams	Ira T.
Finley	Genevieve	Garloff	Henry R.		Fisher	Lora Etta	Marshall	Harry Lee
Finley	L. Belle	Simcoe	James J.		Fisher	Louisa	Kerner	Albert G.
Finley	Leora M.	Matthews	W. C.		Fisher	May Stella	Mowberry	Francis Walter
Finley	Leora M.	Sorensen	Nels		Fisher	Mollie	Holst	Henry
Finley	Louise	Cox	Leslie		Fiske	Elizabeth C.	Horton	Arthur S.
Finley	Vivian Gertrude	Wilds	Jesse S.		Fitch	Blanche	Rohlopp	Carl H.
Finley	Willie Camille	Beasom	John Frank		Fitch	Rosalin L.	Crofoot	Willard H.
Finley	Lovena Frances	Nielson	Anders		Fitch	Virginia Drucilla	Schmiedecke	Henry Rufus
Finn	Nellie L.	Doepfner (?)	Robert		Fitts	Harriet Ann	Pyburn	William Henry, Jr.
Finnell	Lurena Hulse	Callahan	William Daniel		Fitzgerald	Annie	McMinamin	John
Finnerty	Gertrude F.	Bello	Joseph G.		Fitzgerald	Ellen A.	Henelly	Michael J.
Finnerty	Mary Alice	Baccala	Joseph K.		Fitzgerald	Maggie	Underhill	Wm. H.
Finney	F. M.	O'Neil	W. P.		Fitzgerald	Mary	Curtis	William G.
Finnie	Ruth Edna	Thompson	Samuel S.		Fitzgerald	Nell	Stoddart	Lytton
Finsterbusch	Ethel M.	Rice	J. Bryan		Fitzgerald	Nora Gertrude	Farley	William James McA.
Fiori	Frances	Doda	Hobart J.					
Fiori	Francis	Bondietti	W. J. T.		Fitzgerald	Theresa A.	Smith	Julius R.
Fiori	Julia E.	Rogers	Charles W.		Fitzgibbon	Helen B.	Bernhardt	Chas. F.
Fiori	Teresa	Gregori	Peter		Fitzgibbon	Mamie E.	Small	Charles H.
Fisch	Marie	Weber	Henry		Fitzpartrick	Lillian Gertrude	Gleason	Walter Raymond
Fischer	Annie M.	Schenkberg	A. E.		Fitzpatrick	Mary Ann	Clark	Terrence
Fischer	Hilda	Bailey	Eugene B.		Fitzsimmons	Bessie E.	Rodehaver	William W.
Fischer	Mary	Freese	Frederich		Fitzsimmons	Edith L.	Pierce	Joseph G., Jr.
Fiscus	Lois	Post	Myrl		Flack	Rosie	Gercar	Josef
Fish	Jennie, Mrs.	Odle	Samuel P.		Flago (?)	Mary A.	Beeson	Orville W.
Fish	Lucetta A.	Engh	Peter B.		Flarity	Sadie M.	Laton	Edward Lee
Fisher	Ada	Bell	Luther		Flecsher	Minnie R.	Hudson	Kelsey S.
Fisher	C. J.	Spencer	H. D.		Fleming	Nancy M.	McKinstry	Henry H.
Fisher	Claire G.	De Patta	Joseph Miles		Fleming	Selia (?)	Osborne	William Mortimer
Fisher	Elizabeth T.	Petersen	Peter J.		Flesher	Elsie V.	Davis	John M.
Fisher	Ethel Lake	Wooster	John Fairchild		Flesher	Josephine M.	Davis	Ulysses G.

Flesher	L. Maude	Bacon	Arthur D.
Flesher	Nora	Ward	George S.
Flesher	Retta M.	Files	Charles M.
Fletcher	E. J., Mrs.	Cathey	C. L.
Fletcher	Geneva L.	Simpson	Leonard L.
Fletcher	Mary Malsena	Stevenson	Joseph
Fletcher	Ruth Ann	Harrison	Fred Kingsley
Flewelling	Bessie H.	Haub	Chester C.
Flinn	Anna	Hart	Chenowith B.
Flinn	Clarissa G.	Pitt	Arthur A.
Flinn	Frances	Cavanagh	William
Flint	Ella J. (?)	Flint	T. B.
Flippi	Rose V.	Barham	Byrd B.
Flohr	Myrtle Maude	Trine	Wilfred
Flood	Evelyn V.	Baker	Fred H.
Florence	Belle	Thresher	William J.
Florence	Bertha E.	Stewart	Carl V.
Florence	Dora Francis	Thomas	John Joseph
Florence	Eva G.	Walker	Lycurgus
Florence	Lulu	Nystrom	Ard Elan
Florence	Ruth Ardys	Read	George Marvin
Florin	Lucile H.	Abrams	J. William
Flournoy	Emma I.	Foreman	Edward L.
Flynn	Ella Marie	Hadley	William
Flynn	Mary E.	Smith	James J.
Focha	Amelia	Rose	Manuel
Focha	Annie	Millerick	James G.
Focha	Frances Agnes	Furlong	Charles Edward
Focha	Isabel	Castro	Manuel C.
Fochetti	Caterine	Marcollo	John
Fochetti	Theresa	Mahlstedt	August
Fogarty	Ida	Achey	Clarence M.
Fogerty	Annie May	Adams	George Edward
Foley	Josephine	Guadagno	Pompey
Foley	Mary Josie	Kelleher	Cornelius

Foley	Pearl O.	McNeill	Wm. J.
Folger	Alice	Emerson	Mark Lewis
Folks	Ella	French	Jno. H.
Folks	Nellie	Gliddon	William
Follett	Mildred L.	Selvage	Alfred F.
Follmer	Anna	Vanggaard	Hans L. M.
Folsom	Iva Irene	Vail	Bryant E.
Folsom	Mattie	Renshaw	L. J.
Folts	Kathryn Laura Frances	Jenkins	Joseph
Foote	Edna	Garnett	Kennedy Porter
Foppiano	Louise	Arata	Joseph
Foppiano	Magherita	Ratto	Charles
Foppiano	Mary	Cuneo	Joseph
Forbes	Eva L.	Pearson	James R.
Forbes	Mary Jane	Gillett	Charles
Ford	Alice L.	Minto	Lloyd R.
Ford	Bessie, Mrs.	Fitch	John Byron
Ford	Dorothy Louise	Hayes	John Henri
Ford	Lettie F.	Martell	Joseph A.
Ford	Margaret	Von Berg	William J.
Ford	Mildred Agnes	Davis	Clyde Leroy
Ford	Mollie E.	Pursell	John
Ford	Ollie	Todd	Prince W.
Ford	Vergie V.	Race	Benjamin B.
Fore	Mable Edith	Biggs	Frank Leland
Foreman	Annie	Hodges	Henry C.
Foreman	Kate	Gravatt	Wm.
Foresti	Dora	Hayden	Richard
Foresti	Mollie A.	Casini	Neibo
Forgett	Annabel	Huskey	Everett
Forgett	Louise	Vallier	John A.
Formschlag	Tillie Josephine	Newbegin	Herbert Strother
Forni	Angeline	Basileu	Jordan
Forni	Assunta	Tocchini	Arideo

Forni	Josephine	Lafranchi	Frank	Fowler	Gladys M.	Buckmaster	Rlando
Forni	Kate	Babbini	Antonio	Fowler	Irene F.	Bradford	Christopher W.
Fornschlag	Josie M.	Ronsheimer	Henry L.	Fowler	Laura E.	Scripps	John
Forpey	Anna A.	Rien	J. M.	Fowler	Lue Della	Conniff	William Francis
Forrest	Agnes May	Bertoli	Paul Pete	Fowler	Margaret A.	Church	Douglas
Forrest	Annie	Childers	William E.	Fowler	Mary Otis	Fawcett	Thomas
Forster	Lulu L.	Burke	Leo A.	Fowler	Teresa	Stone	Robert L.
Forsyth	M. Margaret	LeBaron	Adelbert J.	Fowler	Viola Augusta May	Schmitz	John
Forsyth	Mary E.	Berglund	Harvey M.				
Forsyth	R. A.	Rankin	J. H.	Fox	Adeline M.	Martola	H. A.
Forsythe	Lillie	Robertson	Dolbert	Fox	Elma, Mrs.	Smith	Commodore P.
Forsythe	Margaret	Mulford	George N.	Fox	Laura	Wempe	Henry Joseph
Fortunati	Mary	Rossi	Frank	Fox	Sadie L.	Urton	John H.
Foscha	Lenora A.	Eckman	Albert R.	Fox	Verna May	Cunningham	Charles John
Fosdick	Mildred Ethel	Thoreu (?)	Gustav Aroid	Foyd	Lucy	Cambra	Manuel F.
Foss	Ethel C.	Saunders	Felix D.	Fracehia	Jiulia	Qualio	Matteo
Foss	Gertrude	Culligan	Francis J.	Fraga	Annie E.	Souza	Joe R.
Foster	Alice, Mrs.	Phelps	John L.	Frahin	Margaret J. C.	Rollin	George A. F. H.
Foster	Bessie E.	Goree	Ernest B.	Frahm	Hertha	Lynch	William Allen
Foster	Blanche	Moore	William J.	Fraim	Daisy, Mrs.	Heryford	Jno. F.
Foster	Caroline	Bruce	William	Francard	Julia	Laurent	Julius B.
Foster	Mable Ida	Sheehan	William A.	Francchia	Josephine	Imperiale	Gianni D.
Foster	Ora C.	Navas	William	Franceschi	Colomba	Micheli	Alfredo
Foster	Rose S.	Bones	Thomas J.	Francesco	Mary Lenora	Derrick	Charles Erwin
Foster	Viola A.	Stephens	Christopher S.	Francesconi	Mary	Zanzi	Antonio J.
Fountain	Ethel	Hussey	William J.	Franceski	Nellie	Brush	Daniel
Fountain	Minnie	Harvey	James H.	Franchetti	Eda	Trombetta	Florindo
Fournier (?)	Alice	Genung	William L.	Francia	Maria	Giacosa	Luigi
Fouts	Elsie M.	Barnum	Clarence L.	Francis	Hattie	Adcock	Abe
Fouts	Emma A.	Jayer (?)	Mentin (?)	Francis	Isabella	Andrew	Dennis
Fowler	Ada Rosella	Bowles	Frank Herbert	Francis	Nettie	Hall	Granville M.
Fowler	Bessie	Sink	Walter	Francischi	Teresa	Howard	William C.
Fowler	Cornelia W.	Gibbons	Alfred Sydney	Francischi	Rosa	Gonnella	Zaccheria
Fowler	Della	Marando	Frank Harry	Francisco	Amelia A.	Guilhot	Bernard
Fowler	Elizabeth, Mrs.	Pearson	James	Francisco	Emma	Bones	Charles H.

Francisco	Mabel Grace	Boyd	James K., Jr.	Fredricks	Carrie	Johnson	John F.
Francisco	Mariana	Martinez	Sylvester	Fredricks	Ella	Hoskins (?)	Edward Sterling
Francoli	Corina Mary	Riboli	Sam	Freebern	Abbe Gail, Mrs.	Arguello	Henry T.
Frandell	Mandi	Koski	Matt	Freels	Julia Louise	Freitas	Antone
Frank	Emilie	Archer	Oliver	Freeman	Clara B.	Anderson	William F.
Frank	Julia L.	Arthur	George	Freeman	Dorothy M.	Forde	John M.
Frank	Marie L.	McCarthy	A. Marden	Freeman	Ella	Gilmore	George
Frank	Lydia E.	Archer	Walter M.	Freeman	Lillian	Cornett	William H.
Frankland	Zita	Smith	Harry D.	Freeman	Lucrelta, Mrs.	Powers	David P.
Franklin	Alta M.	Cook	Ernest E.	Freeman	Lulu	Bryan	Frederick J.
Franklin	Blandine L.	Morris	Wm. H.	Freeman	M. E.	Andrews	Howard
Franklin	Dora	Fulton	Jasper A.	Freeman	Martha E.	Bearden	James M.
Franquelin	Adelaide M.	Bean	Oliver F.	Freeman	Mary E., Mrs.	Graham	Robert W.
Fransioli	Mary	Piccinotti	V.	Freeman	Nadien J.	Gaston	John W.
Franz	Minnie L.	Clark	Samuel Berry	Freeman	Sarah A.	Horr	Riley J.
Franzen	Augusta	Madsen	Neils G.	Freggiro	Christine	Frediani	Angelo
Frary	Adele M.	Bouhaben	Emil H.	Fregulia	Catherine	Giovannetti	Domencio
Frassinello	Angelina	Pardini	Oreste	Frehe	Annie M.	Ahrens	William M.
Frates	Irene	Bettencourt	Joseph A.	Frei	Rosa	Hoppe	Anton
Frati	Celia	Brusa	Carlos	Freitas	Edna Lillian	Lawson	Charles Garfield
Frati	Sarah	Bertoli	Paul	Freitas	Maria	Ferreiro	Jose Gracia
Fratis	Mary E.	Winchester	Walter	Freitas	Rosie E.	Gomes	Antonio E.
Frazier	Mary T.	Hanna	J. G.	French	Francis J.	Forsey	Warren F.
Freandle	Anna	Silvia	Manuel	French	Lenora E.	Stoetz	Frederick C.
Frederick	Hallie	Eldridge	A. C.	French	Meta A.	Chiaroni	Daniel
Fredericks	Emma	Wood	John G.	Frese	Irene A.	Mueller	Frank
Fredericks	Ida L.	Mattei	Valenti C.	Freshour	Irene Martha	Wright	Lee William
Fredericks	Minna	Galleher	John Harry	Freshour	Louise M.	Brooks	Arthur M.
Fredericksen	Anna K.	Laursen	Peter C.	Freshour	Marie A.	Clark	Leonard P.
Fredericksen	Laura B.	Judd	Percy L.	Freshour	Nancy C.	Gilbert	David W.
Frederickson	Mary	Hinshaw	A. G.	Freshour	Sarah Jane	Fitch	Joseph, Jr.
Frediani	Katie	Galgani	Guiseppe	Frey	Anna	Knecht	Tony
Frediani	Teresina	Ridolfi	Vittorio	Frey	Annie M.	Haselswerdt	Harry E.
Fredinani	Edith	Hourcaillon	John B.	Frey	Jennie A.	Heselschwerdt	Vernon W.
Fredrichs	Sophia A.	Barnes	L. J.	Frick	Lucille, Mrs.	Parsons	Arthur Amos

Fricke	Caroline	Heesche	Henry G. K.	Fulinder	Mary J.	Wright	Christopher R.
Frideger	Margaret	Cereghino	Tony	Fulkerson	Alma K.	Fechter	David A.
Fried	Enmma	Haigh	Edwin	Fulkerson	Ida Helen	Cummings	George Lawrence
Fried	Lena	O'Leary	W. F.	Fulkerson	Ida May	Wood	Frank B.
Friedeger	Ellen Agnes	Provines	William	Fulkerson	Linda V.	Barham	Edwin C.
Friedrichs	Mariechen	Lass	Peter	Fulkerson	Mary L.	Wendt	William
Friel	Mary	Friel	Patrick	Fulkerson	Nora C.	Leggett	Henry B.
Friend	Mary E.	McCollam	William	Fulkerson	Laura E.	Badger	Douglas
Friesia (?)	Mary E.	McCollum	William	Fuller	Alice May	Toft	Verne A.
Friis	Elene Christine	Hardin	Harold Jefferson	Fuller	Cora Dickinson	Roberts	John Henry
Frirot (?)	Fanny	Demousset	Armand	Fuller	Dorothy I.	Pentfield	Myron D.
Frisbee	Sarah Howland	Hamilton	Aymer Jay	Fuller	Ellen	Steeland	Peter
Frisbie	Mercie E.	Cornett	N. W.	Fuller	Gratia E.	Smith	Charles L.
Frishman	Regina	Seltzer	Harry W.	Funk	Lena	Knaak	August
Frisk	Hilda T.	Crawford	Albert J.	Furbee	Dora M.	White	Ralph
Fritsch	Katty A.	Peny (?)	A. F.	Furia	Cisara	Boschetti	Centuria
Fritsch	Mary Ealie	Cantel	Eugene	Furia	Elvira	Furia	Alfonzo
Fritsch	Nelly	Hedges	Edward D.	Furia	Ersilia	Albini	Domenico
Fromell	Anita Mabel	Hansen	Elmer	Furlong	Kathryn A.	Marzolf	Frederick George
Fromm	Martha	Armstrong	Alfred E.	Furlong	Margaret M.	Cunninghame	Alexander L.
Frontier	Clara	Moenning	George	Furlong	Nell I.	Norton	Howard L.
Frost	Corda	Martin	Milton	Furr	Maud E., Mrs.	Andersen	Robert
Frost	Emma	Rose	Daniel N.	Furtado	Emma	Macedo	Antone Domingos
Frost	Emma M.	Ingersoll	John W.	Furuta	Tori	Fujimoto	Togro
Frost	Jennie	Dahack	Elsia	Gabriel	Hazel	Bosworth	Bernard P.
Frost	Olive Bernice	Wilkie	Willian P.	Gaby	Emma	Barricklaw	David George
Frost	Phoebe A.	Davis	Robert E.	Gaddini	Elisabeth	Marcucci	Abromo
Frugoli	Lena	Bartolomei	John	Gaddini	Olive	Bacigalupi	Albert C.
Frugoli	Theresa	Guidotti	Francesco	Gaffney	Madeleine	Blot	Louis
Frugoli	Virginia	Brocco	Emil	Gaffney	Mary M.	Putney	Volney M.
Fruitt (?)	Ellen	Lamb	Louis	Gage	Ada Marita	Nepson (?)	William A.
Frusendi	Mary	Modesto	Rovere	Gage	Iva L.	Busher	Walter H.
Fry	Mildred M.	Cozzo	Joseph, Jr.	Gage	Laurina B.	Howell	William
Fryer	Elizabeth M.	Higby	Earl D.	Gage	Mabel	Icanberry	William M.
Fuidge (?)	Rhea E.	Cowan	Kenneth B.	Gage	Vivian Ada	Fish	Franklin Janus

Gaige	Alpha Eunice	Browne	William Frank	Gambonini	Adeline	Ielmorini	Thomas
Gailer	Ada B.	Feliz	Sisto J.	Gambonini	Emma A.	Bolla	Pacific J.
Gailor	E. B., Mrs.	Haukel (?)	Herman, Jr.	Gambonini	Olivia Lettitia	Dado	Atilio Anthony
Gailor	Ima Edna	Martin	Edgar Laurens	Gamborini	Amelia	Guaspari	Domenico
Gaines	Clara H.	Young	Eben F.	Gambroni	Angiolina	Finatti	Guilio
Gaines	Etta	Riedy	Charles C., Jr.	Games	Ruth F.	Young	Thomas G.
Gaines	Lizzie Andes	White	George Richard	Gandola	Mary A.	Luisi	Leonardo
Gainnini	Della	Bertoli	Romeo	Ganmill	May	Patrick	Jessie B.
Gale	Alice	Woods	Robert	Gann	Gladys G.	Cills	Rudolph F.
Gale	Carrie L.	Drake	Floyd G.	Gann	Martha	Cresap	Daniel
Gale	Clara May	Scott	Charles O.	Gann	Martha A.	Hasting	Joe C.
Gale	Eliza Maude	Atkinson	Robert Kavanaugh	Gano	Mary	O'Neil	Michael
Gale	Ellen E. (per signature)	Klingler	George Adolph	Gano	Maud	Martin	Merwin
				Ganske	Mabel K.	Dealy	Charles A.
Gale	Marie F.	Andersen	Peter C.	Gantner	Julia	Cohen	Maxwell
Gale	Mary Ella	McPhail	A. J.	Garbarini	Louise	Merlo	John
Galinda	Mary M.	Avereia	Antonio Silveira	Garbarnia	Lillie	Pagani	John
Gallagher	Alice Louise	Gillogly	William J. S.	Garborini	Annie	Gambogi	Amchese
Gallagher	Loretta G.	Towey	John L.	Garcia	Amelia	Rose	Frank
Gallagher	Nellie Mae	Morris	John	Garcia	Jennie	Perez	Andrew
Gallard	Genevive	Francard	John B.	Garcia	Margaret M.	Bell	Edward H., Jr.
Gallaway	Ella May	Brown	James R.	Garcia	Marie Blasa	Lires	Ramon
Gallaway	Lizzie, Mrs.	Gallaway	John C.	Garcia	Minnie	Rudrigues	Manuel
Gallaway	Nancy E.	Newland	Frank D.	Gardanier	Carol	McMurray	R. W.
Galle	Mary V.	Bobb	H. I.	Gardella	Emily I.	Blazer	C. Lloyd
Gallegher	Sarah	Furlong	Patrick	Gardella	Santina Angela	Solari	Anthony
Galloway	Charlotte	Cadd	Edwin	Gardener	Edith Luella	Johnson	John Christian
Gamage	Lillian Lewis	Fleissner	Hugo Herman	Gardenhire	Grace A.	Schoppe	John C.
Gambini	Emma Annie	Pellacio	Boyd James	Gardenhire	Pearl M.	Nystrom	Carl L.
Gambini	Mary Alice	Hebrard	William J.	Gardner	Dela May	Howell	Ambrose M.
Gambini	Edith Gladys	McGee	Edward William	Gardner	Emma	Daniels	William E.
Gambini	Rose Letticia	Palmer	Will Henry	Gardner	Flora	King	W. E.
Gamble	Bertha V.	Gallaway	John W.	Gardner	Geneveve	Carvalho	Joseph
Gamble	Elizabeth A.	Pitken	Charles S.	Gardner	Ida	Ross	Irvin D.
Gambogi	Eda M.	Baldi	Anselmo	Gardner	Lillie	Walsh	William

Gardner	Lizzie	Dunwoody	Seth M.	Garzola	Lena Frances	Lafranchi	Alfonso
Gardner	Mime	Woods	Geo. E.	Garzoli	Clara Irene	Casarotti	Americo E.
Gardner	Sarah Cornelia, Mrs.	Carrington	Joseph H.	Garzoli	Cora O.	Silva	Joseph W.
				Garzoli	Dora H.	Keiser	Joseph
Garetti	Lena	Dinucci	Romeo	Gaskins	Minnie Maud	Maxwell	Frank Washington
Gargini	Giulia	Dogali	Paolo	Gaspari	Lenora	Fitch	Romualdo A.
Gargini	Laudonnia	Penalini	Frank	Gasser	Pauline K.	Schroeder	Frederick W.
Gargini	Zaira	Lecchetti	Tony	Gastaldi	Elvia	Roppolo	Anton
Garms	Amanda Geraldine	Riede	John	Gaston	Alta Mae	Hyatt	Robert Roy
				Gaston	Hattie Winn	Sales	John
Garms	Pauline	Cole	Lee	Gaston	Kate A.	Schmitz	A. B.
Garnero	Mary	Sartori	John B.	Gaston	Lulu Iola	Steitz	Louis F.
Garr	Mary E.	Robert	Frederic	Gaston	Mary E.	Willard	Thomas H.
Garrett	Hettie	Peatross	Frank L.	Gater	Lillian Edith	Brackett	Raymond Gregory
Garrett	Ida Hazel	Morrison	Lester	Gates	Annabelle E.	Withs	Ernest Hilmer
Garrett	Phrona E.	Bates	Alphonzo	Gates	Caroline J.	Domenzet	Joseph
Garrett	Retta	Gibbs	George D.	Gates	Ethel G.	Dickson	Joshua Bates, Jr.
Garrett	Rouetta E.	Pratt	Henry F.	Gates	Jane Isabell	Ball	Leo Raymond
Garrison	Bertha B.	Long	Harold C.	Gates	Leonora V.	Bruner	Herman D.
Garrison	Carrie	McMillan	Wm. S.	Gates	Lulu M.	Dowling	Charles W.
Garrison	Ellen M.	Lyttaker	Albert	Gathergood	Della Clyde	Lovell	Frank P.
Garrison	Grace E.	Marble	John H.	Gathgood	Nellie	Simpson	James Patrick
Garrison	Jennette J.	Hultgren	John A.	Gatlin	Mary	Troutman	Arthur O.
Garrison	Laura E.	Colburn	Rayman C.	Gatter	Elizabeth A.	Hillam	Frederick J.
Garrison	Lena	Gibson	John R.	Gauldin	Gennevieve	Barnes	Perry S.
Garrison	Ora M.	Choquette	Stephen	Gauldin	Laura	Taveira	John J.
Garrison	Orletta	Ashley	S. Thomas	Gauldin	Laura	Hall	Geo. H.
Garth	Florence I.	Wilson	Wm. E.	Gauldin	Mattie A.	Arnold	Hobart Le G.
Garth	Josephine	Neil	Washington	Gauldin	Minnie L.	Barney	Henry W.
Gartman	Annie	Groskopf	Albert	Gauldin	Nellie B.	Taylor	Charles P.
Gartner	Elsie Louise	Cole	Thomas Hoarse	Gauldin	Nora	Peterson	Anton
Garton	Harriet P.	de Violini	Arduino	Gaver	Bessie Frances	Steitz	Robert Russell
Garvin	Helen	Alexander	Ernest F.	Gavin	Lulu	Pickle	John Andrew
Garvin	Nora S.	Davis	Milton M.	Gavin	Margaret Helen	Hansbrow	George Rutlege
Garwood	Hazel G.	Waterhouse	Robert D.	Gawler	Pearl	Grant	William C.
Garza	Margareth	Henning	Thomas				

Gay	Mary E.	Mosher	Frank	George	Zella	Harris	James William
Gaye	Adele	Cailleaud	Henry, Jr.	Georges	Marie A.	Russell	Hamilton
Gaylord	Eliza	Switzer	John	Georgi	Eva V.	Buchignani	Victor
Gaz	Kittie	Spittler	George F.	Gerali	Elvira	Belli	Angelo
Ge----(?)	Clara M. (?)	Semler	Paul I. A.	Gericke	Agnes Veronica	Cooper	Charles Crawford
Geaney	Lizzie	O'Keefe	Michael	Gericke	Ethel M.	Ames	Earl L.
Geaney	Mary	Mahoney	William	Gericke	Margaret L.	Furlong	Hugh C.
Geary	Eliza L.	Simmons	Robert H.	Gerlach	Elizabetha	Bill	Henry
Geary	Florence	Kisling	Frank	German	Charlotte	Covey	George W.
Geary	Helen J.	Hubbard	William B.	German	Kate, Mrs.	Beebe	Edward T.
Geary	Jean L.	Bundschu	Ralph M.	German	Margaret E.	Meredith	Cyrus N.
Geaver	Nellie	Robinson	Merritt	German	Susan	Coker	Wiley
Gedney	Della	Brackett	J. B.	Gerow	Elsie E.	Mills	Fredrick W.
Geer	Mamie	Cooper	Alfred B.	Gerst	Bertha A.	Cuvrean	Oscar F.
Geertz	Bertha J.	Peterson	Harold A.	Gertosio	Marie	Vannucci	Joseph
Geertz	Josephine	Clausen	Dietrich	Gesel	Anne	Lauman	John
Geertz	Mathilde, Mrs.	Henrichsen	Henry R.	Gestra	Maria	Gestra	John
Geertz	Willhelmine C.	Jensen	Fred P.	Gestro	Marta	Pozzi	David
Geezley	Katie	German	Covington E.	Gethergood	Georgia	Sacry	Harlow D.
Gehlken	Anna	Miller	Charles C.	Ghio	Virginia	Pucci	Victoria
Geiger	Addie J.	Pool	George E.	Ghiozzi	Marie	Biasotti	Luigi
Geils	Elsie May	Carstensen	Charlie R.	Ghiringhelli	Teressa	Forni	Charles B.
Geisbuhler	Ida	Jaeger	Jacob	Ghisletta	Antonia	Cossa	Luigi
Gelhart	Mattie J.	Marsh	Ira M.	Giaconi	Geovanina	Moretti	Joseph
Gellerman	Annie	Rapun	Angel	Gianella	Theresa	Bisordi (?)	Pasquale
Gellerman	Louise	Stockli	Louis	Gianini	Marie	Capucetti	L. A.
Gellerman	Mary A.	Swift	Frederick	Giannecchini	Crotilde	Cia	Silvio
Gelli	Maria	Tardelli	Pietro	Giannecchini	Serofina	Benelli	Lucca
Gemmill	Lillian J.	Miller	Walter	Gibb	Florence H.	Wood	Thomas
Geniser	Elsie M.	Rocha	Joseph F.	Gibbin	Theresa I.	Conner	George W.
Genochio	Elizabeth R.	Crease	Henry George	Gibbins	Lillie M.	Thompson	Morris H.
Gentry	Amanda G., Mrs.	Covington	J. M.	Gibbins	Rosa May	Odell	Frank Edward
Gentry	M. Alice	Magoon	Edward Oliver	Gibbons	Lillie May	Rickard	James Lee
George	Althea L.	Thompson	Charles D.	Gibbons	Mary A.	Hooke	H. W.
George	Laura	Paulsen	Lawrence E.	Gibbons	Myrtle M.	McKillop	Harry C.

Gibbons	Rose Elliot	Kjeldsen	Vernon Edward	Gilbert	Amelia	McDonald	Daniel
Gibbons	Violet M.	Odell	Jesse L.	Gilbert	Caroline	Jones	McMillan
Gibbs	Evangeline C.	Barnett	Walter E.	Gilbert	Cora B.	Walker	Henry L.
Gibbs	Harriet E.	Barnett	Lester H.	Gilbert	Eleanor M.	Lanfear	James A.
Gibbs	Hattie E.	Tauzer	William A.	Gilbert	May E.	Day	Harmon A.
Gibbs	Lizzie W.	Grosse	Guy E.	Gilbert	Minnie E.	Beatty	Edward Waldron
Gibbs	Martha	Larsen	John	Gilbertson	Annie	Doras	Leicester
Gibbs	Mary L.	Hinton	Arthur R.	Gildersleeve	Elizabeth	Faulconer	Joseph C.
Gibbs	Rosa M.	Beach	Riley	Gilen	Anna	Nelson	Martin
Gibbs	Tessie L.	Vonsen	Chris H.	Giles	Lizzie	Lind	Aogost
Gibbs	Zoie Alva	Ford	Edward Franklin	Gilkey	Esther F.	Kern	Harry A.
Gibfried	Emma C.	Williams	Jay G.	Gilkison	Norah F.	Fulks	C. E.
Gibson	Dorothy Irene	Generrilli	Albert J.	Gill	Elizabeth	Cramer	David R.
Gibson	Emily Virginia	Phillips	G. W.	Gill	Fannie	Wilson	Thos. R.
Gibson	Eva L.	Hill	James D.	Gill	Jennie, Mrs.	Burns	Harry David
Gibson	Gladys J.	Kronke	Edward J.	Gillespie	Lulu	Smith	Gerald W.
Gibson	Hazel C.	Feige	Albert H.	Gillespie	Ruth	Stockham	Hugh B.
Gibson	Jeanette S.	Jones	Brainerd	Gillett	Gertrude Edith	Nisson	Harold
Gibson	Kate	Groth	Leopold Frederick	Gillett	Kate, Mrs.	Bones	John Franklin
Gibson	Laura Lee	Grady	Harry Clarence	Gillett	Elizabeth A.	McCombs	Charles W.
Gibson	Lenore C.	Hudson	Clarence D.	Gilli	Emily	Rocchi	Peter
Gibson	Lulu E.	Elliott	Archie E.	Gilliam	Elaine	Spinney	Clifford L.
Gibson	Margaret E.	Bosworth	Fred E.	Gilliam	Emily	Hobbs	Jason
Gibson	Mary Elizabeth	Pitts	Harry	Gillians	Alice	McLaughlin	Clarence Joseph
Gibson	May	Smith	John C.	Gillihan	Anna E.	Pinkerton	John L.
Gibson	Nancy	King	John	Gilman	Barbara	Cox	Earl W.
Gibson	Nona M.	Bussman	William G.	Gilman	Elba Ellen	Duncan	James W.
Gibson	Ollie M.	Parkerson	Fremont E.	Gilman	Lillian E.	Near	James C.
Gibson	Susan A.	Foster	Robert A.	Gilmartin	Josie	Arsistide	George
Gibson	Viola May	Williams	Raymond Philip	Gilmer	Eulalia	Jones	Smith Petitt
Gieg	Louise	Zufall	Frederick	Gilmore	Cassie B.	Johnson	Phillip F.
Giesen	Elsa	Jorgensen	Robert	Gilmore	Flora I.	Taglio	Philip
Gifford	Evelyn Barnum	Hull	Alonzo Clinton	Gilmore	Grace	Hamersley	Garvin
Gilardi	Edith A.	Corippo	Benjamin H.	Gilmore	Lizzie E.	Benepe	Charles S.
Gilardi	Katherine M.	Guglielmetti	Alfred J.	Gilmore	Minerva Ruth	Cline	Arthur Allen

Gilmore	Nettie B.	Peery	Geo. E.	Gleason	Mary Agnes	Furlong	Thomas F.
Gilmore	Sarah E.	Foreman	Park	Gleason	Mattie	Fouts	William V.
Gilooly	Rose May	Mac Lean	Hector	Glenn	Alice	Partridge	Frederick F.
Gilson	Frieda L.	Jensen	John P.	Glenn	Eda, Mrs.	Howard	Charles E.
Gilson	Myrtle Dora	East	Linzey	Glenn	Hazel	Nash	Harry
Gimtley	Emma	Dightman	W. E.	Glenn	Lilly M.	Fahrion	George W.
Gingery	Mandilla	Hays	Edwin B., Rev.	Glenn	Luella	McKinlay	James M.
Ginsti	Julia	Mancini	Massimo	Glenn	Virginia	Rankin	Charles H.
Giorgetti	Nellie	Baiocchi	Nello	Glover	Margaret C.	Barrett	John J.
Giovanni	Clara M.	Malnati	Carlo	Glynn	Agnes M.	Drago	Frank
Gipp	Margaret C.	Devencenzi	Victor	Glynn	Mamie	Blanchard	Frank I.
Girardi	Domenica	Rossi	Giuseppe	Glynn	Mattie E.	Rushmore	Frederick J.
Girt	Petta	Schmitt	Henry	Glynn	Nellie M.	Green	William C.
Gisel	Frieda	Beebe	Louis W.	Glynn	Sarah A.	Farrell	William F.
Gisel	Marie	Papenfus	Reinhold	Gobbi	Rosie M.	Crosta	Mateo
Gisler	Emma	Meyer	Jakob	Gober	Elizabeth	Harkrader	Albert L.
Gisler	Kathrina	Meyer	Benedikt	Gober	Elizabeth C.	Hatton	Charles B. D.
Gist	Fannie Irene	Mead	Fred Ryland	Gober	Elizabeth Tennessee	Fewel	William Cicero
Gist	Lurana	Hammel	Henry				
Gist	Meda	Cannon	Jerome	Gober	Nellie E.	Tully	Pinkney R.
Giudice	Marie	Rosci	Pietro	Gober	Sarah J., Mrs.	Blair	Thomas N.
Giusti	Eda	Cinquini	D.	Gobetti	Kate	Brush	Samuel
Givens	Lizzie	Nichols	H. S.	Goddard	Hattie E.	Goddard	Jesse J.
Givlin	Margret Ella May	Harrington	Charles Winfield	Goddard	Hazel M.	Hills	Percy J.
Gjedberg	Clara	Dean	James Monroe	Goddard	Lillian J.	Rosebrough	William J.
Glahn	Anna C.	Van Frank	Elmer M.	Goddard	Silvia C.	Field	James
Glaister	Blanche E.	Wagner	Otto	Goddard	Viola M.	Crockett	George E.
Glaser	Emma	Holdrich	Hilarius	Godfrey	Ada C.	Odell	L. G.
Glass	Sarah, Mrs.	Morehouse	Arthur L.	Godfrey	Alice E.	Rachford	Arthadus A.
Glaszer	Gertrude J.	Macnair	Douglas	Goding	Mabel Rose	Voelker	Louis
Glatfelder	Lenora M.	Jenkins	Frederich G.	Godman	Ida L.	Austin	Sewell S.
Glatfelder	Lulu	Barnes	H. G.	Godman	Mollie M.	Paxton	Dexter
Glavin	Carmelita	Luhr	Lawrence E.	Godwin	Grace Morris	Waterman	Thomas T.
Glavin	Kittie	Nichols	J. W.	Goenza	Rosa	Rossotti	Domenico
Glazier	Mary O.	Garside	Thomas H.	Goetz	Lena	Mohl	Emil

Goffin	Constance	Strozynski	Teophil	Goodman	Mary	Rud	Jeremiah
Goldman	Edith	Higgins	Raymond J.	Goodman	Susie M.	Swan	Alfred
Goldman	Ida	Emes	Walter H.	Goodner	Nellie	Suetterlin	Lewis
Goldstein	Sarah	Ash	Isador	Goodrich	Mamie	Barker	Ambrose B.
Gollnik	Lizzie	King	Andrew	Goodrich	Rosa Meador	Boida	Lorenzo
Gomberina	Rosa	Maroni	Peter	Goodspeed	Bertha M.	Paff	Charles
Gomes	Alexandrina A.	Mattos	Arthur G.	Goodspeed	Georgia, Mrs.	Johnston	Charles B.
Gomez	Agnes R.	Cabral	Fernando	Goodwin	Agnes L.	Guiberson	Wallace
Gomez	Emily	Silva	Dominic J.	Goodwin	Alma R.	Myers	Joseph S.
Gomzenbach	Elizabeth I.	Muheim	Adolph A.	Goodwin	Caroline Adelia	White	Percy Reginald
Gonella	Florence Marie	Morelli	Morvin Ulysses	Goodwin	Catherine Harriett	Pendleton	Charles Alexander
Gonella	Mary	Howard	Vernon R.	Goodwin	Georgiana K.	Volkerts	Fred L.
Gonella	Teresa	Panelli	Amadeo	Goodwin	Mary Elizabeth	Lewis	Charles Wadsworth
Gonfiotti	Viola	Picetti	Giovanni	Goodwin	Mary Jane	Howard	Emmett Robert
Gongenbach	Elsie	Doyle	Clement A.	Gopcevic	Lucy Louise	Schrender	Duco Anton
Gonsalves	Anna C.	Daveiro	Manuel J.	Gordenker	Loelia	Tietjen	Albert Doremus
Gonsalves	Emerentia I.	Harms	Leland	Gordenker	Martha L.	Romanov	Anton A.
Gonsalves	Emma B.	Silva	Frank James	Gordon	Alice M.	Foster	Clarence E.
Gonsalves	Mary	Simas	John	Gordon	Edith A.	Anderson	James
Gonsalves	Mary E.	Silva	Frank T.	Gordon	Edna Isma	Lyman	William Wickam
Gonsalves	Rose	Daveiro	John	Gordon	Lizzie Jane	Hemphill	William
Gonsalves	Leonor M.	Tobelmann	Henry	Gordon	Mary L.	Philpott	J. F.
Gonzalez	Margaret F.	Miller	Frederick H.	Gordon	Melissa, Mrs.	Andrews	George
Gooch	Florence Irene	Donaldson	Alexander B.	Gordon	Ruby Ethel	Lobb	Lewis
Good	Francis	Patterson	Robert D.	Gordon	Sarah A.	Brooker	Frank Russell
Good	Helen	Lake	D. Delos	Gore	Ida M.	Story	Albert A.
Goode	Lillian	Gray	James W.	Gori	Edith A.	Vellutini	Ray
Goode	Susanna	Swaysgood	John W.	Gori	Rose	Revello	Emilio
Goodell	Mabel Pearl	Thompson	Charles Arthur	Gorski	Lizzie May	Duncan	Mark VanHattren
Goodfellow	Corinne	Strong	Benjamin H.	Gorter	Dorothea	Edgar	Herbert L.
Goodfellow	Thelma Marie	McCrea	James Walter	Goss	Pauline M.	Miles	Elmer Alfred
Goodhue	Esther M.	Weitlauf	Joseph F.	Goss	Stella	Wise	John T. (?)
Goodman	Ada C.	Rogers	Dwight H.	Gossage	Addie	Healy	Edwin R.
Goodman	Addie May	Short	Frank Everett	Gossage	Belle, Mrs.	Cohenour	Joseph Herbert
Goodman	Idell L.	Kettlewell	William W.	Gossage	Carrie B.	Gregg	John W.

Gossage	Ellen C.	Hynes	Wm. H.	Grabs	Lila B.	McCarthy	Timothy
Gossage	Emma L.	Drees	Ernest E.	Grace	Anastasia	Hayes	John
Gossage	Jessie	Lane	Frank J.	Grace	Edith Emily	Hakansson	Axel V.
Gossage	Julia E.	Story	Walter F.	Grace	Ella C.	Donahue	James M.
Gossage	Marjorie	Schooel	Adrian J.	Gracia	Ception	Garcia	Antonio
Gossage	Nellie	Stratton	F. W.	Grady	Katherine Frances	O'Keefe	James Henry
Gossage	Rachel L.	Garbini	Angelo J.	Graeff	Dora	Frasier	Fred A.
Gossman	Ethel I.	Williams	Judge B.	Graeter	Emma	Johnson	Charles D. G.
Gossman	Viola Lucille	Schoenahl	George H.	Graeter	Ida S.	Seawell	Emmet
Goston	Belle	Vestal	Thomas C.	Graff	Lilliebell	Felton	Clarence W.
Gotrig	Stella Marie	Lee	Olaf	Graham	Alice G.	Keig	William C.
Gotschalk	Theresa	Heezen	G. J.	Graham	Beatrice	Donaldson	Philip
Gott	Alice B.	Pritchard	Louis A.	Graham	Bertha	Allen	Robert
Gott	Nancy	Johr (?)	Carlton	Graham	Elizabeth M.	Folco	Eugenio M.
Gott (?)	Laura	Hollar	Henry H.	Graham	Hallie M. Miss	Dutton	George W.
Gotterba	Leona Inez	Leavitt	Albert Henry	Graham	Hazel Maria	Young	David Alonzo
Gough	Annie Emily	Ewing	James	Graham	Ida	Cantel	Eugene Jean Baptista
Goula	Ismay Josephine	Hope	Earl Paul				
Goulart	Maria E.	Brum	Manoel S.	Graham	Ivy E.	Moulton	Page H.
Gould	Bessie E.	Day	William T.	Graham	Katie	Waldeier	Chas.
Gould	Flora Ellen	Otis	Hamilton	Graham	Lettie	Crawford	Thomas
Gould	Gladys V.	Jeffery	Renaldo J.	Graham	Libbie	Fitch	John B.
Gould	Grace M.	Thunbey	Frank W.	Graham	Lillian Fay	Pitzen	Herman Ernest
Gould	Hannah C.	Mordecai	William B.	Graham	Lilly	Fees	Elmer
Gould	Mabel	Lazier	Donald C.	Graham	Lola M.	Armstrong	Edward J.
Gould	Maud	Fiscus	Fred Irwin	Graham	Mary	Sanborn	George D.
Gould	Minnie R.	Fowles	Stephen	Graham	Mary E.	Connell	Chas. H.
Gouley	Lida	Wescott	Oliver	Graham	Myrtle Vye	Smith	Charlie Henry
Gouley	Mollie, Mrs.	DeLong	William L.	Graham	Violia M.	Chittenden	Justin L.
Gourley	Sarah A.	Foster	Chas.	Grainger	Gertrude	Crane	Homer W.
Gow	Blanche M., Mrs.	Gow	Aleck W.	Grainger	S. Margery	Burden	William D.
Gowen	M. E.	Dunlap	Wilson	Grambruna	Mary	Boggiono	Antonio
Goyheneix	Helen M.	Bury	William G.	Grand	Fannie	Hufner	Franz
Goyheneix	Marie E.	Chatard	Philibert	Grandi	Ella C.	Gambini	L. P.
Grabe	Emma	Parker	Charles Benjamin	Grandi	Josephine Emma	Williams	Walter John

Grandi	Marie L.	Williams	Frank E.	Gray	Florence Olive, Mrs.	Davis	Christopher C.
Grandola	Delfina	Peracca	A.				
Granger	Carrie E.	Gallagher	Dominic	Gray	Georgenia R.	Torr	Levy D.
Granger	Cora B.	Parrish	David	Gray	Goldie Irene	Hansen	Herbert M.
Granger	Edith	Hawkes	William	Gray	Harriett, Mrs.	Seymour	Robert
Granger	Ethel	Glady	Thomas	Gray	Lily C.	Byce	L. C.
Granice	Celia Celeste	Murphy	Walter Lewis	Gray	Lotta L.	Allen	John T.
Grant	Effa	Fagan	Shuler F.	Gray	Marion	Gregg	Nelson G.
Grant	Elizabeth	Mortimer	John K.	Gray	May	Ayers	William C.
Grant	Frankie	Gale	Adelbert Orlando	Gray	Minnie M.	McCord	Arthur
Grant	Lillian Alice	Taylor	John Jackson	Gray	Nellie	Peck	George C.
Grant	Mary	Eason	Andrew	Gray	Rosa	Ellison	Charles Eugene
Grant	Muriel Grace	Combs	Henry C.	Gray	Susan	Nissen	Jacob H.
Granucci	Mable	Ungaretti	Adolph	Grearson	Ada	Irving	John J.
Graper	Hazel	Hickman	Wade H.	Greathouse	Emma	Tracy	James R.
Graper	Mabel	Coppedge	Robert	Greaver	Jennie	Meredith	Milton L.
Gras	Anna	Pedeprade	John	Greavor	Betrina	Davenport	Harry A.
Grassly	Clara H.	Becker	Burton F.	Greco	Immaculate	Morley	Virgil
Grasso	Mary	McClure	Isaac	Green	Anna	Wedge	John J.
Graudi	Benigna Clotilda	Piezzi	Benjamin Victor	Green	Belle	Solomon	Peter N.
Gravatte	Katheryn F.	Martin	Paul C.	Green	Birdie	Ducharm	Leon
Graves	Georgia	Bordwell	Fred Albert	Green	Carrie	Lund	Charles
Graves	Laurie E.	Coon	Edward B.	Green	Catherine	Wise	Christpher H.
Graves	Mary A.	Moseley	William W.	Green	Clara	Skinner	W. G.
Graves	Mary M.	Cox	John N.	Green	Emily Augusta	Galvin	George Jay
Graves	Nora B.	Emerson	Harry E.	Green	Filomena	Carvalho	Joaquin P.
Gray	Angie	Downes	Ernest	Green	Frances	Lawrence	George
Gray	Cecil D.	Guptill	William H.	Green	Gertrude A.	Bonham	Willard C.
Gray	Clarissa	Shaw	T. H.	Green	Gretchen O.	Plutt	Charles
Gray	Cornelia L.	Rose	Raymond M.	Green	Ida E.	Wiars	Floyd
Gray	Daisy	Conley	William M.	Green	Kate	Farrell	John T.
Gray	Eleanor	Duncan	John	Green	Lela Isabelle	Overton	Mitchell Ragan
Gray	Ella L.	Swanson	Carl O. R.	Green	Lelah	Overton	Mitchell R.
Gray	Elsie	Nelson	John H.	Green	Lenora	Mello	Joseph
Gray	Florence	Serrott	Marcus	Green	Lida	Marsh	Charles E.

Green	Lovina D.	Anderson	Chris H.	Gregory	Bertha E.	Banfield	William F.
Green	Lucy	George	John	Gregory	Joanna	Brackett	Jack H.
Green	Lucy M.	Crews	Artie C.	Gregory	Louise V.	Morton	Claude C.
Green	Lulah M.	VonHemm	Victor	Gregory	M. A., Mrs.	Ashcroft	J. A.
Green	Mary	Wedge	Joseph	Gregory	Martha M.	Huntington	Horace H.
Green	Mary	Exlay	George	Gregory	Mary Elizabeth	McReynolds	Charles Newton
Green	Mary A.	Liddle	W. J.	Gregory	Mary, Mrs.	Hutton	Daniel D.
Green	May C.	Evans	Roy M.	Gregory	Nettie F.	Penrod	Harry A.
Green	Sarah J., Mrs.	Curtis	James H.	Gregory	Susie	Lent	D. A.
Green	Stella V.	Peckham	George D.	Gregsen	Eliza J.	Butler	Thomas B.
Green	Una	Adams	George H.	Gregson	Carrie D.	Thompson	Edwin H.
Green	Viola H.	Rickett	Charles	Gregson	Delia	Fruits	George Alexander
Green	Clara	Mendonca	Antonio	Gregson	Juanita C.	Butler	Clyde A.
Green	Hazel	Bowers	Herbert Andrews	Gregson	Nellie	Cunningham	George B.
Greenaa	Olive O.	Sackett	Warren N.	Gregson	Ruth Annie	Bollinger	David K.
Greenbaum	Florence	Weeks	Novilla	Greiner	Mary L., Mrs.	Williams	John T.
Greene	Vilette	Bishop	William A.	Greist	Leah Agnes	Blank	John
Greening	Emma R.	Butts	Charles M.	Grennert	Carrie	Cummings	Harvey W.
Greening	Hattie E.	Runyan	Lewis B.	Greott	Marie (?) F.	Bolles	Walter A.
Greening	Jennie	Pritchett	A. W.	Gresham	Gladys Elizabeth	Deas	Joseph Vargas, Jr.
Greening	Laura A.	Adams	J. S.	Gressot	Mabel	Silvia	J. Corea
Greening	Lenna	Chaffee	Jarvis	Grey	Carrie	Bassett	Henry F.
Greening	Nancy Jennie	Heller	William S.	Greyson	Lida	Haley	Robert
Greening	Nellie E.	McChristian	Owen A.	Grider	Eva Rwila	Pollard	Fred Robert
Greens (?)	Florence (?)	Brammer	Jochim F.	Gries	Roberta L.	Freenor	Francis Joseph
Greenslade	Ada Louise	Miller	George	Griess	Caroline	Ludy	Herman
Greensmith	Emily R. M.	Mason	James S.	Griest	Artie M.	Hiscox	Richard A.
Greenstein	Mary	Bernstein	David	Griffeth	Edna O.	Sund	Alfred D.
Greeott	Virginia G.	Cuneo	William J.	Griffin	Annie	Carmody	Thos. B.
Greer	Lizzie A.	Bauman	Edward	Griffin	Ida, Mrs.	Hunt	W. J.
Gregg	Bessie C.	Green	David J.	Griffin	Jessie E.	Bigelow	George A.
Gregg	Mary P., Mrs.	Mersereau	Paul, Dr.	Griffin	Lucile	Anderson	Rex A.
Gregg	Myrtle M.	Adamson	Forrest E.	Griffin	Mamie R.	Morrow	Harrison E.
Gregg	Orbie J.	Archer	Arthur S.	Griffin	May	Stickmeyer	Frank
Gregori	Maria	Frati	Francesco	Griffith	Juanita	Kurlander	Maurice Aaron

Griffith	Loretta R.	Scofield	Frank K.	Grove	Edna M.	Michelson	George L. F.
Griffith	Lucille M.	McComb	George B.	Grove	Emma B.	Hopper	Edward
Griffith	Malinda Ann	Holloway	Isaac Newton	Grove	Leilia E.	Schmidt	Joseph A.
Griffiths	Josie E.	Dickson	Joshua B.	Grove	Phoebe A.	Rickman	Jas. L.
Griffiths	Mary Catherine	Wickershaw	Fred A.	Grove	Sarah Louisa	Porter	Mark Richard
Griffitts	Blanche U.	Cruzan	Donald E.	Grove	Edith May	Wilson	William H.
Griggs	Hattie C., Mrs.	McDaniel	Levi J. M.	Grove (?)	Mary F.	Hamilton	John A.
Grigsby	Jessie M.	Greenlee	John D.	Grubbe	Minnie	Faylor	Orson
Grigsby	Lillian L.	Hayes	Leroy L.	Gruwell	Bessie V.	Wise	Charles W.
Grimes	Ella	Spencer	Henry	Gsobo (?)	Elizabeth	Briard	George H.
Grimley	Eva	McKnight	John	Guenza	Carmelina	Martinetti	Gabriele
Grimm (?)	Jeannie M.	Murphy	James E.	Guera	Henrietta	Cia	Domenico
Grimmer	Cary A.	Thomas	Charles C.	Guerin	Frances M.	Hinch	William I.
Grindell	Hazel Evelyn	Jacobsen	William Robert	Guerin	Ella	Block	Walter Ottmer
Grissim	Lizzie, Mrs.	Hamlin	George O.	Guerne	Edith G.	De Lappe	Fred R.
Griswold	Harriet Eveline	Stanley	Albert Thomas	Guerne	Evalyn R.	Donovan	Ney L.
Grob	Babetta	Rohrbeck	Fredrick	Guerne	Grace E.	Jacobson	Peter N.
Grodhauser	Mary	Jenkins	Gilbert C.	Guerne	Georgia O.	Peugh	Edward Allen
Groh	Katie	Rieb (?)	Peter/Pierre	Guerra	Claudie C.	Studdert	Burton J.
Grohe (?)	Helen S.	Haley	William R.	Gufanti	Rosa	Boldi	Gioseppe
Grohs (?)	Jennie	Chinn	Joseph M.	Guffanti	Paolina	Volonte	Luigi
Grom (?)	Emma L.	Hotchkiss	W. J.	Guggia	Josephine Mary	Dilena	Simon
Grosch	Frieda	Ellinger	Charles	Guglielmana	Lucia	Pelaconi	Guglielmo
Grosgebaur	Louise A.	Mullins	Robert W.	Guglielmetti	Emma Pauline	Pedroni	Homer Angelo
Groshong	Anna E.	Black	Charles A.	Guglielmini	Rosa	Affranchino	Guiseppe
Groshong	Sue	Ellis	Bert Cecil	Guidi	Ida	Ciancio	Giuseppe
Gross	Amelia C.	Tolchard	Henry E.	Guidotti	Annette Jane	Barsotti	Frank
Gross	Elice	Riewerts	Martin Jacob	Guidotti	Arimens	Ridolfi	Casimiro
Gross	Ida J.	Lahue	E. D.	Guidotti	Edythe Ida	Cooper	Harry Anderson
Gross	Ruby	Riley	George	Guidotti	Emma Agnes	Arrighi	Cesare G.
Grosse	Alberta Katherine	Ward	Phil D.	Guidotti	Jemella	Bacigalupi	John E.
Grote	Jennie Estelle	Gibbens	Walter Raleigh	Guidotti	Jennie	Petri	Agustine
Groulx	Florence Mary	Straub	George Augustus	Guidotti	Lizzie	Owens	William B.
Groulx	Jeanne	Searles	Nelson A.	Guidotti	Sarah	Gonnella	Leo
Grove	Blanche	Brown	Fred H.	Guilfoyle	Margaret	Mundkowski	Hans A.

Guilieri	Elisa	Piccinotti	Clemente	Haase	Bertha K.	Clanton	George
Guill	Elizabeth	Clark	Geo. C.	Haberman	Christine	Hanson	William J.
Guillice	Adeline I.	Cook	Glenn A.	Haberman	Gertrude	Bridges	Ira T.
Guirach	Dora Rose	Creagmile	James Albert	Habinger	Irene E.	Foley	Michael A.
Guirand	Ella	Dawe	George C.	Hachett	Ella	Herlitz	Robert
Guirgu	Assunta	Bertolani	Martino	Hacker	Edith Amy	Given	Robert H.
Guissi	Mary	Devoto	Tonni	Hackett	Rosie	Quay	Ah
Guizo	Angela C.	Foletti	Louis G.	Haddlesten	Annie L.	Coman	George L.
Guldager	Annie C.	Hall	Wm. S.	Haddleston	Laura R.	VanPelt	Roy
Gulland	Muriel	Curtis	Charley C.	Haddleston	W. Emma B.	Williams	Willie W.
Gully	Ibie	Kahrs	Lee A.	Haddock	Marion T.	Barnes	Arthur John
Gully	Winona	Bailhache	Nicholas	Hadrich	Elsa Barbara	Lukas	Chris A.
Gum	Hazel Nellie	Hall	Lieuallen J., Jr.	Hadrich	Melani	Haltiner	John W.
Gumes	Bessie V.	Kinley	Basil E.	Hadrich	Pauline M.	Wood	Lilburn Boggs
Gummeson	Grayce M.	Miller	Louis E.	Haeckl	Elene	Farwell	Sidney C.
Gunner	Anna	Johnson	John H.	Haehl	Cora	Davidson	Edward
Guntly	Irene M.	Glover	Albert Carl	Hagan	Mignon C.	Allen	George Harrison
Guntly	Lizzie	Johnson	George W.	Hagen	Emilie	Stevens	Nils
Gust	Mary, Mrs.	Schroni	A. L.	Haggard	Ethel L.	Philbrick	Burt C.
Gustafson	Ellen	Bryan (?)	John Leo	Hagmayer	Beatrice Urania	Moore	Walter Shelby
Gustafson	Esther E.	Craig	Edwin Alfred	Hahmann	Clara Charlotte	Turner	George A.
Gustafson	Esther R. E.	Sjolander	Carl T.	Hahn	Lena	Cain	Walter
Gustofson	Dora May	Strong	James T.	Hahn	Lillian Genevieve	Howell	Olin Kenneth
Gutermute	Elizabeth E.	Plank	Fred F.	Hahn	Mabel L.	Stevenson	Charles A.
Gwaltney (?)	Myrtle Alice	McCarcy	Harry	Hahn	Mary	Hartzel	Joseph
Gwin	Carrie Elizabeth	Lang	Herman Charles	Haigh	Alice Estella	Cook	Reuben Grant
Gwin	Laura M.	Jackson	Guy H.	Haigh	Ethel	Mathisen	Dudley
Gwin	Jessie	Darby	Jasper B.	Haigh	Ethel	Anderson	George
Gwynn	Emily	Pouliu	Louis Ngricole Edward	Haigh	Lena	Evans	C. D.
				Haigh	Minnie A.	Newman	Frank C.
Gwynn	Lillian	Norris	James N.	Hain	Mary Elizabeth	Nelson	Joseph
Haas	Bertha M.	Boyd	Dan	Haines	Helen H.	Harvie	Harold B.
Haas	Louise Dorothey	Hanchette	Edward	Hair	Ruth Marie	Durst	David M.
Haas	Theresa	Blum	Louis	Hakemier	Elizabeth	Heatzelman	John
Haas	Vera R.	Litchfield	Frank S.	Hakes	Colista M.	Stewart	Charlie

Halbinner (?)	Berta	Schmidt	Walter	Hall	Georgia May	Jones	Claude O.
Hale	Caroline A.	Peterson	B. L.	Hall	Gladys	McConnell	Frederick William
Hale	Jean	Conrad	Joseph	Hall	Grace E.	Leighton	Fred H.
Hale	Josephine Emily	White	Edward	Hall	Harriet R.	Weston	Harry McC.
Hale	Laura I.	Boss	George W.	Hall	Jessie	Fullan	Thomas
Hale	Mabel	Byron	Chester	Hall	Kate	Shone	Edwin
Hale	Mabel	Bird	George Francis	Hall	Laura Alice	Meck	William Edward
Hale	Martha	Staedler	Charles	Hall	Lena C.	Tibbetts	Arthur L.
Hale	Martha E.	Neely	Nathaniel F., Jr.	Hall	Lizzie B.	Pickrell	Joseph W.
Hale	Meda Eldora	Ornbaun	Horace Winton	Hall	Lola Jesse	Fox	Henry
Hale	Nannie	McPherson	Charles W.	Hall	M. Isadora	Menefee	Campbell A.
Hale	Samantha Anise	McBrayer	Arthur Lewis	Hall	Mabel G.	Bowbeer	Earl V.
Haley	Birdena E.	Smith	Leon W.	Hall	Mae	Spotswood	Thomas Hopper
Haley	Carrie Estella	Shuman	William F.	Hall	Mae	Hendrix	Harvey L.
Haley	Emma E.	McReynolds	Samuel W.	Hall	Marion Belle	Leroux	Walter George
Haley	Lizzie	Ray	S. M.	Hall	Mary	Hagans	Alfred H.
Half	Rosie	Paltz	Sam	Hall	Mary E.	Pidge	Jeremiah S.
Hall	Aletha	O'Brien	John T.	Hall	Mary Juanita	Groom	Joseph
Hall	Alice E.	Fruitt	Charles E.	Hall	Maud M.	Hinshaw	William P.
Hall	Alice M.	Murray	Howard E.	Hall	Minaral (?)	Westbie	J. M.
Hall	Alma Elizabeth	Graff	Walter Harold	Hall	Nellie	Myer	Anthony R.
Hall	Annetta F.	Zwissler	Frank	Hall	Nellie	Nader	Charles M.
Hall	Carrie E.	Briggs	Ezra	Hall	Nola	Derham	Christopher
Hall	Christina L. M.	Newcom	G. Edgar	Hall	Olivia F.	Petersen	Henry P.
Hall	Clara	Gruenhagen	Gottfried H.	Hall	Rosa E.	Patchett	Charles Henry
Hall	Cora Pauline	Garrett	Albert Walker	Hall	Sara C.	Laughlin	John M.
Hall	Eliza	Mathews	George I.	Hall	Sarah F.	Mapes	Ira C.
Hall	Emily H.	Buhs	Henry F.	Hall	Theodine M.	Olsen	C. S.
Hall	Emma J.	Hovey	Theodore	Hall	Vista M.	Hughes	George G.
Hall	Ensima	Black	Wm. H.	Hall	Lena H.	Hall	Charles A.
Hall	Erma May	Stamer	Julius Ceasar	Hall	Maggie C.	Pettit	Amos
Hall	Ethel Ruth	Nisson	Henry Eric	Hallahan	Elizabeth	Brown	Thomas J.
Hall	Evelyn Louise	McAllister	Floyd Stanley	Halley	Ellen Cecelia	Haskins	William Joseph
Hall	Fannie E.	Williams	Edwin J.	Halligan	Francis B.	Freshwater	Albert H.
Hall	Florence L.	Brunson	Frank L.	Halsey	Edna G.	Willis	Charles A.

Halst	Maggie M.	Adams	John L.	Hamner	Florence	Schoomaker	Abram R.
Haltiner	Babette	Hadrich	Carl F. H.	Hampton	Ida May	Ely	Frank G.
Haltman	Gertrude	Brown	John	Hanbert	Mary	Rugelhuth	Conrad
Halverson	Alice Ethelyn, Mrs.	Brown	Lawrence Edward	Hance	Louise K.	Fitch	Arthur
				Hancock	Mary	Loveland	E. A.
Halvorsen	Laura	Pedersen	Gerhard	Handling	Mary J.	Rush	Edwin B.
Ham	Edith L.	Hopkins	Osmer Clyde	Hanekamp	Anna Maria	Horn	Balthasar
Ham	Julia	Ham	James T.	Hanger	W. Lena	Pomeroy	Campbell
Hamby	Pauline McC	Stout	Charles E.	Hanily	Elizabeth	Dolan	J. L.
Hamell	Cora Jennie	Rains	William C.	Hanke	Beryl Andes	Miller	Emerson Paris
Hamerlund	Hilda	Milton	John L.	Hanks	Alice C.	Meyer	Bruno
Hamill	Mary	Waidmann	John J.	Hanks	Effie L.	Schwan	Harry
Hamilton	Alice	Fennell	James E.	Hanley	Sophie E.	Bowker	William C.
Hamilton	Alice B.	Knapp	Gen W.	Hanlon	Alice Agnes	Ross	George John
Hamilton	Georgia	McClish	John M.	Hanlon	Mae Elizabeth	Johnson	Demus Gale
Hamilton	Georgia Helen	Hamlin	Martin Edward	Hanna	Catherine	Cochrane	John T.
Hamilton	Julia	Upson	Charles	Hanna	Fannie I. (?), Mrs.	Wagers	Coleman B.
Hamilton	Lulu	Barrett	John	Hanna	Lizzie	Thompson	Robert
Hamilton	Mary	Piezzi	Candido	Hannah	Martha M.	Raether	Harry A.
Hamilton	Mary Francis	O'Leary	Edward Frances	Hannan	Margaret Grace	Myers	Henry J.
Hamilton	Nettie	Mersfelder	William	Hannan	Mary	Reilly	Philip
Hamilton	Pearl	Edwards	Ralph Walter	Hansberg	Catherine	Jones	William
Hamilton	Winifred	Young	Harry W.	Hanseb	Agnes M.	Dean	Herbert Burroughs
Hamlin	Emma	Hoar	Charles A.	Hansen	Agnes I. B.	Noland	Alfred
Hammel	Rose M.	Fernando	C. R.	Hansen	Alma Thersa	Werner	John Carl
Hammel	Ruth I.	Bedford	Frederick A.	Hansen	Bessie May	Gilliam	James Mitchell
Hammell	Edna May	Fredericks	Ray Ernest	Hansen	Elene	Holtz	Richard Gustav
Hammerlund	Ada C.	McConnell	Jesse C.	Hansen	Ella M.	Schleth	David F.
Hammersly	May	Petray	Jessie W.	Hansen	Ethel	Udall	C. H.
Hammett (?)	Martha	Bower (?)	Daniel	Hansen	Florence	Beck	Louis
Hammill	Lillian Agnes	Nelson	Charles Oscar	Hansen	Frances	McClure	Walter
Hammill	Lizzie	Vail	F. K.	Hansen	Frieda Elsie	Lassen	Chris
Hammond	Caroline	Moore	John T.	Hansen	Giede	Volkarts	Julius
Hammond	Eva H.	Bailhache	George	Hansen	Helga A.	Kuck	Hans A.
Hamner	Estelle O.	Spragge	David William	Hansen	Henryetta	Guthrie	Thomas George

Hansen	Ingeborg Marie	Jensen	Peter	Harbin	Laura A.	Schwartz	Jedson L.
Hansen	Josie	Knudsen	Conrad	Harbine	Addie	Blazer	John J.
Hansen	Margretha S.	Miller	Rasmus J.	Harbine	Florence Edith	Rutherford	Ernest Stanley
Hansen	Marie	Petersen	Christian	Harbine	Ollie	Plass	E. W.
Hansen	Mary C.	Jones	Milton	Harbine	Susana	Raffety	Abner L.
Hansen	Mary Myrtle	Vaughan	Miller	Harbins	Ella	Scott	Hany W.
Hansen	Meta	Fredrichsen	Cornelius	Harbinson	Emily Gardon	Smith	William Vernon
Hansen	Minnie C.	Winton	Homer W.	Harden	Anna B.	Hawkins	J. R.
Hansen	Olga	Neergaard	Frederick Hartirge, Jr.	Harden	Edna Ursula	Moad	Marshall M.
				Harden	Jinella	Eardley	William J.
Hansen	Poulina	Nielsen	Peter	Harden	Lucinda, Mrs.	McPherson	Thomas
Hansen	Rosa L.	Jansen	Martin H.	Hardesty	Elizabeth N., Mrs.	Olsen	Einar Adolph
Hansen	Sadie M.	Mapes	L. Percy	Hardesty	Susie	Matthews	O. P.
Hansen	Sarah J.	Sodergren	Charles G.	Hardford	Mary	Ahern	Nicholas
Hansen	Ulricke G.	Thiede	C.A. Herman	Hardin	Alice M.	Biggs	George C.
Hansen	Wannoma A.	Tonelli	Albert P.	Hardin	Edith Lourena	Hollis	George Lester
Hansen	Bertha	Moody	Clyde L.	Hardin	Ella I.	Worth	Thomas R.
Hanson	Christine	Haehl	Otto	Hardin	Esther Jimella	Moll	Albert Eugene
Hanson	Cora	Kimes	D. M.	Hardin	Etta	Barry	Norman J.
Hanson	Dora	Simpkins	Reginald	Hardin	Eudora	Upton	Will H.
Hanson	Emelia J., Mrs.	Fairbanks	Julius T.	Hardin	Ida Jane	Corbin	G. Benjamin
Hanson	Eva	Hutchison	Lawrence	Hardin	Julia A.	Gregory	Edwin Stanley
Hanson	Jessie	Samuels	Robert M.	Hardin	Lucinda T.	Denny	Lloyd L.
Hanson	Martha	Hile	Charles H.	Hardin	Margaret	Hale	Peter
Hanson	Minnie	Axtell	Asher E.	Hardin	Nancy	Meagher	John F.
Hanson	Minnie E.	Cook	Harry L.	Hardin	Sarah C.	Benson	Josiah H.
Hapkal	Mary A.	Chittenden	Louis F.	Harding	Edith M.	Lane	Allen S.
Happy	Mary	Bailey	Johnathan J.	Harding	Jennie L.	James	William A.
Haraldson	Elizabeth	Mediros	Frank	Hardisty	Cora Ethel	Colburn	Rufus Paul
Haraszthay	Ida	Hancock	Henry	Hardisty	Daisy D.	Austin	Harry C.
Haraszthy	Eleonor Marie	Dowdall	Leo Edward	Hardisty	Emma L.	Freeman	Albert J.
Haraszthy	Natalia Vallejo	Ringstrom	Sigurd A.	Hardt	Louise	Slattery	John J.
Harben	Jennie E.	Hoover	Leo V.	Hardt	Mamie	Anderson	Haus
Harbin	Amanda	Bailhache	Solon William	Hardwick	Mary	Blosser	Thomas G.
Harbin	Laura	Schwartz	Judson	Hardy	Bessie L.	Hilton	Harry L.

Hare	Lillie	Church	Charlie	Harrington	Anna L.	Nottingham	William T.
Hare	Violet E.	Smith	Wilbert C.	Harrington	Elise	Jackson	Parker L.
Harenisch	Agnes D. M.	Manouk	Charles	Harrington	Florence E.	Stice	I. H.
Harford	Ethel Florence	Dean	Leslie Chauncy	Harrington	Hattie A.	Bryant	Abner
Hargens	Emma	Weltz	John	Harrington	Leila M.	Hopper	Walter E.
Hargreaves	Juanita M.	Brikenstock	Evert F.	Harrington	Ruth H.	Souza	Joseph J.
Harie (?)	Carrie E.	McKenzie	William H.	Harrington	Susan	Young	Warner
Harlan	Margaret B.	Remmel	George E.	Harris	Alice M.	White	James Russell
Harlan	Nevada Judkins	Wilkins	Fred Ellis	Harris	Anna M.	Otton	Stanley M.
Harland	Adeline I.	Frederick	Leonard B.	Harris	Arlein Alice	Reynolds	Emery T.
Harley	Ella	Behmer	John	Harris	Cecile Vivian	Foote	Charles M.
Harley	Emma	Triplett	Geprge A.	Harris	Cora Bell	Hunt	Paul
Harman	Elizabeth	McClude	Roland R.	Harris	Della May	Westen	John
Harman	Louisiana	Pugh	Benjamin C.	Harris	Edith A.	Thompson	Frank B.
Harman	Myrtle	Olts	Frederick W.	Harris	Elizabeth Gertrude	Wrobleski	Ludwig
Harman	Nellie	Steiger	Andrew C.				
Harmer	Althea L.	Focht	Samuel S.	Harris	Ellen M.	McReynolds	Thos. A.
Harmeson	Ella G.	Penny	Charles Edgar	Harris	Elva	Cardinet	Ernest H.
Harmeson	Pearl	French	George Robert	Harris	Etta	Cooley	James F.
Harmon	Belle	Taylor	W. H.	Harris	Eunice Caroline	Campion	Thomas
Harmon	Ella M.	Wright	Winfield D.	Harris	Fern A.	Reeder	Edwin L.
Harmon	Lilly	Bobst	John W.	Harris	Florence Elaine	Webb	Theodore Winthrope
Harmon	Maggie	Boyer	Henry W.				
Harmon	Nellie G.	Conners	Alexander F.	Harris	Gladys M.	Ruoff	Alan H.
Harms	Edith Johanna	Lauritzen	Knudt Broder	Harris	Grace J.	Myers	Joseph J.
Harms	Emma	Hagedohm	William	Harris	Ivy	Ketcham	Lona I.
Harnett	Johanna	Horgan	Patrick	Harris	Jessie	Weeks	Geo. A.
Harny (?)	Eva	Pitt	John W.	Harris	Laura Jane	Lane	Doctor Thomas
Haron	Mary I.	O'Keefe	Thomas P.	Harris	Lorena	Swank	John Wm.
Harp	Caroline	Ogden	William	Harris	Louisa J.	Bruce	Willis L.
Harp	Emma R.	Hillis	John A.	Harris	Margaret A.	Brookshire	Thos. J.
Harper	Grace E.	Weise	Charles C.	Harris	Mary	Rhodes	James E.
Harper	Mabel E.	Phillips	Ernest J.	Harris	Maud	Miller	Charlie V.
Harper	Margaretta W. V.	Malmgren (?)	Carl C. M.	Harris	Maud E.	Berger	Charles O.
Harrigan	Florence Katherine	Eastman	Charles Ward	Harris	Rose A.	Pearson	Walter
				Harris	Ruby	Zimmerman	Paul

Harris	Sarah	Heitz	Joseph	Harvey	Edith A.	Pugh	Alphonzo A.
Harris	Sarah A., Mrs.	Hunt	B. W.	Harvey	Elizabeth E.	Gray	James W.
Harrison	Ada	Williams	Alfred	Harvey	Elnora Abbe	Trudgett	William J.
Harrison	Amanda J., Mrs.	Gaillard	Robert G.	Harvey	Hannah, Mrs.	Wolgamott	Frank
Harrison	Emma	Hausmann	John	Harvey	Helen E.	Squires	Robert L.
Harrison	Emma Burlington	Carlsen	Thorval T.	Harvey	Lillie E.	Stone	Joseph A.
Harrison	Flora I.	Osborn	Porter F.	Hary	Louise M.	Murskey	Frederick A.
Harrison	Florence	Dietrich	Joseph W.	Hasche	Emma M.	Branelenberg	Heinrich
Harrison	Lucy W.	Weatherington	W. A.	Haskell	Clista	Hughes	George
Harrison	Margaret	McCoy	Clyde	Haskell	Jessie T.	Cobb	George O.
Harrison	Ruth	Sinclair	Bertram	Haskell	Ruby Elizabeth	Nisson	Jacob George
Harrison	Viola M.	Loftus	Thomas M.	Haskell	Vera F.	Arndt	Benjamin F.
Harrow	Della	McMath	Ernest Burwell	Haskett	Bessie Anita	Shelton	George
Harrow	Frances S.	Blackman	W. S.	Haskins	Lillie Irene	Gray	Henry Charles
Harrow	Lola M.	Pfister	Wesley E.	Hasnip	Sarah	Bianchini	Giovanni
Harrvy	Mary E.	Prichard	William	Hassett	Carrie J.	Mason	George C.
Hart	Carrie Esther	Banton	James	Hassett	Laurie Caroline	Walker	John Lawrence
Hart	Delphine Antonia	Gardner	Roy Lee	Hassett	Ella L., Mrs.	Cox	Axley C.
Hart	F. E.	Smilth	Samuel	Hassold	Eliza	Petersen	Carl J.
Hart	Grace P.	Barndt	Julius	Hastie	Jessie May	Young	Edwin Guy
Hart	Hattie L.	Fortier	Peter	Hastin	Emily	Owen	Chas. A.
Hart	Myrthena Grace	Corria	Antone F.	Hastin	Lillian	Scheibel	Camille
Hart	Nora	Miller	Fred	Hasting	Clara	Holchester	Paul E.
Hart	Sylvia	Wineott	Rufus	Hastings	Johnietta B.	Leichter	Paul F.
Harte	Lydia J.	Banta	Joseph A.	Hastings	Marguirite Murphy	Roberts	Andrew W.
Hartin	Mary	Kennedy	Charles				
Hartley	Aneita	Estill	Byron Dee	Hastings	Ruby A.	Reavis	Clair W.
Hartley	Nellie Frances	Bowen	Arthur R.	Hastings	Sallie E., Mrs.	Coy	Charles S.
Hartly	Birdie M.	Field	Sydney L.	Hastings	Sarah A.	Batton	John Wesley
Hartly	Edna Augusta	Witherell	Ernest Winfield	Hatch	Blanche	Laymance	George Ebin
Hartman	Hattie	Bray	William	Hatch	Ella Estella	Randall	Franklin Fred
Hartsock	Bonnie P.	Rouse	John W.	Hatfield	Mary J., Mrs.	Lowery	James N.
Hartsook	Ella	Novak	George A.	Hatfield	Sarah M.	Mills	G. W.
Harttrodt	Hilda J.	Meeks	Walter H.	Hathaway	Sarah E.	Poole	William
Harvey	Alice A.	Whitaker	William Harvey	Hattie	Sadie M.	Wood	Ralph S.

Hatton	Blanche L.	Grider	Loran T.		Hayes	Ellen, Mrs.	Trumble	E. S.
Hatton	Carrie M.	Purdy	Lambert		Hayes	Freda M.	Kriedell	Fred W.
Hatton	Mary Jane	Wakefield	Henry Ward		Hayes	Grace	Dinucci	Fred
Haub	Minnie S.	Stump	John A.		Hayes	Hattie	Ford	J. A.
Haubrich	Clara G.	Bauman	Conrad		Hayes	Lillian	Lund	John Oscar
Haufe	Edith M. E.	Strode	J. M.		Hayes	Mae	Ledford	J. H.
Hauger	Perle	Hunter	Rea Baron		Hayes	Mary Isabela	Reese	Thomas B.
Haugh	Marguerite	Holdt	H. Christian		Hayes	May Frances	Dwyer	Harold
Haun	Alice Edna	Berger	Emil Julius		Hayne	Laura	Fenn	Theodore
Hauph	Kittie Luella	Robertson	Henry Alfred		Hayne	Mayme	Strain	John W.
Haupt	Louisa	Marshall	Robert		Haynes	Belle	Briggs	Lawrence E.
Haupt	Mary	Hayden	S. R.		Haynes	Martha L.	Zurcher	Ulysses
Haus	Margaret L. D.	Huson	Willis O.		Haynes	Zoe E.	Cochran	Willis B.
Hausmann	Elta	Vanvicel	Charles W.		Haynie (?)	Annie	Carrington	Homer Bennett
Hautot	Marthe A.	Lacoste	George J.		Hays	Anna M.	Mitchell	Wm. H.
Havenstrite	Irene B.	Templeman	Clarence E.		Hays	Eva Elizabeth	Phillips	Arthur S.
Hawes	Estella M.	Kidwell	Henry C.		Hays	Grace E.	Cochran	Claude T.
Hawkins	Evalyn	Brick	Joseph V.		Hays	Jennie	Field	Walter E.
Hawkins	Linda	Goodsir	Thos. H.		Hays	M. Ida	Tupper	Charles V.
Hawkins	M. L, Mrs.	Anderson	William P.		Hays	Mary Ubia (?)	Rochford	J. C.
Hawkins	Mamie	Wells	Howard		Hays	May	Smith	William E.
Hawkins	Martha S.	Schiller	Peter J. C.		Hayward	Mary O.	Beaulieu	Charles B.
Hawkins	Maud	Knapp	Wm. D.		Haywood	Ruth A.	DeGuerre	Harold
Hawkins	Mildred Claretta	Gustafson	Gustof Sigfrid		Hayworth	Nancy C.	Petray	Frank A.
Hawkins	Nellie	Voorhis	Willard D.		Hazelton	Ruth M.	Hurlbutt	Willard A.
Hawks	Hazel R.	Calkins	Charles F.		Head	Amelia	Patten	Charles
Hawley	Gladys Faye	Showers	Earl F.		Head	Eleanor J.	Page	Edward J.
Haws	Hannah Eleanor	Haws	Alpheus Peter		Head	Frances Gertrude	Finley	Alvin W.
Hawthorne	Esther Gertrude	Gaupp	Edward Philip		Head	Lulu M.	McKune	Otis E.
Hayden	A. A.	McDonald	W. L.		Head	Rosalis	Elkington	Thomas
Hayden	Anna Valentine	Everett	Walter H.		Headley	Louisa E.	Skaggs	Eben
Hayden	Eva	Burroughs	John		Heald	Henriette E.	Brighouse	Thomas H.
Hayes	Alice	Wheeler	David R.		Heald	Sarah E.	Alexander	David N.
Hayes	Anna	Coleman	Gary		Healey	Claire Marie	Sweeney	Walter Thomas
Hayes	Clifton Clay	Huffman	Jacob		Heartwell	Jessie B.	Dean	Carl R.

Heath	Annie M.	Bartosh	William	Helberg	Marie G.	Thomas	Leonard L.
Heath	Annie Mabel	Van de Venter	Frederick G.	Helberg	Valerie Marie	Volquardsen	Leland J.
Heath	Budella W.	Moss	Reginald G.	Held	Henrietta Georgina	Williams	Theodore Thomas
Heath	Maude Blanche	Ker	Robert M.	Held	Mamie	Steevans	C. A.
Heather	Kate	Marlatt	Frank	Heller	Laura E., Mrs.	Coppedge	Charles O.
Heather	Lizzie	Marlatt	Al	Hellman	Edith Mabel	Shatto	Carl William
Heatley	Edna M.	Fitzgerald	Daniel Holland	Hellman	Linda	Haney	Free
Heatley	Eva E.	Drew	Albert E.	Helm	Nancy Maud	Whitson	William H.
Heatly	Gertrude P.	Perry	John A.	Helman	Fannie E.	Oakes	William J.
Heaton	Olive C.	Heaton	William H.	Helton	Lee	Wiley	George Herbert
Hecht	Helen	Kraimer	Isaac	Hembree	Ivy Olivia	Ewing	John Virgil
Heckendorf	Emma	Shearer	Emerson Pratt	Hembree	Mattie L.	Cartwright	George W.
Hecker	Mary Belle	Patterson	Andrew	Hembree	Eliza Ellen	Dudley	Albert Allen
Hedemark	Priscella	Wiedrick	Carl D.	Hembree (?)	Anna D.	Smith	Albert W.
Hefty	Amelia M.	Klaustermeyer	Charles F.	Hemenway	Edna R.	Strain	Frank H.
Hegler	Myrtlye	Cardinet	Edward H.	Hemkel (?)	Emily C.	Remian (?)	Emil H.
Heilfron	Ruth R.	Sullivan	Albert P.	Hemmerle	Frances P.	Thomas	Frank B.
Heill (?)	Amanda Ellen	Hendrick	Wallace	Hemmy	Maria Ursula	Mengelt	George
Heim	Anna	Veuve	Erle L.	Hemsath	Jewel Hermina	McIntosh	Richard Robert
Heim (?)	Florence Elizabeth	Henderson	George P.	Hemseth	Bernardena	Giles	Grant
Heine	Helen	Levy	Joseph	Henderlong	Martha V.	Hansen	Einer C.
Heinrich	Bertha M.	Totten	Harry S.	Henderson	Alma R.	Covey	Alphaeus Vincel
Heinrich	Matilda C.	Johnson	Will E.	Henderson	Clara	Owens	Arthur P.
Heinsen	Letitia R.	Henrichson	Harry C.	Henderson	Mamie	McIntosh	John O.
Heinze	Bertha Emilie	Emmrich	Gustav Moritz	Henderson	Maude Eliza	Ortman	Norman Clifford
Heisel	Nellie	Grofmyer	Henry C.	Henderson	Myrtle May	Mattson	Laurence A.
Heisen	Lillian	Benson	A. F.	Henderson	S. M.	Calhoun	J. W.
Heiss	Henrietta	Bush	Joe	Henderson	Violet V.	Hosmer	Raymond J.
Heitz	Emma V.	O'Bear	Charles W.	Hendickson	Anna O.	Whitaker	James P.
Heitz	Ida M.	Guillie	Edward H.	Hendley	Nannie V.	McKinlay	D. E.
Heitz	Lottie	Stanley	Richard	Hendley (?)	Elizabeth	Young	John S.
Heitz	Sarah Minerva, Mrs.	Runyan	William Smith	Hendrekson	Hilda Kriste	Strome	Morris Olai
Heitz	Tillie/Lillie M.	Stevens	Eldon	Hendren	Lizzie	Burns	Jas.
Helbarh	Terria (?)	Fleishmon	Moses	Hendren	Rebecca	Mc?ammon	Joseph

Hendrichsen	Josephine Thresa	Volkerts	Robert Emory
Hendrick	Maud	Sandberg	John
Hendricks	Ethel Elizabeth	Semeran	Conrad Edward
Hendricks	Lillian P.	Price	George W.
Hendricks	Mayme E.	Adams	William A.
Hendricks	Myrtle	Abbott	Joel A.
Hendricks	Ostella	Traub	Hermann
Hendricks	Sadie D., Mrs.	Mason	Craig M.
Hendricks	Susan E.	Bryant	William Henry
Hendricks (?)	Mary C.	Tombs	John F.
Hendrickson	C. Grace	Cooke	Frank W.
Hendrickson	C. Maud	McCormick	Chalmers
Hendrickson	Clara	Moorehead	Lee
Hendrickson	Etta Pearl	Clark	Edwin Curtis
Hendrickson	Ida	Beveridge	William, Jr.
Hendrix	Matilda Belle	Teague	Harvey Thompson
Henke	Bertha C.	Behler	Benjamin J.
Henneken	Christina	Dushane	Frank L.
Hennessee	Mary F.	Estes	Geo.
Hennessy	Catherine Ethel	O'Neil	John J.
Hennessy	Rose Mary	Danly	Lloyd Elmer
Hennigan	Ida J.	Clayton	S. A.
Henningsen	Johanna, Mrs.	Hyatt	Garrett
Henningsen	Mary	De Groot	Frank
Henrahan	Effie H.	Kirsch	Henry
Henrichsen	Anna M.	Larsen	Peter L. N.
Henrichson	Annie J.	Roberts	Leland S.
Henrickson	Alma I.	Boyson	Simon C.
Henrickson	Anna	Quint	Fred P.
Henry	Amanda B.	Armfield	Tyrus A.
Henry	Cassie	Fitzsimmons	Charles S.
Henry	Catherine	Snow	George Horace
Henry	Ella Etta	Cellarius	William
Henry	Emma Josephine	Smith	Charles W.
Henry	Hallie Edith	Stuart	Harry Edward

Henry	La Veda Lucille	Hellrick	Edward Joseph
Henry	Lennie L.	Peck	John R., Jr.
Henry	Lucile E.	McPeak	Charles E.
Henslee	Marie L.	Gates	Earl J.
Hensley	Mary E.	Lowry	Nicholas M.
Hensley	Vina L.	Chase	John W.
Hentschel	Theresa	Wedge	Jack I.
Hepner	Virginia M.	Barrows	Arthur C.
Heppert	Pauline A.	Wistuba	Otto C. E.
Herbert	Frances H.	Lopus	Joseph
Herbert	Hester R.	Farquar	Frederic Stewart
Herbert	Ina E.	Ball	Walter E.
Herbert	Nellie Augusta	Peters	Oak
Herbert	Retta	Bell	Henry
Herbert	Retta	Wetherbee	Fred B.
Hereford	Gertrude M.	Witham	Albert J.
Hereford	Hattie Elvira	Cole	Vincent Letton
Herger	Martha F.	Craig	Robert Geo.
Herges	Celia K.	Lowe	George W.
Hergeshimen (?)	E. J., Mrs.	Nower	James S.
Herlihy	Elizabeth	Fitzpatrick	Wm. E.
Herman	Alice B.	Cochran	L. P.
Herman	Bessie	Dickey	Arthur E.
Herman	Laura A.	Anderson	August
Herman	Lucilla	Skaggs	Charles Wadsworth
Herman (?)	May Rose	Kennedy	Edward H.
Hermann	Ethel Clifford	Davis	Walter Allen
Herneken	M. J.	Putnam	T. C.
Herrick	Annie M.	Hemler	George E., Sr.
Herrick	Eva Elizabeth	Condrey	Edward Phillip
Herriford	Henrietta	Hudson	Henry F.
Herrington	Mary	Ross	Jesse
Hersey	Cora Pearl	Schneider	William
Hershberger	Ruby D.	Foerstler	William C.

Herterich	Katherine C.	Hale	Eugene C.	Hiatt	Myrtle P.	Cooley	Charles H.
Hervey	Katie	Linebaugh	Columbus	Hiatt	Wanda	Fitzgerald	James G. B.
Heryford	Jessie Marguerite	Halstead	Harry Oliver	Hibbard	Hannah Barron	Sutherland	James Thomas
Herzog	Rosalie	Aussresses	Diderot P.	Hibbitts	Amelia Francis	Byrne	Malachy L.
Heselschwerdt	Amy Lillie	McGrath	Basil William	Hickey	Cathaleen Violet	Heryford	David Hilton
Heselschwerdt	Inez E.	Dixon	Harold G.	Hickey	Ella Berniece	McDonnell	John Joseph
Hespe	Mabel Augusta	Kearns	James	Hickey	Lizzie M.	Stewart	William A.
Hesse	Augusta P.	Duckwortth	HenryAlmon	Hickey	Lulu	Moller	Harry H.
Hesse	Lina J.	Wedde	Harry L.	Hickey	Margaret E.	Stolker	George
Hesse	Marita	Wendt	Leonard	Hicklin	Evelyn M.	Kistner	Loren T.
Hesse	Rachel Elizabeth	Morrison	Alvah Herbert	Hicklin	Mabel Eddie	Siemsen	John William
Hessel	Anna J.	Schneider	Benjamin J.	Hickman	Minnie E.	Chenoweth	A. Roy
Hessel	Eleanor Isabelle	Smith	Roland Hill	Hicks	Alice Coreen	Whitcomb	Clarence J.
Hesseltine	Stella C.	McGeorge	Le Roy	Hicks	Allie B.	Crane	Wade H.
Hession	Minnie	O'Toole	James J.	Hicks	Augusta M.	Shirk	Lawson H.
Hester	Sylvia	Ray	James D.	Hicks	Grace J.	Maxwell	Frank Lawrence
Hether	Christine	Elder	James H.	Hicks	Hattie	Kennedy	David S.
Hetzel	Irene	Rowe	Charles F.	Hicks	Hazel Fern	Toll	Orton Garrett
Hetzel	Olga L.	Nystrom	Sidney A.	Hicks	Henrietta C.	Schneider	William A.
Hetzel	Zelma B.	Roberts	Charles R.	Hicks	Lizzie Amelia	Rubke	Adolph Herman
Hetzil	Mable K.	Merritt	Carl B.	Hicks	Mary Nunn	Hutchison	Lester Earl
Hewald	Elfrida Katherine	Jacobs	Norman Francie	Hicks	Mary R.	Surryhue	B. F.
Hewit	Rosanna	Mead	Wilson Henry	Hiett	Nelia	Henry	James
Hewitt	Emma M.	Badger	Joseph J.	Higby	Birdie	Eason	Joseph A.
Hewitt	Marry E.	Hanley	Harry	Higgins	Adeline	Bice	Fred L.
Hewitt	Mary Jane	Mortenson	Nicholas	Higgins	Carnelia, Mrs.	Carl	William T.
Heyde (?)	Mary J.	Redmond	Martin D.	Higgins	F. Irene	Olsen	John George
Heyward	Nettie	Steinbring	William	Higgins	Gertrude Vivian	Crocker	William Franklin
Hiatt	Josie, Mrs.	Gum	William M.	Higgins	Margaret A.	Drew	Morgan P.
Hiatt	Kate D.	Ahl	Harry Jacob	Higgins	Minnie	Pfaff	Joseph W.
Hiatt	Louvisia	Wheaton	George W.	Higgins	Minnie E.	Martin	Dock
Hiatt	Madge C.	Ingram	Mercer E.	Higgins	Minnie J., Mrs.	Atkinson	Joseph
Hiatt	Maud E.	Plummer	H. E.	High	Minnie B.	Hocking	Frank
Hiatt	Meta May	Murphy	Wallace	Highlander	Irma M.	Moore	Leo A.
Hiatt	Minnie E.	Groshong	Sidney	Higson	Dora E.	Barling	Wm. H.

Higurea	Anna Frances	Salikas	Manuel
Hihu (?)	Kathryn Bothwell	McGroghegan	John Thomas
Hilbey	Catharine B., Mrs.	Sevart/Swart	L. J.
Hild	Annie	Walker	Joseph M.
Hildebrand	Bertha	Rose	Albert
Hildebrand	Lena Rivers	Litton	Roy Burton
Hildreth	Lulu	Pettis	Fred C.
Hildyard	Rosa A.	Reiser	Hugo W.
Hilgereoh	Helen Mildred	Dewey	Victor R.
Hill	Bena A.	Peterson	Peter
Hill	Effie	Carico	John W., Dr.
Hill	Florence S., Mrs.	Hornbuckle	Thomas J.
Hill	Ida May	Tuttle	James
Hill	Mae	Lovell	Walter G.
Hill	Nellie	Clark	James M.
Hillard	Mildred A.	Fellers	Frank L.
Hillbrant	Amy Viola	Wheeler	Marcus Owen
Hillbrant	Nellie	Brooks	Charles
Hillhouse	Elsie	Butts	Raymond L.
Hilliard	Carrie B.	Forsman	William T.
Hilliard	Sarepta E.	Phillips	Joseph
Hillman	Emma A.	Wiseman	Emmet M.
Hillman	Minnie E.	Whittington	Will B.
Hillmon	Katie	Hudson	Alvin P.
Hillson	Louisa	Assenti	Louis
Hillyer	Ethel	Farrance	Charles Evert
Hillyer	Lillian Belle	Jobe	Alfred Ewing
Hillyer	Daisy B.	Adams	William H.
Hilmer	Alma G.	Conger	Glenn A.
Hilmer	Elfreda	Smith	Alfred W.
Hilmer	Lizzie	Krauss	Frederick G.
Hilton	Louisa	Potter	Edmund
Himebauch	Lulu May	Crane	Wade Hampton
Hinckley	Eliza, Mrs.	Wilson	John R.
Hindes	Carrie S.	Ponceitta	Walter F.

Hindringer	Louisa B.	Bauer	Earl F.
Hinds	Marguerite	Furber	William W.
Hinebauch	Allie	Crane	O. L.
Hines	Alice J.	Blake	John R.
Hink	Sarah Anna	O'Sullivan	Eugene
Hink	Catrina	Hunken	John Carl
Hinkle	Katherine Dillon	Morrow	Wm. H.
Hinkston	Alice	Cluver	Henry A.
Hinkston	Ann	Shaw	D. B.
Hinman	Mae	Boyd	Leon G.
Hinoch	Katherine Margarette Minna	Dittmann	Wilhelm E. J.
Hinrichsen	Annie J.	Hadermann	Carl
Hinricksen	Mary	Christiensen	Ernest
Hinshaw	Amanda	McReynolds	Dennis H.
Hinshaw	Fannie D.	Peterson	John L.
Hinshaw	Mattie	Laufenburg (?)	George
Hinshaw	Wilma E.	Eckhart	Percy
Hinton	Violet	Quackenbush	Elmer Plat
Hipsher	Ada	Wertz	Samuel
Hipsher	Lottie C.	Hoadley	Charles W.
Hitchcock	C. Elizabeth	Mason	Frank L.
Hitchcock	Clara G.	Beebe	Elijah W.
Hitchcock	Ida	Ayers	B. F.
Hitchcock	Lavina K.	Anthony	M. J.
Hitchcock	Lizzie B.	Carter	A. E.
Hitchcock	Lottie Belle	Wilson	William Franklin
Hitchcock	Mary Elisabeth	Hanson	John
Hitchcock	Maud E.	Wirth	Fred R.
Hitchcock	Myrtle	Cook	Erle
Hite	Eva B.	Beatie	Walter C.
Hite	Eva Belle	Weaver	Charles Warren
Hixson	Bernice Brooks	Riddle	George Rollins
Hixson	Charlotte J.	Hart	Benjamin F.
Hixson	Maybelle Francis	Symonds	John Richard

Hixson	Mildred Janette	Ledford	Leonard Dowler	Hoegh	Anne Marie	Rickets	Johnnie Peter
Hixson	Zella Irene	Fox	Ancel Elmer	Hoerle	Dora	Wiley	Charles Hazel
Hjelm	Hilda M. E.	Nelson	Erick J.	Hoesch	Margaret C.	Auld	Royal I.
Hoadley	Ida L.	Humbert	Charles E.	Hoff	Emma H.	Frey	John G.
Hoagland	Nellie A.	Montague	Frank P.	Hoff	Georgina Agnes	Rickman	William D.
Hoar	Addie E.	McDowell	James	Hoff	Lydia E.	Smith	Sydney A.
Hoar	Fern	Goodman	Howard W.	Hoffer	Gretchen	Cunningham	William Park
Hoar	Jennie S.	Congleton	A. C.	Hoffman	Emma	Sommers	Jacob
Hoar	Mary L.	Hare	Stephen	Hoffman	Eva Belle	Goodman	Thos. F.
Hoban	Ida N.	Mathiesen	Jesse C.	Hoffman	Gertrude L.	Marier	Edmund L.
Hobart	Jessie Margaret	Leonard	James M.	Hoffman	Louise A.	Long	Alfred G.
Hobson	Louise Jane	Kruse	Frederick Antonio	Hoffman	Margaret, Mrs.	Robison	R. K.
Hobson	Mary L.	Merchant	Thos. S.	Hoffman	Marie J.	Heffner	Edward L.
Hoch	Flora	Vogt	George Henry	Hoffman	Nell M.	Laugridge	Leo J.
Hockensmith	Mary L.	Brott	Edward S.	Hoffmann	Verona	Lawler	Howard T.
Hocker	Alice	Linsley	Winfield S.	Hoffstetter	Albertine	Dietrich	Gottlieb
Hocker	Clara Louise	Nutting	Samuel Edward	Hoffstetter	Eleonore	Scheibel	Julian J.
Hockin	Grace Mabel	Blake	Jeremiah Burton	Hoffstetter	Jeanne M.	Squires	Chester J.
Hockin	Margaret M.	Gambini	William A.	Hogan	Kitty	Perkins	Edwin C.
Hockin	Maude A.	Forsythe	Myrl D.	Hogan	Nora	Waste	John Morton
Hocking	Susie	Spaulding	Henry S.	Hogansen	Dora	Olson	Charles O.
Hockins	Lee	Beck	Edward H.	Hogeboom	Alice B.	Hensley	Harry
Hodge	Minnie C.	Mills	Charles E.	Hogedohm	Johanna F.	Henningsen	John P.
Hodges	Elizabeth F.	Clutterbuck	Ernest	Hogrelius	Clara A.	Dowing	Ludwig D.
Hodges	Ethel A.	Coburn	Ernest A.	Hoirneche	Mary	Albrecht	Asmas
Hodges	Jessie M.	Helfer	George A.	Hoirup	Sine C.	Jacobsen	Neils L.
Hodgins	Kathyrn M.	McDonnell	Charles P.	Hoit	Matilda	Arnold	C. W.
Hodgson	Ada Belle	Rayner	Moses	Holbrook	Helen G.	Odlum	Earl L.
Hodgson	Alice	Bean	Ulysses S.	Holcomb	Daisy	Carter	Raymond
Hodgson	Gladys Esther	Wright	Arthur G.	Holcomb	Edith B.	Sprague	Edwin Elias
Hodgson	Jennie	Samuels	Thomas	Holcomb	F. M.	Kellogg	W. L.
Hodgson	May V.	Darden	L. T.	Holcomb	Lillie Calla	Portlock	Charley Colorado
Hodgson	Ruth G.	Price	Walter F., Jr.	Holcomb	Minnie	Sears	Robert B.
Hodgson	Irene Mae	Futsch	Walter Mecham	Holden	Carrie B.	Cnopius	Louis Christian
Hoe	Elsie	McPherson	August	Holder	Clara M.	Capps	John W.

Holderness	Stella Edna	Smith	Clay Anderson	Holmes	Nellie	Holmes	Charles H.
Holdrich	Emma	Voelker	Henry	Holmes	Nora M.	Crossfield	Archa F.
Holdworth	Gertrude, Mrs.	DuBois	Clarence	Holmes	Rachel	Smyth	Newton V. V.
Holgersen	Hedvig	Hanson	Hans	Holst	Annie	Holcomb	Leonard C.
Holinsteat	Clara Ella	Hawes	William Henry	Holst	Annie M.	Bink	Conrad
Hollahan	Iva	Lackmann	H.	Holst	Annie Mary	Adams	Joseph Walker
Holland	Bella	Burling	Geo. W.	Holst	Mabel	Ungewetter	George W.
Holland	Elsie	Arnold	Harry P.	Holst	Mary C.	Morgan	Samuel M.
Holland	Helen C.	Cassiday	Samuel D.	Holtslander	Lizzie	Cardoza	Manuel
Holland	Josephine	Conniff	Thomas E.	Homann	Augusta W.	Schelling	Alexander
Holland	Mary	Hundley	W. P.	Homerhouse	Alma Margaret	Mize	Cyril F.
Holland	Nettie B.	Goodfellow	John	Hood	Alzina Rose	Christian	Harry Henry
Holland	Rosa Ellen	Banfield	Isaac Newton	Hood	Eva L.	McHatton	Robert L.
Hollar	Flora Dell	Ely	Robert L.	Hood	Laura Frances Beatty	Shire	Jacob William
Hollar	Harriet Ethel	Jones	Lyman C.				
Hollar	Nora	Dahl	Oscar	Hoodly	Eppie L.	Comstock	Herbert G.
Hollar	Viola	Alford	Charles A., Jr.	Hook	Margie	Powers	Frank E.
Hollenbarter	Mary	Millerick	David	Hooker	E. C., Mrs.	Morillo	Peter C.
Hollenbeck	Nella E.	Burghardt	Frank A.	Hooper	Annie T. (?)	Jacobs	Price
Holler	Elizabeth A.	Briggs	Peter C.	Hooper	Harriet	Dietz	Otto Frank
Hollingsworth	Mabel	Jones	Lucas M.	Hooper	Lizzie	Elwell	Charles E.
Hollister	Anna Laura	Miranda	William Melvyn	Hooten	Crystal Abbie	Paxton	John Franklin
Hollivan	Mary	Peters	Manuel	Hooten	Lillian	Butler	Wm. M.
Holloway	Florence M.	Kyburz	Alfred A.	Hooton	Edna	Poulson	William
Holloway	Ida V.	Wilson	John	Hoover	Elizabeth	Davis	Charles N.
Holly	Edna I.	Warner	Raymond E.	Hoover	Louise Booth	Lawler	James
Holm	Ada Louisa	Weber	Frederich Henrich	Hope	Anna M.	Fritsch	J. R.
Holman	Annie	Merrill	George D.	Hope	E. Claire	Hyde	William H., Jr.
Holmberg	Hilda A.	Moore	Oliver C.	Hope	Ella R.	Woodworth	Samuel P.
Holmes	Aetha (?)	Rice	Asbury	Hope	Emma A.	Wright	William A.
Holmes	Carolyn Edna	Powers	Talbot J.	Hope	Natalie	Davis	H. H.
Holmes	Emma Mabel	Douglas	James Herbert	Hopkins	Alma Luella	Dodge	James Arthur
Holmes	Eunice C.	Harding	Reinhardt T.	Hopkins	Clara D.	Wattenburg	Charles S.
Holmes	Minnie A.	Buckingham	T. H.	Hopkins	Florence E.	Scott	George F.
Holmes	Minnie M.	Mello	Louis	Hopkins	Gertrude	White	John N.

Hopkins	Grace J.	Ducker	Barton	Hornbuckle	Kittie	Graves	Bartlette
Hopkins	Kate, Mrs.	Witt	John P.	Hornbuckle	Lulu J.	Lock	Wm. H.
Hopkins	Lottie	Cullen	Edwin Patrick	Hornbuckle	Molly B.	Colbroth	Harry W.
Hopkins	Lulu W.	Zartman	Wm. H.	Horne	Hadie W.	Duerson	Richard C.
Hopkins	M. G. Pearsons	Wolcott	H. M.	Horne	Jeanie R.	Elphick	Roy J.
Hopkins	Mary E., Mrs.	Cash	O. P.	Horne	Mae	Overton	Albert
Hopkins	Ruby B.	Deffenbaugh	Louis M.	Horner	Wilmos E.	Metzger	Joseph E.
Hopley	Juno Clarice	McPike	William F.	Hornschlag	Louise	Nissen	Nahmen
Hoppell	Marie, Mrs.	Starke	John Henry	Horsley	Annie, Mrs.	McGuire	I. N.
Hopper	Bertha	Rhea	J. L.	Horstmann	Ethel B.	Brayman	Willard V.
Hopper	Bertha S.	McManus	George E.	Horwege	Loretta C.	Beveridge	James
Hopper	Clara Jessie	Packwood	Warren D.	Horwitz	Leah	Ringel	Isidor
Hopper	Dora	Taylor	T. H.	Hoskins	Anna May	Neil	Daniel Gilman
Hopper	Emma B.	Nervo	Bartolomeo B.	Hoskins	Annie E.	Skinner	William G.
Hopper	Eva Elizabeth	Lovell	James T.	Hoskinson	Isabel A.	Williams	Phillip
Hopper	Gertrude	White	Charles Henry	Hosmer	Anna	White	Thomas
Hopper	Ida Ione	Cox	Nathan H.	Hotaling	Lillian B.	Austin	Malcolm O.
Hopper	Kate	Pitchford	Ben	Hotchkiss	Anna	Leslie	Charles W.
Hopper	L. Maria	Yeager	Joe D.	Hotle	Effie C.	Ellis	William A.
Hopper	M. Myrtle	Chamberlain	W. Warren G.	Hottinger	Alice M.	Peter	Edwin M.
Hopper	Nancy A.	Groves	Christopher Columbus	Hottinger	Gertrude E.	Barham	Fred
Hopper	Nancy J.	Hardin	Wm. H.	Houck	Mary L.	Holmes	Lester S.
Hopper	Rosa B.	Ludwig	J. Elmer	Houx	Aletha Josephine	Olmsted	John Alexander
Horgan	Julia C.	Crayne	Stephen D.	Houx	Edith Pearl	Monett	Chauncey D.
Horgson (?)	Emma	Gearhart	L. C.	Houx	Ethel L.	Peoples	James A.
Horine	Allie	Goddard	Daniel N.	Houx	Josephine	Hopper	Zachamiah (?)
Horman (?)	Lena Harmon	Anthony	John H.	Houx	Nellie	Coffey	Samuel A.
Hormon	Mabel F.	Curtiss	George C.	Howard	Agnes Julia	Towner	Austin O.
Horn	Anna	Lueger	Ernest	Howard	Amelia C.	Roix	James A.
Horn	Jessie E.	Duerson	Wm. H.	Howard	Beulah	Conklin	Thomas
Horn	Mary M.	Starkie	Alf	Howard	Celia G.	Evart	William P.
Hornbeck	Catherine, Mrs.	Kessing	Clemens	Howard	Clara L.	Walter	Francis M.
Hornbuckle	Ella M.	Pride	William	Howard	Daisy M.	Belveal	Otis E.
Hornbuckle	Harriet	Enders	Charles R.	Howard	Delle	Dickerson	Roy Ernest
				Howard	Edith V.	Baldwin	James M.

Howard	Eleanor Adella	Meads	Willia C.
Howard	Elizabeth J.	Williams	J. B.
Howard	Ella	Soules	Frank H.
Howard	Emily J.	Redmond	Frank Martin
Howard	Ethel May	Fleet	Walter Sidney
Howard	Florence L.	Howard	Alphonse E.
Howard	Jessie	Quiner	John W.
Howard	Juanita V. R.	Murray	Perry Leland
Howard	Lillian	Teaby	Oscar Wm.
Howard	Lucinda	Harrison	G. A.
Howard	Lulu M.	Cox	Hugh
Howard	Mabel C.	Matison	Frank M.
Howard	Maggie	Stutsman	Robert
Howard	Martha G.	Bever	Tunis V.
Howard	Mary C.	Dusick	Albert H., Jr.
Howard	Mary E.	Morgan	Samuel Henry
Howard	Mary Emma	Brown	Ben C.
Howard	Maud C.	Mason	William C.
Howard	Mignonette	Moffit	Lewis
Howard	Nellie	Schweitzer	John
Howard	Pearl	Hickey	Maurice J.
Howard	Ruby S.	Mackey	Edward
Howard	Sarah, Mrs.	Bay	Edward L.
Howarth	Ada	Shaw	Thomas
Howe	Catharine, Mrs.	Clark	J. W.
Howe	Frances	Howe	James Henry
Howe	Johanna V.	Freitas	Anton
Howe	Louise A., Mrs.	Gillon	Charles Mark
Howe	Mary E.	Pettit	Harry M.
Howe	Mary V.	Schwedler	Otto
Howell	Albrnia C.	Morris	Harry B.
Howell	Elizabeth S.	Tuttle	Dexter
Howell	Ella M.	Condict	H. M.
Howell	Elva C.	Churchill	Jabez F.
Howell	Julia E.	Gustafson	Alfred
Howell	Margaret Lent	Canello	Henry G.
Howell	Margaret Lent	Fortson	John T.
Howell	May Elizabeth	Nelligan	Garrett Joy Peter
Howell	Myrtle L.	Green	Perry W.
Howells	Jessie	Bryan	William F.
Howeth	Daisy	Green	Charles
Hoyne	Bessie E.	Leahy	John
Hoyt	Almah E.	Gregson	John N.
Hoyt	Edna	Persing (?)	Charles Frederick
Hoyt	Lillian	Tilden	Henry G.
Hoyt	Susan Effie	Zimmermann	William Frederick Carl
Hrusa	Barbara	Crowley	Cornelius Joseph
Hubart	Jennie E.	Eversole	Abraham
Hubbard	Dell B.	Nelson	Wm. W.
Hubbard	Nancy K.	Burrows	Robt. K.
Hubbell	Maysie	Hamilton	Henry Liberty
Huber	Amalia	Kaelin	Edward
Huber	Cecilia, Mrs.	Shaffer	Ignatz
Huber	Emily A.	Blank	George
Huber	Helena	Blum	Jacob
Huber	Resina A.	Hallenbarter	Frank A.
Huber	Sophia	Sachmann	Charles
Huckabay	Ferne Elizabeth	Chapman	Guy Lee
Huckabay	Maude Sarah	Dixon	Walter C.
Huckins	Ethel Frances	Vestal	Warren Eugene
Hudoff	Rose Martha	Wheeler	Robert Bruce Allen
Hudson	Alice	Finley	Wilson E.
Hudson	Elizabeth, Mrs.	McClelland	Buchanan
Hudson	Flora E., Mrs.	Tyler	Joseph L.
Hudson	Gertrude A.	Owen	B. J.
Hudson	Gladys E.	Pearson	Ralph Wayne
Hudson	Mary E.	Mills	Don
Hudspeth	Alice S.	Clark	William D.
Hudspeth	Dixie	Riddle	John Starr

Hudspeth	Exor	Miller	J. F.	Hulbert	Katherine A.	Britton	Clyde A.
Hueber	Regina	Gangler	Xaver	Hulbert	Laura Emily	Eells	Frank Lorne
Huff	Enola B.	Shelley	William W.	Hulbert	Laura Irene	Hupp	Roscoe E.
Huffam	Hazel May	Menetrey (?)	Charles Louis	Hulen	Lady Maude	Taylor	Clevie Vincent
Huffman	Bessie J.	Churchill	William F.	Hull	Druzella	Wright	Charles W.
Huffman	Cora	Hopper	Henry J.	Hull	Edna Odell	Johnson	Louis Webseter
Huffman	Florence	Farley	Charles	Hultgren	Emma	Bengtson	Carl
Huffman	Mary J.	Tichenor	Everett R.	Hulton	Virginia	St. Ores	Andrew
Huffman	Myrtle	Bosch	Arnold	Hummerland	Christina	Weigand	Charles
Huffmaster	Elmina V.	Orra	Camille Frank	Humphres	Allie L.	Alexander	Rufus
Hufstoder	Mary Belle	Hulbert	Hiram Perry	Humphrey	Agnes	Bains	Gallant
Huggard	Etta	Moore	Warren B.	Humphrey	Marion	Baird	J. G.
Hugh	Flossie	Coker	Charles L.	Humphrey	Rebecca A.	Curtis	Benj. A.
Hughes	Alice Viola	Cox	George Edwin	Hunger	Maria, Mrs.	Knecht	Frederich
Hughes	Edith A.	Crane	William P.	Huni	Sophe	Bertrand	Paul Emil
Hughes	Ellinor Josephine	O'Hara	John Patrick	Hunkler	Amie L.	Brown	Horace E.
Hughes	Estella M.	Hull	Money Elliott	Hunt	Anna L.	Casey	Edward C.
Hughes	Georgia A.	Bagley	Weaver T.	Hunt	Laura Ellen	Farnsworth	Raymond W.
Hughes	Jean	Sheehan	John P.	Hunt	Lois Irena	Gibson	Clifford LaVere
Hughes	Josephine	Pickell	J. R.	Hunt	Luella A.	Acuff	Metcalf
Hughes	Lila Dell	Heitz	James Louis	Hunt	Margaret	Cook	Peter
Hughes	Lizzie W.	Wright	F. N.	Hunt	Minnie	Thrift	Charles W.
Hughes	Mary A.	Neary	George	Hunt	Ollie A.	Ramage	James W.
Hughes	Mary G.	Hensley	F. C.	Hunt	Pearl	Bush	William Herbert
Hughes	May L.	Tonkin	James V.	Hunt	Vitas C.	DuBose	James Gaillard
Hughes	Mayme	Ward	Sydney	Hunter	Ella	Noon	Francis
Hughes	Pearl M.	Cook	Fred B.	Hunter	Ethel M.	Roberts	W. K.
Hughes	Sarah M.	Niego	Louis	Hunter	Helen	Hamilton	Lovell Joyce
Hughes	Virgia L.	Cox	Charles A.	Hunter	Jennie	Peterson	Sash
Hugo	Lydia L.	Nisson	George T.	Hunter	Leslie M.	Noe	William Joseph
Huikston	Annie	Hillis	William Franklin	Hunter	Lola	Kennedy	Ebert L.
Hulbert	Belle	Bonham	Melvin	Hunter	Lutitia R.	Patton	Wm. S.
Hulbert	Eleonora Agnes	Black	William H.	Huntington	Eva J.	Davis	Floyd E.
Hulbert	Fannie O.	Knoles	Rollin C.	Huntley	Birdie J.	Morford	Edward Elmore
Hulbert	Julia A.	Lalanne	John	Huntley	Charlotte Elizabeth	Wendt	John Fred

Huntley	Delia .	Torrance	Dayton
Huntley	Emma	Davis	Jonah W.
Huntley	Gertrude	Turcotte	Clarence Arthur
Huntley	Maude	Schuster	Jacob F.
Hunziker	Emma	Ludwigs	George
Hunziker	Flora	Cooley	Edward A.
Hupus	Josie, Mrs.	Rothkopf	Albert P.
Hurd	Charlotte	Benson	Henry
Hurlbert	Jeannetta	Stender	Christian Henry
Hurlburt	C. W., Mrs.	Waring	Fred W.
Hurry	Mary	Ungerwitter	Henry W.
Hurton	E. Estella	Freeman	M. L.
Husing	Marietta M.	Rayner	Edward Alfred
Husler	Lena M.	Kalish	William G.
Hussey	Anita	Kissam	William A.
Huston	Estella	Kolm	Robert
Hutchings	Susie	Galpin	John W.
Hutchins	Mabel	Herberts	Harvey
Hutchins	Mildred G.	Craver	J. Edward
Hutchins	Minnie, Mrs.	Priest	William H.
Hutchins	Ula Rose	Tyler	Allen Homer
Hutchins	Violet	Mastrup	Andrew
Hutchinson	Annie	Ottmer	Florence H.
Hutchinson	Charlotte	Skinner	Robert Wilson
Hutchinson	Clara D.	Hutchinson	David F.
Hutchinson	Lily E.	Hotchkiss	Douglas F.
Hutchinson	Mary E.	Elkins	Richard L.
Hutchinson	Myrtle	Serres	John P.
Hutchinson	Sarah J.	Fink	Monte C.
Hutchman (?)	Hannah	Rich	E. G.
Huth	Valenteen	Andreasen	Andrew
Hutichinson	Ethel Frances	Norbury	Cecil John
Hutsell	Mary E.	Cooper	John H.
Hutsell	Russie	Rawles	Fred A.
Hutter (?)	Rhoda	Crist	William
Huyck	Pearl	Fricke	Richard
Hyatt	Emma Beatrice	Farahm	John Henry Adolph, Jr.
Hyatt	F. G., Mrs.	Beardslee	John W.
Hyde	Alicia A.	Menihan	Thos. M.
Hyde	Annie E.	McCarthy	Geo. J
Hyde	Cora Lee	Bunney	Alexander, Jr.
Hyde	Francis G.	Cooper	Frederick A.
Hyde	Mary M.	Duncan	Robert A.
Hyland	Elizabeth J.	Mangini	Louis J.
Hynes	Alma R.	Walls	David
Ichtertz	Mary Emily	Bennett	William C.
Icnin (?)	Reyalur (?)	Reedie	Valentine
Iffland	May L.	McVay	John A.
Iice	Nettie Marie	Richardson	Milo B.
Illia	Adele	Albini	Pietro
Imbler	Elsie	Clary	Clarence H.
Imbolz	Frieda	Winkler	Alfred
Infield	Josephine	Kiser	William
Ingalls	Emma	Kruse	James H.
Ingalls	Lillie, Mrs.	Badgley	Sherman
Ingalsbe	Luinie	Bitcon	George
Ingerson	Grace M.	Walters	Martin Edwin
Ingram	Addie Bell	Kennedy	Charles Warren
Ingram	Agnes Pauline	Nickless	Raymond T.
Ingram	Bell E.	Lile	Joseph A.
Ingram	Daisy V.	Smalley	Jefferson B.
Ingram	Ella May	Rodgers	R. F.
Ingram	Emma	Kuykendall	William Stark
Ingram	Kezia	Meyers	Ranie I.
Ingram	May	Kennedy	Joseph Edward
Ingram	Nellie	Cavanagh	John Edward
Ingrim	Delia	McKillop	Dugald
Ingrum	Sarafta (?) I.	Shriver	Isaac
Inna	Matilda	Piezzi	Frank C.

Ioap	Selina Margaret	Thomas	Joe Joseph	Iverson	Hedda	Dokkedal	Niels Peter
Ireland	Grace Elizabeth	Hassett	Jay Vernon	Ives	Agnes	Rogers	Ellis Jay
Irmer	Martha R.	Sutherland	George R.	Ives	Amanda Louise Muller	Moore	Friend Francis
Irvin	Esther	Hart	Albert R.				
Irvin	Ethel	Parkerson	David M.	Ives	Lewaltie	Palmer	Andrew S.
Irvin	Maggie	McCawley	L. E.	Jackman	Madge V.	Rear	George W.
Irvine	Elizabeth	Richmond	Stanley	Jackman	T. A.	Hoyt	Elijah
Irving	Martha	Bowen	John Thomas	Jackson	Allie	Somes	A. W.
Irwin	Edna H.	Farner	David Paul	Jackson	Anna	Roseburgh	Allen
Irwin	Elizabeth A.	Cowles	RAlph	Jackson	Annie L.	Steward	Frank L.
Irwin	Emily H.	Roux	John M.	Jackson	Bertie Estelle	Guldager	Fred H.
Irwin	Gladys	Joseph	William	Jackson	Delia	McProud	Oscar C.
Irwin	Mettie M.	Jones	William Farrington	Jackson	Ethel	Gregg	Art A.
Irwin	Paulina	Mills	Robert	Jackson	Eunice	Trosper	Ernest E.
Irwin	Paulina A.	Mills	Robt.	Jackson	Flora Helen	Hart	Albert Paxton
Isaac	Dora	Grove	Jesse Roy	Jackson	Irene Orr	Wininger	A. W.
Isaac	Eva	Decker	Martin Arthur	Jackson	Lula	Butts	Claude
Isaacs	Clara A.	Purcell	Frank C.	Jackson	Mary	Schumann	F. O.
Isaacs	Dora	Badgley	Ira Walter	Jackson	Mary M.	Courtright	R.
Isaacs	Eva	Purcell	Robert	Jackson	Mina, Mrs.	Jackson	Andrew
Isaacs	Fanny	Covey	Geo. W.	Jackson	Myrtle P.	Kreis	Harry Gailord
Isaacs	Lillie	Cole	W. E.	Jackson	Rosa Ann	Crist	Wm.
Isaacs	Myrtle	Carson	Fred	Jacobs	Amelia A.	Glassman	Abraham B.
Isaacs	Retta	Crockett	James D.	Jacobs	Elba F.	Paxton	John F.
Isaacs	Ruth	Smith	Joel O.	Jacobs	Flora B.	Carston	Godfrey M.
Isaak	Christiana	O'Connell	James	Jacobs	Lena E.	Sharp	Joseph
Isaak	Emma V.	MacKillop	David V.	Jacobs	Lorita M.	Combs	Henry C.
Isaak	Helena	Konig	John	Jacobs	Minnie	Stockstill	George F.
Isaak	Johanna Elizabeth	Potter	Eber Ward, Jr.	Jacobs	Myrtle	Lyman	Eugene
Iselan	Henrietta	Toole	Ralph T.	Jacobs	Nettie Ellen	Leech	Albert Ernest
Isenburg	Hazel G.	Jones	George H.	Jacobs	Ruby	O'Dell	Sylvester
Isham	Tolitha Elizabeth	Mitchell	Benjamin F.	Jacobs	Sarah	Cowen	Frederick S.
Ivans	Laura Alice	Friend	Joseph A.	Jacobs	Stella M.	Bowers	Henry P.
Ivans	Olive Violet	Ducharm	Lambert A.	Jacobsen	Constantine	Grebe	William C.
Iverson	Elsie	Hansen	Carl Christian	Jacobsen	Dorthea	Branson	John

Jacobsen	Frances N.	Evart	Edwin J.	Jasperson	Emma A.	Hessel	Joseph W.
Jacobsen	Hansine	Jacobsen	Richard	Jasperson	Henrietta M.	Foley	Michel J.
Jacobsen	Hedvig	Hedin	Sven Thomas	Jeans	Jessie Lee	DeWitt	Harry Arthur
Jacobson	Dora E.	Beck	John E.	Jefferies	Sylverine	Guglielmetti	Marino J.
Jacobson	Marie E.	Johnson	John W.	Jeffreys	Alva J.	Neyhart	Ralph E.
Jacquet	Rosa Celestine	Mundkowski	Clements Vincent	Jelinski	Mary	Byrne	William W.
Jaggers	Bernice E.	Roberts	Earle L.	Jenkines	Lida M.	Gillette	Russell W.
Jaggers	Mayme T.	Hixson	William J.	Jenkins	Clara Louise	Harrigan	James Daniel
Jakoba	Christina	Kiser	Nicklaus	Jenkins	Hulda	Liggett	Thomas, Jr.
Jakway	Margaretta	Hall	Francis	Jenkins	Jennie L.	Plass	Charles A.
Jalon	Mary	Gonsales	Frank	Jennie	Katherine	Roberts	Benjamin F.
James	Addie Virginia	Moe	William	Jennings	Margaret	Oeltjen	George Henry
James	Allie	McDill	S. F.	Jenny	Sabilla	Bruck	Ernest
James	Blanche	Preshaw	Frank Alonzo	Jensen	Lillian H.	Gibson	Martin R.
James	Edna Craig	Scott	Frank Douglas	Jensen	Alma A. Olivia	Nielsen	Lauritz
James	Ella	Guldin	Fred R.	Jensen	Alma C.	Johns	Robert C.
James	Florence Katherine	Hall	Arthur Lipskey	Jensen	Anna	Bird	Seth J.
				Jensen	Anna L.	Pedersen	Hans N.
James	Hattie	Joseph	Alfred Peter	Jensen	Caroline	Mascho	Leland H.
James	Louisa	Walker	Joseph R.	Jensen	Carrie	Brown	George F.
James	Louisa	Walker	Joseph R.	Jensen	Catherine Marie Doretha	Hienrichsen	Jurgen T.
James	Mabel W.	Perry	Frank				
James	Mamie R.	Penry	John Edward	Jensen	Dagmar	Nisson	Nicklus S.
James	Nora	Smith	James E.	Jensen	Ella L.	Noel	Gus V.
Jamison	Eugenia	Cox	William Martin	Jensen	Ellen	Ducker	William Laurence
Jamison	Mildrem M.	Cox	Winfred R.	Jensen	Helen	Spiller	Bela Richard
Jamison	Myrtle May	Tunstall	William Walter Noel	Jensen	Ida H.	Baxman	Charles F.
				Jensen	Lillian Johanna	Jepson	Hans Alfred
Janssen	Elsie	Beck	Frank Ross	Jensen	Mary	Cannon	Calvin W.
January	Lora K.	Stevens	Henry D.	Jensen	Nellie M.	Vogensen	Johannes
Jappen	Lena Gerdina	Arfsten	Martin Theodore	Jentzsch	M. T.	Whitson	Edward
Jaques (?)	Belinda	Gussman	Santo	Jepsen	Christina	Hansen	August
Jardelle	Bertha	Casteel	J. C.	Jerome	Frances	Ames	Charles S.
Jarnick	Irene Van DeCarr	Romans	Elnathan	Jerome	Theresa	Bright	John Farr
Jarrett	Ellen Luckey	Sexton	George Edwin, Jr.	Jesse	Cecelia	Rhoades	James E.
Jason	Julia	Bregal	Manuel S.				

Jesse	Marie F.	Necker	Byrant Taylor	Johnson	Anna Belle	Richards	Franklin E.
Jessen	Marie	Gregg	George	Johnson	Anne	Mosier	Francis L.
Jessup	Juanita	Kilcourse	John Martin	Johnson	Annie	LeBaron	C. A.
Jewel (?)	Ellie Jane	Patterson	Joshua	Johnson	Annie B.	Von Gafen	William H.
Jewell	Annie	Healy	Frank	Johnson	Annie C.	Frederickson	Hans J.
Jewell	Eleanor F.	Molne	Cuthbert E.	Johnson	Annie T.	Richelieu	James V.
Jewell	Ida	Baker	Asa L.	Johnson	Augusta, Mrs.	Groining	Hyalmar
Jewell	Mary E.	Baumhogger	John C.	Johnson	Belle	Kolb	August L.
Jewell	Sally	Davis	Charles Henry Alexander	Johnson	Bessie	Wilson	Julian
				Johnson	Betty	Malm	Carl
Jewell	Libbie	Englehard	Sam A.	Johnson	Blanche E.	Scott	Miller
Jewett	Emma L.	Clark	Willie L.	Johnson	California I.	McMullin	Thomas F.
Jewett	Ida J.	Silk	Thomas	Johnson	Callie F.	Hicklin	Lieuallen A.
Jewett	May	Laurence	John H.	Johnson	Carinne E.	Carmana	Frederick A.
Jewett	Olive	Greene	William N.	Johnson	Caroline	Root	John W.
Jinks	Harriett M.	Cussins	John E.	Johnson	Carolyn	Mauerhan	John P.
Joachim	Bessie	Campbell	Alexander	Johnson	Cassie B., Mrs. (?)	Klein	Ernest E.
Jobson	Verda Mae Belle	Dont	Clifford W.	Johnson	Clara Belle	Bindt	Rudolph
Johannsen	Emma	Golds	John	Johnson	Cora F.	McPherson	Hal
Johannsen	Francisco	Sammons	Horace F.	Johnson	Cora L.	Howell	Louis V. H.
Johannsen	Johanna	Volguardsen	Detler	Johnson	Della A.	Long	James N.
Johansen	Cecilia	Frus	Hans	Johnson	Dora J.	Cole	George E.
Johns	Anna C.	Elliott	Irving R.	Johnson	Edna Louise	Coppedge	Ernest Frank
Johns	Martha	Cummings	James M.	Johnson	Edna M.	Hemma	Harry A.
Johns	Maude B.	Reed	John Edwin	Johnson	Elizabeth	Higley	John Burdett
Johns	Stella	Johnson	Harry	Johnson	Elizabeth E.	Capell	Chas. W.
Johns	Stella L.	Miller	George E.	Johnson	Ella B.	Adams	Arthur Miron
Johnsen	Nellie M.	Byrne	James	Johnson	Ella F.	McCray	William Lloyd
Johnson	Abbie S.	Palmer	Charles E.	Johnson	Elvira	Baxmann	Arthur V.
Johnson	Ada T.	Bonham	John P.	Johnson	Emma	Lochmer	Joseph K.
Johnson	Addie	Whitaker	John B.	Johnson	Emma	Cobb	Darwin L.
Johnson	Agnes L.	Evans	John	Johnson	Estelle M.	Bemis	Charles G.
Johnson	Alice	Bacon	Charles S.	Johnson	Evelyne Marjorie	Murray	George Willis
Johnson	Alice M.	Sharp	Ernest F.	Johnson	Evie, Mrs.	Johnson	Samuel K.
Johnson	Allie	Lucas	Jacob	Johnson	Florence E.	Hersey	Merrick C.

Johnson	Francis G.	Fernald	Eli V.	Johnson	Mary Caroline	Lindstrom	Henry F.
Johnson	Grace A.	Zane	George Solon	Johnson	Mary E.	Ritchie	Robert
Johnson	Hattie C.	Maddocks	Louis A	Johnson	Mary Hattie	Hawley	William Alexander
Johnson	Helen C.	Newell	Paul C.	Johnson	Mary J.	Pieratt	A. W.
Johnson	Helen M.	Orr	Cornelius Alexander	Johnson	Mattie E.	Matthews	John W.
				Johnson	Mattie J.	Woodcock	Charley A.
Johnson	Hulda	Grandin	Edward	Johnson	Mattie J.	Woodcock	Charley A.
Johnson	Ina B.	Ledford	Frank M.	Johnson	Myrtle	McMillen	Edd
Johnson	Inez A.	Gonsalves	George S.	Johnson	Nan	Bundesen	William
Johnson	Irene	Wilson	J. C.	Johnson	Nancy L.	Colburn	Orlin F.
Johnson	J. A.	Fisk	Chas. H.	Johnson	Nannie	Nelson	William
Johnson	Jeanette B.	Vitale	Charles E.	Johnson	Nellie I.	Estes	William J., Jr.
Johnson	Jennie J.	Sullivan	Asa I.	Johnson	Rebecca	Malone	James H.
Johnson	Jennie N.	Bellany	Severino R.	Johnson	Rebecca T.	Skinner	Hugh R.
Johnson	Juanita Ruth	Mankins	Daniel E., Jr.	Johnson	Rolla May	Kivett	Walter L.
Johnson	Julia	Kemp	Joseph	Johnson	Sarah Elizabeth	Irwin	Thomas Jackson
Johnson	Julia Lizette	Creighton	Charles Oscar	Johnson	Velmer Vermeta	Hull	Silas William
Johnson	Julietta, Mrs.	Hays	Walter Daniel	Johnson	Vera E.	Spittler	Ira J.
Johnson	Kitty	Maybee	Frank E.	Johnson	Vida	Bellah	W. M.
Johnson	Laura	Strode	J. F.	Johnson	Wilma Regina	Armos	Ruel Rogers
Johnson	Laura W.	Cohen	Joel C.	Johnson	Zelma	Palstine	Oliver P.
Johnson	Lillian May	Larsson	Gustaf Adolf	Johnston	Calla F.	Robertson	William D.
Johnson	Lizzie	McClellan	J. A. S.	Johnston	Catherine Barbra	Swain	Triskin Coffin
Johnson	Lizzie May	Karnes	Forest V.	Johnston	Ethel A.	Rowe	Preston
Johnson	Lola V.	Peters	John W.	Johnston	Ethel E.	Hudspeth	James M.
Johnson	Loleta	Shriver	George B.	Johnston	Grace G.	Finn	Robert B.
Johnson	Lucille	Stofen	Wm. J. H.	Johnston	Hattie C.	Willson	Saml. H.
Johnson	Mabel G.	Turner	Fred F.	Johnston	Jennie M.	Burke	John H.
Johnson	Mae	McGhaney	Edward Jasper	Johnston	Leslie Ewing	Robertson	James Calhoun
Johnson	Mamie	Carr	Mark, Jr.	Johnston	Marie A.	Windt	Albert
Johnson	Mamie J.	Tinnin	William Henry	Johnston	Maude B.	Pratt	Earl L.
Johnson	Marguerite	Hills	Walter J.	Johnston	Nellie Josephine	Swetmann	Geo. R. S.
Johnson	Martha	Crocker	J. M.	Jonas	Bess B.	Graves	Zennie B.
Johnson	Mary	Peterson	Hans	Jones	Abigal Akerley, Mrs.	Hudson	David Hill
Johnson	Mary A., Mrs.	Hudson	Arthur T.				

Jones	Belle	Wolff	Charles	Jones	Minnie D.	Sawdon	Samuel William
Jones	Beulah M.	Briggs	Edgar W.	Jones	Myrtle A.	Lee	Alban
Jones	Carrie E.	Adams	Frank E.	Jones	Nell A.	Cromwell	Frederick H.
Jones	Carrie May, Mrs.	Miller	George	Jones	Nellie Bly	Wishart	Claud Vernon
Jones	Celia Francis	Nosler	Karl Emmet	Jones	Nellie M.	George	James W.
Jones	Clara	Ellsworth	Leonard	Jones	Pearl May	Seawell	Earl George
Jones	Clara Ada	Wunsch	Edward Harry	Jones	Rhoda L.	Jennet	Newel
Jones	Edith Margarette	Kelly	Joy	Jones	Samantha A.	Shawver	Clement V.
Jones	Edna M.	Hayes	Bert J.	Jones	Susie C.	Bollinger	Fred
Jones	Edythe E.	Simpson	William Burtis	Jones	Sussie Elizabeth Ellen	Fehrensen	Claude William
Jones	Emma M.	Bray	Lester F.				
Jones	Estella Amanda	Hurlbert	Theron Louis	Jones	Veta	McIntosh	E. A.
Jones	Estella Pearl	Hayden	John S.	Jones	Mary C.	Mills	William J.
Jones	Esther Ann, Mrs.	Seward	Jared	Jonson	Lillie Annie	Rice	Charles Augustus
Jones	Ethel May	Izant	Percy Arthur	Jordan	Amy	Campbell	Walter
Jones	Ethel May, Mrs.	Huebner	Oscar Constantine	Jordan	Grace L.	Tompkins	Charles W.
Jones	Flora M.	Conner	Frank Stanley	Jordan	Louise	Wells	George F.
Jones	Geneva A.	Mitchell	Harry T.	Jordan	Margaret	Stump	Walter G.
Jones	Georgana	Kimes	Rufus Lee	Jordan	Mary	Stump	William Henry
Jones	Hattie R.	Gerow	George E.	Jorden	Mary A.	Lutz	Carl
Jones	Hazel Ann	Jenkins	Charles Francis	Jorgensen	Christina	Moller	Michael C.
Jones	Helen	Wagers	Owen Dallas	Jorgensen	Evelyn L.	Martin	Charles L.
Jones	Helen L.	Waldrop	Joe	Jorgensen	Helen R.	Nelsen	Nels E.
Jones	Jeannette, Mrs.	MacPherson	Stuart	Jorgensen	Magdalena	Hansen	Niels
Jones	Jennie	Shedd	Edward D.	Jorgensen	Violet I.	Ramos	Abel
Jones	Jessie E.	Sylva	William	Joseph	Clara	Sparks	Frank
Jones	Laura H.	Dickson	William H.	Joseph	Flora	Doiza	Joseph A.
Jones	Lillian Beatrice	Holmes	Neal Arthur	Joseph	Inez R.	Sloss	Kenneth A.
Jones	Loretta	Rowan	Charles T.	Joseph	Mae Vera	Gardner	William H.
Jones	Louisa	Bigelow	Calvin	Joseph	Mary	Avilla	Frank
Jones	Mabel	Carvey	Dennis	Joseph	Mary E.	Cook	Roy (?)
Jones	Martha, Mrs.	Jones	Richard H.	Josephe	Maria	Da Roza	Antonio Domingo
Jones	Mattie	Chambers	Peter	Josephs	Emily H.	Canada	Alonzo M.
Jones	May Rodgers	Sager	Edwin Franklin	Joslin	Alma	Flanary	Adam
Jones	Minnie	Eastlick	Wellington B.	Joslin	Eva	Nuckolls	Enoch Marvin

Journey	Nettie Belle	Geisler	Francis Joseph
Joyce	Theresa Alice	Coates	Norman Frank
Jud	Freda L.	Stahl	Emil C.
Judd	Mable Florence	Ditlersen	Albert
Judd	Nettie May	Perigo	Everett James
Judd	Pauline, Mrs.	Baldy	O. Cass
Judkins	Alice M.	Clark	Fred L.
Judy	Emily Virginia	Esterly	Ward Benjamin
Juilliard	Florence Isabelle	McDonald	Mark L., Jr.
Julian	Victoria Susan	McLaughlin	Alexander Douglas
Juncker	Marien	Sorensen	Marinus
Jungclaus	Adele S.	Thoegersen	Theodor H.
Jurgens	May J.	Salzer	Louis A. S.
Jurgensen	Hermina F.	Murphy	Robert M.
Justi	Otilda R.	Gibson	James W.
Justis	Leola	Vander Straten	P. F.
Kady	Mary	Bohmer	Jacob
Kaeintz	Ruby Amanda	Cook	Ralph W. E.
Kaen	Esther	Simmons	Mathew
Kahl	Bertha M.	Mero	Hedly L.
Kahle	Agnes D. J.	Faltin	Wilhelm
Kahn	Alyne D.	Thomas	Harry Willard
Kahn	Bertha S.	Dresbach	William
Kahn	Estelle	Linoberg	Montague L.
Kahrs	Marie	Dabner	Manuel
Kaiser	Charlotte S.	Collins	Frederick A.
Kaiser	Grace	Keefe	Jack S.
Kaiser	Laura Teresa	Meaney	John
Kalen	Charlotte S.	Garrison	Bert L.
Kalkbrenner	Rose	Schmalenbasch	Henry J.
Kameyer	Josie A.	Bunker	Frank
Kamp	Kathryn A.	Rock	Lee L.
Kamp	Nellie N.	Killits	George H.
Kane	Catherine	Bennett	Joseph
Kane	Maggie	Frasier	Malcome J.

Kane	Minnie	Martin	James
Kangas	Justina	Peurala	Isak O.
Kanieri	Anna	Garrett	Thomas
Kapfer	Marie	Winter	Henry C.
Karchner	Mary B.	Prisser	Antone
Karedis	Helen M.	Cominos	George N.
Karev	Mabel	Petersen	William
Karl	Florence	Colbert	William
Karn	Mabel Idelle	Haley	James A.
Karneck	Martha, Mrs.	Williams	Fred
Karr	Kate	Peters	Peter M. A.
Karry	Alice M.	Lunn	Fred C.
Kas	Rhoda F.	Hansen	William C.
Kase	Anna Dorothy	Wolf	Alouis
Kast	Amelia N.	Conroy	Edmund C., Jr.
Kaster	Dena	Derham	Le Roy
Kaster	Julia	Herbert	Fred A.
Katen	Rita R.	Silva	Manuel G.
Kates	Inez	Troutman	Roy R.
Katharin	Agnes	Luchsinger	Peter
Kauffman	Minnie I.	Arnold	John W.
Kaufman	Elsie M.	Hustad	Paul L.
Kaufman	Hazel L.	Gerberding	Howard R.
Kearney	Clara T.	Dowdall	John N.
Kearney	Mary E.	Easley	William P.
Kearon	Annie H.	Olsen	William F.
Keast	Mary A.	Crandall	Walter W.
Keaton	Martha Jane	MacGregor	Allan Peter
Keaton	Norma E.	Palmer	Harold L.
Kee	Mary Elizabeth	Finley	Leon Grover
Kee	Jessie S.	Wallace	Homer
Keechler	Lena K.	Groskopf	Charles E.
Keefe	Annie B.	Neles	William P.
Keefe	Maggie A.	Fitzpatrick	Peter D.
Keefe	Mary	Quinlan	Daniel F.

Keegan	Clara Mae	Evart	Frank R.	Kelley	S. Z., Mrs.	Gray	W. J.
Keegan	Helen M.	Watson	J. S.	Kelley	Virginia Ann	Baine	Lafayette
Keegan	Mattie T.	Schott	Edward G.	Kellog	Ella Francis	Graham	William
Keegan	Marie E.	Trembley	Hubert A.	Kellogg	Anna	Baker	Albert
Keegelar (?)	Mary C.	Powers	David	Kellogg	F. E.	Brown	George C.
Keenan	Anna	Lindsey	Frank	Kellogg	Ida N.	Simonton	C. E.
Keenan	Mary	Piggott	J. K.	Kelly	Elisabeth	Culberson	Harold
Keener	Frances Ellen	Snyder	James W.	Kelly	Emma M.	Martens	Dietrich W.
Keener	Raphaella Acosta	Montgomery	George French	Kelly	Erma Heidel	Forrest	Richard Kenneth
Keese	Lilore	O'Bryan	William H.	Kelly	Evelyn Mary	Weinberg	Louis
Keese	Sada L.	O'Bryan	Leon N.	Kelly	Fannie	Robie	Walter S.
Keffel	Emma May	Shiell	Frank R.	Kelly	Gertrude C.	Plant	Charles E.
Kehoe	Etta	Vitali	Frank August	Kelly	Ida C., Mrs.	Moss	James Marion
Keiser	Josephine M.	Cummings	William J.	Kelly	Lillian Marie	Palmer	George Washington
Keiser	Lena M.	Jones	William H.				
Keithley	Nora	McGimsey	Charles L.	Kelly	Mildred Edith	Howell	James Myras
Keithly	Clara Calvina	Tarwater	Martin	Kelly	Orpah Grace	Ames	Lynwood Passen
Keithly	Lucy B., Mrs.	Lichau	Henry P., Jr.	Kelly	Stella	Day	Louie
Kellaway	Birdie	Anderson	Joseph W.	Kelsey	Florence	Manies	Morrison
Kelleher	Rose C.	Mustain	Terry	Kelsey	Mary H.	Davis	Henry D.
Keller	Annie	Briggs	James M.	Kelsey	Mary, Mrs.	Skiffington	John
Keller	Dora	Marks	Harry	Kelso	Ada E.	Hale	W. D.
Keller	Fannie	Cautel	Louis	Kelso	Alice L.	Hirst	Samuel
Keller	Josie E.	Glass	Hugh M.	Kelso	Eunice O.	Lyons	Thomas J.
Keller	Nevada	Clark	Charles Preston	Kelton	Alice R.	Abraio	William Franklin
Keller	Winifred W.	Meyer	Conrad N.	Kelton	Amy I.	Winsby	Walter Warren
Kelley	Caroline L.	Laird	Fred J.	Kelton	Frances P.	Polley	Samuel W.
Kelley	Emma A.	Miller	Wm. R.	Kelton	Loretta L.	Plag	Leo F.
Kelley	Florence Euyler (?)	DeMell	Joseph	Kemp	Marie I.	Ramsay	William Latimer
				Kemper	Josephine	Johnson	Frederick
Kelley	Hazel C.	Bettega	Louis	Kemper	Sarah E.	Conger	Charles W.
Kelley	Lulu Salome	Detroit	Philip Adam	Kempf	Jennie E.	Heitstuman	Henry
Kelley	Maggie	McDonald	John	Kemster	Minnie, Mrs.	Warner	Joseph L.
Kelley	May	Petersen	Richard	Kenbury	Amanda E.	Stewart	Joseph
Kelley	Millie	Wallace	William W.	Kendall	Emma J.	Groff	William R.

Kendall	Thelma	Brewer	Clyde Clinton	Kenyon	Alice	Keane	Frederick J.
Kendell	Bessie H., Mrs.	Pyne	Henry H.	Keogh	Marion	Crooks	Robert Lee
Kendrick	May Virginia	Walker	Herbert Charles, Jr.	Keohane	Nellie	Horgan	Eugene
Kenison	Mabel E.	Martin	Oscar J.	Keough	Minnie	Penry	Irving
Kennedy	Alice Cary	Dudley	William Seawell	Kerby	Phoebe P.	Dutton	N. T.
Kennedy	Anita Alice	Wright	Carl H.	Kercheval	Irene L.	Tuttle	Clare A.
Kennedy	Ann S.	Archer	James J.	Kern	Josephine	Grossman	Abraham L.
Kennedy	Annie E.	Mitchell	W. J.	Kerr	Margaret G.	Neerguard	Robert C.
Kennedy	Annie M.	Hampton	Robert M.	Kerrigan	Mary J.	Slater	Louis C.
Kennedy	Clara	Switzer	Burton	Kerrn	Ella R.	Boswell	F. C.
Kennedy	Clarice G.	Wood	Lester J.	Kerscher	Monica	Steimer	Joe
Kennedy	Ella, Mrs.	Phinney	George Washington	Kerschner	Juanita Evangeline	Descalso	Luke M.
Kennedy	Emma	Smith	Henry W.	Ketcham	Agnes Grace	Clark	Charles A.
Kennedy	Ethel L.	Johnson	Vernon L.	Ketelsen	Freda	Lebech	Andreas
Kennedy	Eva G.	Jewett	Frank W.	Ketring	Vera	van Gilder	David
Kennedy	Fema (?)	Peterman	Christian	Ketterlin	Marguerite	Roberts	William R.
Kennedy	Ida Belle	Culbertson	John B.	Kettlewell	Jessie Lee	Washabaugh	Grover
Kennedy	Lillie Louise	Warner	Frank W.	Keyes	Mary	Moore	Charles M.
Kennedy	Maggie	Lehn	Louis	Keyes	Mary	Scott	Arthur W.
Kennedy	Mary Jane	Clawson	Chas.	Keyes	Mattie	Haubrich	Benjamin F.
Kennedy	Nellie	Carmody	Fred L.	Keys	Amelia	Adams	Robert S.
Kennedy	Rosa Belle	Bruce	Fred Clarence	Keys	Mary Ellen, Mrs.	Torrance	Joseph Lane
Kennedy	Rosa M.	Cargile	Charles W.	Keys	Nellie	Litton	A. P.
Kennedy	Ruby Gwendoline	Carmody	Chester Arthur	Keyt	Edwina M.	Smith	William J.
Kennedy	Unice Pearl	Ford	Charles	Kidd	Abbey W.	Pool	Kinnie Ditimius
Kenney	Mary	Ravizza	Ernest	Kidd	Alta S.	Manter	Benjamin H.
Kenney	Mary N., Mrs.	Thomsen	Jens	Kidd	Katie E.	Rambo	J. H.
Kenney	O. S.	Smith	John B.	Kidd	Katie Ellen	Rambo	J. H.
Kenniston	Lorena E.	Roe	George Robert	Kidd	Mina	Colton	Frank B.
Kenny	Mary L.	Schmidt	Philip G.	Kidder	Evelyn Agnes	Slocum	Beach C.
Kent	Cassandra M., Mrs.	Ward	Porter	Kidder	Lizzie	McCausland	James
				Kiechler	Josephine	Riebli	John B.
Kent	Winifred L.	Carr	Arthur C.	Kiefer	Clara	Spitler	Burton Andrew
Kenworthy	Elvira Charity	Hall	Harry Willson	Kieffer	Hattie L., Mrs.	Wagner	Frank Hermann
Kenworthy	Vera	Button	Floyd Walter				

Kienle	Loretta M.	Bailey	Douglas A.	King	Laura A.	Peterson	Gilbert D.
Kieser	Agnes	Muller	Joseph	King	Lila	Wilson	Charles W.
Kilgore	Eudora T.	Newman	Geo. W.	King	Mabel Ruth	Goatley	John L.
Kill	Carrie	Walters	Chester J.	King	Margaret	Renstrom	C. W.
Kimball	Anna May	Rogers	Joseph Albert	King	Marie	Owens	E. A.
Kimball	Edna Genevieve	Bingaman	Joseph Wheeler Dores	King	Martha Winifred	Bufton	William Arthur
				King	Mary	Rose	Joe
Kimball	Lulu M.	Hopper	Henry James	King	Mary E.	Ryan	John F.
Kimball	Marie	Vissas	Frank Peter	King	Mary F.	Mendonca	Joseph J.
Kimble	Annie M.	Lawrence	Bert M.	King	Matilda J.	Garrison	Nonnie
Kimble	Delia	Harmon	Robert A.	King	May Louisa	Bromley	Frank A.
Kimble	Mary M.	Harmon	Frank A.	King	Nettie E.	Rickliff	Gus A.
Kimes	Clara A.	Van Keppel	John H.	King	Rhoda M.	Wilson	Truman E.
Kimes	Daisy Viola	Van Keppel	Cornelius	King	Ruby E.	Baughman	Horace Ray
Kimes	Deeda C.	Coats	William B.	King	Sarah I.	Cummings	Harry W.
Kimes	Ethel A. (Mandy)	Jenkins	Henry R.	King	Sarah I.	Goldson	William H., Jr
Kimes	Mabel Ann	Davidson	Roy Frederick	King	Marie Elizabeth	Exley	William
Kimura	Sakae	Kimura	Tokizo	King (?)	Hannah	Taylor	C. H.
Kindler	Amelia L.	Bowers	Joseph Ellsworth	Kingsbury	S., Mrs.	Latimer	Hugh N. N.
King	Annie	Rose	Toney	Kingwell	Avis B.	Fleming	Eddie Ellis
King	Bertha F., Mrs.	Monks	John	Kingwell	Mable	Ratliff	Raymond
King	Blanche Elizabeth	Curran	Phillip Joseph	Kingwell	Phebe M.	Fleming	Frank M.
King	Dorothy I.	Maddocks	Harold F.	Kingwell	Rhoda	Smith	Edwin H.
King	Effie	Gusti	Albert	Kinloch	Mary	Goodrich	Henry P.
King	Emma	O'Dell	Cicero H.	Kinlock	May	Murbar	George
King	Emma Bee	Tollouse	William	Kinnaman	Alta	Young	Fred
King	Esther Florence Violet	Root	Julian Van Cleave	Kinne	Eudora May	Wilen	Alfred John
				Kinne	Lillian Blanche	Rambo	William Dennison
King	Evelyn Irene	Codner	Frank E.	Kinne	Ethel S.	Dennison	Ezra D.
King	Francis A.	Seward	Manuel J.	Kinner	Harriet B.	Howell	W. E.
King	Getrude	Bowen	Lorenzo H.	Kinsel	Dorothy	Morris	George F.
King	Hollis E.	Giberson	William P.	Kinsey	Sarah	Poe	Robert
King	Irene	Lownes	John	Kinyon	Bessie M.	Folsom	Fred Newton
King	Jennie	Pomeroy	Charles F.	Kinzie	Mabel	Smith	Thomas R.
King	Jennie N.	Lambert	Edward	Kircke	Amelia Anna	Bouk	Alva Roy
King	Jessie I.	Dorris	Fred O.				

Kirk	Elise	Dugue	Fernand	Klause	Levina	Stewart	John H.
Kirkbride	Blanche Bernice	Barnett	Marion L. R.	Klaustermeyer	Louise	Peters	Emil H.
Kirkland	Daisy Helen	Hanner	Elmer R.	Klein	Grace Lena	Cunningham	Edmund James
Kirkland	Frances M.	Lampson	Walter A.	Kline	Eletha Alice	Andrews	Robert Shaw
Kirkland	Lizzie	Kelly	David	Kline	K. Isabelle	Bolton	Walter A.
Kirkland	Maria Ellen	Smith	Sydney Vane	Kline	Lena E.	Brown	William E.
Kirkland	Sarah Margaret	Nichols	Thomas J.	Kling	Christine	Christoffel	Jacob
Kirkpatrick	Alice Corena	Robin	Gabriel	Kling	Clara W.	Ronan	Thomas C.
Kirkpatrick	Catherine L.	Wheeler	John C.	Klinger	Edith	Noll	Edward G.
Kirkpatrick	Grace Cynthia	Coulter	Paul	Klink	Vernie Gladys	Gardner	Bernard Rogers
Kirkpatrick	Olive A.	Whitney	Mernie A.	Klotz	Amelia	Sharp	David
Kirlin	Annie E.	Barnett	Frank W.	Klotz	Bertha K.	Ross	Syd C.
Kirmess	Caroline	Galliah	San	Klusing	Emma L.	Rochester	John N.
Kirry	Dora	Heryford	Hilton	Knapp	Alice B., Mrs.	Jones	Walter
Kirsch	Catharine	Samuels	Robert M.	Knapp	Hope Irene	Wasserman	Milton L.
Kirsch	Frances Margaret	Borba	Frank	Kneale	Eva	Von Grafen	Chester
Kirtley	Emma G.	Smith	Charles P.	Kneale	Isabella M.	Weeks	Robert L.
Kirwan	Nellie E.	Bradford	Clifford G.	Kneale	Mona	Urton	John H., Jr.
Kise	Electa E.	Petersen	Edgar	Kneller	Emilie Florence	Brassill	James Frederic
Kise	Ida	Fordemwalt	C. E.	Kniest	Sophie M.	Pattosien	William J.
Kise (?)	Etta	Harrington	Ambrus	Kniffen	Mary M.	Gregory	Harvey
Kiser	Agnes C.	Harris	Robert E.	Knight	Jennie	Frost	Walter C.
Kiser	Edith E.	Hathaway	Albert	Knight	Mary	Crone	Edwin
Kiser	Frances	Riebli	Robert John	Knight	Mary Augusta	Green	Parley H.
Kiser	Hermina	Straub	Frank	Knight	Rosetta	Chappell	Alfred U.
Kiser	Josephine	Kathriner	Paul	Knipp	Winfred	Leach	Roy H.
Kiser	Lillian Rozalia	Silver	Anthney Deering	Knoch	Gertrude O.	Pagh	John C.
Kiser	Matilda	Jakober	Carl	Knolty	Dora Edith	Cofer	Clinton Tice
Kiser	Rose N.	Porter	Albert A.	Knolty	May M.	Fowler	David
Kistler	Lucille C.	Wagy	Earl W.	Knowles	Ada A.	Van den Noort	Walter P.
Kistner	Lena Belle	Smith	Leslie D.	Knowles	Dora E.	Park	William T.
Kittchen	Josephine	Roedert	Charles	Knowles	Lora F., Mrs.	Sylvester	Daniel W.
Kittler	Rose J.	Kinney	William S.	Knowles	Lou	Ward	Clyde E.
Kjar	Helene	Jensen	Niels	Knowles	Nanon	Ellis	William H.
Klaus	Ella	Robinson	John O.	Knowles	Venie	Stumbaugh	Charles W.

Knox	Edith	Cox	John	Koster	Bertha Josephine	Benson	Roy
Knox	Lizzie E.	Ferguson	Angus V.	Koster	Josephine	Peterson	Eric Peter
Knox	Maud Florence	Gibson	David L.	Koutmire	Emma Etta	Coffey	Wm. M.
Knudsen	Elsie E.	Nielsen	Niels A.	Kowski	Johanna Witt	Matson	Arthur C.
Knudtsen	Mary C.	Roerden	William N. F.	Kraft	Emma A.	Thorpe	John D.
Kobler	Rosa	Fischer	Henry F.	Krahmann	Amelia	Helberg	William
Koch	Anna	Shearer	Henry	Kramer	Regine	Lindig	Charley D.
Koch	Anna E.	Evans	E. Esley	Kraus	Mayme A.	Staehli	Edwin J.
Koch	Anna E.	Millar	John W.	Kreamer	Nellie	Dayton	Wm. L.
Koch	Dorothy B.	McAskell	Angus H.	Krepps	Jennie L.	Manuel	George S.
Koch	Emilie E.	Zimmerman	Charles	Kreps	Minnie Elizabeth	Hibbard	Earl Francis
Koch	Kate Anna	Jones	Samuel	Kresky	Dora W.	Van Bebber	James W.
Koch	Mamie	Cook	Charles Edward	Kreutzer	Kate	Lagger	Cesare
Koch	Minnie	Amann	Wendalin	Kricke	Ernestena	Caseres	Albert H.
Koch	Pauline Josephine	Filippini	Emidio John	Kricke	Mary	Shuster	Clarence Lloyd
Kocher	Roselie	Silva	Rufus J.	Kricke	Louisa Mary	Jensen	Alfred J. P.
Kochuke	Margaret Martha	Brodersen	Julius Peter	Kriedell	Amelia, Mrs.	Fields	William A.
Koegler	Elisabeth	Johannes	Herman	Kriedell	Elsie	Johnson	Raymond
Koenig	Lillie F.	Berry	Joseph P.	Kripp	Clara Betts	Landresse	Charles Paul
Kohl	Charlotte	Budde	Frederic/Fritz	Kristensen	Amanda	Tillotson	Arthur Fletcher
Kohle	Minnie	Mills	Wm.	Kroehuke	Clara E.	Halley	James L.
Kohler	Emily Freda	Williams	William Jacob	Kroft	Doretha	Offutt	Charles G.
Kohler	Josephine K.	Skaggs	Charles E.	Krohn	Joeliene E.	McNeil	James F.
Kohler	Mary Elizabeth	Gray	Woodward Martin	Kron	Ebba Levena	Wagers	James Irvin
Kolasa	Stanislaw	Besenthal	Adolph	Kronich	Hannah	Leaner	Maurice
Kolb	Belle	Combs	Monroe	Krounest	Emily	Frellson	Hans
Kolb	Ola	Arfsten	Ben	Krug	Anna Agnes	Brannan	G. Clark
Kolkmeyer	Freda C.	Bundesen	Karl	Krumdick	Jennie, Mrs.	Gill	George W.
Koller	Sanne H.	Myhre	Olaf A.	Kruse	Clara Elise	Pedrotti	Carter L.
Kopf	Victoria Louise	Fenkhausen	W. R.	Kruse	Mary, Mrs.	Smith	John
Kopiske	Amelia	Gard	James F.	Krusick	Eva Angelina	Boysen	William Henry
Kopken	Sophia	Bork	Julius	Kstrom (?)	Annie E.	Royal	William H.
Kopp	Frances M.	Davis	Mac A.	Kubala	Rose A.	Moody	Frank L.
Koppen	Emma C.	Frederickson	Frederick C.	Kubic	Annie	Gaba	Marks
Koster	Anna D.	Campigli	Frank Charles	Kubie	Katie	Hammer	Marquis

Kubie	Lottie	Torr	Mead O.	Lacerda	Mary Augusta	Azevedo	Frank Augusto
Kuehne	Clara	Mullen	James J.	Lachman	Violette	Gilbert	Joseph L.
Kuffel	Elsie B.	Schwartz	Albert John	Lackard (?)	Sarah J.	Skinner	George A.
Kuffel	Gertrude	Fletcher	Andrew	Lacque	Sarah A.	Hanson	Peter
Kuhl	Catharina	Bizzini	Julius	Laereman	L., Mrs.	Willis	Robert
Kuhm	Louisa	Cook	William	Laerssen (?)	Mary Alice	Upton	William Edward
Kuhn	Caroline	Thorpe	James	Lafferty	Lola F.	Laughlin	R. L.
Kuhule	Irene Genevieve	Bettinelli	Silvio L.	Lafferty	Mary E.	Jenkins	William L.
Kulberg	Engre C.	Donogh	Russell W.	Lafferty	Naoma E., Mrs.	Beeson	William S.
Kunde	Alice	Behler	William	Lafferty	Nettie C.	Stout	Wm. E.
Kuner	Bertha	Rehaag	Otto	Laffey	Rose	McDonald	Albert S.
Kunzler	Della Adele	Beck	Hans Madison	Laffourguette	Marie	Donmecq	Ben
Kupper	Melaine	Dupon	Julius F.	Lafon	Henriette	Dufau	Joseph
Kurtz	Amelia	Nimmo	J. H.	Lafore	Marie	Bronnais	Victor
Kurtz	Henricki	Meyer	Friedrich Wilhelm	Lafranchi	Adelina	Sartori	A.
Kurtz	Rosa	Pfeiffer	Frederick Henry	Lafranchi	Clara J.	Pedrotti	Fred J.
Kuykendall	Helen	Romaine	William, Jr.	Lafranchi	Gentila	Sturlini	Leopordo
Kuykendall	Luella (?)	Noffsinger	Wilbur	Lafranchi	Giema	Mazzoni	John
Kyle	Beatrice J.	Gunn	Robert	Lafranchi	Mary	Lepori	Peter
Kyle	Effie M.	Reed	Chas. W.	Lafranchi	Olimpia	Guglielmetti	Cesare
Kyle	Lana E.	Nash	James A.	Lafranchi	Ollie	Martignoni	Walter
Kyle	Maude	Blackburn	Charles Walter	LaFranchi	Sylvia J.	Gambonini	Alfonso Joseph
Kyle	Mildred Baxter	Madsen	Herbert H.	LaFranci	Margaret	Bassi	Giatano
Kynoch	Edna I.	Horrup	Frank J.	Lagan	Katherine J.	Marsh	John P.
Kynoch	Flora	Sherman	Adelbert	Lagomarsino	Katie	Gilbride	Philip Joseph
Kynoch	Lydia L.	Duerson	John T.	Lagomarsino	Marie	Babbino	Thomas
La Blanc	Carrie	Barbee	Elias W.	Lagomarsino	Rosa E.	Lovotti	F.
La Franchi	Anita E.	Gambonini	Arnold	Lagorio	Therese B.	Ferretti	John V.
La Gue	Gertrude	Steffensen	George	Lahne	Gerda H.	Calliman	William G.
La Page	Cora M.	Landelin	Frank W.	Lahr	Lillian	Willis	Mervin
La Vallee	Archange	Jessen	Adolph	Laird	Arminta Arabel	Rose	John Wesley
Labarthe	Madeleine	Sarvoe	Alexander	Lake	Grace E.	Lloyd	Walter A. L.
Labastorde	Jennie	Luque	Peter	Lake	Mabel E.	Schneider	John, Jr.
Label	Dora	Wharton	Henry	Lakeman	Sara C.	Straw	Edwin E.
Lacchetti	Zaira	Rebottaro	Emanuel	Lakey	Aida Belle	Wymore	William W.

Lalanne	Henrietta	Young	Jesse Lindley	Lane	Madge May	Riley	Edward Heald
Lamb	Edna May	Earhart	George Hammond	Lane	Mary C.	Middagh	Ezra Sypes
Lamb	Laura B.	Carman	Cecil C.	Lane	Vera	Nelson	Andrew Thomas
Lamb	Mary A.	Hopper	George R.	Lang	Alice May	West	Charles Nathan
Lamb	Nora	Keslar	Jackson	Lang	Myrtle Ethel	Haskell	Herbert Raymond
Lambert	Clara V.	Bullock	Lewis M.	Lange	Catherine	Lindsey	Elon
Lambert	Donna E.	Farwell	Marcus Morton	Langenour	Irma R.	Lomax	Walter B.
Lambert	Elise Mary	Boyer	Ernest D.	Langer	Alice G.	Garrison	Richard William
Lambert	Estella May	Soares	Joaquin S.	Langhlin	Ida, Mrs.	Cleaveland	Robert Fuller
Lambert	Gussie	Heaton	Robert Bruce	Langstaff	Loraine L.	Trout	Frank M.
Lambert	Lotus L.	Adams	Ross B.	Lannan	Margaret E.	Walsh	Richard J.
Lambert	Mima	Edwards	Matthew	Lannow	Annie	Purcell	Thomas J.
Lambert	Nevada	Jouker (?)	G. G.	Lanpher	Ruth Louise	Landgrebe	Milton William
Lamburth	Ada E.	Hill	George O.	Lansdale	Mary Elizabeth	Bowden	John Wesley
Lamer	Annie, Mrs.	Carrington	George	Lantere	May	Piche	Albert
Lamonte	Idella	Jackson	Bert	LaNuit	Clotina	Rose	Alfred Abel
Lampkin	Lois V.	White	Sidney T.	Lapham	Cornelia E.	Givin	Aneil W.
Lampson	Nellie E.	Holgard	Carl C.	Lapham	Esther	Sturgeon	Wade
Lamson	Jessie	Taylor	Bird E. S.	Lapham	Ethel	Meeker	Robert T.
Lanati	Margherita	Piazza	Martin	LaPlant	Louisa	Cooke	James F. R.
Lancaster	Ellen A.	Richardson	Webster H.	Laplechre	Anna	Vignan	Bernard
Lance	Anna May	Norton	Lewis A.	Lapus	Marie	Milne	Donald
Lancioni	Liza	Pieroni	Sebastiano	Large	Byrtie	Cresap	Gallant
Landgrebe	Pearl	Rubke	William	Largente	Genevieve	Perramont	Louis B.
Landgren	Louisa, Mrs.	Feldman	William	Larsen	Anna	Schmalinbach	Edward
Landgren	Teresa	Millerick	John	Larsen	Dortheaty	Rasmussen	Nels Peter
Landis	Hattie	Barnes	William A.	Larsen	Laura Christina	Christensen	Martin Petersen
Landrus	Edith Lily	Hayner	Ralph Waldo	Larsen	Maria Christine	Larsen	Jorgen
Landsborough	Georgy M.	Whitely	Henry M.	Larsen	Stella M.	Ledford	William F.
Landy	Mary C.	Riley	Michael Edward	Larson	Dora	Hansen	William Adolf
Lane	Grace A.	Giorno	Vincent W.	Lasher	Sarah Lela	Hutchinson	David Kyle
Lane	Gusta	Rose	Frank	Laske	Katherine	Felix	Gustav H.
Lane	Irene J.	Arnett	Vivian O.	Lassey	Grace B.	Nichols	Elmer J.
Lane	Lottie E.	Blackford	Ernest F.	Latell	Elsie Elizabeth	Lange	Niels Frederik
Lane	Lottie Mae	York	Willis Braisted	Latelle	Meta	Suhr	Martin

Latson	Rosilla	Jessen	Christopher B.
Laufenburg	Ellen	Hinshaw	J. D.
Laughery	Martha E., Mrs.	Hottel	Peter G.
Laughlin	Adeline	Thomson	R. Heber
Laughlin	Amanda	Bailey	J. E.
Laughlin	Cynthia E.	Gordon	Reece
Laughlin	Eliza Jane	Brown	Marqus
Laughlin	Ella	Hassett	James T.
Laughlin	Irene J.	Berton	Mars F.
Laughlin	Josephine	Laughlin	Samuel McKendry
Laughlin	Lizzie	McCulloh	Frank
Laughlin	Maesota	Laughlin	Merton
Laughlin	Mellvina	Slusser	Wm. P.
Laughlin	Myrtle	Abshire	Alfred C.
Laughlin	Tina Patoka	Price	Malcolm Eugene
Laughlin	Willa Lee	Cowper	Charles Wallace
Laughuane (?)	Mary	Woods	James A.
Laumann	Millie J.	Wood	Will H.
Launoise	Estella	Stracca	Peter
Laurens	Ida	Rebois	Leon
Laurent	Julia	Gilardoni	Attilio
Lautenschlager	Amelia M.	Driver	Nickolas
Lauteran	Antoinette M., Mrs.	Cobb	Omar O.
Lauteren	Gertrude C.	Johnson	Ernest
Lauz	Lydia (of colour)	Harris	Charles C.
Lavagnino	Mary	Ciezere	Lavagino
Lavege	Mary Jane Laragoche	Grand	Peter
LaVine	Adelaide	Johannsen	Edward Henry
Law	Elmira	Hubseh	Albin J.
Law	Lulu	Wells	John James
Law	Mildred	Rodehaver	Ray H.
Law	Myrtle H.	Mariotte	Paul A.
Law	Nettie M.	Luttrell	H. L.
Law	Phoebe Ann	Perry	Tony

Law	Tammy	Bevington	Walter Clark
Lawler	Alice	Stillwell	Daniel L.
Lawler	Elsie Margaret	Kelly	George Thomas
Lawler	Gertrude M.	Norton	Archibald A.
Lawler	Grace	Akers	Stephen
Lawler	Lucy H.	Drees	Herman A.
Lawless	Anita A.	Wolfstein	Errol P.
Lawrence	Alfa N.	Evey	David D.
Lawrence	Edith	Ayers	Frank
Lawrence	Francis Green	Lawrence	Joseph G.
Lawrence	Georgie May	Kurlander	Sidney
Lawrence	Grace Belle	O'Leary	Archie Francis
Lawrence	Kate Amanda	Elder	Henry Elmer
Lawrence	Katie	Gonsolos	Antonio
Lawrence	Linny Belle	Dalton	Thomas Benton
Lawrence	Louise A.	Miller	John J.
Lawrence	Mabel M.	Burr	Robert L.
Lawrence	Maggie M.	Evans	John D.
Lawrence	Margaret	Wilds	John C.
Lawrence	Martha E.	Walker	John L.
Lawrence	Myrtle L.	Winans	Lewis J.
Lawsen	Cherrosette	Luce	Elmer E.
Lawson	Catherine	Frohmoder	Thomas
Lawson	Cora Edith	Temple	Erle
Lawson	Dorothy B.	Jackson	W. Edward
Lawson	Marion E.	Mehl	Walter A.
Lawson	Mary	Roberts	Logan
Lawson	Rosetta	Freeman	Orin
Lawson	Sarah	Rima	Willard Freemont
Lawton	Anna I.	Perkins	Carlos L.
Lawyer	Mary	Patten	J. O.
Laycock	Vivian W.	Reinhardt	Andrew
Laymance	Leona	Gardenhire	W. H.
Laymance	Margery A.	Nelson	Henry Elvin
Laymance	Sarah Augusta	Heimroth	William Henry

Laymance	Suzanne	Hibbard	Lee	Lee	Emmie H.	Bennett	George H.
Layneance	Charity L.	Harlan	William Christian	Lee	Gertrude May	Rowland	James David
Lazzaroni	Carolina	Quartaroli	Peter	Lee	Hattie	Rowcroft	Francis M.
Lea	Lola	Hixson	Roy H.	Lee	Helen L.	Jones	Thomas W.
Lea	Lola M.	Hixson	Roy H.	Lee	Mamie	Nellist	Frank F.
Leahy	Lillian	Mahler	Henry J., Jr.	Lee	Margaret L.	Hockin	William Henry
Leal	Rose Mary	Rudolph	Fred	Lee	Rachel Orlena	Baugh	Clive Evertt
Leard	Bernice Edna	Black	Homer W.	Leef	Edith F.	Linderman	Clyde E.
Leard	Dora	Metzger	Alfred V.	Leek	Cyntha	Mathis	Henry F.
Leard	Laura J.	Ellis	William C.	Leek	Mary Jane	Davis	Monroe
Leard	Nettie A.	Martin	J. E.	Leete	Margaret S.	Gale	Cecil H.
Leary	Clara	Siefkes	lane Lincoln	Leete	Mattie A.	Singmaster	Edwin
Leary	Mattie H.	Stevens	Horace B.	Leeter (?)	Sadie E.	Hunt	Arthur H.
Leathe	Alice May	Long	George	Leeth	Myrtle	Hays	Marmion
Leathers	LaVerne B.	Swyers	George G.	Leffingwell	Margarett, Mrs.	Nay	Wm. J.
Leavitt	Cecilia W.	Hixson	Charles H.	Leftar	Minnie May	Rutherford	Frank Steven
LeBaron	Beryl	Bliss	Philip P.	Legg	Margaret Ruth	Winsby	Harry Elmer
LeBaron	Grace Eleanor	Moodey	Ross Clarence	Leggerini	Nina B.	Turcatti	Ermino
Lebaron	Laura Mabel	Minor	William Peter, Jr.	Leggerini	Mary	Paolini	Pietro
LeBaron	Mildred S.	Salih	Fred	Leggett	Anna Eliza	Power	Newton Theodore
LeBaron	Sarah	Hassett	Adlai V.	Leggett	Della Z.	Monroe	Raymond
LeCam	Marie C.	Bortone	Michel	Leggett	Donna Z.	Waldson	Wesley W.
Leck	Alis	Kelly	James H.	Leggett	Julienne G.	Woodrich	Robert J.
Leclerc	Emily	Lambert	Charles A.	Leggett	Lizzie M.	Craver	Frank W.
Leddy	Lillian Ruth	Lafferty	Daniel H.	Leggett	Maud Lillian	Bones	Frank M.
Ledford	Anna May	Hendricks	George L.	Legro	Eva Agusta	Pressley	Lawrence Adams
Ledford	Vesta V.	Hedden	Donald	LeGro	Bernice	Downs	Vernon, Jr.
Ledgett	Alvina	Roeters-VanLennep (?)	Frederick T.	Lehman	Lilian H.	Cader	Israel
				Lehmkuhl	Marie, Mrs.	Vellage	Rinaldo B.
Lee	Ada A.	Morrice	Edward	Lehn	Estella A.	Wilson	George D.
Lee	Annabel	Foreman	Andrew Macpherson	Lehn	Marguerite	Chandler	Leo F.
				Lehritter	Annie Louise	Hall	James F.
Lee	Catherine	Thornton	Charles	Lei/Sei	Norina	Briganti	Angelo
Lee	Clyde	Skaggs	Geo.	Leibert	Lorraine E.	Maddalena	Charles J.
Lee	Emma	Johnson	James W.	Leibler	Dorothy C.	O'Neill	Frank H.

Leigh	Amanda J.	Disher	George W.	Leonard	Belle Esther	Sandford	Henry Topping
Leigh	Delia	Ellis	Leander Gilbert, Jr.	Leonard	Emma F.	Starrett	Raymond C.
Leigh	Jennie	Miller	Charles R.	Leonard	Margaret	Tyrell	William Patrick
Leigh	Josephine	Anderson	J. A.	Leonard	Neoma	Wilson	Charles Wesley
Leigh	Mary Ellen	Evans	Thomas	Leonardi	Alphonsa	Gori	Adolph
Leininger	Carrie	Blower	Sumner J.	Leonardini	Teresa	Biasotti	Giovanni
Leininger	Ruth C.	Van Deusen	Malcolm G.	Leonardini	Theresa	Bertossi	Joseph
Leisen	Jennie, Mrs.	Leisen	William C.	Leoni	Giaconda	Nichelini	Benedetto
Leisensing (?)	Ida	Rasse	William	Lepley	Helen Margaret	Willard	Tkomas Kay
Leith	Kathleen	LaDue	Earl Francis	Lepper	Lena	Fiege	Joseph
	Laurence			Lerner	Cecelia	Warshauer	Bernard
Leiva	Irene M.	Benson	Harry	Leroux	Cora F.	Black	Shirley R.
Leland	Maude	Burs	Henry S.	Leroux	Nellie T.	Felt	William W., Jr.
Lelouarn	Celestine	Leibert	Robert E.	Lescure	Julia	Baillesderr	Joseph C.
Lemay	A. Ellen	Coffey	J. H.	Leslie	Jessie	Sutherland	Walter Morton
LeMay	Edna Mercer	Oberte	Frank Wesley	Leslie	Margaret May	Gibbens	Robert L.
Lembke	Louise C.	Rohde	Bernhard F.	Lesser	Anita T.	Kirby	Duncan J.
LeMester	Lula A.	Meyer	Theodore	Lester	Catherine	Sedgwick	George
Lemkuhl	Meta	Pool	Walter B.	Lester	Martha Genevieve	Pfister	Franklin Pierce
Lemley	Laida F.	Monson	John C.	Leszinsky	Estelle	Doss	John W.
Lemmon	Ethel	Biavaschi	Emil	Letold	Alice Mary	Hastings	William Walton
Lemmon	Mary M.	Weeks	Harold Gregg	Letterman	Hattie F. A.	Bath	Thomas
Lencioni	Anonsiata	Simi	Egidio	Levalley	Lena, Mrs.	Howard	Benjamin Franklin
Lencioni	Emma	Landi	Enrico	Leventhal	Gertrude	Dower	John R.
Lencioni	Theresa Josephine	Maroni	George Joseph	Levicy	Ethel	Hudson	H. R.
Lencioni	Carrie	Giorgi	Arthur	Levilt	Mary Ward	Matthews	James Overton
Lenihan	Elsie Mae	Keefe	Thomas	Leviston	Elizabeth M.	Harde	Grant O.
Lenout	Nellie J.	Ebers	Henry F.	Levreau	Hattie La Dow	Bucknell	Bert Monroe
Lentz	Edith	Cook	Leo Francis	Levy	Esther	Tvete	Elmer Leonard
Lentz	Grace A.	Barnett	Harry J.	Levy	Felice	Minton	Wm. M.
Lentz	Lizzie	Waldvogel	Joseph O.	LeWarne	Anna Jean	Allen	Leslie Russell
Lentz	May C.	Greenwood	Harry E.	Lewin	Catherine Ellen	Emerson	George Edwin
Lenzdorf	Mara	Wentworth	Samuel	Lewis	Addie	Arnold	Edward
Leon	Louise	Jackson	Matt	Lewis	Alice	Sallady	Benjamin H.
Leon	Lupe	Blakley	Jesse E.	Lewis	Alletta C.	Anderton	Harry Thomas

Lewis	Annie A. Walter	Lennon	Edward Francis	Lewis	Nellie	Lindley	Charles
Lewis	Cashia S.	Mathorn	Perry D.	Lewis	Nellie M.	Ham	Whitcomb H.
Lewis	Cora	Lawson	Thomas	Lewis	Pearl M.	Cook	William H.
Lewis	Edith Mary	White	Edwin Dean	Lewis	Rachal E.	Keener	John E.
Lewis	Edna	Barker	Richard, Jr.	Lewis	Rebecca	Martin	Josiah
Lewis	Elizabeth	Wallace	Leon L.	Lewis	Rebecca A.	Peters	William F. (?)
Lewis	Emma Isabella	Bayler	Joseph Anthony	Lewis	Sarah A.	Mothern	Fernando C.
Lewis	Etha Lillian	Sani	Julius A.	Lewis	Sarah Jane	Peck	Loring
Lewis	Eva	Moran	Alexander	Lewis	Verbina	Thomas	Howard D.
Lewis	Faye B.	Bolton	William L.	Libby	Martha M.	Benepe	Wesley L.
Lewis	Florence E.	Smith	Christopher Charles	Libel	Frances	Singer	Bertram
				Lichen	Annie E.	Roberts	William T.
Lewis	Georgiana	Dibblee	William Henry	Liddell	Anna	Dickerson	Melvin R.
Lewis	Grayce Edna	Bennett	Edwin George	Liebscher	Lucy B.	Bundy	Pete D.
Lewis	Haltie	Abbey	Bert	Lielien (?)	Rose	Gottlieb	Sam
Lewis	Julia	Cox	Charles	Liggett	Erma E.	Sweeney	Joseph H.
Lewis	Julia	Streeter	Benjamin E.	Liggett	Ora May	Jenkins	Henry
Lewis	Julia A., Mrs.	Wiswell	Nelson L.	Light	Ella	Gibbs	E. C.
Lewis	Katherine E.	Mailer	John A.	Light	Emily Hida	Kelsey	Edwin Joseph
Lewis	Lena	Young	James M.	Lile	Ethel	McAbee	Frank
Lewis	Lillian B.	Rhodes	Orin O.	Lile	Florence Marguerite	O'Dell	Raymond Bluford
Lewis	Lillian L.	Gamage	Jule Crigden (?)				
Lewis	Lizzie	Quinlan	Wm. H.	Lilja	Olive, Mrs.	Anthony	George Francis
Lewis	Lucy	Boyd	George	Lillard	Dora M.	Barker	Frank E.
Lewis	Lydia Mary M.	McDermed	Joseph E.	Lillard	Fleet	Contreras	Baltimore Y.
Lewis	Mabel C.	Benson	Elwin D.	Lillard	La Doske	Stoner	William L.
Lewis	Mabel E.	Charles	Everett L.	Limes	Annie	Francisco	Antone
Lewis	Mabel M.	Catlin	D. Willis	Lin	Seo	Wing	Tong
Lewis	Maretta E.	Ford	Fred J.	Lind	Alma B.	Kahrs	Leander A.
Lewis	Margarite	Zgiaggen	Paul Leo	Lind	Marion E.	Flagg	Rollo E.
Lewis	Martha A.	Nichols	B. T.	Lind	Nina C.	Nelson	James
Lewis	Mary Elisabeth	Mee	Thomas H.	Lindemenn	Sarah B.	Heryford	James W.
Lewis	Mildred Marie	Brayton	Leon Conway	Lindenmeyer	Jeanette O.	Heckendorf	August J.
Lewis	Nannie May	Dinmore	Walter Robert	Lindley	Hannah Melba	Finch	Gordon Wilbur
Lewis	Nellie	Wise	H. Edmund	Lindley	Lillian Leah	Ridley	Norredden Algernon

Lindsay	Edna P.	Hardin	Lexter B.	Litchfield	Martha Irma	Sparkes	William
Lindsay	Mary	Peterson	Manuel	Litchfield	Mary E.	Martin	Frank M.
Lindsey	Estella Blanche	Packwood	Laurel E.	Litchfield	Sophie E.	Scammon	Alexander E.
Lindsey	Georgiana	Comstock	George F.	Littell	Nellie, Mrs.	Mac	M. B.
Lindsey	Margaret Jane	Coleman	John E.	Little	Beatrice G.	Murrel	Sylvanus B.
Lindsy	Coney Gunda	Hancorn	Walter T.	Little	Marie L.	Schmidlin	Martin A.
Lindsy	Phoebe	Huntley	George W.	Littlefield	Mary A.	Williams	Charles Henry
Lineard	Louise I.	Jacquot	Alexander C.	Littlejohn	Dellphine	Treibig	L. G.
Linebarger	Marinda, Mrs.	Brannum	Caswell	Littleton	Mae	Sieberberg	Saul
Linebaugh	Anna G.	Moore	Harold S.	Litton	Mary L.	Laughlin	Joseph W.
Linebaugh	Kate, Mrs.	Bell	Henry	Litton	Nita	Quick	Claud E.
Linebaugh	Mae Olivia	Church	Royal Ira	Lituanio	Marie B.	Belluomini	Matteo
Linebaugh	Mary Jane	Lowe	Dawson	Livemach	Mary F.	Ingalls	John C.
Linebaugh	Olivia Fay	Hall	Oliver Perry	Livernash	Elizabeth A.	Koenig	Frank
Linebaugh	Sarah E.	Parrish	David F.	Livernash	Margaret Theresa	Modini	James Laurence
Lines	Lulu	Dilges	William	Livey	Elizabeth	Wiscarver	Joseph R.
Lingenfelter	Lucy	Gardenshire (?)	S. B.	Livey	Mary	Hammel	Chas. P.
Lingg	Louisa H.	Guder	William C. O.	Livey	Sarah V.	Gill	James W.
Linklitter	Mary F.	Wynn	John	Livings	Flora Estella	Lapum	Oscar Edwin
Linkogel	Ledona Beatrice	McMahan	Grover Cleveland	Livingston	Katherine Rock	Cole	William Lester
Linney	Mary Mabel	Terwilliger	Jesse W.	Livingston	Minnie H.	Hardin	Henry
Linscheid	Emma A.	Old	Robert H.	Livingston	Teresa	Roe	Charles C.
Linscott	Belle	Postel	Carl	Lloyd	Edith VanAllen	Rechoine (?)	Sanford Lee
Linscott	Hazel	Lawson	Ivan G.	Lloyd	Emma	Dennison	Ezra D.
Linton	Fannie V.	Stay	John C.	Lloyd	Emma May	Linebaugh	Robert A.
Linville	Ada	Wisecarver	Thos. J.	Lloyd	Hattie F.	Jessup	Charlie W.
Linville	Lizzie	Wisecarver	J. L.	Lloyd	Irene Mildred	Theobald	Beverly Wescoe
Linville	Pemelia	Munday	Martin E. C.	Lloyd	Julia M.	Schow	Andrew
Lipe	Ina	Armstrong	Roy V.	Lloyd	Kate	Oliver	John S.
Lippitt	Lois Genevra	Proctor	Alexander Henry	Lloyd	Mary Jane	Percival	W. C.
Liscomb	Florence A.	Goddard	Albert D.	Lobdell	Ella	Philpott	William E.
Lisignoli	Marie C.	Crotyogini (?)	Battista	Lobdell	Lily Mae	Nowlin	Ande
Litchfield	Anna M.	Hunt	William C.	Locan	Rubie	Tully	Andrew J.
Litchfield	Cora L.	Hotle	Charles E.	Locatelli	Teresina	Locatelli	Luigi
Litchfield	Laura B.	Coltrin	Hugh C.	Lochetti	Veginia	Rizzi	Luigi

Lock	Mary F.	Cummins	W. E.	Long	Agnes E.	Healey	Joseph M.
Lock	Phebe	Cummins	J. L.	Long	Annie May	Robinson	Nelson
Lockard	Ruby	Barry	Garland	Long	Edna	Hudelson	Warren S.
Locke	Alice	Chartrand	Louis	Long	Evelyn Irene	Roussan	Fred E.
Locke	Beryle Evelyn	Grove	Clarence	Long	Hattie Irene	Dana	Martin V. B.
Locke	Ethel M.	Crist	Henry A.	Long	Lucy A. M.	McWilliams	Eslie B.
Locke	Isadore	Warren	Benjamin F.	Long	Mary A.	Velasco	Joseph A.
Locke	Sadie E.	Wells	Edward E.	Long	Mary Alice	Stone	John H.
Locke	Veravuche (?)	Dibble	Walter	Long	Mary E.	Ross	Harry B.
Locke	Vina?cke	Dibble	Walter	Long	Mary E.	Long	Charles H.
Lockley	Susie	Case	J. W.	Long	Maud R.	McIlwain	Alexander
Lockley	Susie E.	Case	John Wyatt	Long	Minnie A., Mrs.	Lambert	Richard
Lockman	Ella Ray	Allen	Gilbert W.	Long	Hazel Gertrude	Heitz	Frederick Charles
Lockwood	Alice	Brown	Manuel J.	Longo	Mary Florence	Follini	Louis
Lockwood	Beulah M.	Bower	G. N.	Longsine	Addie M.	Wirts	John W.
Lockwood	Cora B.	Brown	Edward A.	Longuet	Louise	Fieux	Constant
Lockwood	Linnie Katherine (?)	Frazee	Henry Dewitt	Longwell	Ethel V.	Robinson	Walton H.
				Loofbourrow	Fern M.	Wallace	Marshall M.
Lockwood	Linnie, Mrs.	Beckner	William S.	Loomis	Nancy	Walker	Fred T.
Lockwood	Mary	Fish	George	Loomis	Ruth Viola	Senteney	Douglas Lester
Locsen (?)	Amelia	Frank	Samuel	Looney	Addie	Bostwick	N. W.
Lodge	Hazel K.	McClish	James B.	Looney	Alice	Jacobs	George
Lodge	Lillian	Stoker	Bert E.	Looney	Curvera M.	Doty	Albert
Loe	Dorothy E.	Byers	Thomas Homer	Looney	Ethel	Ferguson	O. J.
Loe	Elvira R.	Mitchell	James H.	Looney	Laura	Heinrich	Frank A.
Loeffler	Dora	Smith	W. C.	Looney	Mary Elizabeth	Young (?)	James Hiddy (?)
Loeleliz (?)	Susie	Case	J. W.	Looney	Nellie	Macy	William C.
Loenthal	Gertrude W.	Silberman	P. H.	Loop	Amelia	Opfer	Frank A. S.
Logan	Adelia	Corbin	Warren	Loosley	Bonnis	Buchanan	James A.
Logan	Emma C.	Beeson	E. I.	Looson (?)	Ann M.	Fortier	Louis
Logan	Harriet	Laird	H. Spencer	Lopes	Mary L.	Mora	Antone
Loggie	Vida Rebecca	Riley	Earll Thomas	Lopez	Domingo	Sherman	George
Lombardi	Lillien B.	Murray	Elmer J.	Lopus	Evelyn F.	Thorson	Albin T.
Lombardo	Mary Agnes	Spingola	Anthony Lionel	Lopus	Minnie	Giaconini	Americo
Lonergan	Helen Catherine	Ormerd	Lawrence Wellington	Lorenzen	Pauline	Reorden	Eschel Fredrich

Lorenzini	Louise	Giusti	Alfred	Lowrey	Minnie	Fowler	Nicholas R.
Lotriz	Roselia	Shearman	Daniel	Lowry	Jennie	Charles	Isaiah B.
Lottritz	Elizabeth B.	Apiarius	Palmer H.	Loyan (?)	Annie	Blanchard	Frank
Loubier	Louise	Goldspring	Samuel	Loyd	Lillie May	Gilliam	Samuel Jackson
Loucks	Kate Myrick	Baltzell	Alfred	Lozzori	Rosa	Ferroni	Louise
Loughead	Maggie	McNamara	Bernard	Lubas	Marie J.	Boyd	Noah M.
Loughlin	May Ella	Ramos	Andrew	Luby	Mabel E.	Cole	Francis M.
Louk	Katie	Kirkpatrick	Virgil	Lucas	Edna W.	Bruns	Richard F. C.
Lounibos	Annie	Chauvet	Henry J.	Lucas	Leta A.	Conger	Harry E., Jr.
Lourdeaux	Aline	Mouyer	Louis	Lucas	Metta	McCutchan	Fred E.
Loury	Mary	Ford	Barnett	Lucas	Pauline	Eagleson	Welcome E.
Love	Lou Donie	Banton	Belva	Lucas	Ruena Louise	Willett	Frank James
Lovejoy	Jennie L.	Spotswood	Robert H.	Lucchesi	Elvira Rosa	Bianchi	Attilio
Lovejoy	Lillian A.	Stafford	Nelson O.	Lucchesi	Pauline	Damario	Damacati
Lovejoy	Mary M.	Camero	Nathan	Lucchetti	Isabel	Parducci	Adolph
Loveland	Inez Lillian	Locke	Augustus Caldwell	Luce	Carrie	Rios	Benito
Loveland	M. J.	Hansen	Rufus	Luce	Isabella	Tracey	Edward R.
Lovell	Lena Myrtle	Smith	Thomas Theodore	Luce	Jennie D.	Coffman	James T.
Lovell	Mary Jane	Wentworth	Ira Martin	Luce	Marie Antoinette	Mothorn	Pressley Perry
Lovell	Maud	Osborne	William S.	Luce	Mary E.	Day	William B.
Lovell	Sarah	Lovell	John M.	Luce	Mary Elizabeth	Ross	Kemp L.
Lovera	Josephine Clara	Perrari	Frank	Luce	Nina M.	Rose	Guy
Low	Sarah A., Mrs.	Cassel	Wm. F.	Lucero	Lena	Ramos	Manuel
Lowe	Annie	Meagher	Thomas	Luchetti	Maria	Pachinni	Paris
Lowe	Jennie E.	Jones	George H.	Luckenbill	Elise	Muff	John
Lowe	Jessie	Trimble	Herbert	Luckenbill	Sophia	Peutz	Peter H.
Lowe	Teresa, Mrs.	Black	Samuel	Ludmann	Sophie	Glaser	Albert Ludwig
Lowens	Loretta S.	Shattuck	Byron S.	Ludwick	Elma	Lorenze	Albert D.
Lowery	Jennie	Harrington	Daniel	Ludwig	Christine H.	Westlake	Percy W.
Lowery	Mary	Fawcett	S.	Ludwig	Katy	Anker	Neal
Lownes	Mary	Daniels	H. A.	Ludwig	Mary	Neilson	Neils
Lowrey	Cerillda (?)	Gerald	James Thomas	Luebberke	Clara F.	Butler	Samuel Reed
Lowrey	Elizabeth F.	Anderson	Oscar E.	Luebberke	Dora	Keyes	John M.
Lowrey	Florence E.	McAllaster	Fred Shelby	Luedke	Mae Florence	Daniels	George Eaton
Lowrey	Helen W.	Elton	Arthur M.	Luerssen	Alice, Mrs.	Upton	William E.

Luiebberke	Flora	Monte	Tiziano	Lynch	Frances A., Mrs.	Jones	Joseph C.
Lukas	Emilie	McCawley	Lucien E.	Lynch	Maggie	Cornwell	F. J.
Lukas	Emma M.	Bradlee	Arthur S.	Lynch	Mary Stasia	Griesheimer	Charles
Lukas	Lavana Ruth	Leggett	Raford Wesley	Lynch	Tillie	McClellan	Albert R.
Luker	Vesta G.	Williams	William W.	Lynden	Sylvia Vallejo	Cobos	Norberto B.
Luman	Anna Mai	Hill	William C.	Lynn	Florence I.	Reed	Plerry (?) W.
Luman	Mary A.	Hodgson	W. H.	Lynott	laura B.	Williams	Harry
Lumsden	Elizabeth R.	Gillett	C. W.	Lyon	Ada	Pauli	Albert F.
Lumsden	Fannie L.	Bonner	Chas. D.	Lyon	Ada May	Phariss	John B.
Lumsden	Martha Louise	Gamble	Charles Elmer	Lyon	Grace	Thomas	William Edward
Lund	Anne M.	Wilford	Severa L.	Lyons	Helen	Brand	William H.
Lund	Annie L.	Bonward	P. N.	Lyons	Henrietta	Abrott	Fred Henry
Lund	Ovina Sicretta	Heitzel	David	Lyons	Julia E.	Phariss	John B.
Lund	Tove	Stretton	John	Lyons	Maggie E.	Schutte	William Henry
Lundan (?)	Rose	Metzzer	Alfred E.	Lysnar	Edith E.	Lippitt	Frank K.
Lundholm	Esther Leone	Bauer	Ernest William	Lytaker	Anna	McCann	George
Lundholm	Lydia	Cook	De Roy	Lyttaker	Emma M.	Hargreaves	Thomas W.
Lunt	Addie R.	Chapman	Edwin A.	Lyttaker	Irene	Salvador	Anthony M.
Luscher (?)	Marie G.	Hughes	Floyd B.	Lyttaker	Lenora	Casassa	Frank A. J.
Lusetti	Florence	Pianetti	Pio	Lyttaker	Martha M.	Cameron	Charles L.
Lusk	Kate	Johnson	William	Maack	Lily	Frese	Henry
Lussier	Minnie I.	Larson	Sven	Maas	Helene	Joosten	Fred W.
Lutgen	Irene C.	Watson	Ben C.	Mac	Mabel E.	Gregory	Bion S.
Luther	Mary F.	Rishel	William H.	Macartny	Annie, Mrs.	Young	James F.
Lutrario	Maria	Rossi	Rafael	Maccabe	Hilda Susanna, Mrs.	Dupont	Joseph
Luttrell	Florence June	Padula	James L.				
Luttrell	Leita Lorine	Kammeyer	Erich M.	Maccano	Mary	Catelani	Leonori
Luttrell	Ruth M.	Holmes	Ovid	Maccario	Angelina	Toscani	Antonio
Lutzenhizer	May	Williams	Charles J.	Maccario	Katie	Gasperi	Pietro
Lyman	Francian V.	Martin	Russel Sage	MacCaskie	Alice Jane	Deremer	Fred Richard
Lyman	Kate	Guptill	William H.	MacCaskie	Effie	Searcy	George E.
Lyman	Owa (?) E.	Lyman	James H.	Macdonald	Helen Gertrude	Boyd	John
Lynch	Amy	Ross	Benjamin	MacDonald	Nellie M.	Mize	Frederick
Lynch	Elizabeth F.	Huittmann	John O.	MacDonald	Vestina	Luney	William
Lynch	Ella Louise	Haigh	Robert Charles	MacFarlane	Susie W.	Batchelor	David William

MacGregor	Jessie C.	Howland	Gardiner G.	Maebury	Eva Kenworthy	Hampton	William
MacGregor	Mabel C.	Leffler	Herman V.	Maestretti	Claire	Ricci	Joseph
Machada	Catarina	Silva	Frank	Maestretti	Dena M.	Brugge	George E.
Machada	Maria F.	Silva	Carlos	Maffia	E. Milia	Poncia	Martin
Mache	Minnie L.	Morenzoni	Joseph	Maffioli	Catherina	Bordessa	Martin
MacIntosh	Sara	Hardy	Orlando B.	Maggetti	Carrie	Andrews	Walter J.
Mack	Amanda	Wilsey	David C.	Maggetti	Katherina	Scolari	Ernesto
Mack	Florine	Campigli	Albert E.	Maggini	Catterina	Marra	Battista
Mack	Ida	Eberling	C. W.	Maggio	Maria	Dapelo	Luigi
MacKenzie	Blanche	Knight	Reginald S.	Maggioro	Maria Della	Molinari	Giocommo
Mackey	Verda E.	Kuechler	Harold J.	Magnam	Anneta Estella	Mallory	Jacob T.
Mackie	Mary	Connoff	William John	Magnani	Eugenia M	Lindon	Harvey J.
Mackinnon	Grace May	Kelly	Michael F.	Magnani	Paulina Zita	Brunh	Ernest Roy
Maclath	Mary M.	Jackson	Amos	Magner	Ophelia	Stump	Arnold B.
MacLeod	Florence Clara Bell	Tuttle	Lauren Taylor	Magnuson	Mae L.	Nicholas	Ciero V.
				Maguire	Ann Loraine	Holdsworth	Miles E.
Macomber	Pearl A.	Burns	John M.	Maguire	Ethel Adella	Moss	George W.
MacUrton	Ethel	Keller	Vernon E.	Mahan	Genevieve	Halkidis	Sam
Madden	Edith G.	Root	Harold Emile	Mahoney	Ella	Reedall	Thomas
Madden	Elizabeth	Billings	J. F.	Mahoney	Kathleen Cecelia	Taylor	William Joseph
Madder	Lizzie M.	Stafford	Edgar T.	Mahoney	Mary Agnes	Heil	Roy P.
Maddern	Sophia Elgin	Eby	Edwin Dayton	Maidenbaum	Lillian	Dublin	Isidore
Maddocks	Anna Katherine	Smith	Almon Edwin	Maine	Annie	Bargoloti	Louis J.
Maddocks	Erminia	Disher	William F.	Makee	Alvia C.	Jones	Alvie N.
Maddocks	Grace E.	Tredway	Sylvester G.	Malaney	Ella Nora	Finley	Robert
Maddocks	Helen Carter	Graves	Harry Thomas	Malaspina	Mary	Perotta	Ambrose
Maddux	Edith M.	Spindler	Harry A.	Malatesta	Eugenia	Tanner	Charles F.
Maddux	Gertrude E.	McCray	David W.	Malchow	Bertha	Hansen	Henry
Maddux	Lorette	Graves	J. H.	Malcolm	Catherine B.	Cohen	Harold J.
Maddux	Martha E.	Freeman	Wm. H.	Maldonado	Helen	Axley	John R.
Maddux	Martha E.	Current	Thomas David	Maley	Margaret G.	Odegaard	Oscar J.
Madeira	Lulu	Powell	Ransom	Malipeide	Rosie	Moore	Frank E.
Madeira	May F.	Truitt	Harry	Mallen	Kate F.	Long	D. W.
Mader	Constance Marie	Redner	Charles G.	Mallon	Bridget P.	Clark	John Thomas
Madsen	Emelie	Josephson	Frederick	Mallory	Beatrice Irene	Vier	Wm. Joseph

Mallory	Bertha V.	Pierce	Chester R. B.	Manion	Lulu	Taylor	Benjamin F.
Mallory	Edith M.	Kettlewell	Benjamin	Maniz	Cassie	Beach	Alva Frank
Mallory	Ethel S.	Pritchard	Arthur A.	Mann	Lulu	Dodge	Milton
Mallory	Hazel Florence	Barnes	Allen Percival	Mann	Ora	Hayes	Frank
Mallory	Margaret L.	Fishel	John E.	Mann	Embie (?)A.	Bomemann	Arthur F.
Mallory	Nina Leonna	Duncan	Sebastian	Manning	Ella J.	Folks	Charles
Malogani	Sereno	Magatelli	Antonio	Manning	Ellen Ida	Galindo	Joseph Vincent
Malone	Annie E. C.	Sullivan	John R. E.	Manning	Evelyn L.	Kennedy	Floyd
Malone	Edna M.	Siegrist	Frank D.	Manning	Mary F.	Mathews	Alfred F.
Malone	Ellen M.	Goss	John	Manning	May Frances	Wilson	R. L.
Malone	Rosabell K. L.	Wakeland	Walter L. R.	Mansfield	Carrie M.	Ragin	Frank A.
Maloney	Nora, Mrs.	Valerga	Joseph	Mansfield	Maude	Cook	George
Maloney (?)	Kate E.	Stewart	John	Mansfield	Ollie	Pegram	N. J.
Maloof	Margaret Virginia	Simpson	Philip Alan	Mansson	Helen Susanna	Sundstrom	Peter
Malouf	Fifie	Hoster	William S.	Mantle	Susie L.	Mellette	Randolph H.
Malpiede	Angeline	Belli	Harry Alfred	Manuck	Minnie	Lager	Phillip
Malugani	Caterina	Paroli	Antonio	Manuel	Florence I.	Cutter	Ephraim M.
Malugani	Martina	Marci	Jerunoz	Manville	Minnie E.	Mayfield	George W.
Man	Henrietta M. C.	Weske	W. Adolph	Manzaga	Josephine	Pedranti	Theodoro
Manchester	Vieva Florence	Florence	Arthur	Mapel	Belle	Maple	Geo. M.
Mancini	Liduina	Chiappero	Domenico	Mapel	Reba A.	Wilson	Robert J.
Mandarini	Guiseppina	Bertossi	Carlo	Mapes	Leora	Briggs	Hanley
Mandler	Katie	Wedde	Charles M.	Mapes	Annita G.	Garloff	John A.
Maney	Josephine Mason	Hill	Dolph Brice	Marall	Amelia E.	Pollard	Lewis N.
Manfredi	Angela	Paolinelli	Adadino	Marall	Annie C.	Peterson	Carl S.
Mangers	Ester May	Kreutzberg	Robert	Marall	Christine M.	Leach	John W.
Mangili	Mary, Mrs.	Falvey	Dennis	Marango	Verlie Elden	Burton	George Walter
Mangis	Lola E.	Bradley	Byron B.	Marble	Estilla L.	Rose	Charles L.
Mangis	Nora E.	Burke	Abner L.	Marchant	Ethel	Baird	Fred E.
Mangold	Frederika	Meese	Henry	Marcies	Secelia, Mrs.	Robb	James M.
Mangole	Pauline	Frank	Christian	Marcucci	Angelina	Maffei	Italo
Manier	Fanny	Woolley	William C.	Marcucci	Ida	Caretto	Pete
Manin	Mary Ellen, Mrs.	Crow	Edward	Marcucci	Iris Marie	Massei	Guido
Manion	Edith L.	Bates	Vernon G.	Marcucci	Jennie Mary	Church	William Thomas
Manion	Lillie B.	Wheeler	Pleasant D.	Mardon	Alta	Itter	William Henry

Mardon (?)	Nellie	Patteson	Charles L.	Marshall	Grace A.	Havenstrite	Reed C.
Marenghi	Mary	Mergo	Charley	Marshall	Ida May	Groshong	Hal Willard
Marin	Hannah, Mrs.	Tilson	Lemuel R.	Marshall	Irene P.	Maddocks	Fred W.
Marin	Hermina	Asher	Charles Lewis	Marshall	Jennie S.	Clark	James Wesley
Marinoni	Rose L.	Oliveri	Edward	Marshall	Josephine	Cross	F. G.
Marion	Louise E.	Wagoner	Leroy E.	Marshall	Lillian B.	Dorman	William E.
Maritzen	Florence Otilla	Christensen	Harry Edward	Marshall	Lizzie	Snedaker	E. H.
Markell	Helen I.	Baer	Reuben E.	Marshall	Lottie B.	Grewell	E. D.
Markell	Mary J.	Swindell	Joel A.	Marshall	Louise, Mrs.	Nobles	Harmon
Markell	Sarah A.	Baer	Geo. B.	Marshall	Mabel	Hills	Winford G.
Markham	Bridgie A.	Noonan	William C.	Marshall	Marian	Norton	Edward M.
Markham	Sarah J.	Noonan	Henry	Marshall	Mary Alice	Farmer	John H.
Markham	Susan	Gossman	John	Marshall	Mary I.	Lucero	Gilbert E.
Marks	Lena	Borges	George Louis	Marshall	May	Albrecht	Charles
Markwood	Mary F.	Ragan	Thomas C.	Marshall	Sarah A.	Cochran	A. E.
Marmori	Katie	Carter	Albert	Marshall	Sarah J.	Nobles	Harry A.
Marmori	Luigia	Borgo	Filippo	Martell	Lillian L.	Richards	Thomas J.
Marmori	Stella	Maloney	James	Martens	Elise Emma	Speaker	William Melvin
Maroni	Mary	Capitani	Michele	Martensen	Jenny	Petersen	Fedder Nicholas
Marron	Nellie	Deevy	Daniel J.	Martia (?)	Carolin H.	Poppe	Charles J.
Marsh	Adeline J.	Gray	Alvin A.	Martignoni	Rosa	Capella	James C.
Marsh	Dora E.	Cannon	Chester G.	Martin	Alma	Koster	James
Marsh	Kittie	Noyes	Elmer E.	Martin	Amy	Luce	Chas. F.
Marsh	Lulu May	Head	Robert Calvin	Martin	Anna	Scanlan	Jerry J.
Marsh	Mamie	Pacheco	Manuel A.	Martin	Annie Maria	Wyatt	Hiram Jet
Marsh	Myrtle S.	Vallier	Charles Henry	Martin	Augustina	Purisch	Frank
Marsh	Visalia May	Vote	Howard J.	Martin	Aurore	Marin	Louis
Marshall	Anna	Stockwell	M. W.	Martin	Dahmar	Jacobsen	Jacob E.
Marshall	Annette	Rayband	Joseph	Martin	Delphine C.	Patocchi	Benjamin J.
Marshall	Christina	Robertson	Jesse Joseph	Martin	Effie, Mrs.	Hulbert	Harry E.
Marshall	Clara	Fuller	Lyman T.	Martin	Elizabeth Graham	Zoppi	Walter Americo
Marshall	E. E.	Lemos	J. F.	Martin	Elizabeth, Mrs.	Barton	John W.
Marshall	Effie L.	Brunning	John H.	Martin	Ella A.	Gwyn	George P.
Marshall	Elizabeth Ann	Johnson	L. M.	Martin	Ella, Mrs.	Watt	Charles L.
Marshall	Florence B.	Gregory	Ernest Bernhardt	Martin	Emma R.	Earhart	William H.

Martin	Erma	Wallace	Edward		Martin	Rose	Strider	George B.
Martin	Estella M.	Cheney	Edward L.		Martin	Sarah Matilda	Marion	Angelo Nickoles
Martin	Fannie Susie, Mrs.	Curtiss	Thomas E.		Martin	Susie	Dillingham	John L.
Martin	Fanny	Richmond	Henry		Martin	Susie	Max	Albert
Martin	Harriet	Valentin	Joseph M.		Martin	Violet D.	Deu Vaul	Bert E.
Martin	Helen	Smith	Jasper		Martin	Minnie L., Mrs.	Wilson	Henry E.
Martin	Ida Mary	Hoyrup	Rasmus Nielson		Martina	Fontana	Regusci	Pietro B.
Martin	Ida May	Weiss	Frederick W.		Martineaut (?)	Josephine	Nickerson	Charles
Martin	Jennette	Baker	Jesse F.		Martinelli	Mary	Benelli	Joseph
Martin	Jennie	Cunningham	Hugh Ronald		Martines	Maria Lopes	Lopera	Rafael Riviera
Martin	Josephine G.	McHugh	George		Martinetti	Carmelina	Rossotti	Cristoforo
Martin	Laura E.	Stark	George W.		Martinez	Adoracion	Munoz	Mariano
Martin	Lauriana Vieira	Miller	Frans Oskar Gustafson		Martinez	Mollie I.	Anderson	Albert S. J.
					Martins	Libania Jason	Brown	Edward
Martin	Lena	Pedrotti	Faustino		Martz	Belle	Sherman	George W.
Martin	Leona	Bascom	Elmer		Marvin	Evalyne Lottie	Burtchall	Walter L.
Martin	Lita Adele	Sherrard	John Warren		Marzo	Matilda Clelia	Enfield	Joseph Louis
Martin	Lola Lee	Edwards	Clarence A.		Marzolf	Dorothy	Woodson	Jasper
Martin	Lucy	Bidwell	James		Marzoli	Margaret	Gobbi	John
Martin	Mabel S.	Campbell	Boyd		Masciorini	Erminia Agnes	Altenreuther	Leopold C.
Martin	Maria E., Mrs.	Webster	Alba		Masciorini	Florence J.	Petersen	Harold P.
Martin	Marie	Guy-Perret	Andrew		Mascoinini	Lily	DeCarli	Bathista
Martin	Mary E.	Heatly	George O.		Masey	Vesta, Mrs.	Blair	F. M. D.
Martin	Mary Minnie	True	Marvin Edward		Mason	Annie E.	Dudley	W. S.
Martin	Mary, Mrs.	Rudolph	Otto		Mason	Centennia	Emenegger	Frank
Martin	Mathilde	Barnett	Stanley		Mason	Clarice	Vogt	William C.
Martin	Mattie	Webber	Henry C.		Mason	Clarrisa	Mathisen	Henry
Martin	Meron	Shadle	Henry		Mason	Eva	Morris	Walter
Martin	Mildred Mae	Marr	Clyde H.		Mason	Lenna	Avery	Howard
Martin	Millie M.	Caughey	Robert		Mason	Mary Adeline	Thomas	Harry Raymond
Martin	Minnie H.	Hoberg	Arthur O.		Mason	Mary C.	Kunz	George E.
Martin	Nellie	Butts	Alfred		Mason	May Augusta	Green	Robert Franklin
Martin	Nellie	Smith	Albert Perry		Mason	Rossaline L.	Maher	William M.
Martin	Rebbeca Marilla	Gregory	John Shattuck		Mason	Tressie B.	Jackson	Frank
Martin	Rosa	Olsen	Martin		Mason	Violet Belle	Brady	Howard

Massa	Clara	Cook	Levi F.	Matthews	Grace E.	Townsend	James H.
Massoni	Eda	Scatena	Fred	Matthews	Helen	Albright	James O.
Massoni	Laurina	Belli	Ostaguio	Matthews	Ina Marguite	Craig	Albert James
Masten	Helen	Banks	George	Matthews	Jerenia E.	Chitwood	James M., Jr.
Mastin	Mary L.	Meyers	Charles F.	Matthews	Mary E., Mrs.	Townsend	William
Mastrup	Anna Sophia	Brady	William Franklin	Matthews	Mildred May	Vogensen	George
Mastrup	M. Sophie	Haus	Fred C. H.	Matthews	Myrtle	Kelly	James P.
Masvik	Hanna	Christopher	Irvine T.	Matthews	Sarah Francis	Smith	James
Mathe	Marie	Gregoire	Louis	Matthias	Frances L., Mrs.	Gookins	Ernest James
Matheson	Nina R.	Luce	Jirah	Mattison	Mary	Jepsen	Peter
Mathews	Amanda	Chase	Charles Edwin	Matus	Lena	Maloof	John
Mathews	Asentha Vera	Ellsworth	Percy Leland	Matzen	Dora	Evans	Arthur B.
Mathews	Evelyn M.	Questo	Melvin P.	Matzen	Ella	Marcus	Carl Ralph
Mathews	Evy	Masher	John Ed	Matzen	Hannah P.	Obanion	Howard L.
Mathews	Laura	Burris	Luther W.	Mau	Evelyn M.	Paul	George A.
Mathews	May	Dabner	Manuel	Mauch	Katy, Mrs.	Gunther	Frederick A.
Mathews	Salina	Beeson	Isaac R.	Mauch (?)	Matilda Dorothy	Hall	George Herbert
Mathis	Maude	Purcell	Edgar	Maule	Lucinda, Mrs.	Lindner	John D.
Mathis (?)	Emma	Martin	Milo (?)	Maule	Sarah E.	Woodworth	Wm. D.
Mathisen	Ingeburg M.	Frederiksen	Andreas	Maupin	Olive Pearl	Leedy	Chester Clyde
Mathison	Ida E. J.	Martin	John	Mauregard	Marguerite	Lalanne	Louis
Matos	Margarete Etelvena	Brazil	Manuel M.	Maxwell	Eliza B.	Reid	Cornelius
				Maxwell	Elizabeth Belle	Huffman	Daniel
Matos	Mary S.	Pera	Jerry	Maxwell	Lillian J.	Kemler	Andrew C.
Matos	Minnie L.	Malof	John	Maxwell	Mary E.	Darrow	John O.
Matson	Emma M.	Olufs	John H.	Maxwell	Ollie V.	Brown	Charley
Matson	Tinne M.	Petersen	Lorenz	May	Delia A.	Johnson	William A.
Mattaini	Mae Isabel	Menefee	Roderick E.	May	Emily	Willett	Raymond V.
Mattei	Julia	Soldate	Joseph	Mayer	Emily	Colvin	Thomas Floyd
Mattei	Sephina	Greppi	Sylvester	Mayes	Ethelyn Lorena	Hall	George Morrill
Matteri	Marie	Poncia	John	Mayes	Louisa Ellen	Scott	Winfield
Matteucci	Florence	Baitano	Fortunato	Mayes	Pearl Adelaide	Newnham	Albert
Matthews	Edna	Green	Harvy	Mayes	Violetta Verna	Raymond	Elmer Comstock
Matthews	Ella, Mrs.	Adamson	Isaac Newton	Mayfield	Flora	Marsh	Robert Linus
Matthews	Frances B.	Johnson	Geo. A.	Mayfield	Gussie B.	Boyd	Sloan

Mayfield	Maud	Ahl	John	McBrown	Marie M.	Leavenworth	Randolph J.
Maynard	Eva E.	Faribanks	Joseph Frank	McCall	Annie Rice	Thurow	Ameil
Maynard	Grace A.	Nelson	F. Victor	McCallum	Marguerite	Turpin	Frank
Mays	Cora E.	Stump	Charles E.	McCampbell	Sue B.	Perry	Charles B.
Mays	Helen J.	Kirkland	Henry B.	McCann	Eva Theresa	Cahill	James Morden
Mays	Mary E.	Travis	W. W.	McCann	Lerda	Schaumberg	Earnest
Mays	Mattie H.	Blake	John R.	McCann	Rosa E.	Underhill	John L.
Mays	Rilla L.	Coster	George J.	McCanse	Margaret F.	Montgomery	Elmer J.
Mayse	Mary E.	Miller	E. H.	McCappen	Jennie	Bell	Grant
Mayshark	Stella N.	Esslinger	John A.	McCappin	Ellen	Wheeler	Henry Albert
Mazota	Lillie	Ewing	James E.	McCappin	Lavina E.	Grant	Francis E.
Mazza	Angelina M.	Beretta	Angelo P.	McCappin	Ruth Olive	Burke	Claude E.
Mazza	Josephine	Morelli	Antonio	McCario	Minnie	Blackly	Frank E.
Mazza	Louisa	Cattanep	Louis P.	McCarren	Rita H.	Carey	William F.
Mazza	Nilda	Saleme	Raid E.	McCarthy	Edyth Davis, Mrs.	Orr	William Jackson Thomas
Mazzolini	Clementina	Bondietti	Frank				
Mazzoni	Lena M.	Baiocchi	Guido F.	McCarthy	Julia L.	O'Connor	Peter L.
Mazzucchi	Giovanna	Matteri	Peter	McCarthy	Maggie	Brown	Charles A.
Mazzucchi	Giuseppina	Matteri	John	McCarthy	Maggie E.	Schlusser	Martin E.
Mazzucchi	Theresa E.	Brandt	August J.	McCarthy	Margaret	Wells	Ralph
Mazzurchi	Angiolina	Mazzoni	Peter	McCarthy	Tillie	Maxwell	William
McAbee	Hazel N.	Guernsey	Fred R.	McCaughey	Edith	McCown	Albert E.
McAfee	Georgie L.	Gale	Archie R.	McCaughey	Mabel	Cunningham	Wm. N.
McAffery	Helen Agnes	Pancoast	Joseph Lester	McCausland	Amy	Bower	J. Elmer
McAlister	Maggie	Sheldon	Oliver Proctor	McCawon (?)	Caroline	Singley	Frank B.
McAlister	Martha Ann	Knapp	Charles Houry (?)	McChristian	Andra L.	Richardson	John Mead Stanley
McAlpin	Edith S.	Bose	John Edward	McChristian	Delphine G.	Frates	Joseph V. A.
McAlpine	Alice M.	McHugh	John	McClancy	Isabella M.	Cronin	Joseph A.
McAndrews	Winifred	Smith	Fred E.	McClanny	Josie	Swailes	Charles
McAskill	Margaret J.	Comstock	Leslie F.	McClary	Bella	Evans	E. R.
McBee	Fetnie A.	McPeak	Mathew A.	McClellan	Elizabeth L.	Huntington	Harry E.
McBride	Eleinor	Ward	Milton B.	McClellan	Mary E., Mrs.	Baker	Samuel S.
McBride	Elizabeth May	Frost	Harvey Chester	McClellan	Minnie	Goldsmith	Edwin S.
McBride	M. E., Mrs.	Stine	William H. W.	McClellan	Ruth	Gashwiler	L. F.
McBrown	Jenevive	Beggs	William P.	McClellan	S. F., Mrs.	Hasting	Fletcher D.

McClelland	Clara	Hembree	Atlas T.	McCorkle	Mary M.	Johnston	Wm. F.
McClelland	Ella	Welch	F. T.	McCormick	Alice	Kreiss	Frederick W.
McClish	Anna	Thurman	James A.	McCormick	Carrie J.	Smith	Frank J.
McClish	Ella N.	Flack	John A.	McCormick	Flora A.	Stiles	S. A.
McClish	Florence	Brigham	George H., Jr.	McCoubrey	Josephine Eva	Arnold	Floyd Hilton
McClish	Jennie C.	McCracken	Frank B.	McCoubrey	Nettie	Evans	William P.
McCloskey	Ida	Derham	Herbert	McCowen	Mary Louise	Cunningham	Frank Michael
McCloud	Rose, Mrs.	Howland	Thomas A.	McCown	Mary E.	Tibbetts	Gilman B.
McCloy	Irene M.	Williams	Herbert G.	McCoy	Carrie	Beggs	William John
McClure	Arabelle	Briggs	Paul C.	McCoy	Cora	Baxter	Arthur W.
McClure	Emma	Dobel	William L.	McCoy	Dollie	Kuykendall	James O.
McClure	Ethel Dorothy	Welcer	Henry Louis	McCoy	Olive Lee	Pendergast	John J.
McClure	Frankie Ethel	Taylor	Albert Ross	McCracken	Catherine	West	John H.
McClure	Leadith J.	Story	Grover M.	McCracken	Edna E.	Archer	Claud H.
McClure	May	Cunningham	John G.	McCracken	Effie Elizabeth	Nosler	Omer Howard
McClure	Neva	Kenneally	William Joseph	McCracken	Elizabeth M.	Stibi	Paul
McCollough	Amy Leah	Severy	Delmer Elton	McCracken	Emily G.	Archer	Horace E.
McCollough	Mary	Belati	John	McCracken	Louisa	Howard	John B.
McCollum	Jennie	Petty	Frank P.	McCray	Amanda	Buffett	Chas. C.
McCollum	Sarah M.	Phillips	Albert J.	McCray	Bertha A.	Williams	Oliver C.
McCombs	Jessie Frances	Petrie	Maynard J.	McCray	Emma E.	Conners	Alexr F.
McCombs	Luetta A.	Kruse	Fred G.	McCray	Etta	Stuart	William Alvin
McCombs	Nellie D.	Chadd	George H.	McCray	Kate A.	Winter	John D.
McCombs	Leanna Jewel	Collins	Eldorado	McCray	Mary Alta	Siemer	William
McConaghy	Annie N.	Bonnet	Robert A.	McCray	Minerva	Shaw	Isaac E.
McConihe	Ethel M.	Marlatt	Charles E.	McCrea	Anna Bell	Strong	William George
McConkey	Retta May	Stockstill	George F.	McCready	Carrie	Finley	Jefferson
McConnell	May	Swain	Arthur B.	McCready	Laura T.	Black	Martin L.
McCord	Gladys	Talkington	Robert O.	McCreagh	May	La Bossure	Louis
McCord	Henretta	James	Charles G.	McCrimmon	Mildred A.	Wemmer	Albert F.
McCord	Lois L.	Van Deveere	Clyde E.	McCubbin	Elizabeth	Rome	Paul
McCord	Mary E.	Wohrden	Otto Nicholas Thom	McCulloch	Dora Barham	Noble	Ralph Weyman
				McCulloch	Eva	Landree	Roy
McCord	Ora Anna	Toney	George W.	McCumiskey	Florence	Bertolani	Angelo L.
McCord	Ruby D.	Hunkins	Lyle D.	McCurrie	Madeline E.	Ingraham	Edgar

McCutchan	Minnie May	Hall	Adolphus Warren	McDorley	Mary U.	Heafey	John J.
McCutcheon	Elizabeth	Johnson	Gus Charles	McDougall	Annie	James	R. L.
McCutcheon	Hazel Genieveve	Douglas	David W.	McDougall	Louise	Kelso	Edgar Clayton
McDaniel	Emma U.	Ballard	Benjamin F.	McDowall	Mary	Watson	John A.
McDaniel	Olive L.	Bower	Bertram H.	McDowell	Elsie	Kuster	Gerhard
McDermott	Flora A.	Benson	August	McDowell	Hazel E.	Kolb	Clifford A.
McDermott	Marie L.	Macdonald	Leonard C.	McElhany	Florence	Hendricks	J. W.
McDonald	Birdie Ella	Noriel	Zenas	McElhany	Olive E.	Ernest	Albert J.
McDonald	Cora A.	Plum	William L.	McElroy	Luciuda	Skinner	Arthur Tapin
McDonald	Dora D., Mrs.	Kimball	Heman A.	McEwan	Maggie	Lockie	James S.
McDonald	Edith M.	Chamberlain	Selah	McFadyen	Isabel	MacKay	William
McDonald	Elizabeth F.	Wilkinson	John E.	McFarland	Amelia	Brain	William H.
McDonald	Erma Eunice	McGavin	William	McFarland	Dora M.	McGarr	Frank
McDonald	Etta Elizabeth	Stratton	Edward L.	McFarland	Hazel Belle	Towner	Verne Bennett
McDonald	Faith	Hunt	Avery G.	McFarland	Maggie D.	Taylor	Washington H.
McDonald	Flora	Hodgson	Richard	McFarland	Margaret	Canevascini	S. J.
McDonald	Georgia	Stark	Ulysis S.	McFarland	Mary	Garrity	Thomas
McDonald	Helen Maud	Wilson	Thomas William	McFarland	Mary Udel	Noble	Hugh M.
McDonald	Isabelle	Lamay	Alfred	McFarlane	Elizabeth Robina	Langlois	Robert Franklin
McDonald	Jessie F.	Garloff	William F.	McFarlane	Leonore May	Boden	Jack
McDonald	Josie	Hiatt	Charles	McFarlane	Mellie M.	Shanks	Robert M.
McDonald	Joy Bernice	Nielsen	Carl William	McFarlin	Lottie V.	Morse	Harry S.
McDonald	Lillian	Crawford	Russel D.	McFarling	Ethel	Rose	George Washington
McDonald	Mabel	Hamilton	William H.				
McDonald	Maggie E.	Turner	Andrew V.	McFarling	Eva J.	Berkman	James H.
McDonald	Martha	Cowan	Edward	McFarling	Gertrude L.	Pitkin	Charles Addron
McDonald	Mary	Barlow	Richard Wright	McFarling	Jessie M.	Bobst	Richard M.
McDonald	Mary E.	Brooks	Charles Wesley	McGah	Mary E.	Burns	Robt. W.
McDonald	Mary Elizabeth	Monroe	Harold H.	McGahan	Fannie Agnes	Smith	Belden Burt
McDonald	Mary Jane	Howell	George	McGaughey	Fannie G.	Martin	Edgar
McDonald	Mary R.	Cushman	Zacheus (?)	McGaughey	Maggie, Mrs.	Prewett	George W.
McDonald	Phila F.	Wilcox	Frank	Mcgear	Kathleen	Solander	Stewart
McDonnell	Florence Evelyn	McCord	Charles	McGee	Kate	Gillett	Martin
McDonnell	Louise	Decker	Frank William	McGill	Minnie	Fulkerson	Chas. A.
McDonnell	Nellie	Hood	Alexander	McGimsey	Etta Gladys	Shaw	Harry Barrett

McGimsey	Marie M.	Clement	Jesse Edward
McGinnis	Mary	Mason	William H.
McGinsey	Alta	Pauli	Roy A.
McGleshan	Fannie H.	Williams	Jessie E.
McGlynn	Alice A.	Johnson	James E.
McGlynn	Catherine L.	O'Connor	Patrick Francis
McGoldrich	Mary T.	Keenan	Peter
McGonagill	Eunice R.	Heintz	Victor F.
McGovern	Annie Lauretta	Dickson	Frank Maurice
McGovern	Carollynne	Olmquist	John L.
McGovern	Clara Josephine	McMullen	Russell McGarvey
McGowan	Daisy Fedora	Adams	Darwin C.
McGowan	Maggie	Farley	Henry
McGowan	Phoeba, Mrs.	Wells	Pleasant
McGrath	Mary	Hickey	William A.
McGregor	Agnes, Mrs.	Knack	Frederick
McGregor	Edna	Wood	George L.
McGregor	Loella Rea	Burch	George Alexander
McGrew	Irma Merle	Witham	William
McGrew	Lovila A.	Hill	Charles N.
McGrew	Rosella	Hamilton	Charley S.
McGrew	Ruby L.	Collins	Howard J.
McGuire	Mary Elizabeth	Roberts	William Thomas
McGuire	Mary Jane	McCarthy	David A.
McGuyre	May	Hickey	Jerry D.
McHall	Mary Ellen	McGuire	Jacob
McHarvey	Mary	Lee	Rollen M.
McHarvey	Sadie	Cordill	Lewis C.
McHarvey	Wilhelmina	Smith	G. McBride
McHeary (?)	Tammy A.	Chuny (?)	J. M.
McHorney (?)	Mary	Stewart	Horatio N.
McHugh	Bertha E.	Dedmond	Edward F.
McInerney	Isabel M.	Dickerson	George E.
McIntire	Mary L.	Gallagher	Edward H.
McIntosh	Annie	Moore	Robert W.
McIntosh	Clara	Johnson	James
McIntosh	Emma	Estes	Frank H.
McIntosh	Mary Ellen	Legg	W. H.
McIntyre	Ella F.	Minkel	William J.
McIsaac	Wilma C.	Williamson	William C.
McKay	Isabella	Donegan	William
McKay	Margaret	McSweeney	Daniel
McKean	Mary, Mrs.	Mateson	Hans
McKean	Muriel A.	Plum	Claude
McKee	Hattie Bailey	Morrow	James
McKeen	Florence L.	Siemsen	William Jacob
McKenna	Maggie	Hamlin	Charles J.
McKenna	Mary	Vickerson	George G.
McKenzie	Anna M.	Thatcher	Walter R.
McKeown	Alice M.	Sinclair	Carl E.
McKeown	Margaret	Dempsey	Patrick
McKinney	Artie	Otterson	Jack S.
McKinnon	Gertrude E.	Franklin	Benjamin
McKinzie	Eliza Jane	Hocking	James
McKoon	Mary	Winter	Gilbert
McKoon	Vernett	Sink	Wilbert M.
McLain	Agatha F.	Gleason	Leo H.
McLain	Lavina B.	Fitzpatrick	Lawrence F.
McLain	Marjorie Lewis	Chase	Louis Walter
McLaren	Eugenie	Carlisle	Herbert L.
McLaughlin	Kate Theresa	Dowd	George William
McLaughlin	Mary	Murphy	Wm. A.
McLaughlin	Mary T.	Mangili	Henry G.
McLean	Agnes Bertha	Thomas	Robert Franklin
McLean	Ella A.	Madeira	George Madison
McLean	Katie G.	Kruse	August W. T.
McLeod	Amy	McDowell	Wm. J.
McLeod	Cassie, Mrs.	Thompson	Benjamin
McLeod	F. M.	Hollister	George C.
McLeod	Louisa E.	Tevendale	George M.

McLeod	Margaret	McGuyre	William	McNabb	B. M.	Keir	Sherwin
McMahon	Celia E.	Price	William R.	McNabb	Jessie I.	Ayers	Omar
McMahon	Gertrude	Brooks	Walter	McNally	Ella	Kingman	Ralph Elmer
McMahon	Lulu A.	Scoville	Gilbert L.	McNally	Mary A.	Lane	Walter J.
McMahon	Maggie	Guinnar	David Andrew	McNalta	Delia	Becker	W. F.
McMahon	Margaret	Coykendall	Chauncey B.	McNamara	Lydia E.	Willard	Charles A.
McMahon	Rose	Brosnahan	Terrance F.	McNamara	Mary E.	Sullivan	Frank A.
McMannus	Eunice E.	Gwynn	Edward	McNamara	Nora	Rudd	Joseph
McMartin	Mary J.	Garvey	John F.	McNamee	Lenora Margarete	Mann	Ned Frase
McMeans	Alabama	Boggs	Geo. W.	McNear	Clara	Leppo	David Harrison
McMeans	Helen S.	Connor	Edward H.	McNear	Louise	Naffziger	Howard C.
McMeans	Mary Alice	Coman	Robert Grimes	McNear	Miriam	Korbel	Leo V.
McMellon	Mary S.	Gross	Harry B.	McNeeley	Eva	Kruse	James H.
McMenamin	Rosa	Lowary	Joseph F.	McNeil	Minnie Clara	Alten	Wendell
McMichael	Eula	Caughey	Alexander	McNeil	Myrtle Adell	Maas	William George
McMichael	Sofrona Elizabeth	Porter	Benjamin McKindree	McNeill	Bertha L.	Reihl	August C.
				McNeill	Ida E.	Green	Lewis E.
McMillan	Clestia M.	Nelson	Carl G.	McNeill	Viola	Myers	Henry
McMillan	Lena Alice	Scharf	Samuel Joseph	McNeill	Cora D.	Small	Herbert
McMillan	Leonora	Bradbury	Edward A.	McNew	Orpah Belle	Frazier	Elisha H.
McMillan	Sarah Jane	Tuly	William	McNiel	Sarah E.	Terschuren	William
McMillan	Theodora S.	Tiedeman	Claus H.	McNutt	Edith L.	Tennant	Troxel Leroy
McMillen	Cora	McLaren	Richard	McPeak	Dora	McKinney	John H.
McMillen	Gertrude	Ross	George	McPeak	Edna Carl	Luce	George Liddle
McMillen	Helen Martha	Gibson	Herman W.	McPeak	Hattie E.	Allen	D. B.
McMillen	Lillie	Storem (?)	George	McPeak	Jennie	Torrance	J. T.
McMinn	Clara J.	Collins	William A.	McPeak	Minnie	Misener	Albert F.
McMinn	Etta	Foltz	Edward P.	McPeek	Mary I.	Lawrence	James W.
McMinn	Mary Frances	Mayes	John H.	McPhearson	Malinda	Hayes	Jacob
McMinn	Mary M.	Hardin	Lester B.	McPhee	Kattie	Kauffman	John
McMinn	Rosa	Marr	John A.	McPherson	Hazel	Allen	George A.
McMullen	Margaret	Harmon	Charles Reuben	McPherson	Mamie	Shiver	Joseph F.
McMullen	Minnie F.	Hobson	Jerome C.	McPherson	Mary	Patteson	Ezekiel
McMullin	Sara J.	Ragsdale	Bertrand	McPike	Edith G.	Argoud	Alfred L.
McMurtry	Mary M.	Swan	Francis	McQuade	Anna	Jamieson	James

McQuade	Celia	Osborne	Thomas James	Meek	Mary L.	McCutchan	George F.
McQuaid	Louise Delvigne	Orvis	Charles Wilton	Meek	Tina O.	Hawes	William R.
McQuart	Emily	Johnson	Otto H.	Meeker	Clara E.	Jackson	Harry E.
McQuiston	Kate	Petersen	Sheridan	Meeker	Iola	Goodfellow	Lyle C.
McReynolds	Delia	Johnson	David E.	Meeker	Maud L.	Wiley	Warren D.
McReynolds	Emma R.	Upson J. or Z.	Sylvan	Meeker	Maurine A.	Shelley	Louis A.
McReynolds	Lizzie	Guidotti	Giovanni	Meeker	Winifred M.	Frellson	Oscar August
McReynolds	May Violet	Donner	John Carter	Meeks	D. C., Mrs.	Hayward	J. B.
McReynolds	Ruth F.	Hart	Jack E.	Meeks	Sarah L.	Miller	James P.
McReynolds	Susie M.	Stevens	John E.	Meghan	Fannie M.	Devine	Patrick
McReynolds	Virginia	Givens	Archibald Wills	Mego	Jennie Angelia	Haskins	Elmond Sterling
McSherry	Mary	Clifford	John	Mehegan	Margaret U.	Maghetti	Henry A.
McTarnahan	Addie, Mrs.	Fowler	Nathaniel D.	Mehl	Wilhelmina	Stoeckle	William Paul
McVean	Martha M.	Liddle	William S.	Mehlhorn	Martha	Arguello	Alexander
McWilliams	Edith T.	Bruner	Clement M.	Meiling	Bertha M.	Schlener	Carl
McWilliams	Edna Alice	Ballou	Albert L.	Meiller	Hattie	Vandevere	Ralph
Meacham	Elvira F.	Cameron	Donald C.	Meineri	Adelaide	Mentasta	Giovanni (John)
Mead	Alice C.	Hall	Clarence C.	Meineri	Edith A.	Leva	Leo Frank
Mead	Iva H.	Rogers	Howard D.	Meisner	Hattie	Ingham	Arthur Cleveland
Mead	Jenevieve I.	Allison	Jay J.	Melbourne	Lillian	Yandle	William J.
Mead	Susie E.	Atherton	Albert W.	Meldrum	Rachael	Doyle	Fred R.
Meade	Bertha L.	Steinbach	Hermann Reinhard	Melehan	Anna E.	Ayers	Robert B.
Meade	Edna	King	Cecil Ray	Melehan	Ella Gertrude	Childers	Dennis Spencer
Meador	Bertha P.	Rowe	James W.	Melehan	Mae J.	Howard	Frank M.
Meador	Leanora	Henshaw	George M.	Meliza	Opal	Shively	John Edwin
Meador	Nannie	Armstrong	George R.	Melley	Delia	Wollner	William
Mecchi	Mary	Gaspari	Julius	Mellington	Leoleon S.	Ingerson	Lewis Nelson
Mecham	Loretta	Hinkle	H. C.	Mello	Christina	Vier	Manuel
Mecham	Mary I.	Fritsch	Walter S.	Mello	Mamie G.	Perry	Harry W.
Mecum	Alice L.	Houghton	Grover C.	Melson	Josephine	Huntoon	J. R.
Medeiros	Anna	Forcha	Catano Jose	Melson	Mary Ann	Kendall	Albert Kuy (?)
Medeiros	Victoria Gloria	do Rego	Francisco Theodoro	Melton	Elizabeth A., Mrs.	Annis	Wm. O.
				Melvin	Annie, Mrs.	Schmidt	Peter
Medland	Florence F.	Call	Clyde C.	Menary	Kate G., Mrs.	Meeker	Stephen A.
Meek	Mary E.	Rickman	George Thomas	Menary	Mary Katherine	Gamboni	William Robert

Menary	Matilda J.	Hope	John B.	Messner	Irma Seynhaeve	Sholz	Paul G.
Mendenhall	Carrie P.	McPeak	William H.	Metcalf	Amanda P.	Peterson	Columbus
Mendenhall	Florence	Button	Eugene R.	Metcalfe	Mary M.	Cranwford	James A.
Mendenhall	Lola I.	Baago	Edmund A.	Metzler	Alba	Silverthorn	Milo E.
Mendoco	Laura	Decco	Henry	Meyer	Anna	Conrad	Charles Francis
Mendonca	Mary Frances	Healey	Earl F.	Meyer	Annie Dora	Cottle	Harold Bertrand
Mendosiz	Fara	Garcia	Felix	Meyer	Caroline L.	Miller	George R.
Menefee	Emma	Berry	W. P.	Meyer	Catherine B.	Schott	Franklin T.
Menefee	Marinda I.	Knowles	D. C.	Meyer	Clara	Shorey	James Milton
Menefee	Sarah Bell	Meyer	George Homer	Meyer	Doris	Brody	Sam
Menefee	Victoria	Judsen	George Franklin	Meyer	Dorothea	Sumner	Edwin M.
Menges	Lizzie	Sherman	Ulysses Grant	Meyer	Dorothy S.	Laumann	Frank E.
Menighan	Mary P.	Armstrong	M. V. B.	Meyer	Elizabeth	Carrillo	Manuel
Menihan	Gertrude	Hearfield	Harold H.	Meyer	Elizabeth G.	Seed	William Henry
Menihan	Margaret	Woodward	Elmer D.	Meyer	Francis M.	Crawford	Harry F.
Menne	Mary	McAfee	Vernon	Meyer	Ida E.	Smith	R. Press
Menow	Virginia L.	Brockmann	Henry M.	Meyer	Josephine	Enz	Albin
Mercer	Elizabeth	Gerstley	M. Louis	Meyer	Julia T.	Hughes	Alfred G.
Mercer	Eula	Trine	Oliver P.	Meyer	Lilly R. S.	Ferguson	W. R.
Mercer	Simi	Cockrill (?)	Thomas Jefferson	Meyer	Lula L., Mrs.	Porter	William P.
Merchant	Vena Christine	Sears	William W.	Meyer	Marguerite	Bower	William G.
Meredith	Anna Lee	Thomas	Charles R.	Meyer	Mary Josephine	Dupont	Albert
Meredith	Blanche P.	Kimes	Walter H.	Meyer	Rosa	Harhoe	Christian
Meredith	Gladys L.	McAnally	Robert W.	Meyers	Addie	Kenneally	James
Meredith	Helen L.	Tovani	Fred A.	Meyers	Bessie R.	Elliott	Carter W.
Merrick	Eleanor Dorothy	Dodson	William Howard	Meyers	Carleen Marie	McNally	Raymond Gregory
Merrill	Barbara M.	Turner	Angus D.	Meyers	Florence	Wright	Adam
Merritt	Ida J.	Benson	Nathaniel W.	Meyers	Hazel M.	Driver	William W.
Merritt	Many A.	Hickey	Maurice	Meyers	Lorene Emeline	Ellis	Arthur Clarence
Merritt	Mildred Maurine	Parmelee	Lester Vernon	Meyers	Rose	Baley	George Moses
Merritt	Minnie E.	Ingram	Charles L.	Meyers	Sussie	Martin	John M.
Merryfield	Kittie	King	John F.	Meyling	Freda M. E.	Hammermann	George B. G.
Messerle	Nellie	Anderson	Oscar	Mezger	Ethel Irene	Siegel	George
Messerle	Rosa	Massler	George	Michael	Emma A.	Farmer	George
Messing	Rebecca	Morris	Henry	Michaels	Kate	Flohr	Charles W.

Michaels	Mae A.	Campbell	James J.	Miller	Charlotte E.	Parnell	Eben H.
Michaelsen	Mary W.	Klintworth	Edward	Miller	Christina A.	Riebli	Arnold B.
Michaid	Mary, Mrs.	Bledsoe	Isaac	Miller	Cora E.	Fisher	Theodoric L.
Michalake	Barbara M.	Fish	Clarence P.	Miller	Daisy M.	McMillen	John J.
Michalini	Corina	Maffei	Luigi	Miller	Edith Maria	McDonald	William
Micheli	Pia	Micheli	Adamo	Miller	Effie C.	Leard	Robert B.
Michelsen	Agusta	Clark	James H. H.	Miller	Elizabeth	Meyer	Lorenz
Michelson	Magdalene	Peterson	Carl L. C.	Miller	Ella L.	Howe	Joseph
Mickle	Clara A.	Doering	Julius	Miller	Elma Finetta	Smith	George Edward
Middleton	Emma	Milty	Nicholas	Miller	Emily Theresa	Vincent	John Adolph
Middleton	Tilly	Butler	A. B.	Miller	Emma	Buher	Florentin
Middogh	Myrtle	Dickson	David Simms	Miller	Emma	Brooks	George
Migliano (?)	Elizabeth	Bacon	Herbert Wm.	Miller	Emma C.	Johnson	Peter S.
Mignimi	Maria	Balzari	David	Miller	Emma Estella	Baker	Louis Alexander
Mikalier	Isabel	Snyder	James W.	Miller	Emma J.	Thornton	David, Jr.
Milano	Felicita	Savio	Alexandro	Miller	Emma O.	Williamson	Jesse C.
Milano	Teresa	Borziny	Bob	Miller	Esther A.	Courtney	Willard J.
Miles	Lilly B.	Pfeifer	Frederick C.	Miller	Eva Mabel	Edwards	Clarence Alvin
Miles	Mary	Gater	J. E.	Miller	Fawn	Perigo	William
Milford	Ellen M.	Fulmer	James S.	Miller	Florence Emily	Dutcher	Steve Joseph
Millard	Addie F., Mrs.	Dunlap	Joseph B.	Miller	Georgia A.	Peck	Jerome A.
Millard	Carrie G.	Hewett	Clyde A.	Miller	Grace P.	Nystrom	Alfred John
Miller	Alice D.	Scott	Aaron H.	Miller	Hattie E.	Carey	Edward J.
Miller	Alice E.	Stubbs	Edward J.	Miller	Hazel	Blakesley	Franklin C.
Miller	Alice L., Mrs.	Gray	Clarence A.	Miller	Henrietta	Chenoweth	Frank B.
Miller	Amelia	Huff	Henry J.	Miller	Irena B.	Ballard	S. E.
Miller	Annie Wickershaw	Fine	Alex	Miller	Jane, Mrs.	Creagh	Michael
				Miller	Josephine	Grogan	Spencer Jordan
Miller	Bertha	Donovan	Jeremiah C.	Miller	Julia	Ryerson	Reason S.
Miller	Bertha	Groskopf	Albert	Miller	Julia	Johnson	David A.
Miller	Bertha	Reynolds	Scott L.	Miller	Kathleen	Van Fleet	Clark C.
Miller	Beulah G.	Lance	Ora L.	Miller	Laura E.	Barlow	Thomas E.
Miller	Birdie E.	Cnopius	Lewis C.	Miller	Lena	Riebli	Joseph
Miller	Blanch	Vesper	David William	Miller	Lizzie J.	Rodehaver	Geo. W.
Miller	Celia	Wildemann	Johannes G.	Miller	Lois	Lindstrom	Charles Otto

Miller	Louise H.	Purrington	S. W.	Miller	Nancy C.	Hayworth	Ruben F.
Miller	Louise Sunderhouse	Bowman	William Frederick	Millerick	Helen E.	Jensen	Creston H.
				Millerick	Mae E.	Guernsey	Louis E.
Miller	M. Ruth	Patteson	Keith O.	Millerick	Mary	Minahan	William T.
Miller	Margaret	Micheli	Charles	Millett	Nettie J.	Atwater	Edwin L.
Miller	Marion C.	Foster	H. G.	Millingtin (?)	Ollie	Linebaugh	Abraham
Miller	Martha E.	Bohan	Michael	Millington	Anna E.	Clark	Charles E.
Miller	Martha M., Mrs.	Miller	James M.	Millington	Bessie M.	Helton	William A.
Miller	Mary Alice	Ragle	Alexander	Millington (?)	N. M.	Dunn	William A.
Miller	Mary E.	Peterson	Peter	Millman	Mamie L.	Faber	H. Charles
Miller	Mary E.	Butler	Charles H.	Mills	Anna Margrett	Johnstone	Thomas Henry
Miller	Mary E.	Ferguson	Henry O.	Mills	Blanche B.	Cameron	Alan F.
Miller	Mary J.	Berry	Samuel B.	Mills	Catherine Aileen	Wright	Andrew Frederick
Miller	Maud	Brooks	James	Mills	Effa	Espey	George M.
Miller	Maud Irene	Smith	Walter E.	Mills	Emma	Stone	Louis S.
Miller	Maud Marie	Priestley	Frank Louis	Mills	Esther Faye	Taber	John Slattery
Miller	Maude	Whitaker	Mark S.	Mills	Ethel Mabel	Park	William Ellsworth
Miller	Maude	Walgamot	E. J. T.	Mills	Eva	Walk	J. J.
Miller	Minnie	Kivett	David W.	Mills	Gertrude	More	E. R.
Miller	Minnie	Silver	Joseph	Mills	Grace F.	Robertson	Lawrence A.
Miller	Minnie D.	Levy	Robert	Mills	Lucy O.	Pells	Edward O.
Miller	Mrs., Leona	Williams	Charles A.	Mills	Martha Pauline	Duane	Edward A.
Miller	N. E.	Richards	W. E.	Mills	Minnie E.	Stump	Davis Morrow
Miller	Nannie	Michael	George W.	Mills	Ora Anna	Graham	Monon
Miller	Oliva B.	Emrick	George W.	Mills	Sadie	Moller	Henry, Jr.
Miller	Rae	Knutsen	Isaac	Mills	Sadie Florence	Mayers	Irving
Miller	Rosa A.	Behmer	John	Mills	Winifred Alice	Garcia	Agopito P.
Miller	Rosanna	Shiach	D. J.	Millsap	Amanda Jane	Clanton	Thomas D.
Miller	Ruth M.	Muchway	Peter S.	Milne	Hazel A.	Shire	George F.
Miller	Sadie L.	Atkinson	Joseph	Milne	Laura	Benepe	Selden C.
Miller	Sarah A.	Hall	Luke	Milton	Elizabeth May	Middagh	John R.
Miller	Sarah B.	McMillen	Hiram	Minasco	J. Lee, Mrs.	Allman	Joe Peter
Miller	Sophie	Kuhn	Michael	Minch	Marguerite W.	Jones	Seth W.
Miller	Velma Pearl	Willock	Martin Lloyd	Ming	Jennie Woo	Lum	Tsai Yan
Miller	Maggie E., Mrs.	Alten	Pete	Minick	Viola E.	Coutts	John

Minkel	Martha	Cook	William W.	Mize	Vivian Elaine	Spangenberg	Ernest J.
Minkle	Amelia L.	Greaver	Andrew J.	Mizer	Sarah P.	Hart	David B.
Minor (?)	Jessie Irene	Waters	Herbert Joseph	Mizer	Sarah P.	Lynch	James M.
Minter	Lydia W., Mrs.	Shriver	Nathan	Mobley	Anna Dorothea	Magee	Thomas Wm.
Minto	Carrie	Skaggs	Alexander	Moch	Willie Ann	Rawles	Alexander N.
Minto	Ive Pearl	Feldmeyer	Wm. B.	Mock	Julia A.	Neil	Washington
Minto	Mabel	Witschey	Louie	Mock	Margaretta	Hunt	Joseph H.
Miramontes	Genevieve E.	Riley	George N.	Mockel	Anna	Engelland	Detlef
Miramontes	Marie Leanor	Follows	Jack Apperley	Modeste	Julia Charlotte	Archibald	Edward Joseph
Miranda	Lee	Covey	Harmon	Modini	Mary	Beretta	Angelo
Miranda	Mary	Decarli	Antonio	Modino	Angeolina	Sanguinetti	C. B.
Miranda	Pilar L.	Soeder	Leon S.	Moes	Anna Mary	Bee	Louis
Miser	Hannah	Frampton	Charles E.	Moes	Ernestine	Dinucci	Adolph
Mitchel	Sarah	Miller	Henry H.	Moes	Rosa M.	Anthony	William Jas.
Mitchell	Bertie	Overton	Theodore T.	Moldenhauer	Milea	Berndt	Paul
Mitchell	Elisabeth	Mosna	John	Molf	Minnie, Mrs.	Masa	Joe
Mitchell	Ella V.	Stone	Charles M.	Moll	Emilie	Tuomey	Thomas Bernard
Mitchell	Emma E.	Byers	William A.	Moll	Eugenie Sophie	Siebricht	Max
Mitchell	Florence F.	Winsby	Richard C.	Moll	Julie Frances	Sibley	Edward Franklin
Mitchell	Florence L.	Gould	James A.	Moller	Georgine N.	Chambers	David M. C.
Mitchell	Lela Irene	Sayre	Burt Genung	Moller	Thora A.	Jamieson	Daniel J.
Mitchell	Malinda A.	Wall	William Thomas	Molleston	Catheline	Bledsoe	W. O.
Mitchell	Margaret E.	Laughlin	Glen P.	Molleston	Mary Emma	Perkins	Bishop
Mitchell	May A.	Moore	Harvey	Molloy	Minnie	Norton	L. A.
Mitchell	Susan	Marshall	Joseph Gilbert	Molseed	Sarah	Perry	F. O
Mitchell	Trasey, Mrs.	Snider	John Eugene	Monahan	Florence	O'Rourke	James C.
Mitchener	Katherine	Short	F. B.	Monahan	Mamie L.	Carpenter	S. E.
Mitler	Mary E.	Percival	Richard	Monahan	May Elizabeth	Haley	James Lewis
Miyamoto	Shina	Horita	Katsuki	Monck	Euphenia	Peck	Auguste F.
Mize	Adeline N.	Mize	Frederic	Monghette	Angealina	DeMartini	Mansueto
Mize	Amanda	Moore	Geo. W.	Moniz	Marie Eugenia	Maderous	Antone
Mize	Irene Viola	Weinland	H. A.	Moniz	Marion Ursala	Enos	Manuel Joseph
Mize	Julia	Brittain	Norris	Monroe	Adalene S.	Converse	Gervase V.
Mize	Maria	Hawkins	Louis J.	Monroe	Annie	Shaver	Wesley
Mize	Mary	Henderson	Hardin W.	Monroe	Carrie May	Babcock	Kilbern J.

Monroe	Dora B.	Carter	Robert L.	Mooney	Rachael Bertha	Benson	Benjamin James
Monroe	Florence Irene	Wiseman	Richard	Moore	Alta	Moniz	Tony G.
Monroe	Jennie E.	West	Guy H.	Moore	Amanda	Ford	Michael
Monroe	Lois	Clay	E. W.	Moore	Amy L.	King	John
Monroe	Madalene	Morrison	John M.	Moore	Annie	Samules	Thomas M.
Monroe	Mary E.	Coomes	Albert M.	Moore	Annie A.	Price	Charles O.
Monroe	Ora Ethel	Parrish	George Edward	Moore	Belle	Finney	Clarence
Monroe	Rosa Nell	Rogers	Emmet Philander	Moore	Bertha E.	Smith	William J.
Monsees	Jessie L.	Jerden	Arthur G.	Moore	Catharine	Deakin	Henry C.
Monson	Alvine Mathilde	Dombrowski	Johann	Moore	Clara Rosalie	Sherriffs	George
Montague	Eleeta	Gensler	G.	Moore	Edna Junuita (?)	Peralta	Miguel Baldeugro
Montalon	Jeanne	Perelli-Minetti	Anton J.	Moore	Elizabeth	Moore	Thomas W.
Monteith	Marie Loomis	Hewlett	Lewis Clifton	Moore	Ella Jane	Fulton	James E.
Montgomery	Ambrosine	Davis	John H.	Moore	Ellen C.	Morrow	Thomas J.
Montgomery	Frances	Lane	Richard E.	Moore	Emily T.	Griffin	Gerald A.
Montgomery	Rose Bagley, Mrs.	Bradlee	Arthur Seawell	Moore	Essie B.	Buell	Park A.
Montgomery	Sarah	Griggs	Achilles	Moore	Eudora Emogene	Watson	John A.
Montgomery	Zimmie	Currie	Charles W.	Moore	Eva B.	Erving	Richard
Montgomery	Edwinnie	Crommett	Clyde Leon	Moore	Georgie L.	Rose	A. J.
Monticelli	Carrie	Wehrspon	William	Moore	Grace Mabel	Hanson	Hans P.
Monticelli	Emma	Marcucci	Oreste	Moore	H. C., Mrs.	Kirkpatrick	Josiah M.
Monticello	Sylvia C.	Blair	James K.	Moore	Helen E.	Descalso	James R.
Moodey	Rose C.	Hart	Jesse B.	Moore	Henrietta	Howard	James
Moody	A. M., Mrs.	Hubbard	Henry	Moore	Hope	Work	William B.
Moody	Clara J.	Irwin	A. W.	Moore	Huldie Jane	Copps	Willis
Moody	Frances M.	Nussbaum	Thomas W.	Moore	Iva H.	Winter	George Harry
Moody	Georgia C.	Witty	James F.	Moore	J. Maud	Jenkins	Joseph L.
Moody	Jessie Leona	Appleton	Willington	Moore	Jackie Dolores	Tunstall	Edwin Brueton
Moody	Viola	Kraus	Albert	Moore	Jessie Marie	Andrews	Admiral Leonadi
Moon	Carrie	Knock	Malcolm A.	Moore	Leola C.	Pozzi	Archie R.
Mooney	Anna J.	DeTurk	William S.	Moore	Lulie A.	Snyder	
Mooney	Edna	Gossage	H. S.	Moore	Lulu E.	Musselman	William T.
Mooney	Joan E.	Frei	L. A.	Moore	Margaret	Daggett	Mathew H.
Mooney	Mary Ellen	Brown	Robert Henry	Moore	Marguerita	Smith	Thomas M.
Mooney	Mary Tresa	Simi	Angelo	Moore	Marguerite	Aquistapace	Louis

Moore	Martha A.	Shamp	H. S.	Moretti	Irene	Demartini	Albert
Moore	Mary, Mrs.	Watson	C. N.	Moretti	Josephine	Vanoni	Julius
Moore	Maud	Peck	H. W.	Moretti	Linda M.	Tomasetti	Otto
Moore	May T.	Bertino	Thomas	Moretti	Marie Josephine	Thompson	Leslie Earl
Moore	Mollie	Odbert	Frank B.	Moretti	Rose	DeMartini	Louis
Moore	Nettie	Goodrich	Milford	Moretti	Stella I.	McDonald	William M.
Moore	Ollean	Phinney	Charles	Morey	Ellen C.	Workman	John
Moore	Ruby Freeman	Lauge	Walter Harry	Morey	Florence A.	Davidson	F. W.
Moore	Sarah	Gilliam	David T.	Morey	Mary A.	Thorne	Clifford L.
Moore	Sarah Inza	Lambert	Frank	Morgan	Alice L.	Phillips	Ambrose F.
Moore	Zilla C.	Lambert	Henry A.	Morgan	Eva L.	Foster	Joseph
Mooris	Ollie M.	Stouffer	Ira H.	Morgan	Grace E.	Lang	Henry A.
Moors	Pauline S.	Quast	Joseph C.	Morgan	Margaret	Stone	Walter G.
Mooser	Ynez E.	Weaver	Hart L.	Morgan	Marguerite M.	Cherry	Edwin E.
Moraga	Martena	Fitch	Joseph	Morgan	Mattie	Hankins	Samuel S.
Moran	Blanche E.	Garrison	James G.	Morgan	Maud Frances	Talbert	Ernest E.
Moran	Elenor Elizabeth	Bartlett	Fred	Morgan	Nellie W.	Adams	Robert L.
Moran	Florence B.	Decker	Elmer E.	Morgan	S. J.	Moore	C. A.
Moran	Jennie	Wallace	Samuel T.	Morgantini	Katherine M.	Sartori	Simin R.
Moran	Millicent Bertha	Russell	Archie McMarth	Morin	Bertha	Ticoulat	Fred
Moran	Vola B.	Minetti	Charles L.	Morledge	Marie B.	Veitch	Edward I.
Moranzoni	Edith A.	Lamb	George H.	Morley	Elsie K.	Niles	Lee Roy
Morby	Rhoda C.	Swanson	Carl Otto	Morley	M. J. , Mrs.	Hemphill	John H.
Morchio	Eva	Maloof	John	Morretti	Adelina	Patocchi	Olindo
Morchio	Argentina	Guidi	Ismaele	Morrill	Carrie F.	Dutcher	Burt W.
Mordecai	Frances Elizabeth	Foster	Joseph Walter	Morrill	Cassie F.	Dutcher	Burt W.
Mordon	Emma S.	Brooks	Thomas J.	Morrill	Julia Marie	Leathers	Harry Allison
More	Lena	Kline	S. R.	Morrill	Mary Francis	Bidwell	Albert
Morel	Mary Caroline	Gaberil	Manuel Joseph	Morris	Ada Louise	Zandreno	Angelo Gaspero
Moreland	Esther	Leithold	John V.	Morris	Anna	Ford	John
Morelli	Irene	Filippini	Achille	Morris	Anna M.	Koch	John J.
Moreschi	Maria	Maffia	Emilio	Morris	Annie	Mills	Edward C.
Moresi	Angela	Ghigliotti	Fred V.	Morris	Bessie	Meranda	Robert
Moretti	Candeda	Atkinson	William K.	Morris	Delia	Hill	Robert
Moretti	Elisa	Bellesi	Nestore	Morris	Eliza E.	Robinson	William D.

Morris	Emma Allice	Laymance	Henry J.	Mortimer	Anna May	McDonald	Alexander
Morris	Katherine Rice	McGimsey	John Milton	Morton	Carrie	Camron	John T.
Morris	Lavinnia	Rich	George D.	Morton	Dicie M.	Hall	Geo. A.
Morris	Leah Isabelle	Murry	John P.	Morton	Georgia Norene	Dannells	Walter Byron
Morris	Lenora C.	Talamantes	Patrick A.	Morton	L. Permilia Louisa	Morten	A. J.
Morris	Lizzie	McFarland	James	Morton	Lucille Ida	Tucker	Edward E.
Morris	Louie Eva	Andrews	Leslie Watson	Morzoni	Hazel M.	Platt	Charley W.
Morris	Mamie	Dutro	Joseph J.	Moschetti	Louisa	Reinero	Jos.
Morris	Marie L.	Cameron	Donald B.	Moseley	Ella M.	Snow	Philip H.
Morris	Mary C.	Philpott	James S.	Moseley	Lilly Olive	Kahler	William T.
Morris	Mary S.	Frates	Joseph W.	Mosely	Edith P.	Miller	James Z.
Morris	Elvin B.	Devlin	Thomas H.	Mosher	Ella	Herrmann	Ino
Morrisey	Margaret	Kavanagh	James	Mosher	Lucile Ruth	Kirwan	Thomas D.
Morrison	Alice	Swayze	Winfield S.	Mosman	Jessie M.	Gould	George F.
Morrison	Alice J.	Mullin	Edwin F.	Mosna	Anna	Benkiser	Fred
Morrison	Eliza A.	Howe	Baxter	Moss	Meta	Wilde	Louis
Morrison	Junietta	Butcher	Albert W.	Moss	Minnie P.	McDonald	Winthrop G.
Morrison	Katie May	Allan	Frank Walker	Mossi	Annie	Barangini	Charlie
Morrison	Lulu	Jahn	Henry	Mosure	Emma R.	Guenther	C. F.
Morrison	Mary Jane	Dunton	Oscar	Mothom	Claudia Alice	McClish	James Blaine
Morrison	Rosa E.	Staples	M. L.	Mothorn	Herma Booth	Jones	Alfred Benoia
Morrison	Violet	Faught	Jabez	Mothorn	Lizzie	Hinkelmann	Gustav
Morrow	Emma	Hewitt	Ernest E.	Mothorn	Lydia Rebecca	Nunn	Clarence Newton
Morrow	Ethel M.	Fairfield	William M.	Mothorn	Mary F.	Walters	James V.
Morrow	Isabel	Graham	Albert W.	Motroni	Dena	Dow	Archie
Morrow	Jennie	Alexander	John	Motroni	Filomina	Barsi	Santi
Morrow	Maria A.	Kern	Wm.	Mott	Ruth	Smith	Judson A.
Morse	Marie L.	Lamore	Joseph Verrell	Motti	Maddalena	Matteri	Paolo
Morse	Mary	Lenhart	Lee R.	Mouch	Grace	Speer	Harry C.
Morse	Mattie H.	Ong	E. Ralph	Mould	Ella E.	Murphey	John J.
Morse	Maude E.	Pemberton	Johnson W.	Mount	June F.	Ross	Arthur H.
Mortenson	Elizabeth	Rehder	Carl H.	Moxley	Alta R.	Brockelman	Ernest A.
Mortenson	Nellie	Smythe	Thomas A.	Moxley	Gladys Beulah	Edmunds	Clyde Jordan
Morter	Hattie	Jones	Charles H.	Moxley	Roberta Blanche	Milne	Henry Clinton
Morter	Matilda Ann	Wolfe	Avery M.	Moyer	Bertie	Shaw	Clarence

Moyer	Carrie S.	Brown	Rudolph M.	Mulvehill	Margaret	Clary	Dennis G.
Moyer	Eva	Groulx	Albert	Mumma	Lela Maude	Hedrick	Clyde Warren
Moyer	Sybil	Hart	Benjamin F.	Mumma	Marguerite Mae	Weber	Joe C.
Mudd	Althea Arline	Gratto	Frank Richard	Munday	Jessie	Becker	Roy D.
Mueller	Lizzie	Timm	Henry	Munday	Mabel	Allen	John F.
Mueller	Margaretta	Olesen	Christian H.	Munday	Verna Adelaide	Cornett	Ernest William
Muenzer	Bertha	Piezzi	Julius John	Mundkowski	Emma	Neumann	Anton
Mueting	Charlotte Rose	Arville	Archie B.	Munro	B. F.	Macphail	John R.
Mugarrieta	Victoria	Shadburne	G. D., Jr.	Munro	Emily A.	Cooley	Mayberry D.
Mugge	Louise Feltz	Hansen	Peter	Munro	Margaret J.	Adams	Arthur Joseph
Mugler	Frances Helen	Mugler	Albert Miller	Munson	Edith O.	Armstrong	William J.
Muir	Jaunita L.	Schubert	Peter Page	Muntzer	Madeleine	Templeman	John
Muirhead	Janet Irene	Parrish	David F., Jr.	Murbar	Clara	Gardner	Chas. M.
Mulgew	Josephine	Clemons	William L.	Murbar	Mae	Feehan	W. J.
Mulgrew	Cassie A.	Ward	John W.	Murbar	Mattie	Morehouse	J. W.
Mulkey	Bertine	Strebel	William	Murch	Jennie S.	Davis	Daniel O., Jr.
Mulkey	Galdys	Simoni	Albert Joseph	Murdock	Ella S.	Rogers	Will E.
Mull	Ellen	Durant	William	Muriale	Vincie	Peripollli (?)	Joseph
Mullally	Catherine E.	Jones	Patrick C.	Murk	Elizabeth Hazel	Wright	Charles Raymond
Mullen	Ellen	Haran	James	Murk	Mabel	Metcalf	John W., Jr.
Muller	Amanda Louise	Ives	Alfred	Murphey	Margarett L.	Loftus	William
Muller	Anna	Leachman	Ream S.	Murphy	Alice	Ridley	James F.
Muller	Anna	Zeh	Harry	Murphy	Catherine	Wagy	Benjamin Franklin
Muller	Babetta	Barth	Adolf	Murphy	Dorothy Marie	Muir	Guy Edward
Muller	Ethel	Reheiser	Alfred	Murphy	Florence M.	Carter	William A.
Muller	Josephine M.	Wright	Garrett D.	Murphy	Frances M.	Katz	Harry H.
Muller	Louise	Breiling	Alfred F.	Murphy	Francis	Kentzell	James
Muller	Margaret H.	Coggin	Clarence A.	Murphy	Hannah	McDevitt	Edward
Muller	Marie B.	Ketcham	Clarence S.	Murphy	Helen E.	Butler	James T.
Muller	Rose Helen	Flickinger	Andrew Grant	Murphy	Ida May	Grimmer	Louis
Muller	Bettina	Haley	Michael E.	Murphy	Irene R.	Fletcher	Harry A.
Mulligan	Ellen J.	Lay	Henry D., Jr.	Murphy	Jennie	Cameron	Russell L.
Mullikin	Arrilla J.	Marshall	Adam, Jr.	Murphy	Jennie R.	Adams	Merrit
Mulqueen	Lucy M.	Hinds	Loring D.	Murphy	Kate	Fletcher	John H.
Mulqueen	Mabel Park	Riechel	Olaf	Murphy	Lizzie Irene	Rue	Henry H.

Murphy	Mabel Mary	Jentzsch	Carl Waldemar	Myer	Priscilla G.	Dunn	Robert K.
Murphy	Madeline Marion	Dryer	Hiram George	Myers	Alice R.	McClelland	Robert Henry
Murphy	Martha Jane	Tomblenson (?)	Alexander	Myers	Annie, Mrs.	Nagle	Edward
Murphy	Mary Elizabeth	Lelinger	August C.	Myers	Bessie	Duncan	Clarence E.
Murphy	Minnie A.	Moore	Benjamin	Myers	Dora M.	Husler	Edward A.
Murphy	Myrtle	Lemaihe (?)	Louis	Myers	Emily	Kise	Philip
Murphy	Myrtle Violet	Gunn	Charles A.	Myers	Josie M.	Gordon	Frank W.
Murphy	Nellie Agnes	Foster	John Warren	Myers	Katie	Kise	Philip A.
Murphy	Sallie	Murray	Joseph	Myers	Phoeby	McMullen	John
Murray	Alice	Hellrich	Paul H.	Mynatt	Bettie, Mrs.	Bryant	Allen
Murray	Annie E.	McKinney	George B.	Myres	Susanna	Frost	G. W.
Murray	Bertie	Adcock	Samuel W.	Myrick	Eliza	Griest	Peter
Murray	Elizabeth D.	Goodbrake	Christian H.	Nagel	Alvina	Cooke	John Blucker
Murray	Eva	Allenden	Gerald	Nagel	Edna Viola	Hale	Leslie Ravone
Murray	Fodie L.	Hembree	Leon	Nagle	Helen Catherine	Mills	Roy Hudson
Murray	Frances M.	Paulson	Harry A.	Nalley	Ellen Mary	Quinan	Louie Sheppard
Murray	Lola	Clawson	Ardent Benjamin	Nalley	Marion	Kohl	Stanley E.
Murray	Lottie J.	Drake	George A.	Nally	Jennie M.	Daniels	Corel (?) J.
Murray	Louise E.	Zunino	William J.	Nance	Grace A.	Mack	John
Murray	Maggie	O'Brian	John	Nangeroni	Lettizia	Brovelli	Emilio
Murray	Mary	Casey	John	Napper	Maude Ethel	Long	William Lile
Murray	Maud M.	Jackson	Roy E.	Narcizo	Mary	Rodgers	William A.
Murray	Melinda O.	McGimsey	Charles L.	Naselli	Mary E.	Foss	Werner C.
Murray	Sarah M.	Whitney	Benj. P.	Nash	Emma	Schmidli	Joseph
Murroy	Mary R.	Johnson	John P.	Nathanson	Tillie D.	Rawson	Geo. C.
Mury	Elise	Firth	Christopher C.	Nau	Barbara E.	Goethe	William E.
Muschialli	Maria	Pelascini	Lorenzo	Nauert	Fredda	Cline	Thomas J.
Musselman	Frona	Eagleson	E. G.	Naughton	Annie	Miller	John W.
Musser	Edith E.	Lovinggood	Harmon G.	Naughton	Julia M.	Haw	Michael J.
Muthall	Bernice Josie	Keyes	Ralph E.	Navins	Mary	Bradley	Hugh
Muther	Daisy M.	Rockstroth	Frederick E.	Navoni	Johanna I.	Lytjen	Ludwig M.
Muther	Georgie M.	Dibble	Roland C.	Navoni	Lisandrina	Pacini	Francisco
Mutschlechner	Mary	Hollister	George S.	Nay	Abbie M.	Driver	Maurice Leon
Muzio	Olivia L.	Granucci	Frank	Nay	Martha A.	Jackson	Frank
Myer	Mary	Bardell	Luzius	Nay	Mary	Pabst	Roland Benson

Neal	Almatia	Nisson	Christian	Nelson	Mary	Madero	Alvin
Neal	Rita E.	Gartner	Charles Henry	Nelson	Mary E.	Geiorvas (?)	Pete D.
Near	Fannie F.	Twitchel	John E.	Nelson	Octavia R.	Zanazzi	Francis B.
Neardon	Mary A.	Nye	Everett C.	Nelson	Rose B.	Boswell	Ernest J.
Neasham	Anna Leah	Hougland	Ira A.	Nelson	Tekla B.	Beeson	Jesse R.
Needham	Grace	Edwards	David	Nelson	Thyra A.	Gallaway	Alfred J.
Needham	Maggie	Healey	Dennis J.	Nelson	Vera A.	McNeil	James J.
Neel	Jennie	Arfsten	William Arthur	Nelson	Violet	Kelley	George F.
Neely	Flossie F.	Starke	Earle E.	Nelson	Violet Rose	Huffman	James R.
Neergaard	Grace Lovell, Mrs.	Davis	Preston R.	Nerton	Mattie, Mrs.	Ives	Alfred
				Nervo	Remilda M.	Zanzi	Pietro
Neese	Nettie M.	Vanover	William E.	Nesbitt	Chetanna M.	Broder	Lee S.
Neff	Anna K.	Dornin	John C.	Nesbitt	Eva Elizabeth	Denham	Frank P.
Neil	Bell	Calderwood	Henry E.	Nessen	Ana	Mauck	Carl August
Neil	Francis E.	Bradford	Frank	Nettleton	Mabel Irene	Rea	Wilber A.
Nelby	Rose E.	Robinson	Norval A.	Neuendorff	Dora H.	Tolle	Henry G.
Nelsen	Alfena	Osmund	James S.	Neuman	Maggie	Caulfeild	W. Stafford
Nelsen	Emma G.	Gandy	Lemaul J.	Neuman	Sylvia, Mrs.	St. John	Clarence L.
Nelsen	Josepha	Elliott	Daniel	Neurauter	Mary	Usher	John W.
Nelson	Agnes	Muller	Martin	Neurauter	Agnes	Davis	Mack A.
Nelson	Alfreda F.	Stubbe	Fredrick William	New	Rose	Cook	William E.
Nelson	Alice M.	Hall	Walter W.	New	Charlotte Emily	Tunzi	Henry John
Nelson	Alzire	Dogge	Rudolph S.	Newbert	Byrdie Geneva	Boyd	Elmer
Nelson	Carolina	Simpson	Joseph R.	Newbert	Della	Lantz	George F.
Nelson	Christina	Igom	Julius Petersen	Newbert	Dorothy F.	Sawyer	Thomas A.
Nelson	Christine B.	Bjorman	Henry	Newbert	Margaret B.	Martin	Arthur J.
Nelson	Clara	Esaia	Bartholomew	Newbert	May	Rose	Rudolph
Nelson	Grace	Hess	Frank	Newcom	Lena, Mrs.	Crandall	Fred C.
Nelson	Hazel M.	Doss	Earl M.	Newcomb	Irene	Schnabel	Howard I.
Nelson	Irine Mae	Branern	William F.	Newell	Flossie Clair	Berlin	William Herman
Nelson	Jennie	Mullan	Felix George	Newell	M. A., Mrs.	Grant	Frederick
Nelson	Johanna	Ahlstedt	Gustave	Newell	Maude L.	Winkler	Edward C.
Nelson	Josephine Helmer	Poe	Charles Alfred	Newland	Maude L.	Gunn	George Lucius
Nelson	M. M., Mrs.	Capella	James	Newland	Vernie B.	Stover	James E.
Nelson	Margaret Anna	Poe	Edgar Allen	Newland	Winnie Jane	Stratton	Vernon Julian

Newlin	Laura D., Mrs.	Lavell	William T.	Nielsen	Else Christine	Matthiesen	Anton Ludwig
Newman	Bessie E.	Corfield	Thomas H.	Nielsen	Helene A.	Snoke	John Waldo
Newman	Esther H.	Fetterly	Charles	Nielsen	Hertha	Nelsen	Elmer J.
Newman	Marguerite F.	Carden	William Joseph	Nielsen	Lucy	Petersen	George
Newman	Nita Claire	Merrill	John L.	Nielsen	Marie	Bassett	William David
Newton	Jennie, Mrs.	McBee	Nathan	Nielsen	Mattie	McAllaster	Anson D.
Niblett	Metta B.	Cantwell	William L.	Nielsen	Sophia M.	Nielsen	Niels C.
Nichalson	Agnes Maye	Babcock	Joseph L.	Nielsen	Tine	Larsen	L. P.
Nicholl	Gertrude C.	Urban	Kurt	Nielsen	Violet	Chapman	Frank H.
Nichols	Agnes	Petty	Raymond D.	Nielson	Dorothy E.	Heitz	Frank
Nichols	Cynthia	Barnes	Ben H.	Nielson	Emma Marie	Etz	Arthur Kenyon
Nichols	Ida C.	Kelly	Mark P.	Nielson	Grace M.	Heitz	W. F.
Nichols	Lillian Edith	Koch	William B.	Nielson	Hazel	Walls	Sidney Everett
Nichols	Lois	Fidler	Joseph L.	Nielson	Helen Ione	Carr	Elgin Otto
Nichols	Marcia A.	Reed	William Freeman	Nielson	Lenora M.	Mello	William B.
Nichols	Sade Jane	Martin	Robert A.	Nieman	Kathe Else Adelhite	Wigington	John
Nichols	Sarah	Tanner	James				
Nichols	Sarah Margaret	McCammon	Robert	Nieman	Laura B.	Buchanan	John A.
Nichols	Vesta	Ayer	John	Nieman	Rolina W.	Pieper	Richard H.
Nicholsen	Mary Emily Jane, Mrs.	Herring	Elias	Nighturne	Helen M.	Baldocchi	Alfred A.
				Nilansen	Hansine Helene	Jarvis	Morgan
Nicholson	Catherine A.	McCloskey	R. M.	Nilausen	Marie S.	Petersen	Hans N. P.
Nicholson	Rose K.	Allen	Maxwell W.	Nile	Inza E.	Shauer	Leroy
Nickelsen	Naudine	Balzari	J. T.	Niles	Lavania A.	Lambert	Robert Franklin
Nickerson	Emma M.	Treat (?)	James M.	Niles	Nora E.	Rockliff	Edward H.
Nickson	Florence W.	Symons	William	Nillis (?)	Lizzie	Steele	David
Nicol	Harriet J.	Christensen	Christian	Nilousen	Hanna M.	Mathison	Hans Peter
Nicolaisen	Elizabeth	Doyle	Milton	Nilson	Pauline	Larson	Carl
Nicoletti	Listina	Consoni	Alfredo	Nina	Florence Dello	Bertellotti	Pio
Nicoletti	Virginia	Foelone	Domenico	Ninmer	Jennie	Voigt	William Charles
Nicoll	Fannie	Elliott	J. B.	Nippert	Nancy Frances	Gussman	Cass
Nielsen	Anna	Jacobsen	Jacob C.	Niquet	Katie	Bohn	Johannes W.
Nielsen	Anna	Plow	Carl	Nissen	Henrietta	Knudtsen	Sophus
Nielsen	Anna Marie	Cummings	Ralph M.	Nisson	Anna	Linebaugh	William A.
Nielsen	Christine	Asplund	John A.	Nisson	Christine Anna	Mickelsen	Mads Peter

Nisson	Gertrude	Fisk	Charles Grosvenor	Norouha (?)	Maria	Alvernaz	Manuel Brum
Nisson	Irene E.	Nahmens	Simon	Norris	Bertha M.	Bish	Lewis M.
Nisson	Lena	Andersen	Rasmus Theodore	Norris	Celia E.	Keeley	Thomas H.
Nisson	Mary	Mickelsen	Madsen	Norris	Dalia	Black	V. D.
Nisson	Teresa N.	Stolker	Chas. W.	Norris	Emma	Koch	Leroy
Nixon	Leola F.	Zoss	Benjamin	Norris	Erma B.	Garrett	Edward Lee
Nobelli	Philomena	Biaggi	B.	Norris	Hannah A., Mrs.	Coon	Parmenas C.
Noble	Ada	Christensen	Wm. E.	Norris	Henrietta	Francis	Edwin Charles
Noble	Clara Eno	Varley	Edwin Lincoln	Norris	Julia	Lock	William H.
Noble	Frankie L.	Haskins	W. R.	Norris	Mary A., Mrs.	Vaughn	Erastus H.
Noble	Lizzie	Lodge	David E.	Norris	Sarah	Holden	Josiah N.
Noble	Louise Anna	Snook	George R.	Norris	Zona E.	Brink	Johannes
Noble	Madge	Douglas	Alexander S.	Norsworthy	Hattie F.	Lorange	John
Noble	Maude	Haven	Acton	North	Ralphina	McDonald	Mark L.
Nobles	Adeline May	Boyd	John David	Northern	Hattie Belle	Bennett	William Stephan
Nobles	Hattie	Irwin	Joseph W.	Northrop	Lenna May	Carpenter	Laurence
Nobles	Inda J.	Shimm	Andrew J.	Northrup	Mary C.	Platts	John M.
Nobles	Mable C.	Strahle	Herbert B.	Norton	Bessie, Mrs.	Bushnell	John D.
Nobles	Minnie Frances	Livingston	Edward Perry	Norton	Elizabeth	Tyrrell	George W.
Nobles	Pearl E.	Brady	Thomas M.	Norton	Ellen	McCormack	Philip
Noden-schneider	Marie R.	Werth	William B.	Norton	Laura A.	McGawim (?)	Frank P.
				Norton	Philinda	Case	Benjamin Bascom
Noffsinger	Melvina E.	Kuykendall	J. O.	Norton	Wilma Mae	Arata	John King
Nolan	Rose	Fischer	Francis	Nosher	Olive J.	Rouse	Charles J.
Noli	Olymipia M.	McDonald	Bernard John	Nosler	Maude P.	Sullivan	Denman E.
Nonella	Celestine	Crivelli	Alexandro	Notari	Regina	Gambarasi	Edward
Nonella	Olympia	Tresch	Robert	Notingham	Mary Jane	Donel	P. A.
Nonnon	Marie	Laurent	Ernest	Nott	Florence	Thomas	William F.
Nooland	A. A.	Leard	J. B.	Nourse	Susie L.	Guldager	George M.
Noonan	Alice R.	Mecham	Sherman A.	Novelli	Clariee	Bondi	Oreste
Noonan	Elinora A.	Plover	John P.	Nowdesha	Lulu	Ross	Harry E.
Norcross	Alice	Boothe	William N.	Nowell	Hattie A.	Colby	Edwin
Nordstrom	Emily M.	Rasmussen	Lars	Nowlin	Lillie L.	Duncan	William P.
Noriel	Lydia Bell	Miranda	John	Nowlin	Lula L.	Kirkland	Harry B.
Noriel	Susie	Yell	Peter, Jr.	Nowlin	Margaret A.	Case	Benjamin B.

Noyes	Ruby Thersa	Foss	Leonard Rangwell	O'Brien	Eleanor	Robin	Arthur F.
Nuhrenberg	Henrietta M.	Hinze	Victor A.	O'Brien	Elizabeth V.	Garety	Leo J.
Nunes	Adlaida	Trigeiro	Joseph	O'Brien	Ellen	Buckner	E. L.
Nunes	Caroline	Roges	Antone J.	O'Brien	Hattie	Murray	Thomas
Nunes	Lucy	Cabeleira	Antonio Silveira	O'Brien	Katie C.	Carriger	William W.
Nunes	Mary	Nunes	George	O'Brien	Mary E.	Dunster	Frank J.
Nunes	Mary A.	Juzix	Chester L.	O'Brien	Yvonne M.	Row	Charlie E.
Nunes	Mary J.	Vier	Joseph F.	O'Callaghan	Mary	James	George A.
Nunes	Mary L.	Brayer	Geo. H.	O'Celeghan	Frances E.	Eager	Marcus K.
Nunes	Mary S.	Foste	Manuel	Ochsenreiter	Helen L.	Chodrow	Samuel
Nunez	Maria	Simas	Manuel	O'Connell	Kate A.	Willis	John K.
Nunley	Isabelle	Bowman	Thomas Franklin	O'Connell	Marian E.	Tedesco	Charles E.
Nurnberg	Nettie	Souza	Frank	O'Connell	Sarah T., Mrs.	Norrbom (?)	P. G. (?)
Nurse	Mabel	Roberts	Henry E.	O'Conner	Florence L.	Walker	Joseph
Nursement	Nellie Helen	Reynolds	Frank Steven	O'Conner	Amy Joan	Fore	Walter Francis
Nutter	Josephine Hattie	Burtnett	Charles Gordon	O'Connor	Anne G.	Wattles	Samuel Lockwood
Nutter	Laura W.	Roberts	Edward L.	O'Connor	Eleanor Inez	McFarlane	Frederick George
Nutter	Lizzie A.	Johnston	Alexander C.	O'Connor	Florence M.	Craig	Isaac
Nutting	Mable L.	Lyons	James A.	O'Connor	Ida Mae	Walker	Arthur Glenn
Nuyl	Elinor C.	Several	Ferdinand H.	O'Connor	Mary	Doran	James
Nydeffer	Mary, Mrs.	Amrhein	John	O'Connor	Nora	Keleher	Wm. Thomas
Nydegger	Anna C.	LaValley	Elmer R.	O'Connor	Ruth Virginia	Walter	Lawrence H.
Nye	Adelaide D.	Dewey	Gra M.	O'Dea	Carolyn E.	Wagner	Stanley A.
Nye	Anna G.	Pellonini	Fred	Odell	Amanda J.	Combs	John F.
Nylen	Elivira L.	Fletcher	Lee C.	Odell	Edith V.	Richardson	Alexander
Nystrom	Louise E.	VanNess	Fred M.	Odell	Emily A., Mrs.	Rambo	Harrison M.
Nystrom	Pearl Alma	Weyhe	Paul Herman	Odell	Nettie	Bauright	Wilson
Nystrom	Thelma G.	Schlundt	Karl F.	Odell	Ruby	Nerz	John
Oatman	Nellie E.	Robertson	Floyd A.	Odell	Sophrmia	Cox	James M.
Ober	Bessie I.	Averill	Herbert O.	O'Dell	Addie	Patterson	Wm.
Oberfell	Clara	Austen	John O.	O'Dell	Rhoda	Smith	Frank E.
Oberfell	Mary	Cuthill	James Sinclair	Odem	G. A.	Golden (?)	James (?)
Oberle	Katherine	Peterson	Florent S.	Odermatt	Theresia	Fasel	George
Obram	Mary H.	Fitz	Anton	Odle	Jessie Lee	Story	James Augustus
O'Brien	Annie	Massie	Fred B.	Odlund	Anna Othelia	Wand	Joseph

Oehlman	Gertrude Clara	Beckman	Louis Henry	Olmsted	Amanda E.	Thurmond	Richard E.
Oellig	Ruth	Dorroh	Carleton C.	Olmsted	Dorothy J.	Hill	Alexander B., Jr.
Oettjin (?)	Mathilda L.	Sexton	Reg C.	Olmsted	Helen M.	Brown	Wilson J.
Offuit	Ella	Long	R. H.	Olney	Mary Louise	Moses	Robert T.
Offutf	Ella May	Marzolf	Charles Joseph	O'Loughlin	Leah Hester	Brain	Walter Earl
Offutt	Jennie B.	Stephenson	Arlington W.	Olsen	Esther Alena	Beck	Mads Sorensen
Offutt	Rieta J.	Murphey	Harry Bruton	Olsen	Ruth N.	Mayer	Edmond A.
Ogan	Charlotte Louise	Wakeland	Clytus Clay	Olsen	Thora	Flemming	William
Ogan	Mabel Dorothy	Austin	Raymond Thomas	Olson	Clara Albertina	Van Gafen	Roy
Ogan	Pearl	Speers	Chester Burris	Olson	Edyth W.	Merrit	Edson C.
Ogburn	Edith L.	Graves	Edwin C.	Olson	Hulda	Renstrom	Ole
Ogden	Ermon S.	Gibb	James W.	Olson	Mabel B.	Mooney	William O.
Ogilvie	Mable L.	Carter	Lawrence J.	Olson	Mabel E.	Nelson	Alf E.
O'Grady	Mary	Scott	Thomas	Olstad	Anna	Andreasen	James P.
O'Hara	Emma E.	McCormick	Rodney	Olstad	Carrie	Ohnstad	John
O'Heron	Helen	Ragoss	Edward S.	Olstad	Gunhild	McNutty	Edward Francis
Oiler	Mary A.	Norton	John A.	Olts	Myrtle	Jones	Ervon
O'Laughlin	Maggie	Berryman	Samuel	Olufs	Pauline	Tennyson	Martin M.
O'Laughlin	May A.	Bealer	George A.	O'Mally	Mary	Hanlon	Frank
Olbrich	Lou F.	Carillo	Joseph	Oman	Genevieve Ida	Caldwell	William Beatty
Older	Edith M.	Berger	William	O'Meara	Julia A.	Jordan	Harvey S.
Oldham	Mary D.	Odlum	Samuel L.	O'Meara	Mary A. L. (Polly)	Doyle	Frank P.
Oldroyd	Gladys	Pearson	Carl Frederick				
O'Leary	Blanche A.	McGuire	William J.	Oneal	Mary E.	Patterson	James T.
O'Leary	Dollie	Wible	Dean D.	O'Neil	Eva L.	O'Neil	James
O'Leary	Isabella	Lunt	Arnold E.	O'Neil	Susan, Mrs.	Julin	Adolf
O'Leary	Kate	Walsh	Michael	O'Neill	Ella A.	Drapeau	Frank M.
O'Leary	Mary	Kimball	Jerry Whitney	O'Neill	Jennie	O'Neill	James
Oleven (?)	Azora A.	Board	William	Onel	Emma B.	Shreeve	Arthur
Olinger	Helen G.	Palmer	Charles L.	Ong	Kitty D.	Wilkie	Arthur E.
Olison	Georgianna, Mrs.	McReynolds	Stephen	Ord	Ella, Mrs.	Whitlock	Charles J.
Oliver	Laura M.	Wilson	George R.	Ord	Lois	Schnier	William
Olivera	Annie	Ameral	Manuel S.	Orender	Alma May	Elphick	Oscar Frank
Olivera	Margaret	Lawrence	Frank	Orilley	Nellie	Morion	Louis
Olivera	Rose	Perry	John Francis	Orlando	Frances	Novello	Vincenzo

Orlando	Rosa	Camarda	Joe	Oster	Ellen L.	Habenicht	John F.
Ormsby	Ella	Putnam	Jay Rodney	Osterhild	Elizabeth	Thornton	William
Ormsby	Julia	Rose	August	O'Sullivan	Josephine	Butler	Edmund J.
Ormsby	Julia B.	Reese	David J.	Otis	Flora	Blair	Duke
Ormsby	Stella	Griffith	Thomas E.	Otis	Flora E.	Roux	Newton Frank
Ornbaum	Edyth Leoleon	Wiester	Aber Stowe	O'Toole	Mary C.	Scott	John
O'Rouke	Annie E.	Sullivan	David V.	Ott	Rosa H.	Perry	P. P.
O'Rourke	Irene Marie	Starrett	John R.	Otterbeck	Evelyn M.	Montijo	Daniel
O'Rourke	Margaret	Nego	Antone	Ottmer	Adelia B.	Blazer	Charlie
O'Rourke	Teresa	Conley	Philip	Ottmer	Ida F.	Board	Horace D.
Orozco	Julia V.	Bertholdi	Stephen P.	Ottmer	Lora A.	Block	George
Orr	Alberta E.	Cowan	John	Ottoboni	Lena Helen	Matazzoni	Armando
Orr	Jessie V.	Ross	Randall R.	Ottoboni	Rosa A.	Babbini	Ernesto
Orr	Marguerite Ellen	Campbell	Harold George	Oustott (?)	Ruth C.	Dodgson	John C.
Orr	Mary E.	Fay	John	Overhalser	Bettie N.	Shaeffer	N. W.
Orr	Ora A.	Miller	David A.	Overton	Beatrice	Green	Isaac Leander
Orr	Tury	Roller	Carl T.	Overton	Grace V.	Dulac	Enest E.
Orre	Jeanette	Crowley	David	Overton	Harriet L.	Cavanaugh	William M.
Ort	Clara	Temple	Rufus A.	Overton	Jessie	Livernash	Edward J.
Ort	Rosa H.	Keown	George W.	Overton	Laurene	Clark	Leslie D.
Ortman	Clara	Utah	Herman	Overton	Martha Jane Mildred	Burton	Francis A.
Orvis	Ella M.	Northway	Isaac B.				
Osbam	Susan A.	Burk	John C.	Overton	Mary A.	Bowbeer	Benjamin F.
Osborn	Annie	Von Carnap	Otto	Overton	Mattie C.	Holcomb	Alfred
Osborn	Edith	Greaver	Elmer	Overton	Sarah J.	Pohlmann	Edwin G.
Osborn	Eliza M.	Ruhlman	Henry S.	Owen	Jennie Mabell	Briggs	William Henry
Osborn	Elrene	Cobb	Tony A.	Owen	Mary	Buckle	John
Osborn	Leonia E.	Peterson	Fred V.	Owen	Mary M.	Marvin	John F.
Osborn	Mary B.	Nielson	George N.	Owen	Susie	Thomas	T. R.
Osborn	Mary Helen	Speckmann	Herman	Owens	Emma F.	Essig	Frank
Osborn	Zelphia Florence	Patton	Heber	Owens	Imelda C.	Archambault	George E.
Osborne	Angie L.	Bagley	Willard D.	Owens	Leeta	Mello	Frank
Osborne	Grace M.	Chaffer	Chester C.	Oxley	Della	Wilson	David Lee
Osborne	Katherina	McMahon	James	Oxtoby	Alice Josephine	Hageman	Emil H.
Osmon	Oma E.	Roberts	Raymond D.	Oy	Ho	Yim	Fung

Oyen	Ariadne Minerva	Pier	Paul Albert	Palmer	Ethel A.	Reeve	Orson H.
Paccini	Italia	Lucchesi	Francisco	Palmer	Georgia M.	Coffman	Charles
Pacini	Ida	Angelo	Antonie	Palmer	Grace Pearl	Craig	Bert F.
Pacini	Ida	Morini	Ubaldo	Palmer	Ida Eugene	Walker	William Gus
Pacini	Vesta	Nicolai	Carlo M.	Palmer	Jennie, Mrs.	Low	William R.
Packard	Olive S.	Papera	Joseph	Palmer	Lou	Knowles	Albert William
Pagani	Katie E.	Bonardi	Guiseppe	Palmer	Maud Elizabeth	Meeks	George Lawson
Paganini	Carmalita	Guidotti	Leonardo	Palmer	May L.	Showalter	Carl L.
Page	Georgiana	Brown	Alfred	Palmer	Mollie A.	Schuster	Marvin L.
Page	Gladys H.	DeGoa	Victor G.	Palmer	Nirma	Markley	Albert E.
Page	Matilda Jane	Page	Ruben Fred	Palmer	Sarah Emily	LeBaron	Harrison M.
Page	Sarah Jane	Case	Wm. E.	Palmerlee	Edith A.	Simcoe	John D.
Page	Yuma L.	Butler	Thomas I.	Palmieri	Asalina	Peri	Joe
Paget	Lulu G.	Jeffress	James V.	Palmsten	Hildur Elvira	Anderson	George
Paget	Susie H.	Jeffress	John K.	Palucci	Lizzie	Perry	Joseph
Pahaus (?)	Christina	Petersen	Herman	Palumbo	Josephine	Osnato	Frank C.
Pahud	Heloise	Lukas	Israel	Pancio	Domenica	Cerini	Isidaro
Pahud	Henrietta	Stoher	Alfred	Pancrazi	Jule	Paganucci	Adolph H.
Painter	Katie Iowa	Allen	John Harvey	Pancrazi	Minnie E.	Greeley	Benjamin M.
Paisley	Helen Marie	Smith	Walter Frederick	Pancrazi	Josephine Florence	Campodonica	Adolpho P.
Paladini	Amelia	Canessa	Attilo				
Pallady	Bessie	Brooks	Charles W.	Panelli	Angelina E.	Vivarelli	Victor
Pallady	Helen L.	Saul	Roy B.	Panini	Carmelina	Maloof	Charles
Pallady	Ida M.	Legg	Samuel M.	Pannell	Frances M.	Hughes	William L.
Pallady	Nellie G.	Gschwend	Thomas	Pantier	Emma May	Hoffman	Charles T.
Pallady	Ruth Miller	Helin	Charles Edward	Paolini	Eufemia J.	Plum	Arthur W.
Pallady	Viola E.	Legg	Edward T.	Paolini	Maria	Novelli	Elio
Pallo	Victoria	Doe	Edgar A.	Paolini	Mary Innocentia	Lombardi	Joseph Augustus
Palm	Hilja M.	Parkinson	George A.	Papear	Louisa, Mrs.	Deluca	Amadeo
Palm	Hilda A.	McMillan	Alexander	Papera	Eugenia	Papera	Natale
Palmater	Sarah E.	Hess	Albert	Papero	Angelllina	Fava	Lorenzo
Palmer	Annie E.	Waugh	Fred H.	Paradis	Elizabeth	Wild	Charles
Palmer	Caroline Isabelle	Gray	Robert Floyd	Parara	Florence	Forgett	Frank Alma
Palmer	Clara May	Miller	Will Henry	Paravinni	Maria	Leonardini	Paolo (Paul)
Palmer	Edith B.	Miller	Clarence A.	Pardi	Venice	Bartalini	Joseph

Pardini	Emma	Bacci	Amoto	Parks	Tamy (?) H.	Barnes	Edward D.
Pare	Della	Beebe	Thomas E.	Parmer	Clarissa	Gray	Isaac
Parent	Hattie M.	Seligsberger	Sigmund	Parmeter	Mary L.	Matthews	John E.
Parinoli	Annie	Fiori	Antonio	Parnell	Mary	Parnell	Thomas
Parish	Mary Alice	Purvine	Walter S.	Parnell	Ruth	Narron	Roy James
Park	Bertha M.	Cook	William H.	Paroli	Domenica	Magatelli	Domenico
Park	Carrie F.	Price	George W.	Parr	Barbara	Hevel	Christopher
Park	Edith Rae	Johnson	Frank Eugene	Parriott	Lois I.	Buckingham	Edwin B.
Park	Mabell Phoebe	Pfeifer	Harry Edwin	Parrish	Eliza Jane	McNiel	James F.
Parker	Angie F.	Crocker	George S.	Parrish	Harriet	Barnes	George Otis
Parker	Bernice	Sharp	Bay Burns	Parrish	Janet	Williams	Andrew B.
Parker	Bessie M.	Haupt	Louis C.	Parrish	Ruth M.	Sylva	F. H.
Parker	Ella	Moore	William	Parrott	Elsie E.	Cake	Luther B.
Parker	Gladys E.	Paulson	Heyno A.	Parrott	Marguerite Marion	Lampson	Chester William
Parker	Jeanette	Perry	James S.				
Parker	Lulu	Sherriffs	Charles	Parson	Sarah Elizabeth	Brunskill	Ralph W.
Parker	Madge E.	Williams	Charles F.	Parsons	Carrie E.	Sibbald	Emmette Kent
Parker	Mary	Pachini	Alexander	Parsons	Charlotte	Van Alstein	Byron M.
Parker	Maybel	Winkler	George Howard	Parsons	Ella M.	Demman	John R.
Parker	Mildred	Holloway	Clarence	Parsons	Esther Ruby	Currie	Claude Raymond
Parker	Pearl	Akers	Lawrence	Parsons	Hallie A.	Wood	Lucian L.
Parker	Virginia Belle	Cummings	William Frank	Parsons	Lavina J.	McGuire	Oscar Alonzo
Parkerson	Belle	Pedrotti	Louis	Parsons	Leila A.	Lowrey	Frederick D.
Parkerson	Jane Edith	Frutiger	George F.	Parsons	Margaret Jane	Stone	Henry Charles
Parkerson (?)	Eva	Rose	John	Parsons	Mary E., Mrs.	Kalb	August L.
Parkin	Josie, Mrs.	Mason	James W.	Parsons	Nellie	Crumley	Francis M.
Parkin	Marguerite I.	Greaves	Walter	Partington	Lydia H.	Andrews	Geo. Francis
Parkins	Harriett E.	McLaughlin	Oswald R.	Partington	Mary Ellen Frances	Morris	J. E.
Parkins	Tamson	Boerner	Richard F.				
Parkinson	Rosa L.	Jensen	Fred Peter	Partlow	Loella M.	Carrier (?)	Fred J.
Parks	Anna M.	Bock	Walter D.	Partridge	Grace E.	Hays	Ira C.
Parks	Clara Adele	Buechler	John	Partridge	Katherine	Franklin	Alex R.
Parks	Elvira	Hickman	M. S.	Partridge	Marion	Cale (?)	Theodore Webster
Parks	L. F.	Estep	Henry S.	Pasage	Clare	Bury	Joseph L.
Parks	Maria C.	Gregson	Henry M.	Paschal	Ada M.	Cromwell	John T.
				Paschal	Rosa Belle	Fisher	Louis Fredk.

Pascoe	Caroline M.	Finley	Asa L.
Pasero	Christine	Maccario	Tony
Pasero	Margherita	Ponzo	Chiafredo
Passalacqua	Rosa	Passalacqua	Andrew D.
Passalacqua	Silvia	Giannecchini	Louis
Passalacque	Amelia I.	Mecchi	Costantino
Passarino	Dalia	Di Grazia	Giocondo
Passarino	Lucia	Rosasco	Lawrence
Pastorino	Rose Lee	Huffman	Daniel
Patocchi	Olimpia	Consoli	Peter
Patrick	H. A.	Alexander	Thomas
Patrick	Lena A.	Simpson	Oliver S.
Patrick	Lottie F.	Patteson	Frederick E.
Patrick	Rose	Obenauer	Arthur
Patronak	Annie	Sten	Michael
Patronak	Mamie	Almann	John
Patronak	Margaret	Simmons	Laurence Cudbirth
Patrow	Clara May	Bell	Raymond C.
Patten	Elizabeth	Miller	J. S., Dr.
Patten	Julia A.	Haupt	Charles W.
Patten	Luddie	Stuart	Fred W.
Patten	Mary	Cadra (?)	Emil C.
Patten	Mary C.	Willey	Philander L.
Patten	Nancy	Whitchurch	John F.
Patterson	Alma Vivian	Beene	Luther Garnett
Patterson	Bell	Adams	Claude W.
Patterson	Clara	Carrington	Charles N.
Patterson	E. Blanche	Young	Maynard N.
Patterson	Eva May	Smith	Andrew H.
Patterson	Grace E.	Trobitz	Henry E.
Patterson	Hester A.	Heason	George W.
Patterson	Lou, Mrs.	Griggs	Smith M.
Patterson	Martha	Bones	William H.
Patterson	Mary E.	Walls	Alexander
Patterson	Mattie A.	Carey	Charles Edward

Patterson	Maud Alma	Stone	George Cleveland
Patterson	Minnie C.	Ferguson	Clarence M.
Patterson	Myrtle	Smith	Luther N.
Patterson	Pearl Elizabeth	Mosely	Irve Clyde
Patterson	Rita J.	Sinclair	David D.
Patterson	Stella F.	Fay	John P.
Patterson	Tony	Kee	James H.
Patterson	Geneva E.	Green	L. D.
Patteson	Adeline G.	Button	Horace H.
Patteson	Laura	Vaughan	Spruce C.
Patteson	Mollie D.	Caldwell	Samuel T.
Pattison	Jean M. O.	Acker	James W.
Patton	Bertha V.	Bequette	Julian P.
Patton	Edna	Jensen	Alexander
Patton	Emma	Commary	John A.
Patton	Julia Ellen	Wickstrom	Joseph Herman
Patton	Lillian E.	Lowrey	George A.
Patton	Ora Lillian	Ashurst	William R.
Patton	Sadie L.	Woods	Loyal E.
Patton	Talitha Gibson, Mrs.	Petross	James
Paul	Eliza Ann		
Paul	Josephine	Sjogren	Nils M.
Paul	Mabel	Mattiesen	Hermann
Paul	Mary C.	Wolf	Benjamin Hamilton
Paul	Theresa M.	Champion	John E.
Paula	Alexandrina Catherine	Perry	William
Paula	Maria	Brazil	Anthony
Paula	Wilhelmina	Rose	John
Pauli	Della C.	Rowell	Elmer I.
Pauli	Ethel M.	Smith	Thomas Allen
Paulinelli	Emma	Bisordi	Frank
Paulsch	Susie A., Mrs.	Austin	George
Paulsell	Carrie	Roix (?)	Chas. Franklin
Paulsen	Gwinna M. J.	Kerbey	S. A.

Paulson	Anna E.	Offutt	William J.	Peck	Mary H.	Faires	James B.
Paulson	Anna L.	Arnold	Richard	Peck	Mary H., Mrs.	Peck	Thomas M.
Paulson	Ingeborg	Wade	Lars	Peck	Muriel	Gabel	W. E.
Paulucci	Adeline	Perry	John	Pecsenye	Rose C.	Wolfe	Rollin E.
Paulucci	Celistina	Cella	Dominick	Peddrazzi	Margaret	Leete	Orton R.
Paulucci	Marie E.	Beffa	Quillie W.	Pedersen	Annie	Hanson	John G.
Pauluci	Giulia	Bartolomei	Victor	Pedersen	Christine Jensine	McClary	David Reid
Pauly	Helen	Kevan	Frank Charles	Pedersen	Mary Magdeline	Elder	Louis Ely
Paxton	Emza E.	Maner	Marcellus	Pedersen	Meta Marien	Johannsen	George Henry
Paxton	Melinda C.	Dunlap	Joseph B.	Pedigo	Retha Rosalie	Miller	Frederick William
Payne	Adelia M.	Keegan	William D.	Pedlar	Ethel Moran	Stimpson	Stephen A.
Payne	Etta V.	Stevens	Homer W.	Pedotti	Elvira	Sala	Romeo
Payne	Florence E.	Hansen	William	Pedraita	Clara Irene	Meyers	John C. E.
Payne	Hannah J.	Heimorth	Charles R.	Pedranti	Angelina	Ostini	Fulvio
Payne	Maggie E.	Zimmerman	Augustus D.	Pedranti	Estelle V.	Clark	Richard R.
Payne	Mary	Junker	Clarence M.	Pedrelli	Margheritta	Bettinelli	Filippo
Payran	Mary	Henry	George	Pedrini	Clementina	Capitani	Antonio
Peachey	Julia H.	Jones	Parker W.	Pedroli	Antonietta	Bormolini	Louis
Pearce	Martha	Egbert	Warren	Pedroncelli	Emma A.	Trogni	Battista
Pearce	Pearl	Dudley	Albert P.	Pedrota	Rosalia	Pozzi	Martin
Pearson	Lena	Anderson	Peter	Pedrotti	Annabella	Smith	Francis N.
Pearson	Louisa	Hallberg	John	Pedrotti	Annie Teresa	Bino	John
Pearson	Sarah C.	Woolsey	Frank	Pedrotti	Beatrice Margaret	Capucetti	Frank Charles
Pease	Abba	Hansen	Peter E.	Pedrotti	Clara	Bassini	Bernard
Peat	Pearle E.	Francis	Joseph Andrew	Pedrotti	Ernestine B.	Pronini	Isadore
Peatross	Carrie	Badger	Henry L.	Pedrotti	Estella Belle	Brumbaugh	Raymond
Peatross	Florence	Sanborn	Wm. B.	Pedrotti	Lucinda E.	Armstrong	Charley H.
Peck	Annie	Bidwell	James E.	Pedrotti	Mary Angelina	Ghisletta	Antone
Peck	Clara H.	Sisson	William D.	Pedrotti	Mary Olivia	Kessack	John Douglas
Peck	Henerietta	Leona	Frank J.	Pedrotti	Stella Julia	Beaurgard	Harry Julius
Peck	Ida Viola	Baldwin	Charles Ellsworth	Pedrotti	Victoria Edith	Potter	Floyd Joseph
Peck	Louise	Ross	William R.	Peduzzi	Pierina	Guidotti	Giuseppe
Peck	Lulu	Tucker	John H.	Peerman	Alice Elizabeth	Mecham	Harrison Carlos
Peck	Mabel	Eby	Edward D.	Pelaccini	Maria	Albini	John
Peck	Mabel Irene	Terrel	Samuel A.	Pelanconi	Anna	Raviscioni	Theodoro

Pellascia	Mary	Giulieri	Mansueto
Pellascio	Lillie Vergie	Garzoli	William Victor
Pellascio	Vera	Cockrill	Obe A.
Pellascio	Minnie	Calzascia	Emilio
Peller	Placida	Quartaroli	Francesco
Pellini	Perry, Mrs.	Hearns	Charles H.
Pellonini	Costansa	Vivenzi	Giovanni B.
Pells	Agnes Nettie	Faudre	Stuart William
Peloquin	Marie Louise	Mangin	Eugene Louis
Pember	Ethel Marie	Dean	Oliver Franklin
Pendergrast	Noma	Tathan	John
Pendleton	Edna F.	Hartwell	George H.
Penick	Mackie Katherine	Henry	Amos
Penland	Ada B.	Osborn	Arthur G.
Penn	Caroline L.	Brown	Richard E.
Penn	Ida Irene	Gale	Wallace P.
Penning	Mary	Mann	Edward H.
Penny	Olive E.	Evans	Alexander
Penrice	Lizzie R.	Balsley	Iven E.
Penrod	Florence A.	Graheck	George A.
Penrod	Lillie L.	Allen	Merton C.
Penrod	Minnie M.	Raymond	I. B.
Penry	Effie A.	Van Bebber	F. E.
Penry	Lois M.	Van Bebber	George W.
Pensa	Linda	Massaini	Guiseppe
Peoples	Cora M.	Chapman	Elliot C.
Peoples	Josephine Irene	Oster	Walter Henry
Pepin	Jeanette Corine	Hall	George Henry
Pepper	Ada Elaine	Abeel	James Martin
Pepper	Lydia E.	Hart	Victor E.
Pera	Ida	Vannucchi	Paul V.
Pera	Mary	Bacci	Joseph
Perazzo	Celestina	Rigoni	Antonio
Perazzo	Julia	Lauritano	Edward
Perazzo	Mary	Montessoro	Pietro

Perazzo	Rosie	Ferrari	Guiseppe Joseph
Pereira	Calara	Cardozo	Joseph S.
Pereria	Carrolina Amaro	Jardin	Antonio Fernadis
Pereria	Francelina Simas	Silva	Henry V.
Perez	Mary A.	Dutton	Windslow D.
Perinoli	Francesca	Rossi	Chester
Perinoni	Annie	Bianchi	Peter
Perinoni	Lena E.	Willmann	Walter S.
Perinoni	Rose	Franceschi	Ceasre
Perkenson	Hannah	Dumas	Harry Thos.
Perkins	Alice	Wallace	James
Perkins	Blanche	Hipsher	Henry Clay
Perkins	Cora	Jackson	John B.
Perkins	Cora	Reed	G. W.
Perkins	Doris Estella	Peterson	Stuart
Perkins	Eva F.	Davis	Walter S.
Perkins	Fay K.	Kraft	Emil C.
Perkins	Margaret Edna	Eichbaum	Edwin Treat Betts
Perkins	Nettie	Santmyers	James Louis
Perks	Lilly Bevins	Murray	James H.
Perlet	Mildred B.	Grimm	Frederick W.
Permieu (?)	Anna Mae	Taylor	Edmund
Perotta	Eliza	Rosati	Robert
Perotta	Josephine	Girolo	Pietro
Perottini	Mary L.	Columbo	Charles H.
Perottini	Rosa	Merga	Antonio
Perrier	Katheen	Lowry	Chas. E. C.
Perrin	Alice Hollcroft	Kennedy	Willard B.
Perry	Alice L.	Knott	William
Perry	Annie	Saunders	Wm. M.
Perry	Annie	Wiems	Frank Wooster
Perry	Catherine	Anderson	Nicols
Perry	Clara M.	Anderson	Carl
Perry	Della Emma	Rau	Benjamin F.
Perry	Edith Terese	Wells	Edward Ellis

Perry	Elizabeth G.	Kirkman	Claude J.	Peters	Emma	Waddell	William C. H.
Perry	Ellen, Mrs.	Lee	Charles A.	Peters	Flora	Fowler	Lorenzo Gipson
Perry	Emma R.	Ferguson	W. R.	Peters	Frances A.	Scott	Alexander D.
Perry	Flora L.	Wallace	Henry N.	Peters	Gertrude A.	Bones	Francis L.
Perry	Gertrude	Williams	Leland H.	Peters	Kate	Ronsheimer	Anton John
Perry	Gertrude M.	King	Willis James	Peters	Maggie J.	Miller	George W.
Perry	Gussie	Justine	Frank	Peters	Margaret Helen	Andresen	Carl A.
Perry	Hazel L.	Paulsen	Ward C.	Peters	Mary	Lopus	Frank R.
Perry	Isabel	Hall	Henry	Peters	Mary Z. (?)	Ricks	Thos. F.
Perry	Isabel Mabel	Nunes	John Martin	Peters	Elene	Hansen	Peter
Perry	Laurene L.	Wedel	W. W.	Petersen	Annie	Sornsen	Henry
Perry	Leonora A.	Anderson	Joseph A.	Petersen	Annie M.	Ascherman	Charles F.
Perry	Libbie	Remos	Joe Ferreira	Petersen	Annie M.	Boysen	Fred B.
Perry	Lois O.	Stetson	Herbert J.	Petersen	Bertha Elizabeth	Vonsen	Magmus
Perry	Marie Jane	Bacon	Charles E.	Petersen	Carrie S.	Miller	Frank J.
Perry	Mary	Francis	William S.	Petersen	Catharina J.	Seibel	Charles
Perry	Minnie	de Klark	Henry	Petersen	Clara	Meeker	John V.
Perry	Minnie S.	Doss	George W.	Petersen	Dora	Freidrichsen	Peter
Perry	Pearl E.	Felte	William A.	Petersen	Elena	Harms	Alvin
Perry	Rose	Silveira	Joseph W.	Petersen	Hansine	Hermansen	Carl Andreas
Perry	Roseline	Fontes	Manuel Rodgers, Jr.	Petersen	Hattie	Masciorini	Henry T.
				Petersen	Hazel A.	Walter	William C.
Perry	Rosie	Amanso	Antone	Petersen	Hilda M.	Schultz	Fred J.
Perry	Theo M.	Anderson	Seymour E.	Petersen	Lena A.	Nickelsen	Nickels
Perry	Violet	Maliard	Edwin	Petersen	Margaret Marie	Meeks	Everett
Person	Emma	Badenhop	Chris	Petersen	Marie	Bolz	Francis J.
Peruzzo	Jennie	Allegrini	Julius	Petersen	Olive May	Petersen	Peter
Perz	Dora	Dana	P. F.	Petersen	Rosa E.	Steinbus	John W.
Pete	Mary	Rose	Joe	Petersen	Sine	Nielsen	Andrew
Peter	Jesserah	Burgess	James F.	Petersen	Tina	Rasmussen	Rasmus L.
Peterman	Emma J.	Ramey	Henry J.	Peterson	Albertine	Dubois	J. C.
Peters	Ada May	McNair	James	Peterson	Alma Edna	Goyette	William Henry
Peters	Anna Marie	Mates	George Adams	Peterson	Amy	Vecki	Marion
Peters	Elsie K.	Shelford	Erastus Lee	Peterson	Anna	Bundesen	Martin
Peters	Emilie	Nisson	Theodore	Peterson	Annie F.	Linthicum	J. F.

Peterson	Bertha	Geisel	Henry John
Peterson	Bertha E.	Olson	Ernest A.
Peterson	Christine	Isaksen	Linfred
Peterson	Edith V.	Martin	Lauren M.
Peterson	Edna	Rasmussen	John
Peterson	Elizaabeth Cordelia	Jones	James Lloyd
Peterson	Elizabeth E.	Sellers	Lloyd F.
Peterson	Ellen J.	Bowden	J. W.
Peterson	Elsie	Leroux	Robert
Peterson	Emily	Lafranchi	Marino Joseph
Peterson	Ethel	Scheibel	Camille M.
Peterson	Ethel	Hanssen	Louis O.
Peterson	Etta	Collins	Howard Benfield
Peterson	Etta	Mortenson	Hans
Peterson	Eva R.	Schwan	William
Peterson	Frieda Dora	Patrick	James J.
Peterson	Gretta M.	Banks	Ansel W.
Peterson	Hedwig A.	Ogle	Frederick C.
Peterson	Hettie	Carter	James W.
Peterson	Hildur	Steenberg	Louie C. S.
Peterson	Ida	VonGrafen	Charles E.
Peterson	Josephine C.	Swenson	Hugo F.
Peterson	Julia A.	Overton	James W.
Peterson	Julia C.	Anderson	Almer Parker
Peterson	Laura D.	Newlin	John H.
Peterson	Lillie A.	Baker	Charles A.
Peterson	Louella M.	Shields	Carl G.
Peterson	Lucy L.	Conyers	William E.
Peterson	Mabel Violet	Mayze	Joseph
Peterson	Mary	Staley	John C.
Peterson	Maud Endfield	Rhoades	Grover Cleaveland
Peterson	Minnie	Thomas	Howard
Peterson	Nellie I.	Algeo	Andrew J.
Peterson	Pearl	Damon	Henry Stuart
Peterson	Phoebe	Staggs	Franklin
Peterson	Ruby	Wert	William
Peterson	Sonoma	Rodgers	John P.
Peterson	Sophia	Maybee	F. E.
Peterson	Susan A.	Hendrix	Edwin W.
Peterson	Elsie	Huffman	Aaron
Petit	Augusta L.	Donley	Charlie E.
Petiti	Maria	Balatti	Peter
Petray	Gladys Valentine	Ackerman	Charles J.
Petray	Laura May	Bridgford	Chester Allen
Petray	Mary E.	Moody	Wilfrid
Petray	Myrtle E.	Strode	Marcellus E.
Petray	Parthenia	Bonnie	B. F.
Petre	Louise V.	Hughes	Hugh
Petri	Annie	Azzari	Eriglio
Petri	Mary	Sodini	Angelo
Petrich	Agnes	Ferguson	Andrew T.
Petrie	Lottie	Petrie	Charles Russell
Petrini	Lena Lizzie	Lucchesi	Alberto
Pettis	Annie	Gould	Emmet F.
Pettit	Clara M.	Pierce	George F.
Peugh	Christine A.	Yarbrough	Robert E. L.
Peugh	Erba M.	McCabe	W. H.
Peugh	Jemella G.	Hoffman	Freedom W.
Peugh	Jennie, Mrs.	Vail	D. C.
Peyser	Amelia Augusta	Mountain	Floyd
Peyton	Lillian	Dillon	David
Pezzie	Ethel	Mayes	Ernest E.
Pfalzgraf (?)	Justina L.	Schenk	Walter Clarence
Pfeifer	Ruth V.	Nelson	Harold P.
Pfile	Clara A.	Kastens	Herman J. C.
Pfister	Julia	Robinson	T. A.
Pfister	Martha A.	Stacy	Henry Ellis
Pfister	Nellie M.	Kruse	Herbert M.
Pfost	Alice May	Lewis	Joseph Walter

Phair	Helen	Field	Harry B.	Phillips	Maude (?).	Hendricks	Geo. L.
Phariss	Alice	McReynolds	Lewis M.	Phillips	Pauline	Black	Claude Henry
Pharris	Alice	Gardiner	Waldron R.	Phillips	Rosa	Strauss	David
Pharris	Bernice Wilda	Cook	William Irl	Phillips	Sada M.	Oppenhein	Herman
Pharris	Ilma	Harris	James W.	Phillips	Sarah	Hesser	Herman R.
Phelps	Bessie E.	Johnson	John A.	Philpott	Emma J.	Shane	Robert G.
Phelps	Jennie E.	Latimer	Lorenzo P.	Philpott	Gertrude	Bruer	Fred Matthew
Phelps	Mary Agnes	Holmes	Melvin Leon	Philpott	Helen Alzina Lordell, Mrs.	Macy	William C.
Phenney	May	Whitson	George				
Philbee	Rachel N.	Ellison	Charles Edwin	Philpott	May	Webb	Joseph
Philbert	Rosa M.	Cox	Grover C.	Philpott	Alma Blanche	Slater	Leon Darwin
Philbes	Margaret J.	Kelly	John H.	Phinney	Annie S.	Thomas	Isaac
Philbrick	Jean M.	Harman	Roy	Phinney	Emma Jane	Yokam	Wm. Madison
Philbrick	Josie R.	Coy	Charles S.	Phinney	Harriet	Keaton	John J.
Philbrook	Pearl C.	Hobbs	Robert M.	Phinney	Josephine	Harow	Tom
Philbrooks	Lucinda	Buzzell	Albert A.	Phippen	Mary A.	Bush	William H.
Philips	Helene	Steinberg	Sigmund	Piatt	Lela M.	Bradbury	Halta
Philkill (?)	Nell M.	Blogg	Ernest J.	Picchi	Frances A.	Bertolucci	Guido C.
Phillbrook	Martha	Ford	James Russell	Picchi	Pasquina	Micheli	Alfredo
Phillfott	Fanny (?) I.	Foss	Charles C.	Pickard	Annie H.	Bailhache	Arthur L.
Phillips	Flora	Towt	John M.	Pickard	Estelle A.	Stevens	Harrison W.
Phillips	Gertrude	Ebbets	Harry G.	Pickens	Mary	Jenkins	Allen
Phillips	Gertrude E.	McAllister	Kieth (?) M.	Pickett	Helen S.	Harris	Arthur L.
Phillips	Henrietta C.	Lowery	Mansfield B.	Pickett	Mildred Stella	Walters	Claude Willard
Phillips	Ina	Hawley	George L.	Pickle	Bernice E.	Kidd	Joseph L.
Phillips	Katherine Wendell	Dittman	Fred August	Pickle	Blanche	Marshall	Thos. H.
				Pickle	Mary E.	Ball	Wm. P.
Phillips	Letitia R.	Baugh	Ernest	Picknell	Catharini M., Mrs.	Bound	Joseph
Phillips	Mabel	Dickey	William James	Pickrell	Cordie M.	Buttner	Joseph F.
Phillips	Mabel G.	Eachus	Edgar P.	Pickrell	Jessie	Van Buren	Edwin Garrett
Phillips	Mae E.	Belvail	Lewis	Pienucci	Ermeda	Tonelli	Dan
Phillips	Maggie May	Walton	Bert Elsworth	Pierano	Teresa	Gagliando	Andrea
Phillips	Martha	Laurin	Robert	Pieratt	Sarah J.	Perry	George L.
Phillips	Mary E.	Somes	George R.	Pierce	Alice M.	Hunt	Francis Willard
Phillips	Matilda A.	Drees	Gustave A.	Pierce	Augusta	Ganner	James Edwin

Pierce	Bessie	Wirts	Frank
Pierce	Ethel Ruth	George	Harmon Alfred
Pierce	May L.	Floyd	Fred
Pierce	Ruth Hamilton	Seeman	Felix Henry
Pierce	Edna Langley	Berger	Otto William
Pierini	Annie	Sparkes	William
Pierini	Rita L.	Ragle	George J.
Pieroni	Mabel M.	Vaccarezza	Alfonso
Pierson	Dora Cooper	Scott	Alfred William
Pierucci	Clara	Guglielmetti	Noe
Pierucci	Marie	Doglio	Frank
Pierucci	Matilda	Felciano	Manuel
Pietri	Malvina Gian	Pini	Floro
Piezzi	Catherine D., Mrs.	Marks	Thomas F.
Piezzi	Eliza	Lafranky	Morris
Piezzi	Lucy	Lafranchi	Edward
Piezzi	Mary	Braga	Peter
Piezzi	Sabina	Acquistapace	Guiseppe
Pifferi	Anita	Filippini	Basilio
Pigoni	Assunta	Minghi	Guiseppe
Pihl	Jennie N.	Mattson	Martin
Pike	Amanda J.	Cook	Edward
Pike	Dories E.	Porter	Edward I.
Pilastre	Anna Victorine	Norrbom	Ferdinand Mariano
Pilastre	Elisa	Pilastre	Emile
Pillsbury	Harriet	Bischof	Martin T.
Pina	Theresa	Montna	Henry Lewis
Pinches	Marie G.	Berger	Frederick W.
Piner	Sarah F.	Reeves	L. P.
Ping	Kate Lee	Heselschwerdt	Fred
Pinkham	Sara E.	Schofield	Lester D.
Pinkham	Helen	Short	James P.
Pinkus	Tillie	Katz	Robert
Pinoli	Catherina	Bettiga	Pietro
Piotrowski	Elizabeth M.	MacDonald	Gilbert

Pippert	Elizabeth	Parks	John
Pippin	Bessie Leona	Springer	Earl Leroy
Pippin	Josie A.	Brians	Daniel Boone
Pitkin	Ettie A.	Tompkins	Edwin
Pitkin	Nettie J.	Harbine	N. W.
Pitkin	Zelpha Ermah	Upton	Segal V.
Pittman	Ada, Mrs.	Braden	Charley
Pitts	Cora R.	Webster	James Scott
Pitts	Ethel S.	Moody	Arthur W.
Pitts	Mable	Valandigham	Andrew E.
Piutt	Bertha F.	McLean	Walter N.
Pizzotti	Marie R.	Anbucbon	John E.
Place	Bertha E.	Dukes	William A.
Platt	Blanch Elizabeth	Jenkins	Joseph Warren
Platt	Ruth	Tidball	Lewis Eugene
Plum	Bessie Irene	Elliott	Charles Milton
Plum	Elsie	Marshall	Aretus
Pluth	Frances	Schubetz	Frank S.
Poat	Minnie L.	Griffin	H. E.
Pocai	Clotilde	Giusti	Omero
Pocai	Jalinda	Pocai	Felice
Pocock	Eva	Linville	Clement R.
Pocock	Vere V.	Wisecarver	Newton B.
Poe	Ethel	Mars	Charles
Poe	Ina Alma	Churchman	John William
Poe	Rosa B.	Einwalter	Paul
Poehlmann	Helen Mary	Lawler	John, Jr.
Poehlmann	Marie Dorothy	Bailey	Allan Leonard
Poff	Ella E.	Boyd	William M.
Poff	Mary J.	Hicks	George Milton
Poggetto	Giglia Dal	Rivara	Albert P.
Pohley	Adelaide C.	Byrn	George M.
Pohley	Lorena G.	Wilson	William F.
Pohley	Margaret	McCutchan	Geo. F.
Pohley	Margaret F.	Agren	Arthur L.

Pohley	Mary L.	Martin	George A.	Pool	Margaret	Staff	Thomas
Pohlmann	Carlotta Gertrude	Crawford	Edwin Henry	Pool	Mildred Coretta	Stone	Donald Roy
Poile	Matilda L.	Norton	Melville	Pool	Millie L.	Scott	Otto O.
Polhemus	Louisa M.	Murphy	Herman N.	Poole	Hattie	Moran	Joseph
Polk	Josephine, Mrs.	Beales	Edmund	Poole	Mary N.	Norton	Charles R.
Pollard	Catherine	Strandell	Charles O.	Pope	Elizabeth I.	Cavagnaro	Charles V.
Pollard	Jean	McCabe	John D.	Pope	Ella	Peterson	Alva Scott
Polloni	Celia	Grazini	Emelio	Pope	Lillie N.	Collins	David R.
Pomeroy	Eda	Morton	Nathaniel T.	Pope	Mary Delilah	Hixson	John, Jr.
Pomeroy	Irene Byrle	Engelhardt	August George	Poppe	Catherine	Buchan	James E.
Pomeroy	Ollie A.	Henderson	H. Seymore	Poppe	Edna E.	Cooper	Morris B.
Pometta	Florence G.	Anderson	Caesar William	Poppe	Emma A.	Small	Joseph B.
Pomi	Mabel D.	Bellon	Walter M.	Poppic	Sarah Anna	Lundin	Carl Arthur
Pomi	Anonziata	Marci	Luca	Porcher	Marion Louise	Cole	Clarence Eugene
Pomocnik (?)	Minnie	Raabe	A. J.	Porcher	Marion Louise	Mardis	John Harvey
Poncetta	Giulia	Ruggeri	Pete	Porta	Mary	Bertoni	Guido
Poncetta	Rosie	Macrina	Leo D.	Porter	Annie L.	Conger	John I.
Poncia	Maria	Albini	Charles	Porter	Bertha	Gibbons	Estell Ellis
Poncia	Maria	Barela	John	Porter	Carrie B.	Short	William S.
Poncia	Mary	Matteri	Gottardo	Porter	Dorothy Nell	Miller	Leffler B.
Poncia	Mary	Moralli	Bernardo	Porter	Ellen Wood	Searby	Frederick W.
Poncio	Carolina	Bordessa	Dominico	Porter	Katie May	Ingman	John V.
Pons	Bertha	Brown	Horace Herman	Porter	Margaret Olive	Redenbaugh	Birt
Ponyferrie	Madeline	Burton	George M.	Porter	Martha Anna	Hiatt	Robert E.
Ponzie	Madelena	Gesse	Giolio	Porter	Martha Elizabeth	Crigler	Thomas Millard
Ponzo	Madeline	Rovero	John	Porter	Maudie Missouri	Young	William Henry
Ponzo	Margherita	Mangini	Jack	Porter	Nell W.	Clements	Edgar J.
Ponzo	Valentina	Barisione	Baci	Porter	Sarah	Wilson	Charles
Pool	Abby, Mrs.	Bowmer (?)	William	Portlock	Earl	Ellis	Walter A.
Pool	Elba	Beffa	Joseph Edward	Post	C. E.	Drummond	E. W.
Pool	Elizabeth	McKean	George F.	Posvar	Wilhelmina M.	Schachterle	Emanuel J.
Pool	Eva A.	Button	H. H.	Potter	Annie	Potter	James
Pool	Jennie B.	Philbee	Frank	Potter	Charlotte Isabell	Brown	William Herbert
Pool	Luella	Saxby	William Leslie	Potter	Edna A.	Bee	Edward L.
Pool	Mamie	Bruggy	George H. W.	Potter	Frankie	Cockrill	Theodore L.

Potter	Hattie Isabel	Morris	Leslie Lenore
Potter	Josephine I.	Doss	Joel A.
Potter	Mabel E.	Pedrotti	Meryn J. (?)
Potter	Nellie Ann	Perry	Frank L.
Potter	Ruby Elizabeth	Baugh	Douglas Guy
Potter	Susan, Mrs.	Turner	John
Poulsen	Emma Gertrude Mary	Tobelman	Frank Anthony
Poulsen	Maria Francisca	Gale	W. S.
Poulson	Addie E.	Cole	Charles B.
Poulson	Mattie	Ruddick	William O.
Poulson	Nettie E.	Decker	Nias M.
Pound	Jennie G.	Miller	David W.
Powell	Amelia, Mrs.	Smith	Orren Edward
Powell	Elizabeth	Moore	James Henry
Powell	Katie I.	Powell	Jessie R.
Powell	Mabel W.	McDonough	Joseph P.
Powell	Marcella	Gifford	John M.
Powell	May	Ward	Herbert F.
Powell	Nettie	Roscoe	Thomas Howell
Powell	Nila, Mrs.	Stollings	Samuel W.
Power	Mary E.	Alten	Henry
Powers	Adelia	Meyer	William Jacob
Powers	Caroline	Stump	D. A.
Powers	Catherine	Hansen	Carl
Powers	Flora B.	Stump (?)	Leonard P.
Powers	Katie M.	Wooden	George Cooper
Powers	Marguerite	Boyd	Alfred Hillis
Powers	Mary T.	Plummer	Frank M.
Powers	Nora	Jackson	Bernard
Powers	Zelma V.	Knudson	Arthur J.
Pozzi	Caterina	Marino	Filippo
Pozzi	Dora	Albini	Paul, Jr.
Pozzi	Elvezia	Scollaro	Antonio
Pozzi	Lena	O'Connor	Edward W.

Pozzi	Linda M.	Columbo	Romeo M.
Pozzi	Lydia	Santos	Carlo
Pozzi	Lydia C.	Scanagotta	Santo
Pozzi	Margheritta	Bordessa	Davide
Pozzi	Mary	Pozzi	Charles
Pozzi	Rachel	Poncia	Angelo
Pozzi	Rosalia	Campana	Joe
Pozzi	Valeria	Borlini	Augustine
Pratt	Amy	Myers	Arthur W.
Pray	Harriet May	Harmon	Peter A.
Prechecq	Marie	Porcherot	Victor
Prefsey (?)	Rosie A.	Stone	Willard P.
Prendergast	Mamie E.	Whaley	Allen W.
Prentice	Julia C.	Whorton	Richard B.
Preshaw	Florence Evalina	Schluter	William Ernest
Preshaw	Mary S.	Ott	Raymond Lawrence
Pressey	L. Beatrice	Egan	Daniel F.
Pressey	Maude A.	Stone	Charles B.
Preston	L.	Badgerow	Weston
Preston	Lida Margaret	Newhall	Henry Whiting
Preston	Mabel G.	Dean	John E.
Preston	Mary Louise	Goulder	C. N.
Preston	P.	Shear	William P.
Preston	Winifred Wood	Cheney	Ansel Colby
Prestwood	Delia	Hurlburt	Robert H.
Prestwood	Louella M.	Fendner	Edward Ludwig
Pretazzini	Maria	Trusendi	Abramo
Pretorious	Mary	Kingsbury	De Witt
Prevedel	Aurora	Fliori	Anchise
Prewitt	Mabel A.	Gibson	John A.
Priak	Mary Jane, Mrs.	Brannum	Casswell
Price	Beatrice A.	Warrem	Hiram P.
Price	Carrie Francis Park	Brown	Benjamin F.
Price	Estella M.	Hunt	Clyde E.

Price	Laura A.	Alexander	Lawrence	Proschold	Hazel	Cole	W. E.
Price	Lauretta Elizabeth	Goodwin	Albert Michael	Proschold	Myrtle Louise	Tunstall	James Edwin
Price	Lucy M.	Fox	Joseph	Prout	Florence G.	Appleby	Ray
Price	Mable	White	Mansfield	Pruitt	Ethel June	Howard	Clarence
Price	Mary	Bates	Ezekiel F.	Pruitt	Nellie Reba	Elliott	Edward Cyrus
Price	Rose	Hinshaw	A. G.	Prunty	Anna	Rowles	Frank E.
Price	Zellah Lucy	Post	Lucious B.	Prunty	Clara	Sharpe	John W.
Pride	Lorene Graves	Roe	Otis Ira	Prunty	Rebekah Ruth	Pool	Chester Raybouldt
Prien	Florentine A.	Hauck	Harry E.	Puccetti	Clara	Vellutini	Egisto
Pries	Minnie	Petray	Cyrus	Puccinelli	Assunta	DelCarlo	Arcangelo
Priestly	Sophia	Lameneth	Jacob F.	Puccinelli	Clementina N.	Scafani	Laurence J.
Prigge	Mary	Swofford	Grover J.	Puccioni	Julia	Fambrini	Federico
Prince	Helen M.	Burt	Charles Arthur	Puccioni	Lena	Lencioni	Domenico
Prindle	Nellie M.	Stefani	Fred R.	Pugh	Sarah A.	Keithly	Seth T.
Pritchard	Emma Jane	Van der Linden	Peter	Pugni	Ida	Leib	Jacob
Pritchett	Dollie	Haggard	Nathaniel	Pullen	Minnie, Mrs.	Mueller	Charles
Pritchett	Elenor E.	Bryant	John I.	Pullen	Nellie May	Rush	Charles L.
Pritchett	Jennie	Anderson	Leroy	Pullman	Stella Millicent	Post	Robert George
Pritchett	Laura E.	Edwards	Claude A.	Purcell	Eunice A.	Halstead	Jesse S.
Pritchette	Nellie M.	Rose	Frederick C.	Purcell	Gertrude	Hansen	E. J.
Procise	Sarah J.	Mundell	Jackson W.	Purrington	Elizabeth M.	Sinclair	R. B.
Proctor	Alma V.	Overton	Walter B.	Purrington	Ethel	Jones	Lester
Proctor	Clara L.	Helman	L. W.	Purrington	Marguerite	Ballard	John Henry
Proctor	Daisy T.	Reed	C. E.	Purrington	Nellie F.	Tedford	Walter B.
Proctor	Effie L.	Coy	Wm. B.	Pursell	Mary E.	Winder	D. L.
Proctor	Gladys C.	Bertuccelli	Fabo	Purvince	Lew J.	Berry	S. B.
Proctor	Hattie	Foss	Charles C.	Purvine	Alice	Murphy	George B.
Proctor	Julia M.	Cook	Peter	Purvine	Alice	Myrick	H. R.
Proctor	Kate	Leisinger	George Henry	Purvine	Jeannette D.	Lloyd	Louis A.
Proctor	Laura Jane	Martin	Van T.	Purvine	Lena Aletha	McCormack	Percival W.
Proctor	Lenora E.	Reiners	George H.	Purvine	Ruby	Summerfield	Harry A.
Proletti	Giovanna	Mazza	Domenico	Purvine	Sarah H.	Hodges	Edgar W.
Proletti	Giovanna	Papina	John	Purvine	E. Mae	Garretson	John D.
Proletti	Josephina	Decanini	Giovanni	Purvine	Olive	Blanchard	Bowman
Proletti	Mary	Dalpoggetto	Charles	Putchard	Eleanor	Wright	Jed Weston

Putman	Pearl A.	Wells	Virgil L.	Radekey	Revia	Belford	Frank G.
Putnam	Ada	Bickford	Elmer Leonard	Rader	Barbara E.	Scott	David P. H.
Pyle	Anna	Burdick	O. U.	Rader	Elizabeth A.	Barnes	W. P.
Quackenbush	Alice	Wright	Charles L.	Radi (?)	Agnes	Wehrspon	August
Quackenbush	Latha Jane	Quackenbush	R. P.	Radtke	Martha	Rains	Jasper O.
Quackenbush	Luella D.	Lind	Charles W.	Rafael	Lydia	Aliphat	Eugene D.
Quackenbush	Olive	Reynolds	Geo. W.	Rafael	Mary	Armello	Manuel
Quade	Martha L.	Linse	C. F.	Rafael	Rosa	Vigario	Jose Brum
Quadro	Pauline	Rudolph	Edward	Ragan	Mary C.	Christian	Harry E.
Quanchi	Maggie	Tomagni	Charles	Ragan	May	Holden	Charles
Quant	Minnie Myrtle	McDonald	Robert J.	Raines	Anna E.	Woodridge	Galland R.
Quarles	Fay S.	Sheridan	Jud F.	Rainey	Nell E.	Stahl	William E.
Quartaroli	Florence M. E.	Adler	Adam Winkle	Rainier	Ida M.	Morey	Robert G.
Quartaroli	Leonora	Fochetti	Julius W.	Rains	Alice H.	Duncon	Wm. T.
Quigley	Beatrice	Cook	Raymond E.	Rairdin	Virginia C.	Cranmer	George O.
Quigley	Flora Lucinda	Donald	John Hall	Rakestraw	Regina R.	Selleck	William S.
Quigley	Ida M.	Tourady	Joseph M.	Ralston	Alta	Chatburn	Joseph L.
Quigley	Julia M.	Catlin	Lovel D.	Ramatici	Lily	Balzari	James Albino
Quinby	Ella	Bly	Albert R.	Ramatici	Linda B.	Moretti	Camillo P.
Quinby	Elsie	Whye	George W.	Rambo	Esther Irene	Lewell	Luther Enloe
Quinlan	Ellie	Flynn	Patrick	Rambo	Ruby Elvira	Scott	George Leland
Quinlan	Sarah	Manning	John	Rambo	Ruhama	Wolfe	William F. C.
Quinliven	Inza Elizabeth	Wade	Lawrence Dow	Ramos	Annie E.	Pimentel	Manuel J.
Quinn	Addie	Large	Arthur R.	Ramos	Ida A.	Gnesa	Louis, Jr.
Quinn	Frances M.	Kopf	August J.	Ramos	Josephine	Wilson	J. H.
Quinn	Margaret A.	Mietzech	Charles E.	Ramos	Josephine Matilda	Moniz	Manuel Joseph
Quinn	Mary E.	Donovan	A. H.	Ramos	Lena	Pariera	George
Quintero	Annie	Briseno	Ruben C.	Ramos	Leocodia	Santana	Jose F.
Quintero	Felipe A.	Stiebel	Abraham C.	Ramos	Mary	Frates	Joseph A.
Quintero	Florence	Mill	Clarence J.	Ramos	Mary E.	Lemon	Joseph P.
Quotis	Jeanette S.	Hammel	Walter	Ramos	Mary V.	Silva	Antonio M., Jr.
Raab	Minnie G.	LoRomer	J. B.	Ramos	Myrtle Teresa	Grubb	Harry Thompson
Rabe	Edith	Heinshaw	Benjamin P.	Ramos	Roselind G.	Azevedo	William J.
Rabolli	Letitia	Gori	Bruno	Ramsey	Madolin Virginia	Revie	Archie
Rackliff	Ella C.	Litton	William	Ramsey	Mollie	Hitchcock	James E.

Ramsey	R. L., Mrs.	Hixson	W. H.	Rawson	Ella	Fairfield	Wm.
Ramsner	Marie R.	Matthes	Charles C.	Ray	Elsie K.	Mooney	J. William
Ranarde	Lina Francis	Ackerman	Oliver Norton	Ray	Hattie	Dennes	Edward F.
Randall	Aileen L.	Nelson	William Ray	Ray	Juanita I.	Garratt	Mansfield W.
Randall	Eliza S.	Croman	Edward	Ray	Lola Catherine	Cooper	Sarshel Amos
Randall	Fannie J.	Garrison	Will Robert	Ray	Mabel Ella	Ore	Alvin Ray
Randall	Helen Mar	Green	Ira G.	Ray	Marie E.	Hubbard	James L.
Randall	Lottie	Taylor	Arthur J.	Ray	Mary Gertrude	Hellinge	William J.
Randall	Myra E.	Weatherington	Wert C.	Ray	R. Belle	Corliss	Albert
Randle	Etta M.	Halsey	Henry G., Jr.	Ray	Robert M., Mrs.	Munn	Joseph L.
Randolph	Annie A.	Spendler	Otto J.	Rayburn	Hannah E.	Kneiss	Gilbert H.
Randolph	Emma M.	Howard	Roeder M.	Rayhill	Mary	Weeden	James Edward
Raney	Addie M.	Shepherd	L. V.	Raymond	Annie	Mathias	John B.
Ranhin (?)	Jennettia	Scott	Milin	Raymond	Flora M.	Nunes	Manuel M.
Ranker	Bernice O.	Geary	George E.	Raymond	Julia M. Ball	Apostle	Arthur
Ranker	Mildred	Shepard	Irving	Raymond	Mary	Dutra	Manuel S.
Rankin	May E.	Reeder	Charles L.	Raymond	Florence B.	Reed	Henry W.
Ransato	Caroline	Ysunza	Ysmael	Rayner	Polly	Fletcher	James A.
Raphael	Hazel Evelyn	Lezzeni	Joseph Andrew	Razee	Carol Reaha	Cooper	Fred Evart
Rappmund	Cecelia	Westerberg	Carl A.	Razle (?)	Laura Anna	Ragan	Monroe
Rapun	Annie	Benjegerdes	Carl L.	Re	Sibilla M.	Rosa	Paul
Raridon	Katie	Stebbins	Charles R.	Rea	Alice J.	Handy	Percy W.
Rasmussen	Augusta M.	Walther	Walter Paul	Read	Margaret J.	Wood	John G.
Rasmussen	Nell	Jorgensen	John	Read	Hazel G.	Black	Oscar W.
Rasmussen	Sigris	Jasper	Joseph John	Readal	Marguerite C.	Rossi	Petro D.
Rassmussen	Hazel M.	Blik	Ell Carl Dunda	Reading	Lizzie	McLellan	David T.
Rathbone	Lillie Jennette	Thayer	Albert Ernest	Reardon	Mary J.	Chaney	John W.
Raudell	Katherine Antionette	Peacock	Fred	Rebois	Martha	Vidal	Peter
				Rebosio	Adelina A.	Oleese (?)	Enrico
Raulet	Annyta	Angel	Percy	Rebscher (?)	Louise M.	Krayenbuhl	John F.
Raupach	Caroline, Mrs.	Conness	John, Jr.	Rector	May	Requa	Arthur A.
Ravegno	Mary	Ballestra	Johnie	Rector	Zerah	Buckner	Zachariah E.
Raviscioni	Martina	Pelanconi	Domingo	Redden	A. B.	Young	H. A.
Rawlings	Bertha	Heryford	William B.	Redding	Eva Lee (?)	Meeth	Paul J. W.
Rawlings	Pearl	Stewart	David	Redding	Laura May	Sponogle	Charles A.

Redenbaugh	Lydia E.	Morrison	Thomas	Reid	Georgie A.	Sawyer	Elbert R.
Redman	Ethel	Weiller	Robert	Reid	Louise S.	Hopkins	William Hewes
Redmond	Ellen	Dowdall	Richard J.	Reid	Mary E.	Forsyth	Henry M.
Redmond	Loretta M.	Kerney	Joseph J.	Reid	Mattie L.	Anderson	David P.
Redmond	Pauline Mary	Hockey	Albert James	Reid	Opal Marie	Ogle	Millard Byron
Redmond	Zella	E?tola	Arnold	Reidling	Bertha	Hecgman	Gustaf
Redoine	Edith V. A.	Murphey	William H.	Reihl	Marie Madeline	McDaniel	Edgar A.
Redwine	Grace Arella	Rhodes	Samuel Wesley	Reilly	Zel G.	Jones	George B.
Reechler	Bertha J.	Cornelius	Clemens F.	Reimer	Jessie	Clawson	Charles D.
Reed	Carrie B.	Cook	Harvey M.	Reinero	Catterina	Chiotte	Giovanni
Reed	Eleanor	Shattuck	W. J.	Reinero	Mary Elenar	Mosna	Ezekiele
Reed	Ellen F.	Fleischman	Louis E.	Reinhart	Mary J.	Callahan	William H.
Reed	Jane	Stanyan	Charles P.	Relyea	Ida May	Ballou	Miner (?) H.
Reed	Jessie L.	Minyard	Thomas D.	Remer	Bertha A.	LeGoullon	L. C.
Reed	Laura	Hettinger	Charley	Remer	Frances Effie	Butler	Carl Guy
Reed	Maggie N.	Waters	Jeremiah C.	Remesal (?)	Maria	Martinez	Leonardo
Reed	Mary	Mead	Charles S.	Renault	Josephine	Ramos	J. F.
Reed	Mattie Agnes	Frawley	Richard Edward	Renfrew	Anna L.	Bever	Thomas J.
Reed	Ruby	Shaw	Charles B.	Renfro	Ethel Amy	Pratt	Homer Clarence
Rees	Harriet A., Mrs.	Allen	Anderson	Reniff	Mary Flora	Reynolds	Edwin Henry
Rees	Nettie	Lawson	Z. Bert	Renshaw	Myrtle M.	Casaday	Fred W.
Rees	Tina Lynne	Shubert	Charles Arthur	Renstrom	Ida M.	McMath	Sanford
Reese	Della	Dutton	Arthur L.	Renworth	Nora F.	Shelford	Erortus M.
Reese	Emma, Mrs.	Lucas	Joseph	ReSaglia	Mattie	Ferrari	Augustino
Reeves	Caroline Helena	McWilliams	Arthur C.	Resendes	Annita Mary	Colburn	Orlin Merle
Reeves	Maud	Miller	William	Respini	Delia	Hoppe	Joseph Edward
Regan	Elizabeth	McIntosh	Charles	Respini	Flaminia L.	Dado	Arnold Walter
Regan	Mary	Gordon	Frank Hendricks	Respini	Matilda	Reicioli	Achille
Reger	Marie A.	Kothgassner	Joseph M., Jr.	Reubburt (?)	May	Cobb	George G.
Regli	Frances	Joyce	George E.	Reubold	Emma Antoinette	Jauke	Carl August
Rego	Mayme A.	Hall	Harry H.	Rewerts	Annie	Patton	Dexter
Rehill	Catherine	Polgreum (?)	William	Rex	Hulda I.	Cook	Charles T.
Reichlin	Anna	Kryst	Charles	Rexford	Edith	Potter	Harry A.
Reid	Alice	Burnett	William	Reyborn	Sallie E.	Smith	James Z.
Reid	Esther B.	Lockhart	Archie	Reynolds	Annie C.	York	Charles A.

Reynolds	Bertha	Jones	Houston	Richards	Jane	Norton	Charles
Reynolds	Edna May	Kunzler	Edward Theodore	Richards	Josephine	Cook	George M.
Reynolds	Emma	Wetzler	Joseph S.	Richards	Penelope R.	Davis	George W.
Reynolds	Fannie	Dunbar	Charles O.	Richardsen	Sarah Jane	Bleakley	William
Reynolds	H. T., Mrs.	Crescenzo (?)	Louis	Richardson	Blanche C.	Thorn	Samuel A.
Reynolds	Ida M.	Johnson	Charles W.	Richardson	Ella M.	Gables	Chaney R.
Reynolds	Lelia Belle	Perry	Russell Wayne	Richardson	Emma	Blakeway	Horace
Reynolds	Sarah Jane	Quackenbush	R. M.	Richardson	Emogene	Moore	Thomas B.
Rhigetti	Velina	Joppini	Joseph	Richardson	Frances I.	Ross	Loring B.
Rhoades	Alzina	Dias	I. S.	Richardson	Gladys Mae	Hargreaves	Thurlow E.
Rhoades	Georgie A.	Fosgett	Jay Derward	Richardson	Iva B.	Nurnberg	Herbert W.
Rhoads	Nancy	Rodgers	Warren	Richardson	Mabel A.	Campbell	David L.
Rhodehaver	Lulu	Hardin	John M.	Richardson	Mary, Mrs.	Madden	Edward
Rhodes	Clara M.	McAuley	George W.	Richardson	Nettie Gertrude	Mabee	John
Rhodes	Gladys Louise	Rauis	Charles Henry	Richardson	Polly	Gregg	Edward E.
Rhodes	Mary L.	Searcy	Charles L.	Richardson	Vernette	Charles	Geo. W.
Ricca	Angie	Valli	Frank	Richelieu	Edith	Nolan	Albert Wallace
Ricci	Ottavia	Casazza	Ricardo	Richers (?)	Dora	Hoerle	Fred
Rice	Ada Maude	Turner	Robert Wilson	Richey	Ella E.	Leahey	Martin E.
Rice	Charlotte L.	Madison	J. Harry	Richey	Ellen May	Logan	John F.
Rice	Eleanor M.	Skillman	Theodore	Richi	Sarah E.	Dias	Antone
Rice	Eliza Rosedellia	Willey	Elmer James	Richman	Elizabeth Eleanor	Adams	George William
Rice	Eunice	Fowler	Harvey	Richmon	Ida L.	Shelford	George E.
Rice	Mary E.	Corum	Herbert A.	Richten	Stella	Brooks	Walter
Rich	Bernise Irene	Lark	Newton Allen	Rickard	Barbara A.	Elkins	I. B.
Rich	Eula S.	McCombs	William H.	Ricker	Mary C.	Nicoson	Marion W.
Rich	Florence R.	Utley	Frederick W.	Rickert	Sarah	Rickert	Austin M.
Rich	Ira	Gularte	George S.	Rickerts		Hoegh	Hans Matzen
Rich	Nettie May	Harris	Harry J.	Rickett	Clara	Murdock	J. W.
Rich	Rose	Hutchinson	Lawrence	Rickett	Leah	Eckert	Julius M.
Rich	Ida M.	Renstrom	Gottfird	Ricketts	Anice Iva	Badger	Albert Neil
Richards	Anna Belle, Mrs.	Eugley	Walter Arthur	Rickliff	Jennie E.	White	Joseph Ames
Richards	Ella	Scott	Charles Tayler	Rickliff	Serina A.	Wilson	Geo. A.
Richards	Ellen B.	Miller	Harry J.	Rickman	Amanda J.	Ingalls	John C.
Richards	Hannah D.	Buisson	Eugene	Rickman	Nancy S.	Emerson	John S.

Ricksicker	Mary A.	Sheldon	Dextor B.	Riley	Bessie M.	Dixon	R. Dawson
Riddell	Ethel	Plymire	Charles James	Riley	Clara	Sharp	John Henry
Riddle	Belle	Pfister	Nelson B.	Riley	Elizabeth	Lynch	Robert Newton
Riddle	Letitia Bell	Yost	Henry Francis	Riley	Gertrude E.	Adams	John F.
Riddle	Marvele O.	Langon	Michael O.	Riley	Mae	Rosano	Lawrence Antone
Riddle	Rosa M.	Reeder	Frederick Oran	Riley	Mary	Cleary	Edward
Riddle	Sue Frances	Claypool	Stephen B.	Riley	Mary	Lawrence	Horace
Ridenhour	Annie May	Covey	James Walter	Rilf	Marie	Clark	Grant Guildford
Ridenhour	Ella	German	Wm. W.	Rima	Addie	Randall	Lawrence
Ridenhour	Emily	Brown	Thomas P.	Rima	Alta L.	Davis	Fred William
Ridenhour	Pearl L.	Wasson	Earnest George	Rima	Estella	Clark	Robert F.
Rider	Lois E.	Gardenhire	William A.	Rima	Minnie A.	Duncan	William M.
Rider	Marie	Keim	Frederick C.	Rima	Rosa M.	Bonham	James B.
Riding	Hannah	Haas	Joseph G.	Rima	Tina L.	Lawson	J. P.
Riebli	Annie	Lichau	George	Rimmer	Mae	Carter	Harvey H.
Rieck	Mable M.	Meeker	John V.	Rimmer (?)	Cly E.	Rouson (?)	Albert
Riedel	Selma E.	Babcock	Albert A.	Rines	Luella	Davis	Harry A.
Rieffel	Hortense L.	Forest	H. A.	Rinker	Elizabeth	Malnburg	Ira C.
Riehl	Emma S.	Conquest	Earl A.	Rippey	Clara E.	Beall	Asbury
Riemens-schneider	Bertha Henrietta	O'Meara	Richard	Rippin	Doris A.	Hillendahl	Frank J.
				Risk	Jennie	Barnes	Henry
Rien	Sarah Cordelia	Fowler	Edgar James	Risk	Lizzie	Whitlatch	Leonidas
Rietce	Pauline	Dreher	Frank	Risk	Nancy	Moiles	Theodore
Riewerts	Blanche L.	Bundesen	Martin	Risk	Sarah	Kerrison	W. W.
Riewerts	Elsie H.	Williams	Tolbirt A.	Risku	Mary	Revathan	Hardy H.
Riewerts	Marie Josephine	Deiss	William F.	Rissardo	Bervenuta	Perotti	Giusseppe
Riewerts	Meta Josephine	Petersen	Marius Christian	Ristan	Edna M.	Johnson	Ray I.
Riewerts	Pearl	Zumwalt	Ed T.	Ritchie	Maggie J.	Lockhart	Robert
Riewerts	Rose	Nelson	John T.	Ritchie	Mary A., Mrs.	Anderson	George H.
Riewerts	Ruby Camile	Waite	Rolla Howard	Rittner	Carrie Rose	Stricker	Otto Ernest
Riffe	Hazel Idella	MacMurdo	Willis	Ritz	Ada E.	Morrow	John A.
Riffe	Mattie	Conrad	James	Rivera	Inocencesia	Marval	John
Riggs	Anna Belle	Simpson	Vernon D.	Rivers	Adah E.	Hemenover	Dudley A.
Righetta	Elia	Mantua	Jiulius	Rivers	Lillian Pearl	Siegwald	Lewis Walter
Righetti	Mamie	Zanolini	Silvio J.	Rivers	Mabel	Lockwood	Harry E.

Rix	Gladys	Townsend	John	Robertson	Bessie	Lyman	William J.
Roach	Jennie E.	Manney	James F.	Robertson	Daisy	Herbert	Thomas
Roach	Ruth Marie	Steinmetz	Rudolph	Robertson	Fannie F.	Bradford	Robert A.
Robba	Malgerita	Macerida/Macida	Marcallo	Robertson	Florence	Connick	Arthur E.
Robbins	Cora	Lewis	Ralph	Robertson	Ivy M.	Taylor	William D.
Robbins	Esther E.	Willsie	Walter John	Robertson	Lizzie	Morand	Charles Harrison
Robbins	Mabel A.	Rogers	Saml. W.	Robertson	Myrtle	Butler	Osmand W.
Robbins	Marboy (?) C.	Copeland	James	Robertson	Nellie	Lane	Joseph W.
Robbins	Myrtle	Johnson	Okey	Robertson	Olive Pernecia	Preston	Sanford
Robbins	Sarah M.	O'Neil	Henry	Robertson	Pansy A.	Pellascio	Miglio John
Roberts	Clara	Hurst	Leslie E.	Robertson	Pearl	Simmons	Meyer
Roberts	Daisy E.	Marple	Robert J	Robertson	R. E., Mrs.	Yates	Owen C.
Roberts	Edith	Moore	William Washington	Robertson	Rose	Linebaugh	Robert A.
				Robinett	Ida L.	Davis	Ernest J.
Roberts	Edna N.	Elphick	James	Robinett	Mary	Gunther	John Douglas
Roberts	Elizabeth G.	Farley	J. B.	Robinett	Mary J.	Loukemann (?)	Richard
Roberts	Ella G.	Morrison	William L.	Robinett	Ollie	Hamersley	Jay
Roberts	Ella W.	Cowger	William H.	Robinson	Alice	Barnes	Benjamin Franklin
Roberts	Grace M.	Farrar	Edmund H.	Robinson	Amoret Malinda	Butts	Thomas Jefferson
Roberts	Hazel	Elphick	Eugene	Robinson	Anna Catherine	Graff	John
Roberts	Ida A., Mrs.	Pritchett	Gill S.	Robinson	Clarinda Rosalynn	Talbott	Walter Glen
Roberts	Iliace	Turner	Ector J.	Robinson	Cora May	Yerrick	William Henry
Roberts	Katie, Mrs.	Leiby	George	Robinson	Edith G.	Gould	Wm. J.
Roberts	Laura Lavina	Justi	William Alfred	Robinson	Edna Mae	Sheridan	Charles
Roberts	Lola, Mrs.	Hammeken	George L.	Robinson	Ella Caroline	Wade	William Frederick
Roberts	Lucy M.	Johnson	John Leroy	Robinson	Enid R.	Ritchie	Oscar D.
Roberts	Lulla G.	Kneppler	George H.	Robinson	Ethel Lewis	Stickle	Richard Charles
Roberts	Marie E.	Plate	Howard H.	Robinson	Hanah S.	Slater	George
Roberts	Marie L.	Violetti	Richard	Robinson	Helen L.	White	Arthur F.
Roberts	Martha	Spier	Stephen Gile	Robinson	Irma G.	Jepsen	Otto A.
Roberts	Mila M.	Gribbin	Jack H.	Robinson	Isabell	Warn	Ivan R.
Roberts	Nettie M.	Peterson	Elmer	Robinson	Jennie M.	Anderson	William J.
Roberts	Ollie May	Hiatt	Charles G.	Robinson	Jessie	Grove	Ray S.
Roberts	Sadie V.	Winsby	Robert Frank	Robinson	Julia S.	Ford	C. W. R.
Roberts	Tillie	Hartley	William H.	Robinson	Lottie	Strachan	George

Robinson	Mabel Anna	Peterson	William Wilson	Rodgers	Edna Janette	Rose	James
Robinson	Mabel L.	Plummer	Shepherd D.	Rodgers	Julia	Lambert	John W.
Robinson	Marguerite	Poteet	Thomas	Rodgers	Leomiza	Vassar	W. J.
Robinson	Marjorie C.	Bartlett	Frederick D.	Rodgers	Mary	Nachbaur	Jacob Mathus
Robinson	Mary	Clattenbury	Alexander	Rodgers	Mary Ann	Butler	Harry Alfred
Robinson	Mary E.	Laymance	F. W.	Rodgers	Mary Edna	Monez	Manuel P.
Robinson	May A.	Gough	Leo J.	Rodgers	Myrtle	Heitz	John Louis
Robinson	Myrtle A.	Oscar	George	Rodgers	Ruth	Faught	Lewis Cass
Robinson	Pearl	Mahoney	John M.	Rodman	Lieuary A.	Barisich	Peter
Robinson	Rhoda	Scole	Liug S.	Rodric	Carrie	Morris	Edward
Robinson	Sadie L.	Bolton	John F.	Roduner	Alice Evelyn	Cox	John Walter
Robison	Maria S. M.	Rayner	John Edward	Roe	Kate	Ambrosini	John
Robson	Marion Louise	Henley	Elihu Shields	Roe	Martha R.	Ancill	Harold J.
Rocchioli	Angeline	Guidotti	Joseph	Roe	Minnie	Yale	Geo. E.
Rocco	Josephine	Dovo	Joseph	Roebeli	Elizabeth	Sturm	Stingley
Roche	Annie J.	Mahoney	David I.	Roehling	Agnes M.	Allenwood	Frank
Rochester	Carrie A.	Smithers	Asa B.	Roelle	Anna F.	Carner	Ohmer E.
Rochford	Jennie	Morrow	John	Roessle	Stella W.	Burnett	Horace Malcohm
Rock	Anna Marie	Gwin	Walter Edward	Rogers	Annie E.	Smith	James
Rockel	Donna Francesne (?)	Rutland	John Wickins	Rogers	Dora	Osborn	Jesse Alexander
				Rogers	Edith M., Mrs.	Sutphen	Charles E.
Rodd	Dorothy C.	Barber	Lewis R.	Rogers	Elizabeth A.	Dolcini	Charles E.
Rodeck	Louise	Kynoch	Ransom	Rogers	Florence Elizabeth	Schell	Edmund L.
Rodeck	Margaret	Mattley	George	Rogers	Lillian	Osborn	George William
Rodeck	Sarah E.	Shepard	Wm. M.	Rogers	Lizzie L. F.	Goodwin	Charles W.
Rodehauer	Hattie	Skillman	E. W.	Rogers	Mamie	Lane	F. J.
Rodehaver	Nettie T.	Neuman	Paul D.	Rogers	Maud	Fitzgerald	John F.
Rodehaver	Pearl Lenore	Walls	Charles Baxter	Rogers	Myrtie L.	Sutherland	Robert
Roderick	Emma	Winchester	Linsley J.	Rogers	Ottillie C.	Faraoni	Frank
Rodgers	Alvina Maria	Maxwell	William Albert	Roheback	Ethel Hattie	Tucker	Charles Royal
Rodgers	Anna Belle	Moltzen	Albert Christian	Rohleder	Betti	Adler	Hans
Rodgers	Annie	Valine	Joseph	Rohlfs	Frances	Gellissen	Andrew
Rodgers	Carrie	Ballard	Hooker	Rohrback	Clara	Fletcher	Marion A.
Rodgers	Catherine M.	Matthias	Manuel C.	Rohrback	May	Palmer	Charles N.
Rodgers	Edna Isabelle	Bill	Howard	Rohrbeck	Betty	Ritter	John Fred

Rohrer	Nellie	Hedges	S. H.		Rose	Mary	Nunes	Frank
Roland	Hulda E. C.	Ranis	Louis J.		Rose	Mary	Frugoli	Virgilio
Rollins	Lizzie	Westfall	Nelson D.		Rose	Mary A.	Rego	John J.
Rollins	May	Gies	John J.		Rose	Mary D.	De Souza	Tony
Ronalds	Mary J.	Skiff	James		Rose	Matilda	Odell	George G.
Ronard	Etta M.	Wright	Harland E.		Rose	P. E.	Reynolds	John R.
Roncalli	Annie	Campi	Lorenzo		Rose	Rosaline	Rosa	Roque P.
Ronchali	Rosa	Gambogi	Davino		Rose	Susan A., Mrs.	Gordon	James F.
Rondinella	Maria	Depole	Giovanni		Rose	Sylva Clare	Douglas	Thomas James
Ronsheimer	Lizzie	Seegelkin	William J.		Rosen	Lenny	Cooley	Walter S.
Rooney	Mary	Lester	B. W.		Rosenblum	Fannie	Spivock	Will
Root	Hilda	Markopulos	Antonio		Rosenblum	Henrietta C.	Colton	Maury R.
Root	Madeline	Wood	James W.		Rosenbolm	Rachel	Vestal	William
Root	Vida D.	Davidson	Fay L.		Rosengreen	Ingeborg	Wadell	Charles
Roper	Inez	Wheeler	William		Rosengren	Annie	Winroth	Nels
Rorai	Lenora	Niccoli	Silvio		Rosenquest	Matilda Estalla	Holden	John Edwin
Rörden	Ricke G.	Lorenzen	Philip S.		Rosenthal	Nettie	Giovannini	Romeo J.
Rosa	Marianna	Simas	Antone T.		Rosetta	Alice	Johnson	James George, Jr.
Rosasco	Anna Maria	Boitano	Leo		Rosewarne	Elizabeth Serretta	Marten	John Edward
Rosasco	Rosa	Fopiano	Giuseppe		Ross	Ada	Yeager	Clinton
Rosbrough	Lena	Wilson	Frank		Ross	Alice	Kimes	A. L.
Rose	Alice Ophelia	Neely	William Robert		Ross	Alice G.	Stone	Leonard G.
Rose	Anna E.	Nicholson	H. W.		Ross	Alice Isabell	Reid	George T.
Rose	Annie Gertrude	Crotts	Charles Maxwell		Ross	Belle D.	Flint	Willard B.
Rose	Bessie Pearl	Lacey	William F.		Ross	Blessing	Richards	Thomas J.
Rose	Clara I.	Johnson	James F.		Ross	Delta Marie	Olsen	Sidney
Rose	Eldora	Kohr	Robert L.		Ross	Frederica I. (?)	Stone	William T.
Rose	Emma	Baumann	Charles		Ross	Genevieve	Harford	Lyman
Rose	Florence L.	Gray	Fred L.		Ross	Genevieve Loiree	Fitzgerald	John Clayton
Rose	Inez Margaret	Fields	Seraphin F.		Ross	Georgia N.	Moran	James
Rose	Julia	Maitoza	Manuel P.		Ross	Hattie G.	Covey	William
Rose	Laura Alice	Wende	Louis Ludwig		Ross	Hazel M.	Close	William A.
Rose	Lora A.	Yeoman	Gilbert		Ross	Janet A.	Scott	Robert Brough
Rose	Maggie I.	Crotts	Louis U.		Ross	Jennie	Hull	Jerome H.
Rose	Mary	de Avilla	Jose Fereira		Ross	Julia	Kane	John J.

Ross	Laura M.	Covey	Daniel	Rossotte	Aurellia	Acquistapace	Amadio
Ross	Lena	Parsons	Daniel Alonzo	Rost	Marie Margarethe	Roberts	Hubert
Ross	Lizzie	Thomas	David	Rothe	Clarinda	Nelson	Andrew E.
Ross	Lizzie E.	Frazier	Isaac B.	Rothford	Violet	Dysart	Thomas
Ross	Lodema O.	Moore	Ray D.	Rouch	Josephine	Engelberg	Henry W.
Ross	Lottie J.	Jensen	George P.	Rouch	Rosella	Segur	Howard B.
Ross	Louise Lavinia	Smyth	Oscar Andrew	Rountree	Caroline Hawes	Peter	Frederick Lee
Ross	Lucy B.	Alison	Archie	Rouse	Eda May	Cooke	James Hew
Ross	Lydia J.	Noren	Victor E.	Rouse	Iva Irene	Pitois	Julius Lewis
Ross	Martha Jane	Tener	George Porter	Rouse	Mary L.	Somes	Charles A.
Ross	Mary E.	Ritchie	William	Roussan	Florence	Robinson	Peter
Ross	Mary E.	Barnes	Aaron, Jr.	Roussey	Mildred, Mrs.	Fraser	D. Herbert
Ross	Mary M.	Brady	C. H.	Roux	Esther Marie	Nobles	Lee
Ross	Mary, Mrs.	Wilson	Charles Thomas	Roux	Anna G.	Campaglia	Domenick
Ross	Minnie A.	O'Callaghan	Michael	Rovai	Carolina	Barsi	Nichol
Ross	Minnie E.	Ward	James A.	Rovai	Elvira	Pepi	Adolfo
Ross	Nellie	Sylar	George W.	Rovai	Perfette	Tambrini	Alfredo
Ross	Pearl S.	Griffith	Will Samuel	Rovera	Marie T.	Merga	Ambrose C.
Ross	Sadie L.	Walter	Ezra Duncan	Rowan	Albertine	Lindsley	Alfred
Ross	Sue A.	Johnstone	Ralph S.	Rowan	Amy	Wormuth	Martin Elphones
Ross	Vera M.	Abshire	Francis P.	Rowe	Elizabeth A.	Bowers	Edward B.
Ross	Viola A.	Johnson	William R.	Rowe	Gertrude Esther	Wheeler	Arthur Holcomb
Rossi	Alice M.	McCue	Herbert E.	Rowe	Leona V.	Bianchini	Fred P.
Rossi	Angelina	Mancini	Pietro	Rowe	Romina Gertrude	Wilchar (?)	Robert Claudius
Rossi	Christina	Asti	Joseph P.	Rowell	Helen Hale	Ingham	Arthur Blaine
Rossi	Elvera	Albini	Abramo	Rowland	Ethel L.	Thompson	Paul
Rossi	Filomena	Rossi	Isidoro	Rowland	Evealena	Staton	Avery B.
Rossi	Iside	Malaspina	Gustavo	Rowland	Lorena	Pride	D. M.
Rossi	Louise	Brewer	Frank F.	Rowland	Maude	Bailey	Charles M.
Rossi	Luigia	Boldi	Giacomo	Rowlett	Virginia, Mrs.	Charles	Elbert R.
Rossi	Maddalena	Denucci	Angelo	Royal	Carrie E.	Peery	Charles Smith
Rossi	Mary	Balette	Ernest	Royce	Mollie T.	Gamber	A. A.
Rossi	Mary	Bei	Giulio	Royer	Bessie	Wyatt	Francis William
Rossi	Mary	Fiori	Celestino	Rpberts	Rose A.	Troth	Darius B.
Rossini	Mary J.	Varozza	Joseph A.	Rubben	Helene	Abels	Ihuk (?)

Rubenstein	Bessie	Reis	Oscar	Russ	Dora J.	Byrd	J. L.
Rubly	Clara E.	Campbell	William E.	Russ	Lillian	Swett	James E.
Rubly	Nettie E.	Capps	Lennie C.	Russell	Cora	Callenberg	Hugo, Jr.
Rucherson (?)	Emma Rose	Sanborn	W. B.	Russell	Edna P.	Travis	Burton M.
Rucker	Dorothy	Smith	Henry E.	Russell	Eliza F.	McIlree	Alexander
Ruda	Mary	Santos	Fil. G.	Russell	Elizabeth	Dusek	Russell Ray
Rudd	Clara E.	Smith	Frank Robert	Russell	Eveline	Cowan	Samuel Nelson
Rudd	Emma	Cooper	Charles H.	Russell	Eviza A.	Ross	Riddley
Rudd	Minnie A.	Fosgett	Jay Dernard	Russell	Genevieve M.	Taylor	Forrest W.
Ruddock	Kittie M.	Johnson	Martin L.	Russell	Hattie M.	Pierce	Charles J.
Rudolph	Rose M., Mrs.	Gregg	George W.	Russell	Helen Jane	Gillespie	William Breese
Rudolph	Cassaline W.	Swensson	Axel	Russell	Isabelle Adeliade	Livingston	Harry Henry
Rudolph	Elizabeth	Bello	Frank N.	Russell	Lena	Mitchell	Robert Henry
Rudolph	Mae	Chenoweth	Warren L.	Russell	M. A.	Alexander	Lemuel H.
Rudolph	Margarethe, Mrs.	Silva	Antone E.	Russell	Mable C.	Ventre	John P.
Rudolph	Stella M.	Smith	John S.	Russell	Martha Jane	Adams	William J.
Rue	Gertrude Alice	Preston	A. Pierce	Russell	Mary I.	Robinson	Geo. A.
Ruebenack	Ella A.	Levich	George	Russell	Mattie E.	Elder	Newton
Rued	Margaret	Baymiller	Fred C.	Russell	Ruth	Beeson	Willis Lewis
Ruffe	Pauline	McDonnell	Joseph A.	Rust	Madeval Pearl	Junge	Albert Frank Henry
Ruffins (?)	Jessie	Campbell	R. E.	Rutherford	Lucinda C.	Wright	Charles T.
Ruffner (?)	Anna	Bush	Giles H.	Rutherford	Lyle	Hakes	Dorr
Ruggs	Ola	Lawson	Grover Edward	Rutherford	Silvia C.	Sunafrank	Levi
Ruis	Gertrude	Wells	S. E.	Rutledge	Adelaide	Savacool	John W.
Rundell	Rosa	Hoffman	Charles	Rutledge	Florence	Hood	John
Runge	Emma	Runge	Richard	Rutledge	Mary E.	Martin	Dorchester E.
Runyan	Eva E.	Smith	John	Ruttiger	Johanna Adelaide	Olmsted	Frederick Lynde
Runyan	Hattie	Woodson	Ernest E.	Ryan	Catharine	Stevenson	Samuel Fowler
Runyan	Sarah E.	Chitwood	Joseph I.	Ryan	Clara A.	Byers	Judson A.
Runyon	Annie	Kinner	William G.	Ryan	Gertrude K.	Michelson	Andrew P.
Runyon	Mary J.	Brooks	Henry C.	Ryan	Irene A.	Nordstrom	G. A.
Rupe	Gay, Mrs.	Peppin	Benjamin Gray	Ryan	Josie	Gise	Edward
Rupe	Judith	Sowerby	Edward Philip	Ryan	Kate C.	Byington	Charles T.
Rupprecht	Mary Annie	Kelley	John Asbery	Ryan	Mary E.	Pescel	John
Rushton	Coovaa Oral	Logue	James P.	Ryan	Mary Frances	Swisher	James Riley

Ryan	May E.	Sweeney	Daniel M.	Samuels	Jennie	Campion	Thomas
Ryan	Minnie	Boyd	Henry	Samuels	Louisa	Brucker	Martin
Ryan	Ruby Esther	Sullivan	John Patrick	Samuels	Mollie	Fisher	Eugene
Ryan	Violet G.	Pine	William H.	Samuels	Pearl Katherine	Bisbee	George Marion
Rygel	Francisca	Hadler	Henry	Samuelsen	Elizabeth Marie	Byle	Joseph H.
Ryley	Mary Agnes	Fay	Frank	Sanborn	Emma	Faught	John H.
Sabia	Anna Theresa	Saake	Herbert Frederick	Sanborn	Etta Leivee (?)	Banks	Herbert John
Sabia	Camela	Montalon	Paul	Sanborn	Fannie	Schrase	Jacob
Sabine	Doris	Renas	John	Sanborn	Flora L.	Cragun	Wilson H.
Sabine	Flora	Silveira	Leopold	Sandberg	Olga Olivia	McCombs	Aaron Cecil
Sabini	Mary	Carey	John	Sandborn	Vira Ann	Iversen	Iver Alfred
Sacchaz	Jennie	Ceva	Daniele	Sander	Ida D.	LeBallister	Thomas W.
Sackett	Golda Almira	Rudisill	Carrol Everett	Sander	Mary	Mitchell	Charles
Sackoille	Franzes	Wright	Edward R.	Sanders	Hazel Goldwin	Thayer	Philip R.
Sacrey	Mary J.	Dexter	Wm. A.	Sanders	Inda G.	Nobles	David M.
Sacrey	Mary Jane	Tombs	Wm. L.	Sanders	Nadie	Frey	Elmer
Safford	Adeline	Eastman	Fred A.	Sanderson	Carrie	Rea	Cleveland T.
Sagaser	Edith M.	Norton	Samuel R.	Sandl	Annie	Sherman	Carl
Saglaw	Lydia M.	Steffens	Herman D.	Sandoval	Alice	Pedranti	Egidio
Saitone	Maria	Faccini	Giovani	Sanford	Edith V.	Walker	H. C.
Sala	Elena	Proletti	Joseph	Sanford	Lalia F.	Waters	De Witt T.
Salazar	Magdalena Katherine	Starke	Frederick Ralph	Sani	Levy	Penoli	Emile
				Sani	Louisa	Pelleri	Ottavio
Sales	Dora A.	Gaston	Geo. W.	Sani	Marie	Marcucci	Paul
Sales	Geraldine	King	Ernest F.	Santini	Casimira	Furia	Ettore
Sales	Ida M.	King	Theodore G.	Santini	Clara	Rossi	Michele
Salia	Pena	Partrick	Ben	Santini	Gostino	Ramondo	Frank
Salias	Pena	Dwynes	Antone	Santini	Hazel	Ronco	John
Salies	Annie	Carrilla	Cassie	Santini	Mary	Novelli	Sam
Salmela	Helza J.	Hitchcock	Arthur L.	Santini	Orientina	Tedeschi	Luigi
Salmon	Mabel C.	Jackson	Herbert L.	Santos	Gussie	Guidotti	George
Sambrano	Ramona	Navaro	Florentine	Sargent	Ella N.	Farnham	James W.
Sammons	Vivian Belle	Sands	Ralph Merrit	Sarginsson	Edith	White	William L.
Samuel	Dorothy Viola	McCloud	William Elbert	Sarginsson	Nellie Maude	Alexander	George C.
Samuels	Belle	Swisher	L. M.	Sargïnsson	Eva Isabel	Saum	George L.

Sarina	Martina	Tamagni	John	Sbragia	Fanny	Buchignani	Rizieri
Sarmet	Clemence	Rufener	Louis E.	Sbragia	Nanziata	Lencioni	Agostino
Sarori	Elizabeth	Fiori	Attilio A.	Scales	Anna	Bushnell	John D.
Sartori	Elvira	Spaletta	Paul P.	Scales	Lucy O.	Spenser	Frank
Sartori	Marianna	Righetti	Fred	Scanlon	Irene E.	Skow	Harold C.
Sartori	Rina	Maddelena	Fred	Scannell	Grace A.	Edmonds	Francis J.
Sartzer	Augusta	Benson	William	Scaramella	Rosie Rena	Maksente	Victor S.
Sarzotti	Minnie	Bettiga	Bruno	Scaroni	Adelina	Lafranconi	Frank
Sarzotti	Teresa	Debo	Emil C.	Scaroni	Celestina	Cavagna	Joseph
Satterlee	Edith G.	Harmon	James E.	Scaroni	Romilda	Canevari	Adolph
Sattori	Alice	Ruse	Edwin L.	Scascighini	Virginia	Slavich	Antone
Sauer	Carrie	Koffenstein	Jacob	Scatena	Eda Norma	Lippi	Dean Orlando
Sauhbin (?)	Mary Ottis	Webb	William R.	Scatina	Margherite	Massini	Giuseppe
Saul	Sallie Belle	Marchant	Frederick R.	Schachter	Mary	Levine	Abraham
Saunders	Ada Henrietta	Howard	Roe Burdett	Schadt	Josephine M.	Williams	Sheridan R.
Saunders	Ceries Providence	Taylor	James Arnold	Schadt	Marjorie	Messerer	Joseph R.
Saunders	Co?sa Frances	Odell	John	Schaefer	Minnie	Custer	Albert S.
Saunders	Elsie	Hansen	Christian	Schafer	May Catherine	Spencer	Charles De Witt
Saunders	Emma	Maslin	Woolsey	Schalat	Delia C.	Drewes	William P.
Saunders	Lulu Olive	Otterbeck	Nathan Evans	Schalchli	Leona	Brooks	James Monroe
Saunders	Melissa H.	Strout	George A.	Schalid	Julia	Muenzer	Anton
Sauritzen	Leonora	Thomsen	John C.	Schaly	Christina	Enz	Joseph
Savage	Laura I.	Leber	Albert L.	Schatz	Magdelena	Karpfenstein	Jacob
Savercool	Alice	Gladding	Orman B.	Schaumberg	Emma J.	Butin	Charles J.
Savory	Nellie J.	Crane	Price T.	Schaumberg	Nellie	Peck	Clinton R.
Sawtell	Winifred	Meisner	Frank Gustave	Schaupp	Rosa	Rued	Henry, Jr.
Sawyer	Helen I.	Proctor	George A.	Scheibel	Lucy A.	Stetson	Stanley A.
Sawyer	Jennie L.	Bird	Harry	Scheidecker	Carolina	Zweisel	Walter
Sawyer	Nina I.	Wyrick	Harrison L.	Scheiderer	Helen M.	Montgomery	Samuel M.
Sawyers	Annie, Mrs.	Rigby	Robert Perry	Schelbert	Marie	Gerig	Henry
Sawyers	Hazel Marjory	Berryhill	Archie Tanner	Schelling	Elizabetha	Beck	Niels Anderson
Saxe	Vella	Mullikin	Andrew Frederick	Schelling	Marie C.	Birch	Russell J.
Saxton	Edith C.	Zabel	Alexander J.	Schendel	Maude Alice	Kemp	Harry Walter
Saylor	Fern L.	Johnson	Edwin L.	Scherren	Mathilde	Heinicke	Carl
Saylor	Florence M.	Moore	Jesse R.	Schiapacape	Antonia Flora	Barberie	Joseph

Schibi	Margaret B.	Garcelon	W. Scott, Jr.	Schriener	Cora Elliott	Otto	Carl Clemann
Schicoh (?)	Agnes	Brockmann	Henry	Schriver	Ida	Colburn	Frank
Schienmann	Ida	Christiansen	Christian	Schroder	Helene Wilhelmine	Cummins	George Washington
Schifferli	Anna N.	Meyer	Louis C.	Schroeder	Anna M.	Jorgensen	Anton M.
Schilling	Valerie	Arbogast	Ernest	Schrub	Evlyn Violet	Johnson	Gus Charles
Schilly	Hattie	Davidson	Chris	Schudsan	Amalia	Mihan	Leo B.
Schiman	Marion	Hesketh	George William	Schug	Rose E.	Hedges	Benjamin F.
Schindler	Lena Olive	Meador	George Frank	Schuhmann	Johanna	Bill	Philip C., Jr.
Schlake	Lizzie	Light	Elisha	Schuhrer	Wilhelmine	Morton	Harris M.
Schlakes	Anna	Thomas	Walter R.	Schuldt	Ottilie	Tonjes	Henry C. L.
Schlam	Grace M.	Kimball	William N.	Schulkebier	Elsa	People	John Worth
Schlicker	Ida Bertha	Cabeceira	Henry J.	Schultes	Florence G.	Mathers	Wesley
Schlicker	Louisa	Weidner	Wendelin	Schultis	Julia E.	Barnett	Garrett C.
Schlinkmann	Marie	Matzen	Edward	Schultz	Anna	Java	M. Murin (?)
Schloss	Amelia	Shuman	Antone	Schultz	Bertha	Heck	Joseph H.
Schloss	Minnie	Rothschild	Chas.	Schultz	Bertha	Butler	Jesse L.
Schloss	Reda	Stellpflug	Henry	Schultz	Elizabeth	Livernast	John J.
Schmidt	Katherine Francis	Bauman	Charles Henry	Schultz	Ellen A.	Armitage	J. D.
Schmidt	Lena	Pummeroy	Simeon	Schultz	Leonora	DeBolt	John H.
Schmidt	Mollie	Simmons (?)	Mark	Schultz	Marie	Burmann	Adolf
Schmidt	Julia	Smith	John P.	Schultz	Marion Georgia	Colby	Alfred Wright
Schneider	Alice Laura	Evans	William Henry	Schulz	Elsie Anna	Jewell	John Francis
Schneider	Charlotte Alfaretta	Perry	Manuel James	Schulz	Emma Johanna	Rossow	William Fred
Schneider	Elizabeth	Trott	Joseph H.	Schulz	Gertrude E.	Marquis	Thomas C.
Schneider	Katherine	Blackford	Clyde R.	Schulz	Matilda Lucille	Bledsoe	Henry Thornton
Schneider	Marie	Pieratt	W. B.	Schulze	Anna	Weisshand	George W.
Schnittger	Frederika, Mrs.	Reuteler	John	Schulze	Ella Marie	Stafford	Earnest
Schnitz	Louisa, Mrs.	Goeller	John	Schumacher	Carrie Theresa	Lankant	Carl M.
Schoeningh	Elizabeth Ida	Weis	Adam Ignatius	Schumacher	Mary	Lanker	Albert
Schoffield	Nettie E.	Dunner (?)	Martin P.	Schuman	Alice E.	Roberts	Edward F.
Schoningh	Marie A.	Muenzer	John P.	Schurba	Celia A.	Eliggi	Bartolomeo
Schoonover	Alice Edna	Miller	Joseph James	Schuster	Barbara	Muller	Frederick
Schoonover	Ethel Verda	Jeffreys	Thomas Leland	Schuster	Eathel Lyle	Sharp	John Henry
Schow	Bertha	Ernst	John Louis	Schuster	Josie	Delong	Albert N.
Schreeck	Josephine	Stoetz	Charles				

Schutt	Marjan Mathilde	Wessels	Rudolf Christoph	Scott	Ida N.	Orr	Stephen L.
Schutts (?)	Teresa L.	Lee	Charles E.	Scott	Ida Ruth	Worcester	Francis White
Schwab	Clare L.	Kaiser	Frank M.	Scott	Josephine	Rader	Isaih
Schwan	Lennie	Wallis	William T. A.	Scott	Katie A.	Voight	George F.
Schwan	Minnie	Forgett	Fred F.	Scott	Laulu	Baum	Alexander R.
Schwarting	Dorothe Magarethe	Buchi	John Henry	Scott	Laura E.	Brown	Raymond E.
				Scott	Lizzie		
Schwartz	Ada	Weber	Henry	Scott	Lola	Hulbert	Charles P.
Schwartz	Hilda	Proivse (?)	Harry S.	Scott	Lottie	Longsine	William M.
Schwartz	Mary E.	Wolff	Isadore	Scott	Lou Alice	Cramer	Walter
Schwartz	Minnie	Silverstein	Abraham	Scott	Lucy A.	Price	John M.
Schwartz	Margaretha	Koenig	William	Scott	Mabel F.	Atzeroth	Henry
Schwarz	Nellie	Goess	Ferdinand Howard	Scott	Martha E.	Hesse	Fredderick G.
Scieghi	Eni	Rossotti	G.	Scott	Mary Ellen	Foster	Geo. Alonzo
Scollard	Louise	Schulz	Harry Lou	Scott	Mary R.	Rhoades	Charles W.
Scorille	Katie	Cook	John Gilbert	Scott	Maud	Rudad	Samuel
Scott	Agnes	Fleck	G. C.	Scott	Minnie May	Page	Albert Elmer
Scott	Amelia I.	Powell	Wm. W.	Scott	Nora Edna	Miller	Oscar Paul
Scott	Anna Catherine	Heatley	Lloyd Eldridge	Scott	Ruth	Murray	Joseph
Scott	Annie	Rodgers	Henry Cleveland	Scott	Ruth	Petersen	Malcolm E.
Scott	Barbara H.	Weeks	Fred S.	Scott	Sarah A.	Whisler	Abraham, Dr.
Scott	Bernice M.	Ponzo	Peter	Scott	Stella	Riewerts	John M.
Scott	Bertha	Beutel	Christian	Scudder	Edith B.	Cruse	James C.
Scott	Betsy, Mrs.	Brown	Charles	Scudder	Elizabeth	Hayes	James E.
Scott	Cecilia Esther	Jansen	Philip R.	Scudder	Hattie L.	Mills	Asa H.
Scott	Delilah	Fordanse	Henry P.	Scutt	Maggie	Coffey	Charles H.
Scott	Esther	Fuller	Percy V.	Seabright	Elice	Johnson	Otto Henry
Scott	Esther Margaret	Hammon	Charles Howland	Searby	Mary E.	Searby	Henry
Scott	Ethel A.	Brannum	Leonard B.	Searey	Laura Joseph	Kertz	Herbert Joseph
Scott	Ethel G.	Tallman	Lester E.	Searl	Lotta	Less	Alexander S.
Scott	Evaline	Byce	Gideon A.	Searles	Emily P.	Threlfall	John W.
Scott	Harriett	Brown	Samuel	Sears	Ethel Matilda	Austin	Louis Cecil
Scott	Hattie	LaFranchi	Henry G.	Sears	Mary E.	Hassett	Ora T.
Scott	Helen Beatrice	Haberman	Charles Henry	Seavers	Deborah M.	Champion	Stanley W.
Scott	Henrietta, Mrs.	Hubbard	Pearl D.	Seavers	Ida Ruth	Clayton	Howard B.

Seawell	Alice A.	McFarlane	Reginald L.	Senner	Mabel E.	Alfrey	Harry K.
Seawell	Bessie	Boyce	F. O.	Sensebaugh	Rebecca	Brooks	Silas
Seawell	Harriet Ann	Warfield	George H.	Sensibaugh	Armodale	Murphy	Wm.
Sebring	Sarah E.	Garman	James	Senteney	Roxie May	McKinney	Joseph Edward
Sechler	Margaret M.	Turner	Henry C.	Sentiney	Dolly	Reger	Oscar H.
Secord	Velma K.	Pancrazi	Julius	Sephton	Grace	Gilbert	Bret Alexis
Sedgley	Mary M.	Haehl	Carl	Sericano	Julia A.	Landis	William A.
Seely	Martha	Caldwell	John Charles	Sermet	Marie L.	Montano	Constantin
Seeman	Alvina	Goodman	Frank	Sessions	Retta M.	Weller	George F.
Seeman	Bertha	Kayser	Albert H. L.	Setliff	Vida, Mrs.	Hilton	Melville H.
Seeman	Dora	McWilliams	George S.	Seventi	Emma A.	Regalia	Steve
Seery	Evelyn	Evans	Harrison H.	Severy	Edna A.	Kinley	Newton B.
Segueira	Maria	Mattos	Manuel B.	Seward	Evalyn I.	Dryden	William
Seifert	Maud	Fehringer	John	Seward	Laura I.	Hunt	Milton G.
Seipp	Maria S.	Chase	George M.	Seward	Mollie	Gaberel (?)	G. W.
Seiss	Marie Martha	McFadden	Sandy	Sewell	Mildred	Hilgerloh	Sierich
Seito	Oy Guine	Wing	Wong Dott	Sexton	Marie A.	Mahony	H. C.
Sekolsky	Rose	Minsky	Nathan	Seyfferth	Ida	Mentch	Hiram A.
Selinge	Ida Helen	Spalding	Raymond	Seymour	Adeline	Wilhoit	Edward Livingston
Sellards	Evelyne Maud	Williams	Albert D.	Shackelford	Mary Ida	Howard	William W.
Sellers	Annie	Brightenstine	Theodore	Shackelford	Susan	Hart	Hubbard
Sellers	M. Jane	Greves	Thos. N.	Shackleton	Annie	Van Bebber	Park Anderson
Sellers	Mary, Mrs.	Trump	William	Shadburne	Julia A.	Lyons	Cornelius P.
Sellers	Mattie	Geanskag	John	Shade	Ida L.	Hoffman	Walter Roy
Sellon	Violet Mabel	Howard	Henry Ward	Shader	Florence	Bowman	Walter
Selmer	Helene	Pohm	Fritz	Shader	Nellie	Jackson	Hugh L.
Selvage	Eliza Mae	Near	Washington	Shafer	Emma E.	Howard	Calvin P.
Selzle	Lena A.	Gebauer	Charles J.	Shaffer	Fern Rebbeca	DeSelle	Howard L.
Semino	Laura L.	Pezzolo	Ernesto	Shaffer	Inez H.	Powers	George E.
Semler	Marie Phillipine	Bruns	John Henrich Henry	Shaffer	Pansy	Scott	Michel Paul
				Shaffer	Pearl Julia	Floyd	James Andrew
Semper (?)	Susie	Shackelford	E. A.	Shaler	Eliza E.	Dixon	James W.
Semple	Ana L.	Semple	H. C.	Shales	Eva A.	Taylor	James A.
Senecal	Pearl Harrison	Davidson	Fred C.	Shalif	Ruby	Smeegel	Adolph
Senn	Lydia E.	Finch	Frank W.	Shane	Mary Gertrude	Canney	Edward Phillip

Shanks	Amelia K.	Ray	Marion A.	Shaw	Maude May	Church	Jessie Raymond
Shannon	Clara May	Astorg	Louie M.	Shaw	May Francis	Bottomley	Thomas H.
Shannon	Marion F.	Conover	Howard J.	Shaw	May L.	Cowley	Arthur S.
Sharp	Gertie P.	Dayton	John J.	Shaw	Susie M.	Smith	George E.
Sharp	Hazel R.	Gillespie	Vern B.	Shea	Ada	Hughes	Charles T.
Sharp	Mary C.	Sharp	Frank	Shea	Agnes W.	Shankwiler	Henry D.
Sharp	Myrtle	Sharp	John H.	Shea	Alice Jane	McLaughlin	William Joseph
Sharp	Sara M.	Lockwood	James Otis	Shea	Emma Angela	Tukey	William Vernon
Sharpe	Geneva L.	Brown	Charles D., Jr.	Shea	Kate	Hallinan	J. F.
Sharron	Maggie R.	Baker	George E.	Shea	Mary J.	Shea	William
Shatto	Jennie	Mills	Henry J.	Shearer	Annie	Holxer	Ernest
Shatto	Virginia, Mrs.	Rugg	George H.	Shearer	Helen J.	Vincent	Paul J.
Shattuck	Aletha S.	Ellsworth	Henry L.	Shearer	Kitty R.	Russel	John R.
Shaughnessy	Margaret A., Mrs.	Lowe	James Garrett	Shearer	Louisa	Copple	William H.
Shaul	Velma Jessie	Lee	George S., Jr.	Shearer	Rena	Caldwell	Edward J.
Shaumburg	Belle	Hughes	David E.	Shedd	R. J., Mrs.	Fix	J. K.
Shaver	Bertha Catherine	Agnew	Asahel Warner	Sheehan	Helen M.	Sicke	Walter W.
Shaver	Carrie I.	Jamison	H. H.	Sheehy	Lottie	Cromwell	Bert G.
Shaver	Hattier L.	Greentree	Charles T.	Sheffer	Delpha	Miller	George B.
Shaver	Hazel Etta	Smith	William John	Sheffer	Hattie Viola	Rodin	Albert Henry
Shaver	Mabel Pearl	Robertson	Everett L.	Sheffer	L. Etta	Kerfoot	Lester R.
Shaw	Anna Emma	Parks	William Thomas	Sheffield	Cora	Moore	Lewis (?) D.
Shaw	Bessie Lurane	Gibson	Frank Lester	Sheldon	Abbie T., Mrs.	Eastlick	Charles F.
Shaw	Catherina	Simonsen	Theodore	Sheldon	Dorothy P.	de Lappe	Wisley R.
Shaw	Cathryn	Dolph	Peter Joseph	Sheldon	Harriet L.	Dannals	Charles H.
Shaw	Ella L.	Jones	Harlold M.	Sheldon	Mabel E.	Gilmer	William M.
Shaw	Elsie O.	Wheeler	Daniel	Shelfine	Luly	Wyatt	M. O.
Shaw	Georgie P.	McWilliams	Hugh	Shelford	Hanna Odessa	Jackson	Charles F.
Shaw	Gertrude M.	Jones	Clifford W.	Shelford	Hazel	Smith	Clifford H.
Shaw	Grace E.	Williams	William J.	Shelford	Lola L. B.	Enemark	Frank R.
Shaw	Hannah M.	Harrison	Wm. H.	Shelford	Lorena L.	Young	Warner Frederick
Shaw	Helen E.	Royal	Edwin J.	Shelford	M. Effie	Hiatt	Lloyd W.
Shaw	Irene	Gennette	Rene Even	Shelford	Susie Blanche	Lake	Alfred Edwin
Shaw	Lizzie	Williams	Charles Francis	Shelford	Tempie E.	Pettingill	Nathaniel W.
Shaw	Marion H.	Sneyd-Kynnersley	John R.	Shelford	Wilda Mabelle	Moore	Harley La Verne

Shelley	Mabel	Denise	Louis H.	Shire	Catherine	Weltz	William
Shelling	Barbara	Storey	Tunis W.	Shire	Maude Frances	Abbott	George Henry
Shelton	Dorothy Day	Gould	Emerson Weyl	Shiver	Mary Ella	Ore	William Robert
Shelton	Grace	Farmer	Eugene Columbus	Shoemake	Ella	Boyd	Bennie C.
Shelton	Lucy E.	Freeman	Charles E.	Shoemaker	Leonarda	Morini	Frank
Shelton	Rosetta	Torrance	Joseph Lane	Shohoney	Ethel, Mrs.	Mason	William C.
Shenicker	Norma	Sanders	Albert	Sholes	Pearl J.	Bush	William P.
Shenton	May L., Mrs.	Weigel	Samuel M.	Shone	Anna Belle	Strider	Ernest
Shepard	Oliva	Mazza	Ralph	Shook	Frances R.	Schuman	Gustav Moritz Emil
Shephard	Emma E.	Wynn	Alfred C.				
Shepherd	Medora Alma	Collins	Charles Albert	Shook	M. Isabel	Smith	Ira E.
Sheppard	Mary J.	Weston	Robert W.	Shooks	Sarah	Johnson	Alfred R.
Sheppard	Sarah	Ried	Wm.	Shorden	Margart	Schmidt	Peter
Sheridan	Alice	McKinna	Frank	Short	Helen Hutchuis	Auerbach	Howell Bidwell
Sheridan	Sarah C.	Whitcomb	Sylvester E.	Short	Louise Amelia	Krutzberger	Fred
Sherlock	Abbie	Croughin	Thomas	Short	Mary	Bannon	Peter
Sherman	Mary Anna	Hanks	William Wallace	Short	Myra Lydia	Daniels	Herbert Mason
Sherman	Mary M.	Brown	Charles F.	Shortridge	Ethel Mae	Brandis	William G.
Sherrard	Maude H.	Thompson	Charles	Showalter	Belle	Fredericks	George
Sherwood	Delphia L.	Allen	Jay B.	Showalter	Gladys L.	Van Slyke	Wayne T.
Sherwood	Ivah R.	Brown	Carl J.	Showalter	Philister M.	Tomlinson	Percival
Sheuhart	L. B.	Cornagie	Geo. W.	Showalter	Ruth	Newman	Charles William
Shevoskey	Eva	Garoni	Guiseppe	Showalter	Victoria	Hardin	Robert
Shibbetts	Grace Knick	Monsen	Martin	Shreeve	Angie	Johnson	Henry Lee
Shields	May E., Mrs.	Dorsen	Isaiah P.	Shreve	Guineviere L.	Bowers	Colon R.
Shields	Susan	Martin	John A.	Shriver	Ethel A.	Houghton	Albert S.
Shine	A. E.	Helmke	F.	Shriver	Evelyn	Comstock	Harold Earl
Shinn	Anna Helen	Denis	George Edward	Shriver	Loleta	Cox	William Frederick
Shinn	Annie	Jones	Earl Petwin	Shriver	Lorena E.	Stone	Thos. B.
Shinn	Cora	Renfro	Thomas Hendricks	Shriver	Martha Ann	Burke	Nevel Ross
Shinn	Ida	Ferguson	Charles P.	Shudy	Leonora May	Peerman	Miles Hinton
Shinn	Jane	Vasser	Benjamin	Shuhart	Eliza L.	Pritchett	Richard
Shinn	Sophronia	Thompson	Wm. A.	Shular	Ella	Bell	Warren
Shipmon	Mary E.	Howard	Benjamin F.	Shuler	Blanche R.	Cargile	James L.
Shippee	Grace L.	Stock	Victor O.	Shuler	Cecil A.	Cozort	John Gaines

Shuler	Florence M.	Robbins	Ira A.	Silva	Isabel Clara	Silva	Manuel William
Shuler	Georgiana	Hall	H. F.	Silva	Isabelle C.	Cordano	Victor V.
Shull	Beulah B.	Barnes	Jesse W.	Silva	Julia Lopes	Edmiston	Frank L.
Shulman	Lillie	Logan	Walter	Silva	Julia Mendonca	Anderson	John G.
Shulte	Grace Evelyn	Cole	Fred Grant	Silva	Laura	Cascardozo	Frank
Shultz	Mary E.	Cooper	B. F.	Silva	Louise Dalphine	Montgomery	Raleigh Claude
Shurtleff	Helen Emily	Stevens	Henry Cushing	Silva	Lydia	Leonesio	Frank
Shuster	Ivy Irene	Lindsay	Adin Arthur	Silva	Mamie	Tanzi	Sam
Shuster	Jessie A.	Bagley	Donald E.	Silva	Maria	Serpa	Jose Cardozo
Shuster	Margaret A.	Drever	John (?)	Silva	Martha	Brantley	Robert L.
Sibbald	Gertrude	Reid	Archibald	Silva	Mary	Francisco	Antone J.
Sicotte	Maude M.	Reilly	Edward C.	Silva	Mary E.	Lyons	John Joseph
Siegle	Sarah	Lindenbaum	Louis	Silva	Mary M.	Palmer	William H.
Siemer	Minnie	Conners	Charles F.	Silva	Rosa	Souza	Francisco C.
Siever	Alice	Hanley	Frank	Silveira	Louise	Cordoza	Joseph
Sievers	Augusta M.	Harris	Henry R.	Silver	Veris A.	Meyer	Henry C.
Siezle	Kate	Yangling	William D.	Silvera	Mariana	Rose	George
Sighesio	Ida	Prati	Eurico (?)	Silvera	Mary	Poalucci	Frank
Sikes	Viola Bly	Gates	William Henry	Silvera	Mary	Souza	John Philip
Silacci	Dora L.	Mache	Steve A.	Silvera	May Cecil	Webber	Charles T.
Silivia	Leonora	Silivia	John Joseph	Silveria	Rose	Palucci	Louis
Silleman	Annie	Oppenheimer	Samuel	Silveria	Rose M.	Souza	Manuel E., Jr.
Sillemann	Ruth Augusta	Baier	Clemens Loyal	Silvers	Lizzie A.	Herbert	John
Sills	Rhoda M.	Lynch	Bernard C.	Silvers	Rettice	Herbert	John
Silva	Ada	Rudolph	Gustave	Silvers	Susie E.	Turner	W. J.
Silva	Alice May	Madison	John Harold	Silverthorn	Martha Jane	Burgess	Edward Homer
Silva	Anna Pereira	Fortado	Jose Jacinto	Silverthorn	Maude Frances	Helman	Edwin Daniel
Silva	Annie	Leal	Frank Avila	Silvia	Frances	McNamara	Dan
Silva	Annie B.	Peters	Frank	Silvia	Katie	Perry	Antone
Silva	Arnicenda Augusta	Aguiar	Frank	Silvia	Louise A.	Castle	Raymond R.
Silva	Elizabeth	Chrones	Lebertus	Silvia	Mamie	Perry	Toney W.
Silva	Erminda Adeline	Goulart	Baptist Silveira	Silvia	Mary	Battaglia	Lorance Daniel
Silva	Frances M.	Moniz	Frank P.	Silvia	Mary E.	Ash	Emerson F.
Silva	Isabel	Mellow	Frank	Silvia (?)	Maria A.	Coreia	Joaquim
				Silvy	Sarah	Rocca	John

Silzle	Minnie Augusta	Crystal	Richard Randolph	Sinclair	Mary Adelaide	Grove	John
Simansen	Gertrude Marie Dagmar	Monk	Hans Julius	Sinclair	Tenia	McPeak	Harmon P.
				Singleton	Jennie	Frost	Ervin
Simas	Helen	Harvey	John F.	Singley	Gertrude E.	Mills	Easton
Simmond	Helen	Scott	John	Singley	Katherine	Blake	James B.
Simmons	Carrie J.	Haraszthy	Mariano J.	Singley	Mary	Field	John
Simmons	Ella P.	Wade	Albert F.	Singley	Theo. E.	Ford	Earl A.
Simmons	Gladys F.	Dodge	Neal E.	Singmaster	Annie	Scott	William Adrin
Simmons	Jennette Augusta	Goess	George Andrew	Sinn	Carrie M.	McCray	Logan
Simmons	Jennette Augusta	Homer	William Harry	Siorio	Lavinia	Picinnini	Frances
Simmons	May	Guinnar	Jesse W.	Sippitt	Helen M.	Dougherty	S. K.
Simmons	Millie V.	Stone	Bert N.	Sisterna	Victoria	Sills	Armando
Simmons	Susan	Doss	Seth B.	Siston (?)	Kattie (?) E.	Barnes	Henry S.
Simmonsen	Hansine Jacobine	Nicolaisen	Anton	Sjosteen	Selma M. C.	Petterson	F. H.
Simoncini	Emma	Matteucci	Laurence	Skaggs	Bessie Leona	Walk	Edwin Udell
Simoncini	Julia	Casassa	Dominic, Jr.	Skaggs	Clara C.	Adams	Frank T.
Simoni	Julia E.	Perry	Henry L.	Skaggs	Emma L.	Byrne	Marshal H.
Simoni	Mary	Borgess	Antone E.	Skaggs	Nellie A.	Anderson	James H.
Simonton	Cora May	Batten	George	Skee	Mary	Dailey	Lawrence L.
Simpson	Alice C.	Chapman	Charles M.	Skelly	Tessie	Ames	George Spencer
Simpson	Anna E.	Richardson	Izrie Cornelius	Skiff	Pearl Gertrude	Vegas	Joseph Anton
Simpson	Christiana	Peterson	L. F.	Skiffington	Ella B.	Prendergast	Thomas F.
Simpson	E. J.	Turner	J. A.	Skiffington	Estella Sarah	Petersen	Peter Hansen
Simpson	Edith M.	Brown	George L.	Skillman	Eva	Hegler	Gerhard H.
Simpson	Ella	Antrim	Joseph A.	Skinner	Goldie B.	Clark	Albert Earl
Simpson	Ivah	Millar	S. Arthur	Skinner	Grace A.	Palmer	Clarence C.
Simpson	Luella B.	Hansen	Axel O.	Skinner	Mabel A.	Alsbarge	Charles A.
Simpson	Lura, Mrs.	Taylor	Wallace	Skinner	Mary	Dolson	Fred
Simpson	Rebecca, Mrs.	Blakley	James M.	Skinner	Mildred M.	Perkins	Ralph E.
Simrak	Josephine	Rosasco	G.	Skinner	Minnie M.	Clark	Duval L.
Sims	Estelle V.	Weeks	Elbert W.	Skinner	Nellie	Pickrell	George
Sims	Nellie	Dingle	Chas. Edward	Skinner	Pearl Ethel	Lewis	Edwin
Sinclair	Ann Jane	Grove	Edward	Skinner	Ruth	Schmidt	Thomas P.
Sinclair	Clara M.	Jorgenson	Peter C.	Skivington	Emma	Gracy	Charles
Sinclair	Elizabeth M.	Bryant	Jay	Slade	Alma, Mrs.	Koeboom	John Henry

Slaten	Eva	Bement	Leighton W.	Smith	Agnes	Davis	James M.
Slater	Anna L.	Peters	John D.	Smith	Agnes A.	Riddle	John J.
Slater	Louise G.	Dornel	Paul A.	Smith	Aileen F.	Hall	Theodore T.
Slater	Margaret May	Pierce	Harry	Smith	Alethea Beatrice	Smythe	Curtis Moon
Slattery	Frances	LeBaron	Harrison M., Jr.	Smith	Alice	Hall	Walter S.
Slattery	Kate T.	Taber	John S.	Smith	Alice L.	Hickok	James C.
Slattery	Katherine	Shideler	Edwin L.	Smith	Ann Elizabeth	Clayton	Capius Henry
Sleeper	Ruth Severne	Marsh	Clarence Joseph	Smith	Anna Jessie	Anderson	Victor Henry
Sline (?)	Etta M.	Hicks	Edward S.	Smith	Annie A.	Faught	A.
Sloan	Ruby Lucky	Slatter	Albert Edward	Smith	Annie E.	Burnham	A. E., Jr.
Slocum	Nellie M.	Wallace	Freeman M.	Smith	Annie Jeannette	Smith	Samuel John
Slover	Martha E.	Ulrich	Lester A.	Smith	Aurelia Maud	Heald	William T.
Slusser	Irma Gladys	Steele	Ben Leon	Smith	Belle Anna	Black	Wilbur C.
Slusser	Rowana S.	Talmadge	Charles V.	Smith	Bertha G.	Meyer	Lawrence
Smail	Alma	Reid	John F.	Smith	Blanche Ethel	Nordyke	Ollie Theodore
Smaker	Anna Francis	Bagley	Carl Elmer	Smith	Camilla G.	Buxton	Natt
Small	Agnes M.	Cowan	James M.	Smith	Carrie	Gater	J. E.
Small	Alice	Baker	Wm. M.	Smith	Carrie B.	Ebeigh	Henry
Small	Beatrice Margarite	Swearingel	Brady	Smith	Carrie B.	Meeker	William J.
Small	Bernice Dolores	Sholden	Hans John	Smith	Carrie E.	Sanson	William
Small	Catherine Norine	Bulotti	Frederick	Smith	Carrie M.	Boschke (?)	George W.
Small	Emma S.	Henderson	James T.	Smith	Carrie May	Brians	James Cameron
Small	Mabel	Williams	Fred E.	Smith	Catherine (?)	Welling	Charles
Small	Nettie V.	Butchen	W. P.	Smith	Clara I.	Hughes	George W.
Small	Lillie	Van Winkle	William N.	Smith	Clara J.	Towner	Finley
Smalley	Ino Mae	Peterson	Howard Wright	Smith	Dacie R.	Ferguson	Geo. P.
Smalley	Jessie	Cannell	Fletcher	Smith	Daisy	Davenport	P. C.
Smart	Cora M.	Gutermute	David	Smith	Dollie A.	Aiken	Henry S.
Smart	Tamar Ewen	Gloeckner	Charles	Smith	Dorothy E.	Rambo	Milton G.
Smathers	Katherine Mabel	Womack	Charles Henry	Smith	Effa	Anderson	Julius J.
Smidberg	Ellen V.	Matson	Carl E.	Smith	Ellen E.	Davall	Melvin O.
Smillie	Isabell R.	Guild	George	Smith	Elva Marguerite	Pryor	George Ed
Smith	Ada	Locke	George	Smith	Elva Sirena	Burton	John C.
Smith	Adah	Herrick	Emerson Brown	Smith	Elvira White	Rose	Tony
Smith	Adeline F., Mrs.	Gibson	Henry Brown	Smith	Emily G., Mrs.	Griggs	Smith M.

Smith	Emma	Cromer	A. M.	Smith	Julia	Guerne	A. L.
Smith	Emma J.	Gilbert	Charles Robert	Smith	Kate C.	Chambers	Joseph A.
Smith	Essie E.	Campbell	B. F.	Smith	Kittie E.	Mast	C. I.
Smith	Estelle	Yeager	Thomas McB.	Smith	Lenabelle (?)	Nydegger	Frederick R.
Smith	Etta May	Pritchett	Grover Cleveland	Smith	Leona	Crandall	James
Smith	Eva M.	Elkins	Stephen F.	Smith	Lillian C.	Carothers	John W.
Smith	Fannie	Mich	Mike, Jr.	Smith	Lizzie	Obenshain	Emmet M.
Smith	Fannie	Daly	Thomas B.	Smith	Lizzie	Smith	Charles A.
Smith	Fannie A.	Collister	Stanley W.	Smith	Loretta R.	Glover	Harold
Smith	Florence A.	McAlpine	J. K.	Smith	Louise Marie	Beach	Charles Henry
Smith	Frances Elizabeth	Hill	Raymond Moffatt	Smith	Lulu Belle	Wilson	Luther Curtis
Smith	Geneva	Allen	Charles P.	Smith	M.	Bushnell	Edwin R.
Smith	Genevieve	Kincaid	Edwin J.	Smith	M. A., Mrs.	Woodworth	D. W.
Smith	Georgia C.	Buttler	Wilmer	Smith	Mabelle	Renshau	George Bennett
Smith	Gertrude E.	Marshall	H. M.	Smith	Mable Turner	Barre	Charles Munson
Smith	Gertrude R.	Bradley	William A.	Smith	Madeline	Richards	G. W.
Smith	Grace M.	Eckes	Clarence J.	Smith	Mae D.	Costa	Joseph W.
Smith	Harriet E.	Beevers	Robert L.	Smith	Marcia P., Mrs.	Duffell	George
Smith	Harriet Porche	Clewe	William F.	Smith	Margaret C.	Stoney	Gaillard
Smith	Harriet Porcher	Wythe	Stephen	Smith	Margaret J.	Osborn	Arthur P.
Smith	Hattie L.	Goddard	Frank	Smith	Margaret Leone	Sturges	Herbert Knight
Smith	Hazel M.	Brown	James A. R.	Smith	Marie	Morris	Anton
Smith	Helen Amanda	Davis	George Armstead	Smith	Mary	Martin	Joe
Smith	Helen Irene	Soracco	Clarence T.	Smith	Mary	Stovall	Chas. E.
Smith	Helen M.	Imlay	Loren	Smith	Mary	Campbell	Frank
Smith	India	Fuller	Charles E.	Smith	Mary A.	Ellis	James
Smith	Inez L.	Jackson	Elmer	Smith	Mary B.	Plag	Alphonse R.
Smith	Isabel I.	Hansen	Adolph N.	Smith	Mary E.	Gwynn	Wm. A.
Smith	Isabella	Withrow	Charles	Smith	Mary E.	Hart	Robert M.
Smith	Jennie M.	Wright	Walter F.	Smith	Mary F.	Bolz	Phillip C.
Smith	Jennie M.	Varner	Philip E.	Smith	Mary G.	Norris	Charles Claud
Smith	Jennie, Mrs.	Benjamin	William E.	Smith	Maud	Howe	Charles J.
Smith	Jessie Alberta	Furber	John Judd	Smith	Maude	Nutter	Harry L.
Smith	Josephine	Dorman	Den H.	Smith	Maude Alma	Black	Harry Edward
Smith	Josephine L.	Philips	Frank C.	Smith	May E., Mrs.	Cade	H. C.

Smith	Minnie Alice	Kerman	Arthur Thomas	Smithers	Ida V.	Graper	Elmer B.
Smith	Minnie C.	Studley	Chester F.	Smyth	Edith	Lawrence	Chester Earl
Smith	Minnie E.	Hoffschneider	Arthur P.	Smyth	Jennie Elizabeth	Markley	Thomas Cox
Smith	Mollie Rebecca	Evans	Frank Leslie	Smyth	Pashie	Bailey	T. E. C.
Smith	Myrtle V.	Walker	M. B.	Snider	Adaline	Samuelson	Jacob
Smith	Nellie E.	Johnson	Karl V?klar (?)	Snider	Ellen	Vollmer	Wm. F.
Smith	Nellie G.	Nimmo	John H.	Snider	Ellen M.	Throop	Charles M.
Smith	Nellie T.	Collier	Richard B. H.	Snider	Joanna	Crandall	John Calhoun
Smith	Nellie, Mrs.	Hastings	Nelse	Snider	Lucy B.	Amesbury	Geo. M.
Smith	Nettie	Harding	Edward F.	Snider	Naoma	Crandle	Frank
Smith	Nolia Malinda	Davis	Joseph Isaac	Snieckpeper	Lillian D.	McDonald	Joseph F.
Smith	Nova N.	Holman	Charles W.	Snodgrass	Ida M., Mrs.	Cooley	John S.
Smith	Ora	Henderson	Vernon E.	Snook	Hazel Oletha	Snow	William Clyde
Smith	Phena May	Friar	James N.	Snow	Edna N.	Burns	Eugene L.
Smith	Rhoda	Beckett	Frank E.	Snow	Rilla	Smith	James D.
Smith	Rita B.	Walsh	James B.	Snow	Ruby E.	Cleek	Samuel P.
Smith	Rose	McPherson	Bert	Snow	Ruth	Stewart	Alexander
Smith	Roselie	Philbrook	Edward	Snow	Thelma Fay	Carter	Grant
Smith	Rosetta (?) J.	Light	Wm. R.	Snyder	Anna E.	Benton	Louis J.
Smith	Ruth Evelyn	Butler	Carl Guy	Snyder	Beula V.	Ardis	Livy L.
Smith	Sadie V.	Johnson	Howard B.	Snyder	Carrie	Karr	Bert M.
Smith	Sarah	Williams	Burdit Bloomfield	Snyder	Laura	Derrick	Grant
Smith	Sarah E.	Taylor	Edward T.	Snyder	Lila	Whitaker	Scott
Smith	Sarah Eliza	Menefee	John Wesley	Snyder	Sarah Rebecca	Benson	Vernon Henry
Smith	Sonora	Carlton	Thomas	Soares	Mary	Felciano	Antone
Smith	Sophie L.	Palmer	Edward S.	Soderberg	Alice	Knolle	Frans J. B.
Smith	Sylvia Lee	Johnson	Webster	Sodergren	Hilda	Bryan	Joseph
Smith	Violet C.	Ross	Edward T.	Soderman	Susanna	Hillblom	Gottfrid
Smith	Wilhelmina L.	Hopper	David E.	Soedler	Emma B.	Kenney	Martin G.
Smith	Zada	Ott	Leon J.	Softus	Mary	Horrick	John
Smith	Zella	Gibson	Ora Ray	Solari	Isola L.	Hansen	James G.
Smith	Carrie	Morrison	John J.	Solari	Lillian M.	Zanetti	Joseph
Smith (?)	?chn (?)	Baker	Peter S.	Solari	Vittoria	Cavallero	C. L.
Smither	Ruby Pearl	Meissner	Walter Charles	Solaro	Ernestina, Mrs.	Baglietto	Ambrogio
Smither	Wanda	Morrell	Leonard	Soldate	Giulia	Soldati	Eligio

Soldate	Louisa, Mrs.	Bolla	Olympio G.	Souza	Anna Clara	Brown	Charles Alfred
Soldate	Mary J.	Giacomini	Michele	Souza	Caroline M.	Bettencorte	Manuel Martin
Soldati	Adeline	Gilardi	James J.	Souza	Gertrude E.	Ramos	Tony P.
Soldati	Corina	Pomi	Louis	Souza	Mae	Thomas	Frank V.
Soldati	Effie Olympia	Bardoni	Charles Costantino	Souza	Mariana	Rose	Manuel
Soldati	Jennie Ida	Mazza	Romildo Louis	Souza	Marie	Nunes	Joseph
Soldati	May A.	Rees	Fred G.	Souza	Mary	Maria	Jose
Soldati	Palma E.	Gilardi	Americo	Souza	Mary L.	Sauto	Frank G.
Soldati	Vina S.	Nonella	William Joseph	Souza	Matilda	Nunes	Manuel
Solomon	Crescencia Edson	Higgins	William J.	Souza	Rosaline	Cuicello	Manuel G.
Solomon	Hattie C.	Burroughs	David	Souze	Rosa	Ramos	Ralph
Solomon	Lena	Ehret	Alexander W.	Spaggiari	Teresa	Picchi	Pietro
Solomon	Ruth	Howard	Frank E.	Spaich	Julia	Perolini	Joseph Henry
Somerfeld	Clara	Ukena	Bernard	Spaletta	Erminia	Lafranchi	Joseph
Somerholder	Lillian May	Shaffer	Harry Sheridan	Spangler	Annie B.	Duston	Byrne A.
Somerville	Margaret Rodgers	Carey	Albert Brock	Sparks	Emma L.	Brigham	Edward S.
Sommer	Fannie	Zemon	David M.	Sparks	Mattie Belle	Burrel	Wesley Jay
Son	Adelaide	Tyack	Henry	Sparks	Minnie	Hevel	Wm. T.
Songey	Harriet M.	Laddish	H. J.	Spaulding	Laura B.	Gilkey	B. H.
Soper	Clerisa E.	Wilson	Mason Henry	Speegle	Amy	Yates	Albert Edward
Sorden	Mary	McCutchan	George Francis	Speegle	Clara E., Mrs.	Richert	George E.
Sorensen	Anna	Winding	John	Speegle	Florence E.	Woodward	Arthur T.
Sorensen	Emma E.	Schroda	Paul F.	Speegle	Lillian	Isbell	Fred E.
Sorenson	Lena A.	Prickitt	Rowen A.	Speer	May E.	Hansen	George G.
Sorg	Magdalene	Peckelhoff	Henry	Speers	Josie	Hall	George H.
Sorini	Silvia	Nonnini	Petro	Spellacy	Ella J.	Eck	John W.
Sorio	Annie	Bogni	Enrico	Spence	W. O.	Dickson	J. M.
Sornsen	Mary	Petersen	John	Spence	Bessie	Strohmeier	W. H.
Soto	Trinidad	Alford	Frederick	Spencer	Chrystal F.	Grieb	Henry Carl
Soule	Frances	Barnes	Edwin E.	Spencer	Emma V.	Deter	Harry R.
Soules	Edith M.	Strider	Walter E.	Spencer	Florence D.	Townsend	Esmay M.
Sourian	Clara	Queyrel	Ferdinand A.	Spencer	Genovena Nella	Baker	Ralph Weber
Sousa	Mariana R.	Nunes	Manuel S.	Spencer	Katie R.	Healey	Robert D.
South	Philinda, Mrs.	Norton	Wm. M.	Spencer	Mattie E.	Pitkin	Palmer A.
Southern	Lucy, Mrs.	Beasley	Jaba	Spencer	Maude E.	Gobbi	William V.

Spencer	Nonie	Harris	Granville	Squires	Nina Alice	Scafire	Anthony
Spencer	Mabel M.	McMahon	John Henry	Squyer	Ida E.	Ashley	David C.
Spense	Sarah	Nichols	William	St. Clair	Ellen	Bidwell	John W.
Sper	Rosa	Kleeman	John	St. Clair	Lettye	Lane	Ernest
Speyer	Catherine A.	Morton	Raymond A.	St. Clair	Nancy E.	Shafer	J. F.
Spiers	Vera E.	Vossberg	George L.	St. Clair	Stella	Simpson	Hugh G.
Spieth	Anna	Beutel	Gottlieb	St. John	Edith Lenore	Dillon	Isaac Parry
Spiro	Fannie J.	Meyers	Clarence M.	St. John	Florence Marion	Michener	William Lewis
Spittler	Marie Belle	Oxley	James Daniel	St. John	Hattie B.	Doble	John Luther
Spitzer	Clara S.	Frank	C. E.	St. Johns	Anna B.	Whitney	A. L.
Spiuter (?)	Melta	Ruddick	Frank Mortton	St. Leon	Grace	Pagano	John B.
Spofford	Edith E.	Hummer	William T.	Staats	Ida	Hagedohm	Herman B.
Spooncer	Letha P.	Canevari	John J.	Stacey	Angie T.	Merrill	Grant P.
Spooner	Anna May	Robinson	John L.	Stack	Lotta, Mrs.	Morton	Henry
Spooner	Flora V.	Pease	George H.	Stack	Lydia D.	Goodyear	Lloyd S.
Spotswood	Eliza	Donogh	Andrew	Stackhouse	Mary Elizabeth	Lichau	Henry Peter
Spotswood	Hattie B.	Clark	Joseph H.	Staengel	Edna A.	Uland	Ralph F.
Spotswood	Mary Jane	Calder	Alexander E.	Staeubli	Bertha	Buckley	Dennis
Spotswood	Rowena	Short	Walter Clyde	Staff	Katherine	Schuh	Rudolph A.
Spottswood	Ada	Martinelli	Gildo P.	Stafford	Alice E.	Gomes	Joseph
Spottswood	Annie	Harvey	Ira B.	Stagg	Edith	Swygert	David
Spottswood	Minerva Belle	Leppo	O. Frank	Stagg	Perla	Trosper	Arthur L.
Spraggins	Florence E.	Fontch	Bert	Staggs	Phebe	?hreeve (?)	Levi
Sprague	Blanche	Lawford	William E.	Stagman	Anna C.	Bohlin	Bernard
Sprague	Elsie L.	Maddux	Preston	Stagner	Bertha L.	White	William H.
Spring	Harriet, Mrs.	White	George J.	Stahl	Laura B.	Holt	Alva Smith
Spring	Rosenia	Bertram	Arthur H.	Stainin (?)	Anie	McColloch	Wilson
Springer	Catherine	Bahnsen	Daniel	Staley	Ada Lavonia	Kroncke	Henry Carl
Springer	Helena	Hinrichsen	Peter M.	Staley	Cora B.	Rulofsan	Charles Herman
Springsteen	Emma I.	Philbrook	D. C.	Staley	Edna M.	Hardisty	James A.
Spurr	Grace J.	Macdonald	William	Staley	Ethyle M.	McCappin	John A.
Spurr	Rose R.	Davis	George A.	Staley	Mabel Mae	Badger	Percy
Squires	Edith M.	Rabe	Otto C.	Standard	Emma	Walton	James A.
Squires	Ella, Mrs.	Cameron	Henry I.	Standish	Minnie L.	Wilson	John A.
Squires	Esther M.	Sandow	Carl H.	Standlee	Sarah	Sidwell	Chesley

Standley	Alpha Omega	Thorburn	John Francis	Stearns	Ethel A.	Lingenfelter	Charles H.
Standley	Barbara E.	Haas	Henry	Stebbins	Lillian May	Oliver	Abe Lee
Standley	Esther Ramiea	Doty	Archie A.	Stebbins	Malissa	Stockwell	William
Standley	Lillie	Griggs	Reno	Stebbins	Malissa	Stockwell	William
Standley	Sadie R.	Elliott	Chester L.	Stedman	Cora Eugenia	Pitzer	Will Marcus
Stanley	Blanche	Griggs	Alvan Stanley	Stedman	Josephine I.	Nowlen	Thos. C.
Stanley	Ina M.	Santee	Levi	Steed	Martha	De France	John
Stanley	Laura	Ambler	Lawrence J.	Steel	F. C.	Talbot	Holman
Stanley	Mary E., Mrs.	Smith	Thomas	Steel	Margaret A.	Perry	Charles A.
Stanley	Sarah N.	Stine	Amos D.	Steele	Allie M.	Warner	James J.
Stanley	Viola N.	Griggs	Justin S.	Steele	Cora Lovina	Mudget	Charles Austin
Staples	Anna	White	Dell	Steele	Effie M.	Campigli	Albert E.
Staples	Charleen G.	McGowan	James E.	Steele	Etta	Morrison	George W.
Staples	Viola B.	Mason	Marshall E.	Steele	Grace Olney	Fox	Francis Gordon
Stapp	Dovey	Likins	James L.	Steele	Jennie	Lundy	Harry
Stapp	Margaret	Shoemake	Omer T.	Steele	Julia	Willits	Frank Bartlett
Starbuck	Emma Grace	Hughes	John S.	Steele	Margaret Mae	Marshall	James M.
Starck	Bertha	Brandt	August	Steele	Ruth	Hubbard	Clyde H.
Stark	Clytie D.	Robertson	Frank C.	Steele	Viva B.	Forrester	Henry A.
Stark	Margaret	Price	Harvey James	Steenberg	Maria	Erickson	Albert
Stark	Rebecca Marilla	Martin	William Ira	Steer	Marian	Dent	William
Starke	Agatha Augusta	Kaiser	William Henry, Jr.	Steeter	Floretta N.	Cantrell	Joe W.
Starke	Anna Frances	Hall	Albert E.	Stefani	Carrie	Del Prette	Ferdinando
Starkey	Elizabeth M.	Tobin	John J., Jr.	Stefenoni	Maria	Lavio	Dazio
Starkey	Josephine P.	Davis	J. Harris	Steffens	Elizabeth Marie	Soares	Manuel Leo
Starky	Catherine	Sherman	Frank J.	Steffes	Emma A.	Norman	Cyrus J.
Starr	Lillie M.	Reynolds	Walter D.	Stegeman	Julia	Genelle	Emanuel Ignacio
Starr	Vera L.	Bowen	R. Hunt	Stegemann	Katherine R.	Hardin	Clarence E.
Starrett	Anna Letta	King	Chester James	Steger	Betty	Mallory	Herbert W.
Statey	Virginia	Shortridge	Elisha S.	Steger	Daisy	Karnes	Ernest
Staton	Cora W.	Bonney	Alfred T.	Stegman	Helene A. H.	Hayne	Harry Henry
Staudard	Ceripta A.	Hanks	J. D.	Stegmuire	Helen V.	Bruch	Calvin C.
Staup	Fannie B., Mrs.	Jackson	William G.	Steifel	Matilda L.	Despain	Silas M.
Stavosky	Bertha Elsie	Osborn	Frank C.	Steigeman	Mary Gertrude	Bohlin	Frank Anton
Stearns	Edythe Belle	Keeler	Nedwyn	Steiger	Hermina A.	Bayler	John R.

Steiger	Rosa	Bohni	Frederick	Stevens	Jennie	Eckman	John
Stein	Katie	Prowse	Harry S., Jr.	Stevens	Louisa E.	Allis	Edmund C.
Stein	Nora L.	Brockowsky	Otto R.	Stevens	Louisa June	Bray	Elisha Jessie
Steinberg	Maude	Erntson	Martin	Stevens	Mamie	Hudson	James
Steinberg	Nellie	Smead	Lloyd	Stevens	Mary E.	Shurtleff	Thomas
Steiner	Lesetta	Rufli	Fred	Stevens	Mary E., Mrs.	Hinshaw	Hugh B.
Steiner	Theresa	Sigrist	Peter Hansen	Stevens	Nettie	Harrington	James
Steinhorst	Amelia	Mezger	Adolph	Stevens	Sophia M.	Slater	H. F.
Steinmetz	Sophie C	Straub	Charles	Stevens	Stella M.	Grosjean	Camille, Jr.
Steitz	Julia C.	Fox	Louis H.	Stevens	Susie M., Mrs.	Huffman	Hezekiah
Steller	Rossella A.	Coe	Fred R.	Stevens	Virginia Francis	Millstead	Silas Augustus
Stemer	Anna	Foreman	Charles	Stevenson	Annie M.	Upham	F. F.
Stemple	Alfaretta	Finley	Jackson	Stevenson	Grace	Borgwardt	August
Stemple	Henrietta E.	Clark	Mathew	Stevenson	Kathryn	Ross	Edward M.
Stemple	Lucretia M.	Gore	Alonzo J.	Stevenson	Lucy	Showalter	O. F.
Sten	Annie E., Mrs.	Yoakin	Charles Franklin	Stevenson	Mary M.	Hodgson	Joseph E.
Stender	Jeanette	Curran	William H.	Stevenson	May Frances	Barkway	Henry Thomas
Stenrud (?)	Nellie J.	Dinsdale	George D.	Stewart	Agnes R.	Batchelder	Thaddeus
Stephen	Mabel Alice	Ables	Horace T.	Stewart	Bertha F.	Fearns	Lawrence H.
Stephens	Isadora V.	Sinclair	Neil	Stewart	Caroline F.	Curtiss	Albert Melton
Stephens	Mary A., Mrs.	Turner	Noah H.	Stewart	Edith Belle	Stage	Albert M.
Stephens	Mary H.	Silva	Frank	Stewart	Edith J.	Liston	Van Wyck
Stephens	Oma E.	Lyman	James H.	Stewart	Elizabeth	Moritz	Meyer
Stephens	Sarah V.	Cullen	Fred T.	Stewart	Elizabeth A.	Wieder	Fritz
Stevens	Bertha Anna	Wright	Alfred Charles	Stewart	Emeline E.	Lecost	William A.
Stevens	Carla	Dryden	William Robert	Stewart	Esther	Seeley	John Stewart
Stevens	Catherine M.	Kiser	Antone	Stewart	Lettie May	Bones	Albert E.
Stevens	Emma Edith	Justice	Augustus Lorenzo	Stewart	Lillian E.	Cline	Henry C.
Stevens	Eva L.	Crandall	George A.	Stewart	Lizzie F.	Stewart	James C.
Stevens	Flora M.	Rough	Bennie	Stewart	Lydia	Morris	John
Stevens	Florence May	Sedgley	Charles Loring	Stewart	Mary A.	Gutscher	Joseph
Stevens	Harriet Ann, Mrs.	Chadwick	James W.	Stewart	Mary L.	Ortman	William Henry
Stevens	Helen E.	Merrithew	Robert	Stewart	Myrtle	Peck	Lowell N.
Stevens	I. A., Mrs.	Brunk	Hezekiah	Stewart	Neva	Ayers	Archie
Stevens	Intha May	Burmeister	Charles H.	Stickel	Katie	Meilicke	Carl H.

Stidum (?)	Etta,Mrs.	Duffield	Fred
Stieper	Mary	Jacobsen	Niels
Stiles	Bertha M.	Matlock	Walter J.
Stiles	Louisa Isobel	Ellis	John Arthur
Stimmel	Cecelia	Ingram	William F.
Stinchfield	Florence V.	Derrick	Herbert D.
Stinchfield	Mary G.	Driver	Clarence A.
Stine	Joysa R.	Davis	Frank N.
Stine	Syvia C.	Davis	Adelbert A.
Stinson	Elizabeth	Miner	Edward P.
Stinson	Fannie Barbara	Gownig	Clement O.
Stites	Harriett Estelle	Hill	Herman Gordon
Stites	Katheryn I.	Brooks	C. E.
Stites	Sarah Effie	McDonough	Michael
Stochini	Severina	Tognacca	Damiano
Stockdale	Lena A.	Herron	Frank C.
Stocker	Dora	Brunner	Robert
Stocker	Katherine H. Maur	Patterson	Fred Henry
Stocker	Mabel Agnes	Porter	Joseph Samuel
Stoddard	Fannie A.	Stone	Wm. Lewis
Stoeker (?)	Emma	Henrichsen	Theodore
Stoetz	Louisa	Leabo	Benjamin
Stokes	Alice Lizzie	Page	Percy V.
Stone	Ada Myrtle	Ames	Louis
Stone	Agnes	Conlin	William George
Stone	Alice	Denchy	Cornelius
Stone	Ella	Cozad	Samuel L.
Stone	Erma Josephine	Watson	Glen H.
Stone	Genevieve Amelia	Mitchell	Merle Ellsworth
Stone	Gladys C.	Cuopius	Eugene B.
Stone	Grace E.	Hartsock	Freedom E.
Stone	Grace E.	Morrell	William L.
Stone	Harriett Ethelyn	Rhodes	Carlton Eugene
Stone	Hattie L.	Holliday	James E.
Stone	Isabelle R.	Schelling	George C.
Stone	Judith A.	Kane	John W.
Stone	Lillian Agnes	Hopkins	Alban David
Stone	Margaret Cynthia	Toney	Elias
Stone	Marie Genevieve	Stone	Alfred J.
Stone	Nora	Barrett	Francis E.
Stone	Prisila M.	Arbuckle	Cyrus P.
Stone	Rachel Abby, Mrs.	Stockton	Isaac Newton
Stone	Sarah Jane	Gifford/Gilford	Francis M.
Stone	Sardmier (?)	Bones	John F.
Stone	Sidney S.	Coffman	John Isaac
Stone	Stella	Halman	William C.
Stoner	Tessa B.	Arlett	George
Stony (?)	Susie	Newman	George Washington
Storenetta	Ida M.	Caylor	John J.
Storenetta	Minnie	Zanini	Attilio
Storer	Flossie	Cox	Clarence J.
Storey	Bertha A.	Harris	Arthur M.
Storey	Frieda G.	Boyer	Otis J.
Storey	Grace Dudley	Guntz	Joseph A.
Storey	Laura L.	Proctor	Charles Ira
Story	Gladys E.	Gowans	Andrew, Jr.
Story	Ida May	Jacobs	Cameron
Story	Myrtle J.	Atchinson	Fred R.
Story	Susan	Allen	Henry C.
Story	Verinda Belle	Gossage	Joseph, Jr.
Stottlemyer	Rena Ada	Davis	Harry Edward
Stouder	Helen M.	Kanode	John O.
Stoughton	Elizabeth Carlon	Hemsath	Jack Henry
Stout	Clara Edna	Hardin	William Graves
Stout	Lizzie	McCutchen	Stanley S.
Stout	Mary Ellen	Carleton	John M.
Stover	Lillian D.	McCormack	William H.
Stowe	Anna F.	Kistler	Ray S.

Stradling	Julia	Clarke	P. F.	Strother	Cora E.	Robinson	Frank E.
Strahan	Emily A.	Kidwell	Paul M.	Strother	Joanna	Lehn	Charles
Strait	Marie A.	Crocker	S. K.	Strother	Johnie	Walton	Charlie P.
Stranford	Elva L.	Ruddock	Edward J., Dr.	Struter	Ruth Florence	Cooper	John Harmon
Strasser	Lizette C.	Crips	Melvin T.	Struve	Martha Olga	Gallagher	Frank George
Stratton	Mary Clair	Teel	Charles Cummings	Strzeleeki	Clara P.	Szemanski	Frank C.
Stratton	Susie I.	Elder	Ralph D.	Stuart	Annie M.	Roy	Anthony
Straub	Augusta	Santos	Frank Francis	Stuart	Isabel	Denis	Foster
Straub	Lottie	St. John	Carl Madison	Stuart	Lydia J.	Hiatt	Thos. L.
Straut	Angelica E., Mrs.	Sayre	Morton S.	Studdert	Angela Gertrude	Edwards	Herbert Hereward
Strayer	Esther	Stauffer	Howard A.	Studdert	Mary E.	Niklas	Max
Strebel	Minnie	Smith	Joseph Charles	Studdert	Susie Estella	Edwards	Henry Seymour
Strebel	Susie	Tamagni	Frank J.	Studley	Alsy	Concerse	Earl Flower
Streeter	Emma I.	Brady	Thomas M.	Stump	A. E.	Williams	John D.
Streeter	Lydia Allen, Mrs.	Patton	John	Stump	Carrie Annell (?), Mrs.	Inman	James Thomas
Streeter	Myrtle R.	McDougall	Edwin J.				
Streeter	Elzada Rose	Nosler	Claud Earl	Stump	Clara A.	Park	John C.
Stretch	Mary Ellen	Gregganis	James Sargent	Stump	Dottie	Hottinger	Bernard F.
Strickert	Alvina Agnes	Duff	Harry Arnold	Stump	Jessie M.	Murray	John A.
Strickirt	Martha F.	Koenig	Frank	Stump	Katie	Muse	George W.
Strickler	Ida Grace	Akers	Earl L.	Stump	Kittie M.	Ross	August C.
Stridde	Bertha C.	Wetmore	Henry D.	Stump	Lottie E.	Witham	George Edward
Stridde	Thyra	Hall	Halbert P.	Stump	Margaret A.	Burke	James G.
Strider	Cora E.	Stoffal	Claude P.	Stump	Martha E.	Keirn (?)	Henry W.
Strider	Saddie	St. John	William L.	Stump	Mary C.	Brown	Richard
Striver	Alice E.	Fronk	Edwin B.	Stump (?)	Susie	Carpenter	Jay W.
Strobel	Lillian L.	Surryhne	Robert H.	Sturgeon	Irene	Lafont	Walter Thomas
Strobridge	Emily May	Sanders	S. C.	Sturgeon	Lena, Mrs.	Wright	C. T.
Strode	Julia M.	Quigley	Fred G.	Sturgess	Sarah A.	Goddard	J. P.
Strode	Theresa E.	King	Thomas Riley	Sturla	Angela	Guffanti	Amedeo
Stroll	Evelyn	Castiglioni	Peter	Sturn	Bessie	Silva	Samuel J.
Strome	Hilma	Jacobson	Jens	Stympson	Ethel V.	Glidden	Willard W.
Stromme	Lena	Sorensen	Anders	Suchowski	Helen	Giannini	Harry
Strong	Eva L.	Smith	Boys J. C.	Suetta	Elizabeth H.	Crandell	Clarence F.
Strong	Lizzette W.	Gillett	Charles	Sugarman	Fannie	Golub	Dave

Sugarman	Fannie Gertrude	Robinson	Joseph	Sutherland	Annie Beulah	Lichan	Arthur Lincoln
Suggs	Rosalene (?) C.	Rohn	Silas M.	Sutherland	Della	Garrison	Charles S.
Sugher	Ida	Brown	Frank Cornelius	Sutherland	Ella C.	Braugher	Oscar H.
Sugker	Eileen H.	Pitt	Daniel W.	Sutherland	Hilda A.	Escola	Charles A.
Suhling	Sophie	Briggs	E. C.	Sutherland	Irene	Rhoads	Frank S.
Suhr	Meta	Rengstorff	Henry Frederick	Sutherland	Mayme H.	Goldsam	Matthias G.
Sullivan	Amanda J.	Harrison	Frank M.	Sutherland	Monica C.	Waldron	Warren B.
Sullivan	Andrea, Mrs.	Deini	Leonardo	Sutherland	Sarah M.	Weaver	Albert W.
Sullivan	Anna	Riddle	Charles	Sutluff	Harriett	Hughes	B. C.
Sullivan	Ella	Mego	Edward	Sutten	Pearl	Feldmeyer	Clemens A.
Sullivan	Juanita	Silva	Anton F.	Sutton	Anna Eliza	Cavanagh	Stephen Patrick
Sullivan	Kate	Counihan	Jeremiah	Sutton	Annie	Middleton	Walter V.
Sullivan	Leatha J.	Coyan	Wilson S.	Sutton	Etta A.	Hamilton	William A.
Sullivan	Margaret Catherine	Davis	William L.	Sutton	Ione M.	Witter	Clyde E.
				Sutton	Mary F.	Stearns	Charles D.
Sullivan	Mary	Ferguson	Edward J.	Svenson	Anna D.	McConnell	Hugh
Sullivan	Minerva	Newell	Charles Ellis	Svilovivh	Evelyn N.	Dailey	Le Roy C.
Sullivan	Nancy E.	Crabtree	Albert H.	Swadeling	Josephine Alden	McDonald	George Alfred
Sullivan	Nellie	Dunbar	Lee A.	Swain	Annie	Rose	Frank
Sullivan	Nellie	Ames	Benjamin J.	Swain	Lena G.	Brush	Frank A.
Sullivan	Prescella M.	Ingham	A. H.	Swain	May McConnell	Houts	Orrie Leonard
Sullivan	Saphronia C.	Street	James H.	Swan	Dora	Miller	John
Sullivan	Annie	Weber	Peter	Swaner	Bulah	Fielding	Edward Joseph
Suman	Belle, Mrs.	Hamer	Sylvester T.	Swank	Susie	Groshong	Walter E.
Summ	Erna Georgia	Marion	Vernal Kennet	Swann	Florence	Driesbach	F. K.
Summ	Amelia	Millerick	Phillip	Swanson	Alma A.	Olsen	Henry C.
Summerfield	Hattie R.	Anderson	James G.	Swanson	Ella L.	Wilson	Frederick C.
Surryhne	Alice Mabel	Gregson	Luke B.	Swanson	Hilda	Easter	James Marcellus Thomton
Surryhne	Barbara Stuart	Mead	Albert Miller				
Surryhne	Beatrice	Roehl	Arthur	Swanson	Louisa	Day	John
Surryhne	Mary Elizabeth	Rickard	Wm. M.	Swanson	Matilda	Corippo (?)	Steve
Susoff	Lucile A.	Flynn	John J.	Sweeney	Mae	Shinn	William McF.
Sussman	Marie	Rathbill	Joseph H.	Sweeney	Malina, Mrs.	Perry	Joseph M.
Sutherlan	Grace Elizabeth, Mrs.	Bierer	David William	Sweeny	Ellen A.	Hannan (?)	Patrick
				Sweet	M. E., Mrs.	Patterson	William
Sutherland	Anna Belle	Richardson	Clarence E.				

Sweetnam	Evelyn Mae	Chandler	Haven Burwell	Tallman	Ida	Taylor	William Ernest
Sweetsen	Alice L.	Howell	Frank M.	Talmadge	Hattie May	Ayers	George Lemuel
Sweetser	Violet Marda	Haigler	Albert Chester	Tamba	Annetta	Bonetti	Joseph
Sweitzer	Audrey M.	McNamara	James J.	Tann	Catharine A.	Brown	Wm. M.
Swenson	Gyda S.	Melson	J. R.	Tantet	Josephine	Pierre	Peter
Swift	Ethelyn Irene	Green	Walter Thomas	Tapscott	Mary Emma	Edmunds	Clarence
Swift	Lizzie	Gensler	Goodkind	Tartter	Frances	Eckel	Tobias Lewis
Swisher	B. Clifton	Deuprey	Munson	Tarwater	Alberta	Rayner	Aaron
Swisher	Kathleen	Poppe	Raymond George	Tarwater	Emma Louisa	Hudson	Daniel Bertnette
Switzer	A. E.	Carter	Geo. W.	Tarwater	Ida	Laughlin	Merton
Switzer	Avis V.	Brown	Frank W.	Tate	Feliciatadad, Mrs.	Miller	John
Switzer	Beryl	Jason	Anton	Taughter (?)	Regina	Nelson	Thomas Arthur
Switzer	Ivy W.	Hasenberg	William F.	Tavilai	Rossina	Paulucci	A.
Sydnor	Eva	Rideout	Walter R.	Taylor	Abby	Park	Collins
Sydnor	Roberta	Porter	George K.	Taylor	Alice B.	Ricklifs	Peter H.
Sykes	Lillian R.	Leffmann	Julius W.	Taylor	Annie	Monroe	Peter
Sylva	Emelia Emma	Allen	Frank	Taylor	Annie	Patten	Thomas J.
Sylva	Mary M., Mrs.	Perry	John	Taylor	Brooksie A.	Earl	John H. P.
Sylva	Mary F.	Perry	Joseph L.	Taylor	Clara E.	Perkins	Harry F.
Symcock	Lizzie	Winton	John B.	Taylor	Effie J.	Mueting	William F.
Syme	Annie	Fuller	Harve	Taylor	Emily B.	Myring	W. H.
Symmonds	Rowena Evelyn	Steilberg	Walter Theodore	Taylor	Ethel	Fitzgerald	John J., Jr.
Symonds	Gertrude J.	Green	Jonathan	Taylor	Eva	Nosler	C. E.
Szalay	Emilie	Richter	Frank	Taylor	Florence H.	Schwobeda	John L.
Szalay	Rosa	Alapi	Hans	Taylor	Georgie A.	Hansen	Frederick E.
Taber	Susie A.	Stahl	George C.	Taylor	Hattie Florence	O'Brien	Arthur Thomas
Tabor	Bessie	Hulsey	John B.	Taylor	Jennie E.	Carrie	Henry C.
Taft	Georginia (?) A.	Maxwell	Ernest Edgar	Taylor	Junita Eyleen	Blakley	Albert Edward
Taft	Mary	Winston	Edwin L.	Taylor	Lela Marjorie	Carrington	Olo Robert
Taggart	Anna M.	Shoemake	Omer G.	Taylor	Lena P.	Crabtree	Albert F.
Talbot	Allena	Clark	George F.	Taylor	M. Rachel	Scott	Archibald
Talbot	Eliza P.	Fouch	Albert	Taylor	Martha Nina	Cummins	George Arthur
Talbot	Tabitha A.	Tyrrel	Horace W.	Taylor	Mary E.	Sullivan	Miles J.
Talkington	Gladys	Cole	Harold	Taylor	Mary Easter	Sherrard	Henry Clayton
Tallman	Lulu M.	Robins	William C.	Taylor	Mary Ellen	Torrance	Joseph L.

Taylor	Minnie G.	Crawford	William E.	Terry	Mary A.	Tucker	M. G.
Taylor	Nina R.	VanBeber	Charles E.	Terry	Mary Jane	Gordon	William
Taylor	Orlean Martha	Miller	Cecil Jesse	Terry	Nora L.	Black	Walter C.
Taylor	Vivian	Butler	H. G.	Terry	Pearl Edna	Townsend	C. W.
Taylor	Cordelia J.	Gibson	James	Teters	Dora G.	Brown	Henry W.
Taylor	Mary L.	Petray	Geo. W.	Tew	Clara N.	Moser	Charles E.
Taylor	Minnie S.	Gale	Milton C.	Tharp	Martha C.	Sales	Wm. S.
Taylor (?)	Elizabeth	Livingston	Charles S.	Thero	Edythe Alma	Sloan	Robert W.
Teaby	Leonnora	Lafrenz	Henry	Thibadore	Jean M.	MacFarlane	Earl R.
Teaby (?)	Ora A.	Dittmore	Clarence A.	Thierkoff	Florence	Craib	William Joseph
Teaford	Emma I.	Whitney	Charles E.	Thing	Annie D.	Reese	William E.
Teale	Grace Louise	Clifford	George Bassett	Thing	Sarah J.	Barnes	Thos. J.
Tebbs	A. L.	Anderson	Vinson	Thistle	Bell	Foley	Michael
Teel	Ida	Blakesley	Claude	Thistle	Lizzie	Muller	Frank M.
Teineira	Rosa	Ennis	Frank	Thoman	Mary D.	St.Clair	C. A.
Tell	Ida Amanda	Forsberg	Hans Peter	Thomas	Alice Leoenia	Playle	Frederick Augustus
Tellefson	Dora	Crandall	Charles I.	Thomas	Anna E.	Fairchild	Leon H.
Teller	Mary H.	Purrington	Joseph M.	Thomas	Cora	Laurance	George A.
Temple	Anna	Mann	Thomas L.	Thomas	Elner	Pickrell	Armour
Temple	Christie	Clary	Paul Dennis	Thomas	Florence L.	Laumann	Arthur H.
Temple	Ethel	Williams	William	Thomas	Grace E.	Mundee	George E.
Temple	Mary Hutton	Keeling	Frederick	Thomas	Hazel B.	Brownscombe	Travis D.
Temple	Rosamond	Clary	Thomas Peter	Thomas	Irene E.	Snyder	John E.
Temple	Ruth	McLeod	Alfred W.	Thomas	Mabel Clare	Murphy	Ralph Everett
Templeman	Agnes M.	Allen	Harry R.	Thomas	Margaret E.	Hoeck	Frederick W.
Tennant	Rose Anna	Mills	Jas. Byron	Thomas	Mary E.	Rambo	Franklin
Tenney	Irene J.	Goodman	Howard W.	Thomas	Mary H.	Schaafsma	Herman F.
Tenter	Elizabeth Mary	Bilstein	Alfred George	Thomas	Minnie Frances	Fechtelkotter	Harry B.
Tenter	Fredericka	Hood	Thomas Bergin, Jr.	Thomas	Myrtle	Helberg	William E.
Tenter	Minnie Marie	Price	Orrie Thomas	Thomas	Nettie E.	Adams	Alfred F.
Terrel	Flora Mabel	Drake	Albert Eli	Thomas	Ora A.	Flesher	Harry
Terry	Annie	Broomfield	Byrd	Thomas	Rachel A.	Churchman	John W.
Terry	Della	Lelounarn	John	Thomas	Rosa Belle	Shook	Roy L.
Terry	Elsie M.	Povey	James A.	Thomas	Ruth Esther	Shearer	Lovick Pierce
Terry	Margareta Gertrude	Silveria	Antone Joseph	Thomas	Sarah A.	Glaister	Middleton P.

Thomas	Tilda S.	Williamson	Frederick F.	Thompson	L., Lieut.	Wallin	G. P., Capt.
Thomas	Vera Jewell	Beck	George N.	Thompson	Laura	Stanger	Amos H.
Thomas	Vivian G.	Fortado	Lawrence F.	Thompson	Laura A.	Fields	Fred S.
Thompkins	Carrie	Clark	Wm. E.	Thompson	Laura M.	Maddox	Samuel W.
Thompson	Agnes L.	Genther	Jeremiah	Thompson	Lenore E.	Price	Ellis F.
Thompson	Alice	Robinson	Frank L.	Thompson	Lillie	Hetzel	Carl
Thompson	Alice M.	Armstrong	Thos. E.	Thompson	Lizzie	Collings	Walter
Thompson	Anna F.	Finlayson	James	Thompson	Lucy Myrtle	Lovell	William Ferdinand
Thompson	Annie	Poulson	Andrew	Thompson	M. Ruth	Elzey	R. H.
Thompson	Annie	Martin	Rasmus	Thompson	Mabel B.	Hovey	Albert Theo
Thompson	Bertha M.	Sealock	J. T.	Thompson	Mabelle Clair	Stagner	Walter A.
Thompson	Carrie W.	Vaughan	W. H.	Thompson	Martha P.	Haehl	Walter L.
Thompson	Catherine Ruth	Creagmile	John Cowan	Thompson	Mary E.	Carrillo	Frank Joseph
Thompson	Cecile C.	Karcher	Myron M.	Thompson	Mary Evelyn, Mrs.	White	Constantine F.
Thompson	Charlotte	Gilbride	Rodger James				
Thompson	Christie D.	Bentley	Rufus W.	Thompson	Mattie M.	Lyman	Chas.
Thompson	Edith Lillian	Reed	Joseph Raymond	Thompson	Maude Elnora	Abshire	Alfred Cecil
Thompson	Eleanor S.	Parker	John W.	Thompson	May	Wilcox	Clarence Clay
Thompson	Electa G.	Wendt	Milton	Thompson	May	Gray	Elmer
Thompson	Elma Pearl	Haberfelde	Albert Valentine	Thompson	May I.	Case	Drury G.
Thompson	Ethel M.	Rathbone	Leland S.	Thompson	Myrtle C.	Gibson	James W.
Thompson	Evvy M.	Potter	Joseph H.	Thompson	Sophia	Fredson	Israel
Thompson	Fannie Jane	Bennett	Glover Henry	Thompson	Thelma Gertrude	Kaye	Charles Ivan
Thompson	Fannie S.	Davison	Henry W.	Thompson	Vera A.	Curtis	Thomas J.
Thompson	Florence L.	Cutter	Charles Samuel	Thompson	Virginia C.	Whittaker	Alan Dean
Thompson	Francis E.	Dillon	Charles E.	Thompson	Willie A.	Robertson	Frank D.
Thompson	Gertrude	Hoffer	Virgil	Thomsen	Alma Erna (?)	Burchard	Karl Sieden
Thompson	Harriett F.	Williams	Chas.	Thomsen	Elsie Loraine	Hansen	Elmer
Thompson	Heneretta	Moran	Jack Willis	Thomsen	Johanna I.	Jacobsen	Jacob E.
Thompson	Ineaz M.	McDowell	Harry E.	Thomson	Sadie May	Swisher	James Riley
Thompson	Ione G.	Briggs	Albert D.	Thorgood	Vera G.	Meldi	Paul E.
Thompson	Irene Ethel	Butts	Robert Samuel	Thormann	Martha T. H.	Fenner	Henry
Thompson	Josie M.	Brady	Jerry F.	Thorn	Blanche	Thrum	Edward Charles
Thompson	Kate	Christie	Frank B.	Thorn	Carletta Jane	Swygert	Isaac
Thompson	Kate Elizabeth	Reisinger	William Harry	Thorn	Matilda Jane	Sharp	James Earl

Thorn	Myrtle L.	Winsby	John H.	Tisolin	Louise	Fadeli	Angelo
Thorne	Grace G.	Carter	Herbert Eaton	Tittus	Phebe	Gleason	Cyrus S.
Thornton	Alice Louise	Porter	James Francis	Titus	Clara R.	Titus	George A.
Thorogood	Esther	Colburn	Joseph	Titus	Seba	Bachelder	Horace
Thorpe	Anna	Hunger	F. J.	Toal	Rosanna	Hulbert	Clarence E.
Thorpe	Louise E.	Bird	Jesse	Tobin	Alice M.	Leathe	Frank C.
Thorsen	Carrie D.	Sinclair	Henry G.	Tobin	Clara J.	Philips	James H.
Thorton	Thusa	Bledsoe	Robert R.	Tobin	Ella M.	Thornton	J. R.
Thrasher	N. J.	Starett	Robert	Tocchini	Julia	Bonugli	Peter
Thrift	Laura	Briggs	George S.	Tocter (?)	Cynthia	Steubbell	Orten
Throckmorton	Margaret M.	Bisinger	Hubert G.	Todd	Clara	Todd	Hugh G.
Throop	A., Mrs.	Throop	C. W.	Todd	Mary E.	Allen	Anthony
Throop	Emily M.	Cole	Henry L.	Todd	Ruby Angeine	Mann	Guy Chester
Throop	Fannie C.	Flournoy (?)	William H.	Todfield	Fannie	Glazer	Henry
Thrush	Nettie	Keykendall	Henry Clay	Tognacca	Lizzie	Dei	Peter
Thuesen	Camilla	Robinson	Morton E.	Tognaldo	Elvizia C.	Bolla	Romelio G.
Thum	Lillian, Mrs.	Thomas	Mathew Akin	Tollini	Celestina	Guffanti	Domenico
Thurman	Alice	McCracken	Marshal N.	Tolman	Mary E.	Seward	Anson J.
Thurman	Anastasia	Frost	Norman Seaver	Toltschin	Clara	Hall	Eugene F.
Thurman	Mabel D.	Warner	Frederick A.	Tomasi	Eda Marie	Witham	Francis Leo
Thurman	Margaret	Blackburn	George	Tomasi	Johanna Mary	Gilardi	Andrew Richard
Thurman	Nellie	McClish	Ralph	Tomasi	Linda O.	Jobe	Thomas F.
Tibbetts	Elsie Maude	McCaughey	Howard Cyril	Tomasi	Virginia	Respini	Attilio
Tibbetts	Josephine	Stacey	W. J. B.	Tomasini	Lila I.	Thompson	Rudolf A.
Tiede	Mary	Miller	Geo. F.	Tomassini	Josephine	Spaletta	Domenico
Tiedemann	Martha B.	Collischonn	Otto	Tomazio	Maria	d'Abreu	John Silveira
Tiers	Ethel Maggie	Happy	Abraham	Tomblinson	Gertrude Annie	Dibble	Lawrence Levinice
Tiers	Olive	Pixley	James	Tomblinson	Hazel Loreta	Kimes	Edward Thomas
Tillman	Margaret	Donner	George Jacob	Tomblinson	Mary Elizabeth	Teaderman	Edward
Timme	Millie, Mrs.	Davis	Henry A.	Tomblinson	Myrtle	Buchanan	Frank T.
Timme	Ora E.	Barrett	Albert	Tombs	Nellie M.	Mason	Robt. A.
Timmons	Eva Ethel	Constantine	Arthur Philip	Tomenski	Anna M.	Schwarz	Frank R.
Tindall	Frankie	Chappell	Emmet	Tomka	Meta Martha	Ludtke	John Emil
Tippe	Louisa, Mrs.	Woodruff	Henry	Tompkins	Maude May	Smith	John T.
Tiscornia	Caterina	Cuneo	Antonio	Tonelli	Josie M.	Peri	Settinio (?)

Tonelli	Lena	Paolini	Oreste	Towle	Emma S.	Gober	Benjamin F.
Toney	Ada	Barnes	John B.	Towne	Florence	McAnear	Saml. F.
Tonini	Assunta	Piccinotti	Clemente	Towner	Myrtle June	Jessen	Paul Frederick
Tonini	Erma	Roof	William A.	Towner (?)	Adeline	Lewis	Washington J.
Tonini	Nellie C.	Hardin	J. Rolla	Townsend	Mary Ann	Greig	David
Toogood	Henrietta	Shannon	James T.	Tozer	Iva M.	Katen	William L.
Toomey	Agnes V. D.	Heinkel	Herman Frank	Tracey	Amy M.	Christian	Charles E.
Toomey	Mary Ellnor	Lane	James Albert	Tracey	Olive	Bronson	William M.
Toppini	Marie V.	Feillers	Daniel	Tracy	Hazel J.	Dart	William E.
Torance	Sarah	Keran	J. N.	Tracy	Phoebe Mabel	Ridenhaur	Hilton Baker
Torelli	Pollonia	Giovani	Galliani	Traeger	Mary E.	Insel	A.
Torgelson	Anna	Bewick	William Young	Traeger	Orah Dell	Langpaap	Max
Torliatt	Marie Blanche	Cobb	Omar Otto	Tramor	Marie A.	Gardiner	Charles W.
Torliatt	Theresa	Jewett	Augustus Leroy	Trautner	Frances	Bacon	Jay S.
Toroni	Katie	Scarpellini	Elvezio	Travers	Emma	Gibson	Gardie L.
Toroni	Mary	Ricci	Germano	Traversi	Isolina	Tunzi	Natale
Toroni (?)	Edith	Canobbio	Ferdinando	Traversi	Josephine E.	Worth	Cletus C.
Torpey	Mary Alice	Osborne	Clifton L.	Traversi	Laura	Simoni	Dan
Torr	Agnes Leona	Benson	H. Urban	Treadwell	Alicia E.	Lando	Frank
Torr	Ida May	Gray	Thos. H.	Treadwell	Sarah E.	Harrigan	G. W.
Torr	Lottie Mae	Zacharias	Ben	Treehan	Catherine R.	Bryant	Albert James
Torrance	Maggie	Robinson	Frank	Treehan	Ellen A.	Packard	Otto B.
Torrance	Nellie	Smith	Arthur E.	Tremblay	Laura M.	Barceloux	Henry J.
Torre	A. C.	LeCarn	F.	Trembley	Evelyn A.	McNamara	James E.
Torrence	Lydia A	Coon	Robt. W.	Trent	Maude S.	Harris	Leon F.
Torrence	Mary E.	Keys	Samuel H.	Trice	Maude	Spaulding	Lewis Wetmur
Toschi	Nella	Tocchini	Armindo	Trimble	Lucy E.	Young	George Albert
Tostevin	Emma Beatrice	Shular	Clarence H.	Trimm	Estella Louise	Sneed	Richard Herbert
Totman	Ruth M.	Davison	Robert W. S.	Trine	Iona O.	Smith	James R.
Totten	Marie Ida May	Stafford	Alvin	Tripp	Anna M.	Terrill	John W.
Totten	Rinda O.	Stark	Henry R.	Tripp	Grace A.	Lynch	George L.
Totten (?)	E. A. T.	Hockin	William	Tripp	Lillian C.	Coggins	Chas. W.
Totton	Ella	Morrison	Francis George	Trisse ?	Caroline, Mrs.	Graumlich	John Y.
Towla	Ada	Turner	Alfred	Trojacek	Anna	Novak	John
Towle	Elizabeth Ellen	Stockstill	E. F.	Trondsen	Emily Rowena	McGimsey	Charles R.

Trondsen	Ruth	Carpenter	Clair W.	Tunstall	Martha N.	Wilson	William H.
Tronoff	Helena L.	Jacobsen	Thomas S.	Tunzi	Albina	Biagggi	Antony
Trotman	Eva Blanche Muriel	Girtaner	Alfred	Tunzi	Emma M.	Caseri	Robert A.
				Tunzi	Geneva M.	Bassi	Amando G.
Trought	Ruth	Smith	Edmund	Tunzi	Lily B.	Canepa	Ben
Trowbridge	Alice Gertrude	Scott	George Walter	Tunzi	Natola	Pasquini	Giovani
Trowbridge	Grace Tyler	McCustion	Bert James	Tuomey	Mary E.	Pozzie	Morris Canstantini
Trowbridge	Leslie A.	Brown	William M., Jr.	Tupper	Emma E.	Thomas	Massey, Jr.
Trowbridge	Mabel Bertram	Dohn	George Arthur	Tupper	Hattie	Cooper	Geo. W.
Trowbridge	Olive R.	Trusty	John F.	Turley	Ethel L.	Shringer	Ellis C.
Troxell (?)	Laura Josephine	Owens	Jessie Marvin	Turman	Margaret S.	Donnely	John Z.
Trubody	Clara C.	Hoffman	George W.	Turner	Ada Marie	Cook	Shelby Erington
True	Eliza W.	Jennings	Edward B.	Turner	Belle	Edwards	Alfred Atherton
Truett	Josephine	Darby	Jasper	Turner	Bessie L.	Patrick	Ernest J.
Truitt	Emma S.	Petray	Edwin A.	Turner	Bettie, Mrs.	Murphy	Henry
Truitt	Eva	Lancaster	John	Turner	Frances A.	Lang	Robert A.
Truitt	Sarah E., Mrs.	Truitt	John R.	Turner	Harriette M.	Owenby	Francis C.
Trunz	Josephine A.	Luce	Guy R.	Turner	Jennie B.	Croll	E. E. W.
Trusendi	Laura	Barilani	Guglielmo	Turner	Laura A.	Huffman	W. H.
Tryon	Elizabeth	Knaff	Henry Richard	Turner	Lizzie P.	Reynolds	James
Tucker	Anna May	Witham	Charles Henry	Turner	Lucille C.	Empey	William A.
Tucker	Harriet E.	Gilman	P. E.	Turner	Mabel	Nobles	Philip
Tucker	Jennie Augusta	Warren	Frank Adelbert	Turner	Maggie	Webber	David Gould
Tucker	Jessica B.	Barre	Lyman C.	Turner	May M.	Marshall	Frank L.
Tucker	Mary Ellen, Mrs.	Reynolds	Wm. H.	Turner	Ruth H.	Shearer	George Edwin
Tucker	Mona E.	Murphy	John	Turner	Sussie	Thomas	Louis George
Tuel	Beatrice P.	Stempnack	Martin	Turner	Verona Marie	Anderson	Irvine John
Tullar	Diadama Helen	Butler	John Walter	Turner	Zilda	Pettis	William Francher
Tullar	Mary	Pool	C. E.	Turner	Minnie L.	Martin	John Milton
Tully	Alice J.	Campbell	Arthur B.	Turner (?)	Delia	Wallace	Willis
Tully	Catharine	Christopher	Jas. C.	Turnidge	Martha A.	Cropley	R. T.
Tully	Louise B.	McCord	Rollin Burdette	Tuttle	Edith M.	Bailiff	John D.
Tully	Theresa Anna	Ware	Elmer Benton	Tuttle	Mary	Holst	Jacob E.
Tunsen	Edith L.	Larsen	Thomas A.	Tuttle	Nellie Mabel	Patton	Carlyle Gill
Tunstall	Annie	Miller	Benjamin F.	Tuttle	Lilla R.	Allen	Gerald M.

Twitchell	Henrietta Genevia	Billett	Frank E.	Usseglio	Catterina	Frugoli	Virgilio
Tygart	Laura	Truell	George	Utman	Hazel E.	McKinley	Charles. C.
Tyler	Jennie B.	Pool	Walter B.	Utt	Mary E.	Harris	Richard A.
Tyler	Leatha Ruth	Frei	Walter C.	Uttley	Juanita I.	Herbert	Vanscoy P.
Tyner	Myrtle	Uslar	Rossney Edward	Vacchieri	Lucia	Norette	Domenico
Ubaldi	Rosa, Mrs.	Recchia	Vincenza	Vader	Elsie	VanSyckle	Lynn V.
Uboldi	Rosa	Volonte	Eliseo	Vadon	Bertha E.	Lambert	William A.
Udall	Lola Maud	Marlatt	Perry Edward	Vail	Emma	Shaver	Eli S.
Uhlenberg	Catherine M.	Jorgensen	Harry I.	Valandhan	Mary	Combs	Alvin Roots
Ullman	Edna	Borman	Noel	Valdes	Vincent E.	Conners	George W.
Ulrey	Wava	Hebbron	Elton Benson	Valentine	Christine	Eagle	Edward
Umbarger	Edith May	Townsend	Robert Floyd	Valentine	Frances	Avellar	Jose
Underhill	Allene R.	Britton	Leland M.	Valenzuela	Mary	Burghard	G. F.
Underhill	Angie A.	Rogers	Walter E.	Valiant	Annie	Nagel	Alfred Richard
Underhill	Catherine	Ducker	John	Vallaiga (?)	Irene	Regalia	Pete
Underhill	Geneva	Rogers	George W.	Vallejo	Lulu E.	de Emparon	Ricordo
Underhill	Hazel Marie	O'Brien	Pam Joseph	Vallier	Emma M.	Elphick	Clarence R.
Underhill	Mary	Eagle	W. F.	Vallier	Maye	Stepp	Jesse N.
Underwood	Pearl Alphia	Licht	George J.	Vallier	Rose	Peters	Herman
Unger	Daphne E.	Jenne	Christian J.	Van Allen	Emeline C., Mrs.	Lewis	J. F.
Ungerwitter	M. Gretchen	Belden	Ralph Austin	Van Aukin	Laura	Head	Walter W.
Ungewitter	Maggie E.	Showalter	Oscar N.	Van Brocklin	Emma J.	Smith	Alfred
Ungewitter	Olive H.	Steen	Victor V.	Van Buren	Stella	Burger	Calvin
Upson	Ella Evaline	Jones	Lewis Eugene	Van de Water	Grace M.	Goldman	Leon
Upson	Florence M.	Young	Silas H.	Van Der Strateu	Pauline Marie	O'Meara	Peter James
Upson	Kathryn	Hughes	Thomas M.	Van Doren	Mary Francis	Nerton	John N.
Upson	Lucy	Hawthorn	Loyet/Loyel A.	Van Keppel	Mary L.	Ellis	Edward
Upson	Sabra E.	Powers	Phineas F.	Van Keppel	Nellie	Ward	Charles. D.
Urhr	Chlara M.	Bray	Elyah C.	Van Riper	Catherine	Barr	William Holt
Uristen	Annie M.	Grady	W. D.	Van Vicel	Bertha L.	Banks	Earl Arthur
Urquhart	Irene Lois	Parker	Harry Beacher	Van Vicel	Pauline	Brown	Lynn R.
Urton	Elsie S.	Meyer	William J.	Van Winkle	Alice M.	Heryford	Reuben M.
Urton	Eunice D.	Barnes	Aaron H.	Van Winkle	Edith	Thompson	Bert
Usher	Mary J.	Sullivan	P. George	Van Winkle	Evalena	Miles	William J.
Ushman	Frederika	Blair	John				

Van Winkle	Lettie	High	Arthur Desten
Van Winkle	Lola	Campbell	C. I.
Van Winkle	Olive	Leek	Charles E.
Van Wormer	Clara G.	Sucher	Victor E.
Vance	Elizabeth F.	Vann	Edward S.
Vandeleur	Mayme Alloysious	Fisher	Isaac Willard
Vanderkarr	Daisy M.	Murray	Ruby E.
Vanderkarr	Eva Lena	Strode	Charles A.
Vanderlieth	Violet V.	Ward	Fred C.
Vanderstreaton	Louise	Thomas	Frank P.
Vanina	Tilly	Chiotti	James
Vanlanding-ham	Maud	Peterson	James C.
Vann	Belle	Porter	Sam Duncan
Vannucci	Algi	Luciani	Pete
Vannucci	Florinda	Martini	Narciso
Vanoni	Ermine	Morelli	Giuseppe, Jr.
Vanoni	Margheritta	Spadini	Battista
Vanoni	Ynez Dorothy	Moy	John Daniel
VanWormer	Charlotte E.	Fulwider	Earl N.
Varneo	Clara J.	Coon	John T.
Varney	Helen	Bradford	D. J.
Varrell	Cora M.	Thurston	Julius Tinny
Vascaressa	Henrietta M.	Lightner	Raymond J.
Vasconi	Angela	Seghesio	Edovardo
Vassar	Agnes Aileen	Honton	Paul Noel
Vassar	Emma	Snediker	Fred L.
Vassar	Etta	Holst	James P.
Vassar	Lizzie	Daniels	Fred J.
Vassar	N. J., Mrs.	Moore	C. P.
Vaughan	Bertha J.	Harlan	Charles E.
Vaughan	Jessie A.	Chaney	William Henry, Jr.
Vaughn	Belle, Mrs.	Crowell	Albert
Vaughn	Louisa F., Mrs.	Bledsoe	Linn
Veale	Margaret	Biggs	George C.
Veale	Margaret A.	Ott	George Herbert
Veasne (?)	Anna	Christansen	John
Veganogo	Angelo	Gardella	Joseph
Veira	Mary Agnes	Mathews	Alvaro Brown
Velasques	Mary	Avjona	Daniel J.
Velazquez	Carmen	Figera	Louie
Vellutini	Lizzie	Dinucci	Richard
Vengenviter (?)	Sarah	Wilson	Louis
Venon	Nora G.	Boyse	Clarence
Ventura	Mary Francis	Horgan	Edward Timothy
Verbeke	Mary Virginia	Osmon	Albert
Verdisio	Flora	Secondino	Capra
Versell	Carolyn J.	Bales	Marion
Verzasconi	Basilia	Verzasconi	James
Verzasconi	Bessie	Ferrari	Tealue
Verzasconi	Clotilda	Malandra	Mauro
Veschi	Claudia	Rossi	Anselmo
Vest	Pearl Maud	Drysdale	Robert Hugh
Vestal	Lena	Hall	William Clyde
Vestal	Blossom	June	H. J.
Vianesi	Angelina	Milanesio	Virgilio
Vicari	Clara	Giacconi	Santi
Vicari	Elvira	Tovani	Romoaldo
Vicari	Evelena	Russell	Charles Wesley
Vicari	Lillie E.	Sutherland	Elmer M.
Vickery	Nellie G.	Abra	Jack W.
Victor	Julia C.	Foste	Manuel V.
Vieira	Francisca	Freitas	Joao M.
Vieira	Maria Joseph	Avila	Joao Maria
Vier	Angeline Genevieve	Borba	Emanuel Ignacio
Vier	Clara	Clark	Harry A.
Vier	Clara Ellen	McDonald	Marshall Bell
Vier	Flora	Felciano	John
Vier	Mary	Nunes	Joseph J.

Viera	Flora	Peters	Frank W.	Von Pokrzywnicki	Hattie	Levy	Alexander
Viera	Mary	De Maura	Antonio				
Viestentz	Alma A.	Davis	J. M.	Von Skatnicki	Anna C.	Purvine	Percy
Villot	Rose J.	Zulberti	Clement	Voris	Isabell Alice	Allenberg	Ferdinand Arthur
Vinal	Mary Olive	Strause	Asher E.	Vosilotos	Louisa Agnes	Hutchinson	Edward Lincoln
Vincent	Irene	Meincke	Herman F.	Voss	Anna K.	Lee	Richard A.
Vincent	Louise Cecile	Poulson	Peter Walter	Voss	Clara C.	Wheeler	Alonzo H.
Vincent	Mary C.	Dunne	Robert H.	Vought	Agnes E.	Wieberts	Duvall C.
Vineyard	Bonnie	Young	J. W.	Voutron	Bartha Barbra	Gotzsek	Albert Henry
Vinyard	Olive Barr	Etherridge	Cecil William	Vragnizan	Margaret	Valerio	Martin
Virgil	Martha E.	Leich	James L.	Vrismo	Edith	Rocca	John
Vitale	Louisa	McGuire	Laurence B.	Vrooman	Mae Baldwin	Forbes	Cleveland
Vitali	Camille	Tognotti	William	Waage	Ollie A.	Arvold	Louis
Vitali	Eleda	Lunardi	Giovanni	Waddell	Isadore Belle	Harris	Eli
Vitonsek	Hazel Peryl	Brown	Edgar Allen	Wade	Bernice	McAfee	Lorn Charles
Vivarelli	Minnie	McCombs	Edward O.	Wade	Daisy E.	McEowen	John W.
Viviani	Georgia	Marchetti	Nicoderro	Wade	Grace E.	Bettini	Alessio J.
Viviani	Maria	Bianchini	Bernardino	Wade	Juniatta, Mrs.	Mallory	George Brown
Viviani	Marie	Edvardo	Bettelotti	Wadsworth	Alice Maud	Hunt	George Walter
Vizitel	Eva	Silverstein	Max	Wadsworth	Anna M.	King	Lochiel M.
Vocke	Anna	Rossi	John F.	Wadsworth	Helen Octavia	Noack	Max F.
Vogel	Camilla A.	Kirstein	Max	Wadsworth	Mildred Jeanette	Crossley	Edwin Hall
Vogel	Olga T.	Mane	Paul	Wagenblast	Alice E.	Johnson	Henry
Vogt	Anne D.	Crane	Richard Henry	Wagers	Arla Marie	Phillips	Harold F.
Vogt	Gertrude G.	Cockrill	Robert L.	Wagers	Candace	Smith	Walter McIntyre
Vogt	Margaret	Dreisback	William E.	Wagers	Martha Elizabeth	Ferguson	Erwin Emmet
Voight	Hannah E.	Guill	Etna E.	Wagner	Alma	Morris	Ernest
Voigt	Margaret M.	Guirin	Stephen I.	Wagner	Annie E.	Flockhart	Joseph J.
Voigt	Wilhelmina	Taggart	Louis Edw.	Wagner	Ella Marie	Warden	Robert Audley
Voletti	Maria	Alberti	Francisco	Wagner	Frances M.	Maxwell	Watson B.
Volkerts	Ida Emelie	Seavey	Robert Tustin	Wagner	Jessie Adeline	Bates	Frank Earle
Von Arx	Emma	Brown	Chester B.	Wagner	Julia	Morrison	John H.
Von Berg	Annie	Gledhill	Ernest B.	Wagner	Louise	Quigley	Francis E.
Von Grafen	Nellie	Bugbee	Bert	Wagner	Mazie	Lawson	Perry Alexander
Von Kassinger	Elsie R. M.	Petersen	Harry	Wagner	Meta Anna	Peterson	August

Wahl	Louisa	Atlon	Theodore F.	Walker	Margaret I.	Bacon	Mark J.
Wahrman	Augusta	Megonigil	Eli	Walker	Marion E.	Crawford	Roy S.
Waite	Ida Luella	Ronsheimer	Charles William	Walker	Olive	Brown	Ralph
Waite	Thenia	Hunter	William Crittenton	Walker	Pearl	Roads	James H.
Wakeland	Maggie E.	Fonts	Lee	Walker	Carrie Belle	Bloch	Albert
Walce	Mary	Nelson	Eddie	Walker	Nellena E.	Fraser	James Grant
Walce	Pauline	Condeff	Gerry	Wall	Ada M.	Dake	John A.
Waldorf	Maude, Mrs.	Burgess	Loiuis L.	Wall	Ella	Legg	Samuel M.
Waldron	Kate	Ashley	William T.	Wall	Florence V.	Cheney	Thomas W.
Waldrop	Julia Andrews, Mrs.	Sherrett	Edwin	Wall	Jennie	Martin	T. J.
				Wallace	Annie E.	Matthews	Charles W.
Walds	Jennie	Brown	Charles W.	Wallace	Catherine	Sims	Ruben L.
Walker	Addie L.	Glatfelder	Clement	Wallace	Clara Nannie	Tew	Martin Ckasey
Walker	Alice Yetta	Schroder	August P. H.	Wallace	Elizabeth J.	Fike	N.
Walker	Alma	Ellis	William	Wallace	May Etta	Chase	Ralph Noble
Walker	Dasey	Allison	Samuel	Wallach	Jane Eloise	Rawles	Ernest Everett
Walker	E. L., Mrs.	Briggs	C. A.	Wallburg	Edna Elizabeth	Healey	Thomas James
Walker	Elizabeth H.	Graunlick (?)	John	Waller	Eva Myrtle	Hayes	Charles Ronan
Walker	Elizabeth H.	Cobb		Wallin	Eva M.	Maddux	Burt
Walker	Elizabeth H.	Burgett	William	Wallis	Lena, Mrs.	Campion	George W.
Walker	Ella M.	Barnes	Louis G.	Wallman	Georgiana	Dolcini	Joseph Samuel
Walker	Emily M.	Sylvester	Chester W.	Walls	Grace E.	Drennon	George
Walker	Eva	Andrews	Albert	Walsh	Clara	O'Brien	Timothy V.
Walker	Evelyn I.	Musante	Louis S.	Walsh	Dixie Edith	Astredo	Anthony Dominick
Walker	Florence J.	Dunsmore	Harry O.	Walsh	Elizabeth C.	Venable	Walter L.
Walker	Hazel	Faylor	John F.	Walsh	Inez E.	Smith	Chester Ariel
Walker	Hazel E.	Baumeister	Carl A.	Walsh	Irene F.	Rogers	George W.
Walker	Hazel L.	Anderson	Ellis R.	Walsh	Nora	Banton	James
Walker	Katherine E.	Jacobsen	Frederick	Walsh	Rose	Gaffney	William
Walker	Laura I.	Weeks	Albert B.	Walsh	Sarah	Cunihan	John
Walker	Linda M.	Zizak	Cosmos P.	Walsh	Sarah Jane	Kulberg	Andrew John
Walker	Louisa	Simpson	Duncan	Waltenspiel	Virginia R.	Williams	Burt V.
Walker	Lucy	Brush	Wm. T.	Walter	Hannah	Newman	Oliver M.
Walker	M. P.	Sears	G. C. P.	Walter	Irene M.	Walls	David Burns
Walker	Margaret B.	Gill	Robert J.	Walters	Audry V.	Hendry	Howard W.

Walters	Catharine	Dorman	Ira	Ward	Margaret M.	Holmes	Chas. H., Jr.
Walters	Mary E., Mrs.	Sutton	Silas N.	Ward	Mary	Russell	Frank D.
Walters	Pearl	Marshall	Manuel J.	Ward	Mary A.	Small	W. H.
Walters	Sianea (?)	Lunney	Phillip	Ward	Mary J.	Madeira	W. R.
Waltham	R. M., Mrs.	Curtiss	Thomas Edson	Ward	Maude N.	Wheeler	Walter J.
Walton	Ida O.	Davis	Charles Marion	Ward	Mayme N.	Williams	Ernest L.
Walton	Louise Evelyn	Guth	Gustave John	Ward	Mina B.	Haselton	C. O.
Walts (?)	Elizabeth	Horne	David	Ward	Nellie Lorain	Karnes	Percy
Waltz	Rena P.	Pierson	George M.	Ward	Polly A.	Gibson	Henry
Wanaka	Leona E.	McKibbin	George M.	Ward	Rosine T.	Linz	Adelbert G.
Wanderer	Myra Francis	Sheridan	Frank Joseph	Ward	Sarah A.	Black	George H.
Warboys	Irene	Bufford	Lawrence	Ward	Sarah, Mrs.	Haubrich	Leonard
Ward	Ada E.	McCutchan	William H.	Warden	Ella M.	Jones	Charles W.
Ward	Ada L.	Ackerman	Clarence M.	Ware	Helen	Fraser	George Willard
Ward	Alice I.	Hemenway	Daniel D.	Ware	Lilla	Gallaway	Alfred Russel
Ward	Annie May	Elliott	Frank Edward	Ware	Mabel	Polastri	Richard B.
Ward	Bertha E.	Small	William H.	Ware	Margaret	Lyon	Arthur J.
Ward	Bertha May	Evans	Samuel C.	Waring	Jane L.	Shepherd	J. Avery
Ward	Cleone	Hyman	Frank J.	Warner	Alma	Anker	Erik Jessen
Ward	E. May	Denton	Paul R.	Warner	Augusta, Mrs.	Darby	Jasper N.
Ward	Elizabeth R.	Webber	Charles J.	Warner	Cora E.	Frost	Martin
Ward	Elizabeth, Mrs.	Alford	Erastus	Warner	Henrietta Mary	Grindle	Monroe Woodard
Ward	Estella G.	Peckham	Alton L.	Warner	Kate	Vallier	George A.
Ward	Gertrude	Keller	J. Bryant	Warner	Mary E.	Byerly	Frank F.
Ward	Gertrude Alice	Boding	Raymond O.	Warner	Mary E.	Davis	G. W.
Ward	Hattie May	Little	Wilbert James	Warner	Maud	Murray	Archibald Benjamin
Ward	Henrietta	Burtchaell	George C.				
Ward	Jessarce Wyman	Williams	Albert Robert	Warner	Minnie E.	McCargar	H. S.
Ward	Jessie M.	Barnett	Montie	Warner	Pearl C.	Wilson	John H.
Ward	Julia Ann	James	Thos. J.	Warner	Rebekah	Ferrell	John
Ward	Katie E.	Ketcham	Orven C.	Warner (?)	Madova (?)	Morgan	Hugh
Ward	Lalitte I.	Davis	Percy E.	Warren	Addie J.	Hasty	Charles H.
Ward	Lillian Belle	Domine	August F.	Warren	Anna L.	Patterson	John R.
Ward	Lulu E.	Westwood	Cecil F.	Warren	Bessie E.	Kendall	James
Ward	Mabel F.	Du Vander	David H.	Warren	Edith G.	Heitz	Howard L.

Warren	Emma Louise	Allen	Frederick William
Warren	Harriet J.	Sonnikson	Henry N.
Warren	Kate A.	Newberry	Cyrus R.
Warren	Lizzie Eyerkuss	Rogers	Lynn E.
Warren	Mary L.	Lampson	Augustus
Warren	May	Cook	Andrew J.
Warren	Ollie A.	Andrews	George B.
Warren	Sarah B.	Moody	Edward Elmer
Warren	Sarah M.	Treece	J. A.
Washburn	Brenda L.	Pool	Frank Johnson
Washburn	Catherine Faith	Marks	Walter Randolph
Washburn	O. E., Mrs.	Hall	George
Washburn	Rose May	McLean	George Graham
Washington	Carrie C.	Salesbury	George W.
Wass	Jessie E. R., Mrs.	Hall	George A.
Wasserfallen	Anna	Baumgartner	Leonhard
Wassman	Ida	Buleis	Wesley
Waterbury	Ada Muriel	Foster	Lewis Keyston
Waterman	Florence M.	Pitt	Clarence L.
Waterman	Gertrude M.	Frisch	Finnly W.
Waterman	Ida E.	Hotz	Ralph O.
Waterman	Leora L.	Seavy	Frank W.
Waterman	Luella	Wilkins	Reuben F.
Waterman	Melvina B.	Bailhache	J. Temple
Waterman	Orena A.	Wiley	Sterling P.
Waterman	Tempy	Calderwood	Ambrose
Waterman	Wylda S.	Kuchmann	Henry, Jr.
Waters	Ella L., Mrs.	Robinson	William C.
Waters	S. J., Mrs.	Nay	L. G.
Watkins	Annette A.	McCan	Francis A.
Watkins	Nellie	Jenkins	Gilbert C.
Watson	Alvania	Jamieson	B. T.
Watson	Elizabeth E.	Foelker	Adam H.
Watson	Emma	Pease	Richard Henry, Jr.
Watson	Josephine	Ferguson	W. W., Jr.
Watson	Lola Etta	Fried	Henry W.
Watson	Mamie	Cameron	George H.
Watson	Margaret	Graves	Ben F.
Watson	Mary, Mrs.	Caughey	John
Watson	Sarah	Hoffman	Alfred H.
Watson	Susan Gordon	Thole	William Carl
Watt	Agnes	Guilfoyle	John
Watt	Chrissie L.	Clark	Harry H.
Watt	Margaret M.	Harper	John
Watts	Edna E.	Oliver	Gordon F.
Watts	Margaret E.	Russell	Howard S.
Watts	May	Cabarrubia	Frank
Waugh	Armina	Monroe	William Henry
Waugh	Lenna M.	Carden	Arthur G.
Weatherington	Myrtle Alberta	Cauckwell	Isaac Newton
Weatherly	Julia	Dad	R.
Weaver	Adeline	Pugh	Alphonzo
Weaver	Anna Alberta	Hunt	Eugene Warren
Webb	Adelie Marie	Pomon	Nick D.
Webb	Annie S., Mrs.	Peck	Orson
Webb	Fanny	Heine	Louis William
Webber	Annie	Pool	Charles Elbert
Webber	Jennie, Mrs.	Wescott	Nelson
Weber	Alma Pearl	Jacobs	Walter Wyrt
Weber	Josephine E.	Clement	Walter L.
Weber	Louise M.	Rubke	Grover C.
Weber	Marie Emma	Tunstall	Robert N.
Weber	May	Snook	Daniel
Weber	Rosa	Artner	Michael
Weber	Ruth B.	Lunger	Walter E.
Weber	Sophie A.	Lowell	George R.
Webster	Anna	Anderson	Robert Marion
Webster	Charlotte E.	Mitchell	Joseph
Webster	Mary F., Mrs.	Fix	J. K.
Wedde	Henrietta	Irwin	William M.

Weddige	Mary Ann	Palmer	George	Welch	Lois L.	Cameron	Wallace A.
Wedel	Lillian	Rodehaver	Ray Harold	Welch	Mary A.	Pace	William Russell
Wedemeyer	Dorothy E.	Hansen	Andras	Welker	Alice	Angelo	Wallace P.
Wedge	Alice Flora	Sousa	Alfred Joseph	Weller	Eva U.	Gardner	Albert E.
Wedge	Clara B.	Davello	Tony J.	Weller	Margaret	Mitchell	Frank S.
Wedge	Josephine M.	Davello	Joseph L.	Weller	Ina K.	Walker	Lyle A.
Wedge	Mamie C.	Harmon	Russell J.	Welley (?)	Nora	McCray	Armund W.
Wedge	Mary Adelaide	Valadao	John M.	Welling	Mabel Bell	Wallin	George Earl
Wecd	Edna M.	Hughes	Louis D.	Welling	Rose A.	Ellis	Arthur
Weeks	Alice M.	Thompson	Westley	Welling	Susie Mae	Colombo	John Edward
Weeks	Anna M.	Jenkines	James H.	Welling	Zella Ella	Robertson	William Jean
Weeks	Effie	Lacque	Frank	Wells	Alice Maud	Jasper	Gustavus A.
Weeks	Frances E.	Morse	Stephen C.	Wells	Emma G.	Reimer	Fred
Weeks	Jean C.	Patchett	John M.	Wells	Gertrude H.	Nelson	Andrew, Jr.
Weeks	Josephine	Proctor	Walter L.	Wells	Grace Eva	Boysen	Charley M.
Weeks	Laura Jane	Burginger	John Frank	Wells	Ida	Gregg	Augustus I.
Weeks	Stella	Rae	Robert S.	Wells	Julia Ann, Mrs.	Pool	John Silas
Weenfield (?)	Bessie	Stewart	Henry	Wells	Leora E.	Weston	Henry F.
Wehrspon	Carrie	Barsi	Nichol	Wells	May	Groves	James H.
Weidman	Emerine	Dean	Lewis F.	Wells	May F.	Norris	Charles G.
Weigant	Winnie	Wohlers	Otto	Wells	Myrtle B.	Oehlman	Christopher G.
Weigel	Esther D.	Huntt (?)	George E.	Wells	Olive	Gustafson	Carl G.
Weinberg	Emma A.	Muat	William F.	Wells	Stella Evlin	Cobb	Clarence Leroy
Weinberg	Gussie	Ormond	Charles K.	Wells	Winnie M.	Staley	Charles E.
Weinreich	Ann, Mrs.	Clark	James R.	Weltz	Katherine	Crowell	Elmer Harlow
Weir	Mary Gertrude	Bailey	Terry Elmer	Wendt	Katherine B.	Morton	Dudley D.
Weirick	Nellie G.	Goodenough	Raymond F.	Wendt	Mollie	Leggett	Charles F.
Weise	Hattie A.	Luttrell	Frank M.	Wendt	Paulina	Fulkerson	Richard
Weishand	Margaretta	Klein	Christian	Wendte	Felicitas E.	Buegge	Harry
Weismann	Alvina	Ackermann	Anton	Wenger	Selma	Kornmuller	Wilhelm
Weiss	Laura	Overton	William M.	Wentworth	Hattie	Thurman	George
Weisshand	Alvina Christina	Gray	Joseph Allen	Wentworth	Ida H.	Grove	Arvil T.
Welch	Effie C.	Lapham	Matthew	Wentzy	Bessie F.	Bodin	Walter B.
Welch	Eva	Swift	Grant R.	Werano	Wisenta, Mrs.	Masgado	Jose
Welch	Grace M.	Coggins	Andrew H.	Werenberg	Dorthea	Lund	Aage F.

Wergand	Loretta M.	Kamp	Daniel W.	Weymouth	Corrinne	Hodge	Levi Francis
Werick	N. Tewella M.	Deloran	Jefferson	Weymouth	Mae Z.	Boulden	Frederick N.
Wernecke	Katie	Marchisio	Delfino	Weythman	Lucretia Elizabeth	Kingwell	Alfred Leslie
Wernecke	Katie	Dont	Joseph	Whallon	Lielia E.	Brown	John
Werner	Marie	Babbino	Fred	Wharton	Nellie E.	O'Neil	John T.
Werner	Meta	Helberg	William	Wheatley	Bertha	Nystrom	Swan A.
Werner	Nora, Mrs.	Kennedy	William A.	Wheatley	Besse Maude	Kinyon	Reuben H.
Wertheimer	Elza L.	Wiltse	Geo. E.	Wheeler	Alta	Lewis	Ray A.
Werts	Gertrude D.	Wallberg	Alfred F.	Wheeler	Anna	Estes	John E.
Wescoatt	Alice Clare	Cahill	James Felix	Wheeler	Anna L, Mrs. (?)	Tarwater	Lemuel E.
Wescoatt	Jennie, Mrs.	Ruggles	Austin	Wheeler	Edith	Shook	Martin B.
Wescott	Mamie	Banks	James A.	Wheeler	Ellen J., Mrs.	Walsh	David
Weselsky	Tillie	Crigler	Walter M. D.	Wheeler	Evelyn S.	Ashe	William W.
Wessels	Ruth B.	Andersen	Phillip N.	Wheeler	Frances L.	Matthias	Henry G.
Wesson	Justice O.	Kerr	Newton	Wheeler	Grace Gertrude	Miller	Melvin Stanley
West	Catherine	Stibi	Paul	Wheeler	Harriet S.	Knipp	Ruscher A.
West	Florence H.	Stewart	Ellsworth R.	Wheeler	Isabella M.	Dana	Fred C.
West	Mary	Andrews	A. J.	Wheeler	Juanita	Georgi	Ralph A.
West	Mary	Welch	Charles	Wheeler	Julie	Judd	Charles A.
West	Minna (?) M.	Winfield	Clarence R.	Wheeler	Kittie May	Terrell	Clyde
West	Nellie G.	Clark	H. O.	Wheeler	L. V.	Winning	J. W.
Westenhaver	M. E.	Jordon	Addison D.	Wheeler	Lela Alpha	Baldwin	Clyde R.
Westgate	Ivy	Scott	William W.	Wheeler	Mattie	Reaty	Thomas L.
Westover	Irma L.	Hoffman	Walter A.	Wheeler	Maude	Fulkerson	Bruce C.
Westover	Minnie Merle	Lannom	Clarence Worton	Wheeler	Myrtle	Cook	Andrew Joseph
Westwood	Inez V.	Gwaltney	W. B.	Wheeler	Nellie Ethel	Hyatt	Will Carlton
Westwood	Mary Ellen	Hebrard	Henry Hepolet	Wheeler	Vera	Johnson	Nels A.
Wetherbee	Elizabeth C.	Lewis	Jere	Wheeler	Winifred Lois	Starke	Arion Stanford
Wetmur	Olive M.	Hoyt	Jesse D.	Whipple	Jennie E.	Conkling	Glenn R.
Weybright	Anna	Bernard	Robert L.	Whitae	Mary Dena	Root	Percy Martin
Weyhe	Dora	Fairclo	Richard	Whitaker	Elsie Day	Miller	Henry Maurice
Weyhe	Edith E.	Nendick	Leroy C.	Whitaker	Julia H.	Lichau	Ernest A.
Weyl	Clara	Fonts	Fred	Whitaker	Kate	Phillips	Walter L.
Weyl	Nellie	Mayer	Frederic D.	Whitaker	Lottie N.	Bouneau	Louis
Weyman	Cletys	Ausmus	Delbert	Whitaker	Rena Pearl	DeRose	William

Whitaker	Rhoda M.	Hershberger	John F.	Whitson	Luella	Wholey	William N.
Whitcomb	Annie O.	Garrison	Ross J.	Whittaker	Hazel	Woodhouse	William John
Whitcomb	Lelia A.	McElwain	Arthur E.	Whorton	Minona	Sparrow	David
White	Almira Leigh	Wilson	James S., Jr.	Wiberg	Betty	Dietert	Rudolph H.
White	Amy F.	Bainbridge	Clarence E.	Wichman	Ida B.	Gibson	Edward E.
White	Anna R.	Smith	Harold U.	Wickersham	Mae S.	Bergevin	Alexander M.
White	Barbara	Wichmann	George Nicklos	Wickersham	Mary Catherine	Dowler	Allen Lewis
White	Blanche Mabel	Valverde	Frank	Wickershaw	Lizzie C.	Maclay	Thomas
White	Cora Belle	Dugan	James Oliver	Wicks	Malinda J.	Smith	James M.
White	Elsie	Smith	E. S.	Wieberts	Kate, Mrs.	Joy	William H.
White	Florence	Cromwell	William O.	Wiedemann	Minna Margaret	Mitchell	Harry
White	Isadora M.	Maddalena	John H.	Wiegand	Mary	Mathiesen	Fred
White	Jennie L.	McPeak	William H.	Wiener	Sophie	Wiener	Louis
White	Julia Emma	Bogard	William J.	Wiers	Margaret E.	Stemper	Ira G.
White	Loma A.	Krenzer	Thomas C.	Wiers	Mattie Theresa	Melehan	Daniel John
White	M. Cadona	Hall	John W.	Wiess	Bertha	Gibbins	Lue Amos
White	Marie C.	Smith	Frank T.	Wight	Ida M.	Bronson	Harry R.
White	Mary E.	Waters	James	Wightman	Cora B.	Norton	F. B.
White	Mary Ellen	Mills	Hiram B.	Wikman	Charlotte	Northey	Frank T.
White	May E.	Lewis	Samuel B.	Wilason	Edith	Tanner	Lewis
White	Myrtle Amelia	Schofield	Silvanus Whitteney	Wilcox	Edith M.	Gardiner	Bevil F.
White	Rachel	Hubbard	Junius H.	Wilcox	Grace E.	Bond	Charles Allen
Whitechurch	Julia E.	Musgrave	Benjamin F.	Wilcox	Susan, Mrs.	Goodrich	Francis M.
Whited	Retta A.	Witherell	William L.	Wilder	Elizabeth Gertrude	Hutchings	Edward Thomas
Whitehead	Florence Estella	Christiansen	Walter				
Whitehead	Mary A.	Randolph	George E.	Wilder	Lois	Ryan	Edmund S.
Whitehead	Sophia I.	Ormsby	Martin P.	Wilder	Olive Converse	Terwilliger	Perley Snow
Whitfield	Ida Furgus	Warner	Milton Bell	Wileg (?)	Sizie	Thomas	Samuel
Whitlatch	Leila M.	Bolz	Albert W.	Wilen	Lillian C.	Hazlett	Herman C.
Whitlock	Sophia, Mrs.	Mansfield	Col. L.	Wilente (?)	Phoebe A.	Peckenpah	H. H.
Whitmore	Margaret	Starkey	Edward C.	Wiley	Minnie H.	Leggett	Elmer E.
Whitney	Inez Luella	Perelli-Minetti	Antonio	Wilfley	Rhoda A.	Boyd	B. C.
Whitney	Innis L.	Pyne	Henry H.	Wilhelms	Anna Mary	Olsen	John
Whitney	Mabel L.	Lowe	Hugh O.	Wilhoit	Mary Ellen	McGuire	Nathaniel
Whitney	Marcella	Wheaton	Charles B.	Wilke	Anna Louisa	Norden-Wells	Guernie

Wilke	Emma L.	Grover	William A.	Williams	Ellen, Mrs.	Clevenger	Thomas P.
Wilkensen (?)	Elizabeth	Shedden	Thomas M.	Williams	Emma E.	Sonniksen	Carsten
Wilkes	Mary E.	Crane	Tarlslm (?) L.	Williams	Emma Lee	Orr	John Francis
Wilkie	Grace E.	Christie	Wilfred A.	Williams	Ethel	Johannsen	Clyde M.
Wilkins	Alice East	Roberts	George Frederic	Williams	Ethel B.	Seaman	Murvin B.
Wilkinson	Charlotte E.	Whitson	J. S.	Williams	Ethel Maude	Hamilton	Rush Emmor
Wilkinson	Emma J.	Stine	Charles E.	Williams	Ethel V.	Pheby	Robert F.
Wilkinson	Eva	Jackson	E. N. B.	Williams	Etta C., Mrs.	Burke	Joseph
Wilkinson	Jane	Gregg	Isaac	Williams	Florence	Wheeler	Joe G.
Wilkinson	Leonora F.	Blackwell	Edward E.	Williams	Francina	Owens	James
Wilkinson	Mildred	Hobson	Myron	Williams	Hattie F.	Tellesen	John
Will	Esther E.	Tully	Edward J.	Williams	Ila I.	Wilson	Allan T.
Willams	Alma R.	Griggs	Arthur O.	Williams	Iva Selina	Ducheneau	Fred
Willard	Cordelia	Taylor	O. A.	Williams	Jennie	de Souza	Jose
Willard	Nellie C.	McLaren	Duncan T.	Williams	Jennie C., Mrs.	Smith	Ellis H.
Willard	Susan Alice	McBride	David	Williams	Julia C.	Grandi	William H.
Willet	Nora M.	Libbey	William S.	Williams	Laura Emily	Cragin	Charles Chester
Willey	Fannie B.	Leggett	William Alexander	Williams	Lotta A., Mrs.	Coats	Charles A., Jr.
Willey	Laura Rosella	Green	John William	Williams	Lottie E.	Leithman	Louis L.
Willey	Mamie E.	Kruse	Charles C.	Williams	Lucy	Moore	Joseph H.
Willey	Mary A.	Hoeck	F. P.	Williams	M. C., Mrs.	Curtis	L. A.
Williams	Ada M.,Miss	Spring	Elias W.	Williams	M. J., Mrs.	Green	Geo. E.
Williams	Adah	Drucks	Edward S.	Williams	Margaret	Avery	W. J.
Williams	Alice L.	Carpenter	Perl R.	Williams	Margaret A.	Stewart	Charles W.
Williams	Bird (?) Maud	Starr	Simeon Elias	Williams	Margaret L.	Russell	Mitchell J.
Williams	Caroline	Williams	Thomas Jefferson	Williams	Mary	Joseph	Tony Peters
Williams	Caroline T. D.	Blackburn	Frank L.	Williams	Mary	Tabor	James
Williams	Carrie	Brown	Thomas Howard	Williams	Mary Amanda	Weeks	George
Williams	Carrie	Wosser	William Streeton	Williams	Mary C., Mrs.	Crigler	W. E.
Williams	Clara C.	Lane	William J.	Williams	Mary E.	Spradlin	Earl Leroy
Williams	Daisy Dean	Lovell	William I.	Williams	Mary E., Mrs.	Lewis	Saml. R.
Williams	Daisy P.	Morrison	William	Williams	Mary J.	Phillips	James J.
Williams	Edna Merle	McFarlane	Walter C.	Williams	Mary L.	Metzler	J. A.
Williams	Elizabeth S. B.	Stratton	William A. T.	Williams	Mary R. M.	Caseres	J. O.
Williams	Ellen M.	Sargent	Abe L.	Williams	Mary S.	Slossen	Joseph

Williams	Mattie M.	Bailhache	Frederick	Willits	Anna	Hill	C. S.
Williams	Maud Jeannette	Kidd	Edward Martin	Willsie	Lydia	Austin	William G.
Williams	May	Petray	Edwin A.	Willson	Anna M.	Coffman	N. B.
Williams	May E.	Childers	Eugene Lester	Willson	Annie W.	Hall	Harry L.
Williams	Minerva	Gilliam	David Taylor	Willson	Emma L.	Richardson	F. A.
Williams	Nada Roll	Evans	William	Willson	Nellie, Mrs.	Adamson	Isaac N.
Williams	Nelle	Stroud	Fred	Wilsey	Edna M.	Toomey	John T.
Williams	Nellie (?)	Rice	Thomas	Wilsey	Ida M.	Davis	Alphonse G. W.
Williams	Ottoline M.	Poulsen	Otto A.	Wilsey	Sarah	McGrew	Samuel
Williams	Rebecca	Blackman	Samuel	Wilson	Ada May	Parr	William
Williams	Sarah	Greeott	John	Wilson	Agnes	McCoffrey	Bernard
Williams	Sophia S.	Weise	John H.	Wilson	Alice A.	Davie	Henry A.
Williams	Stella Price	Cake	Charles M.	Wilson	Alice Charie (?)	Curry	Sylvester James
Williams	Willmina	Berry	Samuel C.	Wilson	Amy	Allen	John W.
Williams	Kate D.	Goodfellow	Thomas C.	Wilson	Austie Lea	Kelsey	Earl Ellsworth
Williams	Sarah I.	Harrison	Robert H.	Wilson	Bertha L.	Johns	Cecil D.
Williamson	Agnes Lucretia	Rielli	Serfino	Wilson	Bertha Melville	Pedrotti	James Stephen
Williamson	Camella	Cheyney	Earl H.	Wilson	Charlotta	Witt	Andreas
Williamson	Carrie A., Mrs.	Ware	H. W.	Wilson	Clara C.	Wilson	Wilbur P.
Williamson	Christina Isabelle	Zurcher	Henry	Wilson	Daisy	Emery	Fred A.
Williamson	Cynthia A.	Barton	John W.	Wilson	E. Marguereitte	Grove	Elliot W.
Williamson	Dorothy E.	Mayo	Larry G.	Wilson	Edith, Mrs.	Rose	John
Williamson	Emilia L.	Compton	Theodore J.	Wilson	Edna M.	Everett	Harry D.
Williamson	Florence E.	Arrowood	Daniel A.	Wilson	Eliza Ann	Churchman	Schuyler
Williamson	Laura A.	Woolsey	Carl C.	Wilson	Elizabeth Ellen	McKay	Loran
Williamson	Pearl L.	Thomas	Alfred R.	Wilson	Elizabeth Elsie	McKinnon	Alexander W.
Willis	Harrietta T.	Atkins	L. G. F.	Wilson	Ella G., Mrs.	McAninch	Harry
Willis	Lillian A.	Emmons	Edward L.	Wilson	Emma	Geary	William W.
Willis	Lulu	Dillingham	John Lee	Wilson	Emma A.	Osborn	Elwood
Willis	Mabel	King	James	Wilson	Ethel Claire	Jensen	August Adolph
Willis	Margaret M.	Barry	William R.	Wilson	Ettie Sarah	Kirkland	Joseph B.
Willis	Mary	Bigsby	Milton S.	Wilson	Florence I., Mrs.	Hansen	Paul B.
Willis	Mary Elizabeth	Long	Charles H.	Wilson	Frances M.	Pool	Clarence A.
Willis	Ruth E.	Fuller	Wm. F. H.	Wilson	Gertrude	Peck	Lester O.
Willis	Sylvia I.	Henzi	William	Wilson	H. Isabella	LaDue	Valloise A.

Wilson	Hannah J.	Beales	George F.	Wilt	Carolyn J.	McConnell	Joseph P.
Wilson	Hattie	Fairbanks	Joseph F.	Wilt	Ida M.	Phillips	Norman D.
Wilson	Hattie A. (?)	Farley	James B.	Wilztmann	Lulu	Fisher	Fred W.
Wilson	Helen	Johnson	Glen	Winans	Blanche	Rhoades	Martin Luther
Wilson	Helen A.	Frey	Herbert R.	Winans	Luella M.	Dickson	Frank B.
Wilson	Inez M.	Hilderbrand	Walter G.	Winant	Pauline	Gregoire	Joseph
Wilson	Iris V.	Monti	Chester H.	Winchell	Laura A.	Mattei	Richard C.
Wilson	Iva Selina	Lithwin	August	Winder	Rose	Vaughan	William S.
Wilson	Jane	Parsons	Jedson	Winder (?)	Eva	Watson	John H.
Wilson	Jennie	Berry	C. S.	Winders	Jessie M.	Tice	Harry H.
Wilson	Jennie M.	Hogg	William G.	Winding	Sina	Hansen	Hans
Wilson	Jessie E.	Dickmann	Charles H.	Windsboro	Hattie M.	Waggoner	Oscar F.
Wilson	Jessie Frances	Anderson	James Orrin	Windsor	Sarah A.	Filbert	Major (?)
Wilson	Josephine C. B.	Ramella	Joseph	Wing	Belle	Murray	William Henry
Wilson	Lillian Wallace	White	John James	Winkler	Ada E.	Randall	Harry E.
Wilson	Loretta	Hopper	Elmer Merton	Winkler	Clara A.	Duncan	James E.
Wilson	Marela	Farmer	Geo. L.	Winkler	Florence Estella	Armstrong	Harry George
Wilson	Margaret Jane	Jessen	Emil Thomas M.	Winkler	Hattie L.	Marshall	Thomas H.
Wilson	Martha E.	Farmer	B. F.	Winkler	Jennie	Williams	George S.
Wilson	Mary	Farley	James H.	Winkler	Martha, Mrs.	Henderson	Fred S.
Wilson	Mary Mitchell	Carter	Andrew Jackson	Winn	Hattie M.	Gaston	William H.
Wilson	Mattie E.	Scott	John A.	Winn	Rosa Clara	Church	Claude Leslie
Wilson	Mildred Irma	Laughlin	Gail Everil	Winquist	Annie S.	Blackburn	Allen H.
Wilson	Minnie	Griffith	Alonzo B.	Winsby	Della Hazel	Thorne	John Harland
Wilson	Nancy E.	Heffron	Fred H.	Winsby	Ruby Ann	Thorn	Elmer H.
Wilson	Nellie K.	Birch	James F.	Winslow	Geraldine M.	McCrystle	Arthur B.
Wilson	Olive E.	Pohley	Joseph Chas.	Winson	Isabelle M.	Haskett	Max H.
Wilson	Reno	Hull	Guy L.	Winter	Alice Maud Mary	Wall	John Abernathy
Wilson	Rose Hanhart	Brown	Orson Dana	Winter	Annie M.	Harper	Charles H.
Wilson	Saidie E.	Gibson	Robert P.	Winter	Emily Elizabeth	Thronsen	Harry William
Wilson	Sarah Maria	Churchman	George	Winters	Elizabeth M.	Vinal	John T.
Wilson	Serena A.	Kean	J. B.	Winters	Mary, Mrs.	Stephenson	N. H.
Wilson	Sophia	Cormer	Frank F.	Winters	Theresa I.	Leathers	G. N.
Wilson	Sue Frances	Robinson	Lorenzo Dow	Winton	Edith May	Duncan	Elmer A.
Wilson	Susan Emily	Butler	Thomas B.	Winton	Fannie	Gutenberger	Jacob

Winton	Flora A.	Mills	William Leslie	Wolcott	Luella M.	Prince	J. B.
Winton	Leticia A.	Hodgson	David R.	Woldemar	Anna	Runge	Louis
Winzell	Kate A.	Cockrill (?)	John L.	Wolf	Adeline T.	Turner	William F.
Wirts	Alazuma J.	Sindmaster	Jacob E.	Wolf	Allena	Showalter	Clarence H.
Wirts	Elizabeth Bernice	McAuley	George William	Wolf	Anna Marie	Brown	Frank G.
Wirts	Mary Alice	Neep	Walter Scott	Wolf	Marie	Nielson	Carl
Wise	A. F., Mrs.	Brown	Charles A.	Wolf	Marie	McLaughlin	Bernard H.
Wise	Goldie	Anderson	Joe	Wolf	Pearl L.	Schuhmann	Paul G.
Wisecarver	Norma Eugenia	Fleming	Paul X.	Wolfe	Effie Maude	Scott	Walter Claude
Wiseman	Edna O.	Bradlee	Arthur S.	Wolfe	Eliza	Gibson	Charles W.
Wiseman	Juanita L.	Wymore	George H.	Wolfe	Jessie Adell	Pearl	Herbert
Wiseman	Susie	Cook	Herbert E.	Wolfe	Katie	Price	Orville J.
Wiser	Macel	Marchisio	Enrico F.	Wolfe	Katie	Paul	James W.
Wisnom	Margaret	MacKenzie	Hugh Fraser	Wolfe	Maude	Watrous	Charles F.
Wiswell	Hattie F.	Reed	Quincy	Wolfe	Minnie	Storey	Gustav C.
Wiswell	Wyima (?) Florence	Blaisdell	Harry Lee	Wollemann	Freda Ehrlich	Rockteschell	Rudolph H.
				Wollitz	Leopoldine Christine	Jurs	Louis
Witbro	Cathrine	Rose	William				
Witherell	Catherine, Mrs.	Duarte	Nicholas	Wolseth	Minnie C.	Price	Perry W.
Witherell	Laura Jane	Cox	George Mervon	Wolter	Ruth E.	Walters	William S.
Witherell	Minnie E.	Andrews	Vernon	Wonacott	Esther B.	Clark	Frank
Witherspoon	Cornelia E.	Hansen	Maurice	Wood	Addie	Price	Ellsworth
Withycombe	Ethel	Baker	David	Wood	Allie S.	Kennedy	Charles W.
Witt	Ellen V.	Fries	Theodore	Wood	Alta L.	Jones	George F.
Witter	Laura	Smith	J. D.	Wood	Clara Edith	Lee	Walter
Wittkoff	Annie	Westphal	Henry	Wood	Enid	Ruggles	Lester Wallace
Wittkoff (?)	Mary A.	Bailey	Frank R.	Wood	Francis A.	Davis	Edward J.
Wittkopf	Martha I.	Stallings	Ivan	Wood	Georgia	Pritchett	Gill S.
Wittkowski	Christine Janette	Bundesen	William Frederick	Wood	Hazel Bea	Dominick	Herbert
Wittkowski	Frieda	Larson	John Benjamin	Wood	Hellen	McIntosh	Andrew
Wittkowski	Magda F. A.	Petersen	Peter C.	Wood	Irma V.	Warren	William H.
Wittkowski	Anna	Bartsch	Charles	Wood	Laura, Mrs.	Whitby	Edgar Reed
Wittman	Alice E.	Pippert	Peter	Wood	Mae R.	Morey	Charles H.
Wittmann	Maria	Maxwell	Michael	Wood	Marie E.	Faylor	William P.
Wolcott	Edna Irene	Cottle	William Leonard	Wood	Marie L.	Paludan	Charles T. A. O.

Wood	Mellicent	Deutch	Edward	Woolf	Rhoda Ann	Wilfley	Thomas J.
Wood	Minnie M.	Jackson	Luther	Woolley	Ethel M.	Schofield	Ernest P.
Wood	Myrtle	Snyder	Lloyd K.	Woolsey	Louise	Dodge	Harold Carew
Wood	N. Pheobie	Mitchell	J. Wright	Woolsey	Marie Louise	Dwinelle	C. H.
Wood	Sarah Louisa	Sewell	I. L.	Woolsey	Ruth	Finley	Ernest L.
Woodard	Helen E.	Miebach	Hans	Wooster	Carrie A.	Gobbi	Charles W.
Woodbury	Alice Gertrude	Driver	Edward L.	Workman	Reta L.	Turner	Robert M.
Woodcock	Lee	Myers	George	Workover	Edwine C.	Disbro	Ernest F.
Woodcock	Maud	Matthews	Oscar F.	World	Dolley	Burnett	A. J.
Woodruff	Clara J.	Bledsoe	A. J.	Worms	Alice D.	Harris	Earl L.
Woodruff	Eva B.	Hoffman	Fernando	Worthington	Louise	Sampson	Joseph M.
Woods	Clara	Rivers	Charles	Wrede	Cordina	Robinson	John
Woods	Elizabeth, Mrs.	Clokey	Robert	Wren	Marcellina	Oakes	Oswald F.
Woods	Ethel Blosom	Harvey	Marion Wilson	Wright	Angeline	Brown	J.
Woods	Katie	Blakley	Thomas F.	Wright	Clara C.	Savage	Nelson E.
Woods	Lily B.	Cook	Grover C.	Wright	Daisy A.	Lea	Clarence F.
Woods	Madge	Robinson	Chas. A.	Wright	Ella	Ellison	Ebert R.
Woods	Mary A.	Courtney	John George	Wright	Ella, Mrs.	Wright	Winfield
Woodson	Leona Eleanor	Carroll	Wm. F.	Wright	Elois	Catendo	Albert G.
Woodson	Pearl Alphia	Mulhall	Henry John	Wright	Emma A.	Churchill	H. Harry
Woodward	Bess Van Alst	Bogle	Samuel S.	Wright	Eva Pearl	Glasgow	Sumner E.
Woodward	Carlotta	Waibel	Fred L.	Wright	Eveline	Cox	Jessee C.
Woodward	Edith May	Whyers	Floyd R.	Wright	Flora Agnes	Cummings	Frederick Merritt
Woodward	Irma Frances	Wallis	Joseph Allen	Wright	Grace Anna	Bridges	Isaac Newton
Woodward	Jessie	Hitchcock	LeRoy V.	Wright	Jennie A.	Williams	John A.
Woodward	Lillian Pearl	McConnell	Mark	Wright	Katherine	Coolidge	George Harry
Woodward	Mattie M.	Ferguson	Charles T.	Wright	Lizzie	Petersen	Augustus
Woodworth	Eva M.	Schlombohm	Heinrick F.	Wright	Mary Edith	Rechel	William Arthur
Woodworth	Katie	Goodman	George R.	Wright	Myrtle J.	Stewart	William H.
Woodworth	Mary	Drummond	R. S.	Wright	Nellie J.	Davidson	W. W.
Woodworth	Ola	Tucker	George F.	Wright	Nellie M.	Poulson	William P.
Woodworth	Rose E.	Meeks	Walter B.	Wright	Nellie Wilson	Frellson	Walter B.
Wooldridge	Elvira	Wright	Henry Clay	Wright	Neva F.	Hinkleman	Fred G.
Wooler	Lillie M.	Purcell	James	Wright	Olive	Allen	Evan R.
Wooley	Emma E.	Cotrell	Charles William	Wright	Ruth E.	McDaniel	Victor G.

Wright	Ruth Irene	Clarke	Leslie Albert	Yancey	Ruby V.	Borri	Lodovico Vincenzo
Wright	Sarah Bernice	Welch	Robert Charles	Yancy	Eveline	Tolman	Ambrose P.
Wright	Sarah E.	Shelden	Frederick N.	Yangling	May	Miller	Carl L.
Wright	Viola May	Hollingsworth	Dale Raymond	Yarbough	Georgia J.	Holt	John A.
Wright	Violet E.	Clementz	Fred A.	Yarbough	Saddie	Litton	H. B.
Wrottero (?)	Edith	Aylsworth	Niles W.	Yarbrough	Ethel B.	McMichael	Rice F.
Wulferdingen	Edna M.	Nixon	Ernest L.	Yarbrough	Mattie	Laughlin	A. P.
Wulff	Cecile I.	French	George Bonzana	Yarbrough	Virginia J.	Howard	W. H.
Wuthrich	Antoinette L.	Kerr	James A.	Yarnell	Eloise I.	Grosse	Guy N.
Wyant	Birdella	Phillpott	Frank	Yates	Alice D.	Chapman	Thomas A.
Wyatt	Amanda	Wyatt	William T.	Yates	Amy May, Mrs.	Conner	Arch C.
Wyatt	Beatrice A.	White	Harvey S.	Yates	Edith	Peterson	U. G.
Wyatt	Catherine	Buell	Robert	Yates	Francis	King	Fred
Wyatt	Lelia	Wren	Carl	Yates	Mabel	Taylor	William Thomas
Wyckoff	Cora	Fallon	John D.	Yates	Pearl	McGarvey	Laurence Thurman
Wyckoff	Emma	Kinsey	Harvey C.	Yates	Rena	Seeman	Hans Peter Otto
Wyckoff	Maggie	Ganter	Clinton E.	Yeager	Carolyn E.	Helman	Louis W., Jr.
Wylie	Arrie L.	Warner	Daniel R.	Yeager	Cynthia Eleanor	Beasley	Russell L.
Wyllie	Annie E.	Starrett	John A.	Yeager	Elizabeth, Mrs.	Strang	Fred William
Wyllie	Beatrice	Lowrey	Thomas J.	Yeager	Eulalia M.	Jones	Henry M.
Wyllie	Ella T.	Purvine	Frank C.	Yeager	Susie	Burgess	Alauson T.
Wymore	Elaine C.	Green	George E.	Yeargin	Eleanor M.	Rader	John B.
Wynne	Alice	Snyder	Edward de F.	Yengling	Ella C.	Gobbi	Julius James
Wyrick	Blanche Christina	Boysen	William Henry	Yerger	Hazel	Drake	Lewis
Wyrick	Louine	Pharriss	Samuel	Yerzykowicz	Clara F.	Roberts	Leonard W.
Yagemann	Henrietta P.	Brooks	Elmer E.	Yob	Rosa	Fisher	Charles
Yager	Barbara	Jones	Evan	Yocka	Lillie B.	Ripley	Isaac D.
Yager	Birdie L.	Hitchcock	John R.	Yockey	Bessie	Moltzen	Thomas
Yager	Elfleda J.	Sellars	Lewis E.	Yokman	Katherine	Yosting	Fred
Yager	Stella L.	Plag	Albert J.	Yokum	Ida May	Nance	Charles W.
Yakovleff	Catherine	Hubbard	George F.	Yori/Jori	Mary	Camenzind	Lewis
Yancey	Delia	Sinder	W. A.	York	Edna Cora	Williston	Edwin Parks
Yancey	Emma B.	Morrow	Joseph A.	York	Eva P.	Pfaff	Louis
Yancey	Laura Russell	McGuire	William J.	York	Inez M.	Scatena	Humbert
Yancey	Minnie M.	Esaia	John B.	Yost	Bertha	Schmitt	Carl

Yost	Rosa	Rothlisberger	Hans	Young	Myrtle L.	Allenden	William H.
Youh (?)	M.	John	Charley	Young	Neva	Hood	James G.
Young	Adah	Robbins	Charles H.	Young (?)	Minnie E.	Kolliker	Fred
Young	Adeline	Bojorques	John	Youngs	Naomi E.	Ward	John H.
Young	Agnes	Conemac	Byron Patrick	Zabel	Angeline	Percy	Francis
Young	Alice G.	Pierce	Harry M.	Zalud	Annie C.	Brooks	William H.
Young	Amelia, Mrs.	Young	Michael	Zamaroni	Egidia	Fillppini	John
Young	Blanche	Howard	Carl C.	Zamaroni	Jennie	Lauritzen	Kundt
Young	Coila	Newman	Max	Zamaroni	Jessie	Beffa	Tony
Young	Cora B.	Lopus	George E.	Zamaroni	Lillie	Beffa	Tony
Young	Corinthia A.	Chamberlain	Albert F.	Zamaroni	Elvira	Flohr	Charles William
Young	D. A.	Young	Jacob A.	Zambelich	Nettis, Mrs.	Proprovich	Christ
Young	Edith A.	Goewey	Charles H.	Zampa	Dorotea	Chelini	Americo D.
Young	Eliza V.	Williams	Jerome B.	Zanderina	Virginia	Bella	Angelo
Young	Elizabeth T.	Rogers	John Henry	Zandrina	Rosa	Gallo	Lorenzo
Young	Emma	McCoy	John M.	Zanini	Flomena P.	Rosselli	Genesio
Young	Emma P.	Young	George W.	Zanini	Maria	Martin	Leopold
Young	Flora E.	Dar	David	Zanolini	Josephine L.	Siemer	Fred
Young	Flora E.	Meek	Nathan T.	Zanolini	Polonia	Zanolini	Michael
Young	Flora M.	Morse	Daniel G.	Zanoni	Delia	Beltrami	Lorenzo
Young	Gladys	Smith	Grant	Zanoni	Elvezia F.	Mezzera	Paul P.
Young	Hazel	Holst	James	Zanoni	Lena	Leoni	Placido F.
Young	Irene E.	Ogden	Lauren E.	Zanoni	Lillie	Fesso	Antonio
Young	Ivy M.	Lonkey	Lloyd C.	Zanoni	Teresa	Zachetti	Giuseppe
Young	Jennie N.	Brooks	Cicero C.	Zanzi	Annie	Bacchini	Romeo
Young	Louella St John, Mrs.	Faudre	Crocket	Zanzi	Irene	Zanzi	Pietro
				Zappa	Anna	Righetti	Leno
Young	Lucy M.	Preble	Fred T.	Zappa	Mary M.	Berruti	Emilio
Young	Mable Estella	Rouse	Rufus Sydney	Zartman	Katie	Rankin	Lowry E.
Young	Maggie I., Mrs.	Bruening	Charles	Zearns	Mary	McCandless	Robert
Young	Maggie J.	Meyers	Chas. H.	Zehringer	Adel	Barr	John
Young	Margaret L.	Davis	Edward W.	Zeigler	Minnie Florence	Menefee	William Alfred
Young	Mattie Isadora	Lawson	Oliver Lester	Zeiph	Anna Zanona	Baker	William J.
Young	Maude E.	Harris	Edward E.	Zell	Martha S.	Maddrell	Lepolde S.
Young	Mertie E.	Wilson	Henry H.	Zeller	Stella R.	Keig	William S.

Zeni	Fausta	Greppi	Louis
Zerga	Jane Lily	Voiles	William H.
Zika	Mary	Temple	Albert
Zilhart	Ella F.	Blaney	John W.
Zimmerman	Alma	Rohrer	Isaac Harley
Zimmerman	Emma A.	Petersen	Thomas S.
Zimmerman	Frances H.	Gross	Ludwig
Zimmerman	Maggie E.	Webb	William Edmund
Zimmerman	Therese	Hobbie	John F.
Zimmerman	Elizabeth	Benedetti	Conrad
Zolski	Agnes M.	Toole	William T.
Zonsius	Mabel Grace	Wilson	Lorenzo J.
Zopetti	Vittoria	Bartoli	Efisio
Zumwalt	Berenice I.	Martin	Frances W.
Zumwalt	Dora	Huntley	John S.
Zunino	Madalena	Quartaroli	Frank
Zunnino	Annie K.	Emery	Vernon V.
Zurcher	Irma	Ardoin	Victor
Zurcher	Lucy	Southern	Elmer T.
Zuur	Gustine Helen	Bryant	George Gilbert
Zuver	Annie, Mrs.	Wilbert	Peter
Zweifel	Edith Bertha	Silk	George Henry
Zweifel	Elsie M.	Raven	Theodore M.
Zweifel	Lena	Walker	Albert
Zweifel	Lulu Rosa	Butcher	Charles Walter
Zweifel	Minnie L.	Small	Ernest Archibald

Other Heritage Books by the Sonoma County Genealogical Society, Inc.:

CD: *Sonoma County [California] Records, Volume 1*

Early School Attendance Records of Sonoma County, California, Beginning 1858

Early School Attendance Records of Sonoma County, California, Volume II: 1874–1932

Index and Abstracts of Wills, Sonoma County, California: 1850–1900

Index to Naturalization Records in Sonoma County, California, Volume 1: 1841–1906

Naturalization Records in Sonoma County, California, Volume II: 1906–1930

Index to The Sonoma Searcher*: Volume 16, No. 1 to Volume 28, No. 3*
(Including Index to The Sonoma Searcher*: Volume 1, No. 1 to Volume 15, No. 4, SCGS, August 1993)*

Index to Vital Data in Local Newspapers of Sonoma County, California, Volume 1: 1855–1875

Index to Vital Data in Local Newspapers of Sonoma County, California, Volume 2: 1876–1880

Index to Vital Data in Local Newspapers of Sonoma County, California, Volume 3: 1881–1885

Index to Vital Data in Local Newspapers of Sonoma County, California, Volume 4: 1886–1890

Index to Vital Data in Local Newspapers of Sonoma County, California, Volume 5: 1891–1899

Index to Vital Data in Local Newspapers of Sonoma County, California, Volume 6: 1900–1903

Index to Vital Data in Local Newspapers of Sonoma County, California, Volume 7: 1904–1906

Index to Vital Data in Local Newspapers of Sonoma County, California, Volume 8: 1907–1909

Index to Vital Data in Local Newspapers of Sonoma County, California, Volume 9: 1910–1912

Indigent Records in Sonoma County, California 1878 to 1926, Volume 1: The Indigents

Indigent Records in Sonoma County, California 1878 to 1926, Volume 2: Taxpayers Who Certified Indigent Need

Marriage License Affidavits, 1861–1921, Sonoma County, California, Volume I: A–F

Marriage License Affidavits, 1861–1921, Sonoma County, California, Volume II: G–M

Marriage License Affidavits, 1861–1921, Sonoma County, California, Volume III: N–Z

Marriage License Affidavits, 1861–1921, Sonoma County, California, Volume IV: Index to Bride's Surname

Militia Lists of Sonoma County, California, 1846 to 1900

Santa Rosa Rural Cemetery, 1853–1997

Sonoma County, California Cemetery Records, 1846–1921, Third Edition

Sonoma County, California Death Records, 1873–1905, Second Edition

Sonoma County California Reconstructed 1890 Census

The 1930 School Census of Sonoma County, California

www.ingramcontent.com/pod-product-compliance
Lightning Source LLC
Chambersburg PA
CBHW082039230426
43670CB00016B/2706